THE **GUINNESS** BOOK OF
MOTORBOATING
FACTS AND FEATS
& origins & development of motor craft

Kevin Desmond

Guinness Superlatives Limited
2 Cecil Court, London Road, Enfield, Middlesex

THIS BOOK IS GRATEFULLY DEDICATED TO

MICHAEL DOXFORD

A TRUE PATRON OF THE ARTS AND SCIENCES

Editor: Anne Smith

Layout: Bernard Crossland Associates

Copyright © Kevin Desmond and Guinness Superlatives Ltd 1979

Published in Great Britain by Guinness Superlatives Ltd
2 Cecil Court, London Road, Enfield, Middlesex

ISBN 0 900424 86 9

Guinness is a registered trademark of Guinness Superlatives Ltd

Typeset, printed and bound by Hazell Watson & Viney Ltd, Aylesbury, Bucks
Colour separation: Newsele Litho Ltd, Milan

ACKNOWLEDGEMENTS

The author wishes to acknowledge the following, to whom he is indebted:

Ailsa Craig Marine Division; Frederick Andrews; Antique & Classic Boat Society; Avon Inflatables Ltd; Scott Bader Ltd; F. Bamford & Co. Ltd; E. P. Barrus Ltd; W. Bates & Son Ltd; BEAMA; Beaufort Air-Sea Equipment Ltd; Beaverbrook Newspaper Group; Berthon Boat Co. Ltd; Sir John Betjamin; Boeing Marine Systems; Boxley Engineering; British Aluminium Company Ltd; British Film Institute (National Film Archive); British Hovercraft Corporation; British Red Cross Society; British Seagull; Brookes & Gatehouse Ltd; Henry Browne & Son Ltd; Bruntons Propellers (Sudbury) Ltd; Ray Bulman; Arturo Chiggiato; John Chitty; Chrysler; Church Missionary Society; D. W. Cooper; Cornwall County Library; Cory Lighterage Ltd; Cougar Marine; Thomas Crimmins Inc; John Crouse; John Cundell (*Model Boats*); R.F.D. Inflatables Ltd; Daimler-Benz Gesellschaft; Department of Trade; Walt Disney Productions; Alan Dowling (Hull Central Library); Du Pont de Nemours SA; *Electrical Times*; Electronic Laboratories Ltd (Guy Dixon); Elliott Turbomachinery Ltd; Fairey Marine Ltd; E. Fattorini; Madame Daniel Fernandez (Arcachon Library); FIAT; Capt. Sir Ranulph T-W-Fiennes Bt FRGS; Hong Kong Fire Services Department; London Fire Brigade (Jim O'Sullivan); *Fishing News*; Fletcher Marine; Francis Searchlights; Peter Freebody & Co.; Gardner & Sons Ltd; M. J. Gaston; Laurent Giles & Partners; Morgan Giles Ltd; Glastron; Greenhithe Lighterage Co. Ltd; Grimsby Central Library; A. E. Hagg; Halmatic; Brian Hillsden (Steamboat Association of Great Britain); Honda UK Ltd; Ray Hooley (Rustons Lincoln); John Philip Huck; Hunting Group of Companies (Chris Simmonds); ICI; Imperial War Museum; Institute of Marine Engineers; JBS (David Parkinson); *International Ship & Boatbuilder*; International Yacht Paints; Library & Museum of the Order of St John; Library of Congress; Johnson Outboards; Police Constable John Joslin (Thames River Police, Wapping); Lazar Kay; Kelvin; Kelvin-Hughes; Jim King; Kingston-upon-Hull Central Library; R. D. Kisch; Kort Propulsion Co. Ltd; G. E. Langmuir (Clyde River Steamer Club); the Law Society; Leeds Central Library; Bill LeFeber; British Leyland UK Ltd; London University (Senate House); Port of Lowestoft Research Society (A. J. Page); Lucas Marine; S.H.G. Marine; 3M; Neil Macdonald (Hoverclub of Great Britain); Hugh McKnight; Sq. Ldr R. J. M. Manson (Historian, RAF Marine Branch); GEC-Marconi Electronics Ltd (Mrs B. Hance); Mariner Radar; Maschinenfabrik Augsburg-Nürnberg AG; Musée de la Marine (Paris); Mercury Marine; The Meteorological Office; Ministry of Fisheries, Food & Agriculture; Charles H. Mistele; Mitchell Library (Glasgow); *Motor Boat & Yachting*; NAEBM; National Motor Museum (Beaulieu); National Science Museum Library; Negretti & Zambra Ltd; Asahitaro Nishimura; K. W. Norris; Norwich Central Library; Rosalind Nott; William Osborne Ltd; E. W. Paget-Tomlinson; Cdr C. F. Parsons; James Penick Jr; Tom Percival; Perkins Engines; Petters Ltd; Keiran Phelan; Cyril Posthumous; Officine E. Radice Sp.A; Rampart; G. Honnest-Redlich; James S. Robinson; Edmund, and Edmond de Rothschild; Royal National Lifeboat Institute; Royal Yachting Association; D. M. Russell (Marine) Ltd; A. Rutherford; Sabre Engines; Bert Savidge; SBBNF; Baron Hans von Schertel (Suparamar); Schottel-Werft; Bill Seebold Jr; Selva Outboards; Bill Sheaff; Constance Babington Smith; T. G. Smith (HM Customs & Excise); SMMT Ltd; Lt. Col. J. N. Blashford-Snell MBE, RE; F. H. Snoxell; Société Zodiac; Stone Manganese Marine Ltd; R. A. Storey (Modern Records Centre, University of Warwick); Geoffrey Streets; Stuart Turner Ltd; Heron Suzuki GB Ltd; Swada (London) Ltd; Swiss National Tourist Office; Tannoy; Tarquin Yacht Co. Ltd; Timber Research & Development Association; W. & J. Tod Ltd; 20th Century-Fox Film Group; UIM (José Mawet); Veteran Car Club of GB; Leo Villa OBE OSJ; AB Volvo Penta; Lord Howard de Walden; Thomas Walker & Son Ltd; Watercraft; Watermota Ltd; G. L. Watson Ltd; Ian Wellcoat (HMS); Dinah White (Camper & Nicholsons); William P. Willig; WD & HO Wills; Windboats Ltd; Windermere Nautical Trust; World Ship Society; Yamaha Motors; Yanmar Diesels; Yarrow (Shipbuilders) Ltd.

To my translators: Alex Albani; Mady Etienne; Friedrich Irmer; Carlo Galluzzo; Siri Botha. To Antoine Sire, French Motorboat Historian. To my Art Editor, David Roberts; and to my Editor, Anne Smith.

CONTENTS

FOREWORD

SIR MAX AITKEN, Bt, DSO, DFC

It was in the 1930s that I first saw a race for unlimited-engined powerboats in Detroit. This was the APBA Gold Cup and to see those boats travelling at over 100 mph was certainly one of the most thrilling and exciting spectacles you could imagine.

At home in England, whilst my brother Peter Aitken raced cars at Brooklands, I owned a motorboat with a 12-cylinder Thornycroft engine which started with compressed air and it always caught fire! However, it was fun travelling along the South Coast at 40 mph.

In the years following the Second World War, having been a front-line fighter pilot, for relaxation I went sailing with my friend Uffa Fox. In 1954 the Ship and Boat Builders' National Federation decided to organise a boat show, separate from the Motor Show, at Olympia. With certain misgivings about undertaking such a venture on its own, the Federation approached me as Managing Director of the *Daily Express* and asked if we would be prepared to underwrite the costs if these were not recuperated at the end of the show. We agreed, provided that the words 'Sponsored by the *Daily Express*' appeared on the official catalogue. The 1955 National Boat Show was an immense success. Today, the number of exhibitors has quadrupled and the Boat Show is in its 26th year.

The first Boat Show had displayed some powerboats unable to stand up to wind and wave. I was able to enjoy, as a spectator, the Miami/Nassau Offshore Powerboat Race, where boats had been built to stand up to rough seas. I returned home, enthusiastically determined to start our own 200-mile offshore contest, Cowes to Torquay.

If Kevin Desmond's book has revealed one thing, it is that motorboating should never merely be defined as a wealthy minority enjoying a hybrid and sometimes dangerous sport. It is the result of a total revolution in waterborne transport. Speed from the motor-power in lifeboats, fire-floats, fishing vessels, tugs and canal craft, has moved them with ever greater efficiency towards their goal.

Despite the seemingly insurmountable problems to be overcome, as one maiden voyage for the pioneering of an innovation in hull or engine design succeeded another, there grew an accumulation of pride in marine engineering progress towards the service of mankind.

The number of lives saved and cared for by the motorboat far outweighs those that it destroyed.

With the boom in post-war motorboat traffic on the seas and inshore waterways of the world, the need for greater reliability in marine engines and for manoeuvrability in tight corners, for increasingly sophisticated methods of ship-to-ship and ship-to-shore communication, and for alert efficiency from such essential organisations as pilotage, police, coastguards and lifeboatmen – have today become more important than they ever were in previous decades.

It must, therefore, become the responsibility of every individual who is benefitting from motorboating today, to show the utmost respect for the natural conditions of the sea and courteous consideration for those countless others, with whom he is sharing it.

London 1979

1 THE ORIGINS OF MOTORBOATING

STEAM

The first experimental steamboat is reported to have been that belonging to Comte J. B. d'Auxiron (1728–78). From 1770, d'Auxiron had become interested in the pioneer aspirations of Dr Denis Papin and others, and had retired from the French Army determined to put his ideas into practice. He prepared detailed plans and specifications in 1771, which were submitted to the Minister Bertin, Comte de Bourdeilles, and approved of.

As a result, the Société d'Auxiron was formed in 1772, with the Marquis Claude de Jouffroy d'Abbans and the Comte Charles M. de Follenay as co-partners. Auxiron obtained a 15-year concession 'pour appliquer la force de la pompe à feu à faire remonter les bateaux sur les rivières', provided that his plans were acceptable to the Academy of Sciences.

Construction of a craft began in December 1772 on the River Seine, near Paris; J. C. Périer was appointed to report on its progress to the Academy. By 1774 it had been fitted with a twin-cylinder 'atmospheric' steam engine, and taken to Meudon; but on 8 September, just before the trials, the counterweight of a beam fell through the bottom of the hull, and the vessel foundered. Sabotage was suspected, the project fell through, and d'Auxiron fell ill and died at Paris in 1778 – some say of a broken heart.

The first boat to be moved by the action of steam was that built by J. C. Périer (1742–1818) at Chaillot, near Paris, in 1775, for an experiment on the Seine. The Périer craft was powered by a steam engine with 8 in (203 mm) diameter cylinder and some device to obtain rotary motion for two paddle-wheels. But its 1 hp was insufficient to propel the craft upstream and Périer abandoned his ambition, returning to developing steam engines for land use.

The first successful steamboat was the *Pyroscaphe*, designed by Marquis Claude de Jouffroy d'Abbans (1751–1832). His first and abortive experiments were carried out in June 1778 on the River Doubs with a 43-footer (13·1 m) fitted with two inclined steam cylinders, but with an inefficient propulsion system.

Five years later, in collaboration with Comte Charles de Follenay, Marquis d'Abbans produced his second wooden twin-paddle steamer – *Pyroscaphe* (literally 'Fire-Boat'). The hull (LOA 149 ft (45·4 m) × B 14·9 ft (4·5 m) × D 3·2 ft (1 m)) with its 13 ft (4 m) paddle-wheels was built at Ecully, near Lyons, whilst the engine, with its horizontal double-acting cylinder (bore 25 in × stroke 77 in) was constructed by Frèrejean et Cie of that town.

On 15 July 1783, *Pyroscaphe* paddled up the River Saone, near Lyons, by steam power for 15 min against the current. D'Abbans' progress was held back by lack of money and the French Revolution, until 1816 when, assisted by his son Achille F. E. de Jouffroy, the 65-year-old Marquis obtained a patent and built the flat-bottomed, round-bilge *Charles-Philippe*, a highly ornamental steam launch (complete with dragon's figurehead and ornamental paddle-boxes). On 3 December 1816, the *Charles-Philippe* made her first successful upstream trial on the River Seine at an effective 6·7 mph (10·8 km/h), despite a defective ratchet mechanism. Neither the *Charles-Philippe*, nor the *Perseverant* (built by the Jouffroys in 1818) was a commercial success. The aged Marquis died in Paris in 1832, a disappointed man.

The first steamboat to prove herself capable of real commercial service was the *Charlotte Dundas*. Built of wood in 1801 by Alexander Hart, at Grangemouth Dockyard, Stirlingshire, to the order of Lord Dundas of Kerse (1742–1811) and named after his Lordship's daughter, *Charlotte Dundas* measured LOA 56 ft (17 m) × B 18 ft (5·5 m) × D 8 ft (2·4 m). Her engine, built and installed by William Symington, the British pioneer of marine steam propulsion, drove a single paddle-wheel, placed at the stern of the vessel in a recess 4 ft (1·2 m) wide and 12 ft (3·6 m) long, the whole housed-in. The double stern carried two rudders, which were controlled by a steering-wheel in the forepart of the vessel.

In March 1802, two loaded vessels, each of 70 tons burden, were successfully towed by the *Charlotte Dundas* on the canal for a distance of 19·5 miles (31·4 km) in 6 hr against a strong adverse wind. Despite this satisfactory performance, the canal owners decided that any benefit resulting from the use of steam tugs would not compensate for the damage that would be done to the canal banks by the wash of the paddles. The proposal to use steam tugs was therefore rejected.

William Symington was reduced to poverty and died at London in 1831. The *Charlotte Dundas* remained laid-up for many years in a creek of the canal, and in 1861 she was finally broken up.

Charlotte Dundas *(Science Museum, London)*

The first commercially successful steamboat was the *Clermont* (1807), born as a result of collaboration between Robert Fulton and Messrs Boulton, Watt & Co. This vessel (first known as the *North River* steamboat) was built by Charles Brown of Carlears Hook, on the East River, New York, to the order of Robert Fulton (1765–1815), as the outcome of study and practical experiments in steam propulsion carried out by him on the River Seine, Paris.

The trial trip of the 133 ft (40·5 m) *Clermont* was on the River Hudson on 17 August 1807, between New York and Albany, with speeds of 4·7 mph (7·6 km/h) being reached. After her completion, *Clermont* ran as a packet on this same route until the end of the season. In the winter of 1807–8, she was rebuilt and refitted, and continued to run on the Hudson for seven years. Her nominal 20 hp engine had one cylinder, supplied by Messrs Boulton, Watt & Co.

The first paddle-steamer to venture out onto the open sea was the 103·3 ft (31·5 m) *Phoenix*. In June 1808, she steamed from the Hudson to Philadelphia. She then ran as a packet on the River Delaware, between Philadelphia and Trenton NJ, until wrecked at Trenton in 1814.

The first of the American lake steamers was the *Vermont*, built by Messrs John and James Winans, at Burlington, and launched in 1808 for public service on Lake Champlain. Under Winans' command, *Vermont* entered service in June 1809 between St Jean, Burlington and Whitehall. On 15 October 1815, she sank near Ile-aux-Noix, in the Richelieu river. Her machinery was recovered however, and sold to the Lake Champlain Steamboat Co. who placed it in their new vessel, the PS *Champlain* (1816), which was also built by the Winans brothers. In 1817, the same machinery was removed for the second time and sold to the Lake George Steamboat Co. to be installed in their paddleboat, the *James Caldwell*, which was the first to run on Lake George, and remained in service until 1820.

The first Canadian steamboat was the PS *Accommodation* (1809), built at Montreal by the brewer John Molson (1763–1836), a native of Lincolnshire, and his two British partners, John

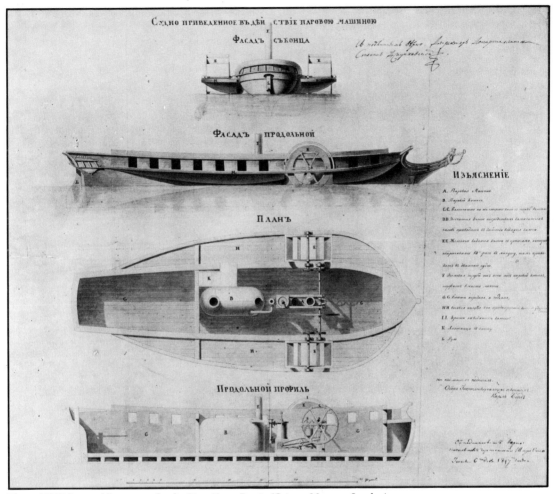

Plans of 1817 for a paddle-steamer for the River Neva, Russia (Science Museum, London)

Bruce (shipbuilder) and Capt. John Jackson. The vessel was launched on 19 August 1809, and completed two months later for service on the St Lawrence River. The vertical steam cylinder and piston were cast of iron and turned at the Forges de Saint-Maurice at Three Rivers, whilst the smaller parts were made in Montreal. She was fitted with berths for 20 passengers with a crew of six men.

On 1 November 1809, commanded by John Jackson, with the French-Canadian river pilot Amable Laviolette, *Accommodation* left Montreal for her maiden trip. She arrived at Quebec after a 66-hr journey, 30 hr of which had been spent at anchor. The distance of 160 m (257 km) was thus covered at a mean speed of 4·45 mph (7·16 km/h). The local newspaper commented:

'It is obvious that her machinery, at present, has not sufficient force for this river.' In the French version of this report, *Accommodation* was described as 'la chaloupe a fumée' or 'smoke launch'!

The first steamboat to run on the river Mississippi was the PS *New Orleans*, built at Pittsburgh by Nicholas J. Rossevelt in association with Robert Fulton, and launched on 17 March 1811. She entered service on the Mississippi in October 1811, and continued to run between New Orleans and Natchez until wrecked on the 14 July 1815.

The first steamboat to run commercially in Europe was built on the Clyde during 1811–12 to the order of Henry Bell (1767–1830) who had submitted proposals to the British Admiralty in 1800 for the steam propulsion of vessels. Soon afterwards he received a visit from Robert Fulton, who was then at work in France. With a crew of nine men, the 51 ft (15·5 m) *Comet* was built of wood at Port Glasgow by Messrs John Wood & Co., and launched on 24 July 1812. Powered by a single-cylinder 4 hp engine, *Comet* made a trial trip from Greenock to Glasgow – a distance of about 20 miles (32 km), in 3 hr 30 min. Also in August 1812, Bell advertised her for public service on the Clyde, between Glasgow, Greenock, and Helensburgh.

Later she was withdrawn from the Clyde, and in 1816 she was in operation on the Firth of Forth. In 1819 Henry Bell used his vessel to establish steam communication between the West Highlands and Glasgow. On 15 December 1820, on one of her trips from Fort William, she ran ashore at Craignish Point and was totally wrecked.

The first 'steam packet' on the River Thames and the first to cross the Channel to France was the *Margery* whose keel was laid down in 1813 by Messrs Archibald MacLachlan & Co. to the order of Messrs William Anderson and John McCubbin, merchants of Glasgow. *Margery* was launched in June 1814 at the Dumbarton yards and ran for a short time on the Clyde, before being sold to Messrs Anthony Cortis & Co. of London. She entered the Thames in January 1815, much to the astonishment of Naval crews anchored in the estuary and of the London public.

Captained by Anthony Cortis, this first 'steam packet' maintained a public service between London and Gravesend on alternate days; but Capt. Cortis had to be replaced before long, simply because he was not a licensed Thames Waterman. *Margery* was laid up several times for repairs, and in March 1816 she was sold to Messrs Andriel, Pajol et Cie, of Paris, renamed the *Elise* and refitted for service on the Seine. Under the command of Capt. Pierre Andriel (who later introduced **the first steamboat service on the Mediterranean**, with the *Ferdinando Primo*), and with Anthony Cortis and Mr W. Jackson also on board, the *Elise* steamed from the Thames in stormy weather to Newhaven. She left Newhaven on 17 March 1816, battling her way across the Channel in the face of

southerly headwinds, and reached Le Havre the next day, after 17 hr at sea. On her arrival in Paris she was met by scenes of much enthusiasm. She later re-descended the Seine and started public service between Rouen and Elbeuf.

The first steam warship was the *Demologos* (1814), an armed vessel intended for coast defence and to break the British blockade. The plans show her sides pierced with 20 portholes, armed with 32-pounders to fire red-hot cannonballs. She was 140 ft (42·7 m) LOA and 24 ft (7·3 m) in the beam. The Napoleonic War ended before *Demologos* was completed and so she never saw action.

The first steamboat to be built in Prussia was the PS *Prinzessin Charlotte*. She was a double-hulled wooden vessel, constructed by John Rubie at Pichelsdorf, near Spandau, for the Patentierte Dampfschiff Gesellschaft, and she was launched on 14 September 1816. The vessel was intended for use on the rivers Elbe, Havel and Spree, and entered service on 6 November 1816.

The first steamboat in the Mediterranean was the *Ferdinando Primo*, built of wood at Naples by Messrs Giuseppe Libetta and Adolfo Wolff, and launched on 24 June 1818 for the newly-formed Società Napoletana Pietro Andriel. She sailed from Naples in October 1818 under the command of Capt. Andrea di Martino, and with a British mechanic on board. Her arrival at Genoa and her manoeuvres at that port attracted much popular interest. She left Genoa on 30 October with 10 passengers, and arrived at Marseilles five days later, the first steamboat ever seen in that port.

The first steam-propelled vessel to sail the Atlantic, or indeed any ocean, was the famous American auxiliary PS *Savannah*, built of wood at Corlears Hook, New York, by Francis Fickett, and launched on 22 August 1818. Fitted with three tall masts, this vessel also carried a steam engine of 90 ihp and one cylinder. She ran her trials in March 1819 off Staten Island. She left her home port on 24 May 1819, bound direct for Liverpool under the command of Capt. Moses Rogers who had been at the helm of the PS *Phoenix*, the first steamer on the open sea.

Savannah carried no passengers, but stowed 75 tons of coal and 25 cords of wood. She persevered across the Atlantic, under sail, with the occasional use of her paddles, at a mean speed of about 6 knots. On 17 June she was seen off the coast of Ireland, and reported as a ship on fire. Her log-book on 18 June contains the admission: 'No cole to git up steam'. However, she recoaled at Kinsale and steamed on to Liverpool, where she arrived on 20 June. It was recorded that 'The *Savannah*, a steam vessel, recently arrived at Liverpool from America, the first vessel of the kind which ever crossed the Atlantic; she was chased the whole day, off the coast of Ireland, by the *Kite* Revenue cruiser on the Cork station, which mistook her for a ship on fire.'

The first steamboat to cross the Atlantic under power, as opposed to the auxiliary sailing ship *Savannah*, was the *Curaçao*, 127 ft (38·7 m) LOA, a wooden paddleboat of 438 tons, built in Dundee, Tayside in 1826 and purchased by the Dutch Government for the West Indian mail service. *Curaçao*'s voyage, begun in April 1827 from Rotterdam, Netherlands to the West Indies, lasted 22 days.

The earliest incident in which a steam-driven ship was involved in fighting was in 1824 when the paddle-wheel tug *Diana* operated during the First Burmese War. While the soldiers attacked the Burmese stronghold outside Rangoon, Lieut. Kellett in the *Diana* attacked the enemy's flotilla of war-boats.

The earliest known race for steamboats took place at Rothesay in 1827 when the Northern Yacht Club offered a cup 'for the Swiftest Steamboat' at their Regatta at Rothesay on the Clyde Estuary. The race was won by the *Clarence*, built locally that year by Robert Napier.

Nevertheless, in 1829 the Royal Yacht Club (founded in 1815 as the Yacht Club, later to become the Royal Yacht Squadron) passed a resolution: 'No vessel propelled by steam shall be admitted to the Club, and any member applying a steam engine to his yacht shall be disqualified thereby and cease to be a member.' The proposal to allow steam yachts had been made by a founder member of the Club, Thomas

Assherton-Smith of Andover, Hampshire. When it was thrown out he left and started steam yachting by himself.

The Royal Yacht Squadron relented slightly but grudgingly when, in 1844, a resolution was passed that: 'No steamer of less than 100 hp shall be qualified for admission into, or entitled to, the privileges of the Squadron.'

The first of two steamboats to be successfully propelled by a marine screw in 1837 was the 31 ft (9·5 m) *F. P. Smith* of 6 tons, built at Wapping for her owner, an inventive farmer from north-west London called Francis Pettit Smith, who had patented a single-threaded screw-propeller with two complete twists resembling part of a large corkscrew, which spun in a recess at the stern of the ship.

During trials on the Paddington Canal, half of the wooden prop snapped off and to the surprise of her crew, the *F. P. Smith* steamed all the faster. Smith thus designed a metal screw, consisting of one complete turn instead of two. Fitted with this new screw, his namesake prototype was able to make short trips from London to Folkestone at 5·5 knots.

In 1838, the Ship Propeller Company was formed and built the SS *Archimedes* with a Smith helical screw of 5 ft 9 in (1·75 m), turning at 139 rpm. On trials the vessel attained a speed of more than 9 knots; she accomplished the circumnavigation of Great Britain and made a trip to Oporto, North Portugal. For his enthusiastic promotion and work towards the practical introduction of screw propulsion, Smith received a Knighthood in 1871.

The second of two steamboats to be successfully propelled by a marine screw in 1837, possibly at exactly the same time, was the 45 ft (13·7 m) *Francis B. Ogden*, which was fitted with a screw, designed and patented by an ex-Swedish Army officer called John Ericsson. In 1837, this craft, named after the US Consul at Liverpool, towed the *Surveyor* and three members from the Board of Admiralty up and down the Thames at an average speed of 10 knots.

Ericsson's second experiment was with the 70 ft (21·4 m) *Robert F. Stockton* (named after a Captain in the US Navy), built of iron by Messrs Laird Bros in 1838, which attained a speed of 13 knots with the tide on the Thames.

Model of John Ericsson's screw propeller of 1837 (Science Museum, London)

When Ericsson was informed by their Lordships of the Admiralty that his ideas for screw-driven steamships were impracticable for the Royal Navy, Messrs Ogden and Stockton had no difficulty in persuading the inventor to move to America. Thus the *Robert F. Stockton* had soon crossed the Atlantic under canvas, to begin many years of reliable service as a New York steam tug, the *New Jersey*. By 1843, 13 river steamers with the Ericsson propeller were in use in America.

The first screw vessel constructed by the Admiralty was the *Rattler* in 1843; this sloop-of-war, weighing 888 tons, was built at Sheerness Dockyard in 1841–43 and installed with a 200 hp engine which drove a screw measuring 9 ft (2·7 m) in diameter, which was steadily shortened from 5 ft 6 in (1·7 m) to 1 ft 3 in (0·4 m) as this reduction was found to increase efficiency.

To test relative efficiencies of the screw and the paddle-wheel, a sequence of trials, including races, took place between 1843–45 in which performances of the *Rattler* were compared to those of HM paddle-sloop *Alecto*, the two vessels being 176·5 ft (53·8 m) long, with 32·7 ft (9·9 m) beam and a displacement of 1140 tons each. **But their most famous trial of all** came on 3 April 1845 when two vessels were tied stern-to-stern and both steamed full ahead, the *Rattler* towing the *Alecto* stern foremost at a speed of 2·8 knots. This tug-of-war was not totally conclusive because the engines of the *Rattler* indicated 300 hp and those of the *Alecto* only 141 hp.

A more equal test took place on 20 June 1849 when HM screw-corvette *Niger* (with 400 nominal hp, four-cylinder engines) 'tugged' HM paddle-sloop *Basilisk* (with 405 nominal hp, two-cylinder engines) astern at 1·46 knots for one hour in the English Channel. Both vessels displaced some 1050 tons and had a length of just over 190 ft (57·9 m).

North Sea, 1845: Rattler *towing* Alecto *astern and proving the superiority of screw propeller over paddle-wheel (Science Museum, London)*

Racing between American paddle-steamers on the Mississippi was frequent in the 1840s. The first adventure of the *Cornelius Vanderbilt* (owned by her namesake) was to accept the challenge of 'Live Oak George' Law, owner of the opposition boat, the *Oregon*, and the sporty 'Corneel' sent his boat out into the river for a friendly brush. But she came back beaten; the *Oregon* won by various well-known tricks of piloting, burning pitch under her boilers, and lashing an anvil to the safety valve!

Announced races between paddle steamboats drew betting money from areas that had never even seen a steamboat; newspapers covered the races as sporting features, and results were included in foreign news dispatches.

The fastest long-distance Mississippi trip on record was made between New Orleans and Cairo (1080 miles (1738 km)) by the *Eclipse* at a speed of 14·38 mph (23·1 km/h). This was in 1853.

The time made by the *Robert E. Lee* from New Orleans to St Louis (1027 miles (1653 km)) in 1870, in her famous race with the *Natchez*, was **the best on record**, in as much as the race created a National interest. The *Lee* left New Orleans on Thursday 30 June 1870 at 4.55 p.m. and landed at St Louis at 11.25 a.m. on 4 July 1870 – 6 hr 36 min ahead of the *Natchez*. The officers of the *Natchez* claimed 7 hr 1 min stoppage on account of fog and repairing machinery. The *Robert E. Lee* was commanded by Capt. John W. Cannon and the *Natchez* was in the charge of that veteran southern boatman, Capt. Thomas P. Leathers (see p. 73).

Arguably, **the most popular and well-known paddle-steamer in American waters** was the 260 ft (79 m) *Mary Powell*, built by M. S. Allison at Jersey City in 1861: rebuilt and lengthened to 300 ft (91 m) in 1874, and again rebuilt in 1882. Powered by a Fletcher-Harrison vertical beam engine (bore 62 in × stroke 12 ft), under favourable conditions, *Mary Powell* was able to run 25 mph (40·2 km/h). On 7 August 1874 she made the trip to Poughkeepsie, a distance of 75 miles (120 km), in 3 hr 39 min 15 s; actual running time 3 hr 19 min. In 1881, she made the trip to Rondout in 4 hr 12 min, a distance of 92 miles (148 km). In 1915 she was used on special service duty, stopping at Bear Mountain and later going on to Kingston. She

Steam-driven paddle-wheeler, built by Abdela & Mitchell, probably for use in South America (Hugh McKnight)

was sold out of service in November 1919, and was finally broken up at Kingston, New York, during 1923.

A race which was unique in the annals of the Royal Yacht Squadron took place in 1868 when Lord Vane's yacht, *Cornelia*, raced Mr Talbot's *Eothen* for £100 – both vessels powered by steam.

'The fastest steamer in the world' was the description given by the London *Times* to the 87 ft (26·5 m), 330 hp Thornycroft steam launch, the *Sir Arthur Cotton*, which on 14 April 1874 was officially timed on the Thames along Chiswick Reach at 25·08 mph (40·36 km/h) downstream and 24·15 mph (38·87 km/h) upstream – giving her a mean of 24·61 mph (39·61 km/h).

Between 1884 and 1890, **steam-launch races** were held at the Dartmouth Regatta for boats under 30 ft (9·1 m); they were regularly won by launches built by Messrs Simpson-Strickland & Co. of Teddington – but never at a speed of more than 8 knots.

Steam-launch races were also held during the 1880s on the River Seine, organised by the Cercle de la Voile de Paris (Paris Sailing Club).

The most exciting races between steamcraft took place between the ocean liners across the Atlantic in the 1880s. For example, on Wednesday 18 September 1889 the Inman liner, *City of New York*, the White Star liner, *Teutonic*, and the Anchor liner, *City of Rome*, all left New York harbour together, at 2 p.m. Considerable sums of money were gambled on the rival steamers, both from the land and by those on board, especially on the first two.

On the night of 24 September at 9 p.m., *City of New York* was first sighted off Browhead – the time taken to make the crossing a little over 6 days and 2 hr. The *Teutonic* passed the Browhead just under 3 hr later.

One year later, almost to the day, *City of New York* and *Teutonic* had a 'return match'. *Teutonic* left New York just 20 min after *City*, to arrive at Roches Point just 20 min after *City* had arrived. This might have been a dead heat if the *Teutonic* had not claimed to have travelled a route 21 miles (33·8 km) longer.

In 1885, the 94 ft (28·6 m) American Herreshoff-designed torpedo boat *Stiletto* made one 8-hr test run at 23 knots. On 10 June in the same year, *Stiletto* raced and beat *Mary Powell* in a much publicised sprint race – *Mary Powell*'s supporters claiming that *Stiletto* would not have maintained her lead had the race been of longer distance.

The most famous British high-speed launch which is rated as **the fastest Umpire's launch on the River Thames** is the 47 ft (14·3 m) steel-plated *Hibernia*, built in 1894 by Simpson-Strickland & Co. for R. H. Labatt of Henley and fitted with a Des Vignes two-cylinder reciprocating steam engine (bore $7\frac{1}{8}$ in × stroke 6 in). On one trial she is reported to have attained some 27 knots.

Mr Whittaker's private steam yacht, Angela, *built by Camper & Nicholsons in the 1880s (Beken of Cowes Ltd)*

The fastest ever American steam launch was Charles R. Flint's aluminium and mahogany 132 ft (40·2 m), Mosher-designed *Arrow*. With a beam of only 12·5 ft (3·8 m) and 3·6 ft (1·09 m) draught, engined with two 3500 hp reciprocating steam engines, this express yacht was timed, in Spring 1903, along a US Government Measured Mile to a speed of 39·13 knots.

The very first steamboat ever launched on an African lake was the *Ilala* on 12 October 1875. The story which led up to this momentous event began 20 years before.

A steam launch called the *Dayspring* had been sent on the third Niger Expedition in 1857 and although used to start the Niger Mission ended up a wreck in 1877.

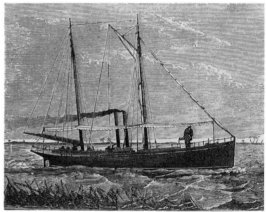

David Livingstone's Ilala *on Lake Nyasa (1875) (Mary Evans Picture Library)*

For his second Zambesi Expedition of 1858, sponsored by the British Government, David Livingstone intended to find a navigable route up the Zambesi River, using an 80 ft (24 m) river launch built of steel at Birkenhead, and named the *Ma-Robert* after his wife, Mary. Foiled by the impassable Quebrabasa Rapids, Livingstone and his argumentative crew turned the leaking and 'asthmatic' steamer about and entered upon an exploration of the Shire River, only to be turned back by further cataracts after a 200-mile (322 km) journey. Thus Lake Nyasa was discovered on foot in September 1859.

In 1860, after assembly of a new steam launch called the *Pioneer*, Livingstone steamed up the Ruvuma River as an alternative route to Lake Nyasa (now Lake Malawi), but after only 30 miles (48 km) Ruvuma became too shallow for the *Pioneer* and again Livingstone had to turn back. Determined that the presence of a steam launch on Lake Nyasa would put pay to the slave trade, Livingstone now put nearly all of his own savings into paying for another vessel, which he called the *Lady Nyasa*. But in 1862 even this third craft failed to steam more than 156 miles (251 km) up the Ruvuma; so she was taken back and up the Shire River to be dismantled and carried in sections past the cataracts. Unfortunately, on 2 July 1863, the British Government recalled the expedition. Livingstone, despite illness, tramped on foot for 700 miles (1127 km) and then, with a scratch crew, steamed his own *Lady Nyasa* for over 2000 miles (3220 km) across the Indian Ocean.

After Livingstone's death in 1873, the Nyasa Mission, formed to continue the suppression of the slave trade in East Africa, approached Alfred Yarrow's Boatyard at East Poplar, River Thames and commissioned a 55 ft (16·8 m) long, 10 ft (3 m) beam, twin-engined, £1600 steam launch to be called the *Ilala*, after the place where the late Dr Livingstone's heart had been buried. She was light with a shallow draft, capable of being dismantled after a rough journey up the Zambesi shallows. Her parts were then to be bodily carried by 800 men through 60 miles (96 km) of forest, to avoid the cataracts, and re-assembled, launched into the Shire and steamed into the lake, 1400 miles (2253 km) inland. This was accomplished. Thirty-three years later the last dhow, full of slaves, was captured on Lake Nyasa and slavery was practically abolished.

Le Stanley was made to the order of H. M. Stanley when he was exploring the Congo and required something bigger than the *Ilala*. Stanley foresaw that the vessel would have to be assembled and taken apart repeatedly – so Alfred Yarrow's Boatyard built her in nine sections, each small enough to be shipped out to Africa, and each capable of floating by itself. When an obstacle was met, the sections were unbolted and each had four wheels attached to it, converting it to a wagon – otherwise, nine wagons. *Le Stanley* steamed on the Congo River by 1884.

The first steam launch to be used for missionary work outside Africa was the London Missionary Society's *Ellengowan I*, purchased in 1873. She worked on the coast of New Guinea up the Fly River, and to and from Australia until 1880.

The first steam launch to be used by the Church Missionary Society was the *Dove* in 1874, unfortunately wrecked on the way to Mombasa. The *Highland Lassie*, an 80-ton sailing yacht with auxiliary steam power was used as a despatch boat between Mombasa and Zanzibar in 1876.

The first full twin-screw steam launch used by the Church Missionary Society was the *Daisy*, initially used to explore the Wami and Kingani rivers in 1876.

The first steam vessel to cross the Antarctic Circle was HMS *Challenger* in 1874, two years and two months after her departure from England.

The world's last, sea-going passenger-carrying paddle-steamer still in operation is the *Waverly*, built in 1947 by A. & E. Inglish Ltd of Glasgow as a 'new luxury steamer' of 695 tons, to carry 1350 passengers at 17 knots using steam reciprocating machinery. Built specifically to re-open the Three Lochs Tour, the LNER's principal Clyde Tourist route, she was withdrawn from service by Caledonian MacBrayne and is owned by the Paddle-Steamer Preservation Society.

The longest surviving Swiss steamboat is the 138 ft (42 m), 90-ton, *Rigi*, built by Ditchborn & Mare (London) in 1847 for the Lake Lucerne Steamship Company. In 1893, after 45 years of service between Lucerne and Fluelen, *Rigi* was given a new Escher-Wyss engine with oscillating cylinders, a new boiler and new paddle-wheels. When she was finally taken out of operation in 1952, after 105 years of service, *Rigi* had travelled, with over six million people, some 675 300 nautical miles (more than 30 times round the world). She is now a restaurant for the Swiss Transport Museum – some of her parts being 131 years old.

The longest surviving paddle-steamer, wholly within the Victorian era, was the PS *Industry* (LOA 68 ft (20·7 m) × B 11 ft (3·3 m) × D 8 ft (2·4 m)). Built of scotch oak in 1814 by Messrs William Fyfe of Fairlie (near Glasgow), her gross tonnage was 52 tons. She was the sixth steamer to be built on the Clyde, and was powered by a Thomson single-cylinder, 10 hp, 'side-lever' engine, complete with copper boiler. She began her life carrying goods between Glasgow and Greenock. In 1828 she had a new Caird engine fitted although the spur gearing for driving her paddles was retained – regrettably, because the noisy cogs were continually giving way and had to be replaced; *Industry* was thus nicknamed the 'Coffee Mill'.

During the next 50 years, this steamboat changed owners frequently – at one time she was owned by the Clyde Shipping Company. In 1873, when Messrs Steel & McCaskil presented her to the Glasgow Chamber of Commerce, at 59 years-of-age, *Industry* was even then admired as the seventh oldest steamer in the world. Soon after, with the frame of her starboard paddle damaged by a collision, she was left to rot in the mud of Bowling Harbour; her hulk was still to be seen there in the late 1890s, whilst her second engine had been taken out and re-erected in Kelvingrove Park, Glasgow – to commemorate early steam navigation in Glasgow.

The oldest steamship in the British Navy was HMS *Wildfire*. At 186 tons, 198 hp, she was originally built for the General Post Office in 1826 at a cost of £9658 and christened PS *Watersprite*. She used to carry mail from Dover to Calais. She was accepted into the Navy in 1938, when the GPO gave up running steam packets. HMS *Wildfire* was employed for many years as tender to HMS *Duncan*, flagship of the Commander-in-Chief at Nore. In January 1888 when she was condemned as unfit for further service, HMS *Wildfire* was 62 years old.

Early photograph, taken c1845–50 by a member of the Norwich-based 'Brotherhood' (Chairman: T. D. Eaton), showing the Norwich–Yarmouth paddle-steamer

The longest surviving Scottish steamboat was the *Glencoe* (ex-*Mary Jane*), built in 1846 for the Stornoway run and still in regular service on the mail run from Mallaig and Kyle of Lochalsh to Portree, Skye until Spring 1931. She was 85 years old. **The second longest surviving steamboat** was the *Glengarry* (ex-*Edinburgh Castle*), built in 1844 and in service on the Caledonian Canal from 1845 to 1927. She was 82 years old. **The third longest surviving Scottish steamboat** was the *Iona* of 1864, continuously in service on the Clyde and West Highland routes until the end of the 1935 summer season. She was 71 years old.

The world's oldest active steamship is the *Skibladner*, which has travelled on Lake Mjøsa, Norway since 1856. She has had two major refits and was built in Motala, Sweden.

The oldest steam vessel in Great Britain is the Bridgwater Docks Scraper boat, *Bertha* (LOA 50 ft (15·2 m) × B 13½ ft (4·1 m) × D 4 ft (1·2m)), built in 1844 to the designs of Isambard Kingdom Brunel by G. Lunnel & Co. of Bristol. Displacing some 60 tons, *Bertha* had no steering and used cables to dredge backwards and forwards from the quay walls to the centre of the dock. Still working in Bristol until the late 1960s, the *Bertha* is now afloat at the Exeter Maritime Museum.

The oldest steam launch in operation is the 41 ft (12·5 m) *Dolly*, raised from Ullswater, Cumbria in 1962. Originally owned by Alfred Fildes in the 1850s, *Dolly* sank in about 40 ft (12 m) of water during the great frost of February 1895. She was discovered in 1960 by sub-aqua divers and on being brought to the surface it was revealed that both her single-cylinder engine and Scotch wet-back, return-tube boiler were still in place, and that her pine on oak carvel construction was still sound. She is presently at the Windermere Steamboat Museum, founded by Mr G. H. Pattinson.

The oldest steam launch, with her original machinery, on the Lloyds Register of Shipping is John Issac Thornycroft's iron-hulled Boat Number 5, *Waterlily*, built in 1866. Measuring 42 ft (12·8 m) she still has her original single-cylinder engine (6⅛ in bore × 7 in stroke) and vertical boiler. She was fully restored by Vosper-

Thornycroft apprentices in 1977, undergoing successful speed trials at both Gosport and the Beaulieu River. She is at present on show, as a static exhibit, at the National Maritime Museum, Greenwich.

The second oldest steam launch in Lloyds Register of Shipping, with her original machinery still in operation, is the 71 ft (21·6 m) iron-hulled *Raven* (1871), presently at the Winder-mere Steamboat Museum. **The third oldest steam launch with her original machinery** is Thorny-croft Boat Number 9, the *Cygnet* (1872), 29 ft (8·8 m) LOA, and presently owned by Turks of Kingston.

Whilst the 1500 gross tons *Ruahine* (1865), owned by the Panama, New Zealand and Australian Royal Mail Steam Packet Company, was one of **the earliest twin-screw steamships**, and twin-screw craft were being used by the Admiralty in 1867, possibly **the earliest twin-screw steam yacht** was the 65 ft (19·8 m) TSSY *Esperance* (1869) built on the Clyde by T. B. Heath & Co. for the great Furness industrialist, H. W. Schneider, when he came to live at Bow-ness. Presently at the Windermere Steamboat Museum, *Esperance* is **the oldest boat on Lloyds Register of Shipping**.

STEAM TURBINE

The first full-scale craft to be propelled by steam turbines was the 100 ft (30·5 m) steel-plated *Turbinia* built in 1894 around the designs of the Hon. C. A. Parsons, inventor of electric-generat-ing steam turbines as used for the lighting on streets and in ships. *Turbinia*'s toothpick hull was developed from experiments made by tow-ing 2 ft (0·6 m) models across a pond with a fish-ing rod and line, and then by a self-propelling 6 ft (1·8 m) model with a wound-up rubber band.

Constructed at the Sheet Iron Works of Brown & Hood, overlooking the River Tyne, *Turbinia* was engined with a 2000 hp radial-flow engine and boiler built at Heaton. After one year's trials on the River Tyne (where Parsons eventually solved the problem of cavitation by replacing the single prop-shaft with three shafts, which were fitted with three 18 in propellers apiece and driven by three tur-

Turbinia, steaming at 33 knots (Richardsons, Westgarth Ltd)

bines in series) in April 1897, *Turbinia* was officially timed at 32·75 knots over the Measured Mile, accelerating from 0 to 28·5 knots in 20 s and decelerating in 35 s.

Their Lordships of the Admiralty remained unconvinced over the practical superiority of the turbine as compared to the most efficient steam reciprocating engine then in use.

Therefore on Sunday 27 June 1897, at the Diamond Jubilee Review of Queen Victoria at Spithead, where no less than 27 miles (43 km) of 170 ships were ceremonially at anchor, Parsons accelerated his red and yellow *Turbinia* to some 34 knots and sped along the lines of battle-ships and cruisers with HM picket boats in futile pursuit. *Turbinia* was at once recognised as the **'fastest vessel afloat'**, and not long after her return to the Tyne, the British Admiralty opened negotiations with the Parsons Marine Steam Turbine Co. for the building of a turbine-driven destroyer.

Sir Charles Parsons (1854–1931) (Richardsons, Westgarth Ltd)

The first steam-turbine craft built for the British Navy was HM torpedo-boat destroyer *Viper*, fitted with no less than five prop-shafts; in July 1900 *Viper* clocked a speed of 37·113 knots on an Admiralty Measured Mile.

ELECTRIC

The first paddleboat to be propelled by an electric motor was designed and built by the Russian physicist, Prof. Jacobi in 1839, with Tsar Nikolas of Russia as his patron. The large engine was made up of electro-magnets – initially activated by a Daniell galvanic battery, but with more successful results from a Grove battery of 128 couples, wherein zinc plates were dissolved in acid.

Although the Jacobi boat paddled up the River Neva, near St Petersburg at some 2 mph (3 km/h), the machinery emitted such toxic, nitrous gases that her crew, choked and asphyxiated by these sickening and suffocating fumes, were obliged to stop their observations!

The first French paddleboat to be propelled by an electric motor, activated by a bank of Grove batteries, was tested on the Bois de Boulogne Lake by M. de Molins in 1859 – but without success. It was not until accumulators had been invented for collecting and storing electricity that electric boats became a practical possibility.

The first trial of Trouvé's electric boat on the River Seine (26 May 1881) (Mary Evans Picture Library)

Gustave Trouvé (1839–1902) (Mary Evans Picture Library)

The first successful screw-driven electric boat was designed and built in 1881 by a Frenchman, Gustave Trouvé, who had taken out his first patent on 8 May 1880.

On 1 August 1881, Trouvé reported to the French Academy of Sciences that: 'A 5 kg motor, activated by six Fauré-Planté accumulators was, on 26 May 1881, placed in a launch 18 ft (5·50 m) long and 4 ft (1·20 m) beam, carrying three people, which achieved a log speed of 2 m 50 downstream to Pont-Royal and 1 m 50 upstream. The engine was activated by two banks of bichromate-potash batteries, driving a three-bladed propeller.'

That Trouvé's electric motor was positioned astern, directly over the rudder, and was easily detachable from the transom by simple pintle-and-gudgeon type fittings, made the Trouvé motor **the first successful detachable – or outboard – motor ever built**.

On 26 June 1881, Trouvé again tested his launch on the Bois de Boulogne lake – this time with a four-bladed 28 cm diameter propeller, driven by Bunsen-plate, Ruhmkorff-type batteries charged with one part hydrochloric acid, one part nitric acid, and two parts water in a porous vase to lessen the emission of nitrous fumes.

The speed, as measured by an ordinary log, read 492 ft (150 m) in 24 s; but after a running time of 3 hr this had dropped to 492 ft (150 m) in 55 s; after 5 hr this had further fallen to 492 ft (150 m) in 65 s.

Trouvé exhibited his 'Motor and Screw' at the Paris Exhibition of 1881.

The first English-built, electric-powered, screw-driven boat was the iron-hulled *Electricity* (LOA 25 ft (7·6 m) × B 5 ft (1·5 m) × D 2 ft (0·6 m)) which went on her maiden trip on Thursday, 28 September 1882 on the Thames from Millwall to London Bridge and back. *Electricity* was designed by Mr A. Reckenzann CE, and built for the Electrical Power Storage Company at Millwall to accommodate 12 passengers.

Power came from 45 electric Planté accumulators (40 lb × 10 in × 8 in), modified by Messrs Sellon and E. Volckmar to total 96 volts and supply power for 6 hr at 4 hp to two Siemens D3 dynamos with regulators and reverse gear, and belt-drive a Collis-Browne type 20 in (0·9 m) water-screw of 3 ft (0·9 m) pitch at a power reduction from 950 to 350 rpm. Either, or both, motors could be 'switched into circuit' at will.

Electricity's accumulators could be re-charged whilst she was at anchor, by wires which came across the wharf from the factory bringing currents generated by dynamos set up in the works.

Whilst the powerplant was below the seats and floorboards, the steering was managed by the same person who operated the switches, seated in a central cabin. With the absence of steam, making a warning whistle obsolete, an electric bell was installed in its place.

On *Electricity*'s maiden voyage, Gustave Phillipart Jr attended to the engines, whilst Mr Volckmar, Silvanus P. Thompson and an engineer were the only others on board. She made a speed of 8 knots upstream and proved herself eminently manoeuvrable.

The first – and last – convertible paddle/screw-driven electric boat, *La Sirene*, was constructed in 1882 by Gustave Trouvé for M. de Nabat. She was 29 ft (9 m) long with a beam of 5·9 ft (1·8 m), and she attained a regular speed of 9·3 mph (15 km/h), being used two or three times per week.

The first time an electric boat entered a sporting event was at a Yacht Club of France Regatta held on the River Aube, south-east of Paris on 8 October 1882. Only five minutes before gun-fire for a sailing contest, the Trouvé boat raced over the 4000-yard (3200 m) course in 17 min, making four turns around the buoys.

Electricity, the first English-built electric-powered boat (1882) (Mary Evans Picture Library)

During the exhibition held at Vienna, Austria in 1883 an electric launch, constructed by Messrs Yarrow of Poplar, East London, called the *Beni*, gave rides to as many as 45 passengers, up and down the River Danube.

In 1888, Customs Officers of the old Chinese Empire, realising the silent superiority of an electric motor over a 30 hp clattering steam launch, during the tricky process of catching an opium smuggler unawares at night on his junk, commissioned a 49 ft (15 m) steel-plated Trouvé launch of 8 tons displacement, and capable of 11 mph (18 km/h), to be transported out to Shanghai Harbour. Equipped with an electric headlamp with a range of 3·7 miles (6 km), this launch was exhibited at the 1889 Paris Universal Exhibition.

The first sea-going electric launch was a 29 ft (8·8 m) cutter, into which the French Admiralty installed accumulators and an electric motor for trials in Le Havre harbour in 1887. Calculating that the total weight of electric machinery was 100 lb heavier than the equivalent steam machinery necessary, it was not long before they abandoned their trials.

The largest electric boat ever built in the 1880s was the *Viscountess Bury* (LOA 65 ft 6 in (20 m) × B 10 ft (3 m) × D 1 ft 10 in (0·6 m)) of 12½ tons displacement. She was launched from Maynards Boatyard, Chiswick on Monday 8 October 1888. Designed by Mr W. Sargeant to carry upwards of 80 passengers comfortably, *Viscountess Bury*'s 200 Electrical Power Storage Company's accumulators, each with a capacity of 145 amphours, powered two motors designed by Mr M. Immisch to convert electrical energy into 7½ hp at 1000 rpm and drive her twin, three-bladed props at 600 rpm; she thus had enough electrical energy sufficient with one charge to travel for 10 hr at 6 mph (9·6 km/h) as regulated by the Thames Conservancy bye-laws. It is believed that Viscount Bury himself was Mr Immisch's patron, because in 1889 Immisch acquired the lower part of Platts Eyott Island on the Thames, near Hampton, and built a generating station there – this was the beginnings of the Immisch Electric Launch Company.

Today, some 90 years later, the *Viscountess Bury*, petrol-engined, is stationed at Ely, near Cambridge and runs trips on the River Ouse.

HRH Queen Alexandra, wife of King Edward VII, on board the electric launch, The Angler, *flagship of the Andrews fleet*

The first electric launch to be built for the Royal Navy was called the *Electric*, built in 1891 by Messrs Woodhouse & Rawson of Kew for harbour use and to convey troops from place to place in Chatham Dockyard. That same year an 80 ft (24 m) river barge was converted into a floating charging station on the Thames, with a semi-portable steam engine/dynamo, generating enough power to charge six launches simultaneously. This was particularly advantageous during regattas such as Henley Royal.

During the early 1890s, it is reported that a M. Flaurin constructed a 52 ft (16 m) electric launch with a 60 hp electric motor, capable of travelling 30 nautical miles at 10 knots top speed, and 200 nautical miles at 5 knots. The boat weighed 3·6 cwt.

In 1898, the Russian Navy operated half-a-dozen sea-going British-built electric launches, one of which, a 32-footer (9·7 m) carried 42 Fauré-King accumulators, driving two 5 hp motors at 7 knots for 4 hr, or 4½ knots for 10 hr.

The most popular period for the electric launch was the turn of the century. Whereas in 1888 there were six charging stations on the Thames, by 1902 there were over 20 on land, and two floating barges.

The Immisch Electric Launch Company had a hire fleet of over 50 launches, ranging from 20 to 65 ft (6 to 20 m) in length, with a passenger capacity of four to 80 persons. The accumulators – T23, B15, E19, C7's – were manufactured by the Electrical Power Storage Company to drive Immisch motors of from 1½ hp up to 12 hp, at 65, 95 and 120 volts – and give with certainty a run of 30 miles (48 km) at 6 mph (9 km/h), on one charge, half up and half down-stream.

The Thames Valley Launch Company of Weybridge, with its Managing Director, Mr W. Rowland Edwards, offered 40 launches for hire, many of which were fitted with the Edwards reversible, feathering propeller. Messrs Andrews & Sons of Maidenhead had a fleet of 12 electric launches, each one named after a freshwater fish, except for the flagship which was called *The Angler*. Apart from these 100 launches on the Thames, between Teddington Lock and Oxford (93 miles (150 km)), a number of provincial corporations purchased electric boats for use in their ornamental parks. The first electric launch on Waterloo Lake (Roundhay Park, Leeds) was the 70 ft (21 m) *Mary Gordon*, named after the Lady Mayoress of Leeds who launched her in 1899. She had a maximum load of 75 adults or 120 children. From 1896 the English Lake District had a number of electric launches for hire, with the Irish and Scottish Lake Districts following suit; some British-built launches had been exported to Venice.

Between 1892 and 1910 the Electro Launch Company of Bayonne, New Jersey (USA), founded by Henry Carse, built a great many electric launches, eg a 55 ft (16·8 m) twin-screw electric cabin yacht, capable of running 125 miles (201 km) on one charge of the storage batteries.

In 1911, John Delmar-Morgan, an electrical engineer and expert in DC traction, installed a petrol-electric drive in his boat *Mansura*, modifying and updating that installation in 1926, without change until his death in 1948. With *Mansura*, he made a number of long-distance ocean cruises, without trouble, around the coast of England.

Even today, a number of electric launches are still plying freely on the lakes at Hangchow in the People's Republic of China – estimated from their construction and type of battery to be over 60 years old, and used on an environmental basis – Hangchow being a scenic beauty spot.

The most important cause behind the decline of the quiet, clean, environmental electric launch in later decades was the development and ease of maintenance of the marine oil engine (however, see p. 242).

J. J. Etienne Lenoir (1822–96) (Mary Evans Picture Library)

INTERNAL COMBUSTION

The first boat to be powered by the internal combustion of a mixture of air and petrol inside the cylinder was built by the French inventor, Jean Joseph Etienne Lenoir (1822–1900), for M. Dalloz, manager of *Le Monde Illustré* newspaper, in 1865. The 40-footer (12 m) boat was equipped with a 6 hp Lenoir engine, and despite its low speed and high petroleum consumption Dalloz used it on the Seine for two years to commute from Paris to Charenton.

In 1880 the American inventor, Brayton, is reported to have installed his version of the internal combustion engine in a boat.

The first German motorboat was 20 ft (6 m) long and built by engineer/inventor Gottlieb Daimler. It was installed with a 1 hp gas engine, and went on trials along the River Neckar at Cannstadt in August 1886. Public prejudice against petroleum spirit, fostered by the destructive nature of naphtha launches, forced Daimler to make his initial trials in utmost secrecy, with the engine being installed at 2 a.m. in the morning and quietly taken out again around 5 a.m. when the first riverside dawn commuters were sighted. Its transportation to and from Daimler's works had to be of an extremely covert, backstreet nature!

Gottlieb Daimler's first motorboat (1886); on board, between chauffeur and engine, are Daimler and Maybach

Within two months, with no previous examples on which to base his design, Daimler innovated and patented a new position for the prop-shaft of his motorboat, thus lifting speeds above the initial 6 mph (9·6 km/h).

To abolish prejudice and fear that his motorboat might blow up, Daimler fixed porcelain knobs round the gunwhales and wired them together, thus 'tricking' the local people that he was only experimenting with an electric launch. The Daimler craft was thus ludicrously credited with 310 miles (500 km) *on one charge*!

The first French motorboat, was a converted iron-hulled steam launch called the *Le Volapuck*. It was installed with a twin-piston, single-cylinder engine, complete with primitive magneto and gearbox, by the engineer/inventor Fernand Forest in 1885, and received its Navigation Licence from Michael Levy and Mr Walckenaer of the Ministry of Mines in December 1886, after a trial trip from Auteuil (near Paris) out around Billancourt Bay and back.

The second and last motorboat to be designed and constructed for J. J. Etienne Lenoir was built by Luce of Argenteuil to 27 ft (8 m) length over 5½ ft (1·65 m) beam, and fitted with a two-cylinder Lenoir engine on the Beau de Rochas cycle, built by Messrs Rouart brothers (concessionaires of his last patent). Ignition was by battery, bobine and spark plugs. Christened *Le*

Lenoir, the boat was launched in 1887, and after trials on the Seine was sent to the Le Havre Marine Exhibition where it made the journey from Le Havre to Tancarville twice a week at 9 mph (14 km/h).

The first motorboat to navigate Lac Leman (Geneva) was the 33-footer (10 m) *Kansas*, built by Fernand Forest for an American called Nicod and installed with a twin-cylinder 6 hp Forest engine to travel at an estimated speed of 10 mph (16 km/h). Because petroleum was then

Two-cylinder, horizontal engine, with magneto ignition on board Kansas *(1887)*

prohibited in Switzerland, Forest and Nicod made do with 13 gallons (59 litres) of 'legal' benzine and *Kansas* duly motored away from the Tour de Peilz, one springtime day in 1887.

The first motor auxiliary was commissioned from Forest by Georges Gallice, late in 1887. Her hull was built by Pere Wauthelet, her engine used a primitive coil ignition. She was christened *Ellen* and launched into La Rapée in May 1888. After voyaging some thousands of miles, *Ellen* figured afloat at the 1889 Paris Universal Exhibition, in the Class 65 Pleasure-Boating Section, alongside Le Lenoir, a Daimler motorboat, and a Benz motorboat, being demonstrated on a temporary lake near the Pont d'Iena.

Forest also claimed to have pioneered **the first ever yacht's motor dinghy/davit** for *Phebe*, M. E. Mallet's 155-ton schooner, also in early 1888. Constructed by Durenne in 2 mm galvanised steel, this 21-footer (6·5 m) dinghy was initially powered by a twin-cylinder horizontal Forest engine, replaced in 1892 by a four-cylinder type; she was still motoring in 1906 – 19 years later.

By 1888 Daimler had built three demonstration motorboats, one of which, the *Rems* (named after a tributary of the River Neckar), he personally demonstrated to officials of Baden-Baden on the 3900 sq yd (3600 sq m) Waldsee. He also built a motorboat to the order of Prince Otto von Bismarck, Imperial Chancellor of the newly-united Germany, called *Marie*, to be used on Bismarck's Friedrichsruh lake.

Although he had sold another 32 ft (10 m) launch to a private customer, Daimler could not resist the temptation of demonstrating its 12 knots in front of the German Emperor during the fêtes on the Wannensee near Potsdam – this was against his customer's express wishes. When the owner found out, he obtained a writ. To serve that writ, an officer on board a steam launch attempted to chase the Daimler, which was manned by Daimler's son Adolf, the engineer Bauer and the Englishman, F. R. Simms. To the delight of the onlookers, the steam launch failed hopelessly to catch the motorboat.

The first motorboat to appear on the River Elbe at Hamburg was the 23-footer (7 m) *Die Sieben Schwaben* (The Seven Swabians), powered by a

A Daimler motorboat on the River Neckar at Esslingen

V-twin-cylinder, 2 hp Daimler engine and manned by Gottlieb, Adolf Daimler, and the engineer, Alfred Lewerenz. On 15 October 1888, *Die Sieben Schwaben* made a profound impression as it followed the steam tugs which pulled the *Kaiser Wilhelm II* on a journey through Hamburg.

The first Hamburg firm to order a boat equipped with a 2 hp Daimler engine was the well-known sailcloth and rigging firm Canel and Son. The boat was built at the Edouard Hopner Yard in Steinwarder. This vessel was the prototype of the Hamburg harbour launches that were soon commissioned for conveying light goods from cargo vessels to various warehouses.

In America, in 1888, Ransome E. Olds (of 'Oldsmobile' fame) installed a two-cylinder gasoline motor in a launch.

The first engine to be successfully run using paraffin vapour was built by William Dent Priestman and his brother Samuel of Hull, England in 1886 in consideration of the prejudice held by insurance companies against petroleum spirit. The first boats to be installed with Priestman Oil Engines were barges, tugs and a couple of fishing boats – in 1888.

The same year, Messrs Alfred Yarrow & Co. of Poplar, East London, were experimenting with their 'Zephyr' launch, with its generator and engine moved by the continual reprocessing of petroleum spirit from liquid to vapour to liquid, etc – with no apparent wastage of fuel.

The first twin-engined motor yacht was the
Djezyrely (LOA 54 ft (16·4 m)×9 ft (2·7 m)),
constructed by Abel le Marchand of Le Havre
in 1888 for the Marquis d'Ure d'Aubais. Installed with two Rouart-Lenoir engines, totalling
16 hp, the *Djezyrely*'s first voyage from Le
Havre to Paris during the cold winter was a
revealing one. Although the engine worked well,
the carburettor, which had been installed on
deck so as to take away the fumes from the
interior cabins, became totally iced-up, giving
the engineer M. Crebassac no end of trouble!
Once in Paris, he moved the carburettor below
decks before taking this motor yacht to the
Mediterranean by canal, then to Constantinople.

During the 1889 Paris Universal Exhibition,
it was Gottlieb Daimler's meeting with Messrs
René Panhard and Emile Levassor, whilst
demonstrating his boat on the artificial lake,
which led to the production, a couple of years
later, of the first Panhard et Levassor motorcar.

**The first Daimler motorboats to be shipped to
Russia** were running on the Dnjester and Dnjepr
Rivers by 1890.

**The first motorboat to be powered by a six-
cylinder Forest engine** was *Tonton II* (1890).

In 1890 Daimler's English friend, Frederick
Simms, ran the *Toni*, a very lightly-built
mahogany launch, fitted with a four-cylinder
nominal 5 hp Daimler engine, which he later

*Cannstatt, the first Daimler motor launch to be imported to
England*

claimed had reached a speed of 13·4 mph
(21·5 km/h). On 6 May 1891, Simms arranged
for **the first Daimler launch to be imported to
England**; this was the *Cannstatt*, powered by a
2 hp V-cylinder engine. Refused permission to
exhibit her on the Serpentine, the Welsh Harp
or the Crystal Palace Lake, Simms gave trial
runs on the River Thames between Charing
Cross and Westminster, and also exhibited her
at the Henley Regatta.

In May 1892, fully aware of the public prejudice against petroleum spirit, Simms applied for
permission from the Metropolitan District
Railway to moor the 'steam launch' (!) *Cannstatt*
at Putney Iron Railway Bridge pier at £1 per
month. This was innocently granted him. At the
same time another launch, the *Daimler*, with a
5 hp, four-cylinder motor, was imported from
Germany and purchased by Simms' wealthy
friend, the Hon. Evelyn Ellis of Datchet. The
installation had a surface carburettor and tube
ignition, whilst ahead and astern drives were
operated by means of sliding, rubber-coned
friction clutches. Ellis exhibited *Daimler* locally
that June on Eton Commemoration day in front
of the British Aristocracy, also at Henley
Regatta, and again in Southampton Waters. In
July 1892, Simms & Co. successfully submitted a
tender for supplying the London County
Council with a motor pinnace (LOA 37 ft
(11·2 m)×B 8 ft (12·4 m)×D 3 ft (0·9 m))
which was soon built by Watkins & Co. of
Blackwall and powered with a 10 hp, four-
cylinder Daimler engine. During her trial over

F. R. Simms, the British motorboat pioneer

the Measured Mile at Erith, with Simms and Sir Alexander Binnie (LCC Chief Engineer) on board, this £748 pinnace clocked a speed of 9 knots. From the resulting publicity, Simms was soon being approached by engineers and boat-builders, such as Moffats of Gloucester, who wished to do business.

Elsewhere in Europe, Daimler motorboats were making their maiden voyages. In the sum-mer, a Daimler motorboat made a voyage round Sicily – a journey of some 360 miles (580 km); the booklet describing this voyage had a pro-found influence on the Italian motor industry. The Cannstadt Daimler Co. also began business with Jules Renaud & Co. of Sydney, Melbourne & Antwerp for **importation of the first motor-boats to Australia**.

The first motorboat to be used by the French Navy was a 27 ft (8·3 m)Forest-engined dinghy for the *Magellan*, built and officially tested by Engineer Vermand in 1892.

The first petrol-driven outboard engine in the world was the *Motogodille* ('Stern-Oar-Motor'), tested by its Parisian inventor, Alfred Seguin, in the SNG garage in Geneva, Switzerland in 1892.

In Spring 1893, the 30 ft (9 m), 4 hp *Twaddler* and the 23 ft (7 m), 2 hp *Plucky* were imported to London via Bremen, and with his newly-formed Daimler Motor Syndicate Ltd, Frederick

Simms now received permission from the Metropolitan District Railway Co. to occupy Arch No. 71 under the Middlesex end of Putney Iron Bridge at an annual rental of £25 p.a. Here H. van Toll and several other workmen prepared to repair and fit 'hot air motors' into launches, using lathes driven by a 6 hp gas engine and portable forge. But no sooner had Alfred Powell, Manager of the Metropolitan Co., dis-covered that Simms' Daimler launches were fuelled by petroleum spirit, then 'for reasons of safety' he gave notice to Simms 'to remove them from our pier at your earliest convenience possible'.

In an attempt to calm his fears, Simms sent Powell several testimonials in praise of Daimler launches – including one from the celebrated Baron Barreto – and also took out an insurance policy with the Northern Assurance Company, particularly covering Arch No. 71.

By this time, after arrangement with Messrs Carless, Capel & Leonard, who were supplying Daimler customers with a launch spirit of specific gravity 0·690, Simms decided to give this fuel the distinctive trade name of petrol.

Also in 1893, William Steinway, of New York, later famous for his superbly-constructed pianos, imported and installed Daimler engines in launches at his workshops on Long Island.

In December 1893 M. Behr, naval attaché to the Russian Government, commissioned a 29 ft

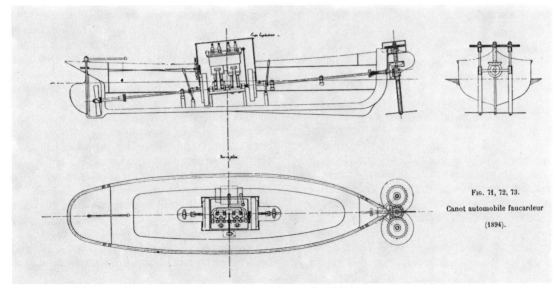

Fᴵɢ. 71, 72, 73.

Canot automobile faucardeur

(1894).

Canot-Automobile Faucardeur ('water-weed-cutting, automobile canoe') of 1894

(9 m), 8 hp launch from Fernand Forest, destined for the port of Nicolaief. Forest built this launch in steel to the plans of the Russian Imperial Navy and her 7-knot trials took place on the Seine in such cold weather that she had to push aside lumps of ice!

In 1894, Jules Mesurer commissioned a 26 ft (8 m), 8 hp, four-cylinder launch from Forest which at one end turned the screw and at the other a cutting-disc mechanism for clearing weeds from the pond in Edmond de Rothschild's magnificent Armainvilliers estate. Forest called this **the first 'Canot Automobile Faucardeur'** ('water-weed cutting automobile canoe')!

Also in 1894, Dr Fred Lanchester, English engineer/inventor, had his single-cylinder, 800 rpm engine installed in a boat built by Slaters of Folley Bridge, Oxford, to drive a stern paddlewheel. **This first British-built motor paddleboat** went on her trials in the spring of that year.

Although the Paris Sailing Club (Cercle de la Voile de Paris) had organised a race for two Daimler motor launches in 1889, **the first regatta race for motorboats** took place in Nice (France) during the 1894–95 Season. The local newspapers had announced a yachting race, and many spectators pressed onto the quays and promenades. But instead of the large yachts turning up at the starting line, all they saw were four four-cylinder motor-dinghies from the yachts *Gipsy* (Count Biscaretti), *Colibri* (André Chauchard), *Jolie Brise* (Georges Gallice) and *Saint Andrée* (Paul Chauchard). The race was won by the *Jolie Brise* motor-dinghy at a speed of 9 knots.

In 1895 **the largest Daimler motor-sailer yet seen** was built by Summers & Payne for a Mr Beatty of Bassett, near Southampton. Called the *Alice* (LOA 41 ft 5 in (12·6 m) × B 8 ft 5 in (2·6 m)) she was built of oak frames and mahogany planking. She was lugger-rigged and her twin-screws were driven by two 10 hp, four-cylinder Daimler engines, with petrol tanks holding 60 gallons (273 litres) and sufficient for a run of 300 to 400 miles (500 to 650 km). Twin engines gave her 9 knots, whilst one engine, a speed of 7 knots. In her trips to Devon, London and Southampton over the next decade, *Alice*

Alice, a Daimler-engined motor-sailer of 1895

became well known on boating circles, even though by the end of 1895 there were some 600 Cannstadt-Daimler motor-launches running in Europe.

The first 'bona fide' paraffin-engined yacht was the *Arcadia*, designed by Herbert P. Blake of Southampton in 1896.

Also in 1896, basing their design on the Daimler petrol engine, the American Motors Company (AMC) of New York introduced their 'Portable Boat Motor with Reversible Propeller'. This was **the first US petrol-outboard**. One version was a single-cylinder, 1 hp air-cooled unit, weighing about 50 lb. The other was a twin-cylinder unit developing 3 hp at 600 rpm, weighing about 75 lb. With this motor, AMC claimed that a 16 ft (5 m) dory could travel at 6 mph (10 km/h). Twenty-five engines were made. The ignition system was made up of an induction coil and dry batteries, which alternately flashed an electrical charge through a set of electrodes mounted in the cylinder head.

In Europe, to solve the problems of tube ignition, Frederick Simms and Walter Bosch teamed up to produce the Simms–Bosch low-tension magneto ignition – this innovation acted as a great boon to launch owners, many of whom had their motors converted to the new system. In 1896 the expanding Daimler Motor Syndicate left Putney Railway Arch No. 71 and took premises on Eel Pie Island, near Richmond, for the building of motor-launches. But with motorcar production at Coventry as a priority, the Eel Pie project was found uneconomical and the premises disposed of in 1897 and losses written off at £841.

Alfred Burgoine of Kingston-on-Thames was more successful when he imported the 30 ft (9 m) *Puteaux*, the first launch engined with a 137 cc air-cooled engine, developing 4½ hp at 2000 rpm as designed by Count Albert de Dion in France. Purchased by Roger Fuller, *Puteaux* could carry 12 passengers at some 8 mph (13 km/h); she was **the first of many de Dion motor-launches** that were to be seen on England's rivers during the next decade.

It was not long before the advantages of taking in water to cool a launch engine were proven over the land-influenced system of air-cooling.

One of the most popular American engines in the late 1890s for what the Americans had already begun to call 'automobile boats' was the single-cylinder two-cycle 'Monarch' motor, designed and built by Henry Lozier; other US makes were the Wolverine and the Michigan.

In 1899, the Daimler Motor Co. Ltd of Coventry issued a catalogue of launch motors, with starting and reversing gear, shaft, stern-tube, and propeller. For a 17 ft (5 m) launch they recommended their 1½ hp single-cylinder engine (plus installation and fittings, etc – £85), whilst for a 40 ft (12 m) launch, their 10 hp twin-cylinder engine (plus installation and fitting, etc – £336).

DIESEL

The first boat ever to be powered by a diesel engine was the French canal barge, *Petit-Pierre* (1903), belonging to the iron founders MM Hachette and Driout. It was the culmination of a design programme which the 45-year-old German inventor Dr Rudolf Christian Karl Diesel had initiated ten years before when, after taking out his patent for a Rational Heat Engine, he signed an agreement with Heinrich von Buz, Director of the well-known German engine factory, Maschinenfabrik Augsburg, allowing him the facilities to build an experimental engine and the opportunity to establish favourable deals with foreign licensees.

The first 10 ft (3 m) prototype engine, built in 1893, nearly killed Diesel and his colleagues

Dr Rudolph Diesel (1858–1913) (MAN Augsburg)

when it exploded on the test-bench. By 1896 that original engine had been redesigned several times and rebuilt twice, when a new design was made and on 17 February 1897, on the advice of Rudolf's wife Martha, the Rational Heat Engine was re-named the DIESEL engine and had its first official, public test. This 25 hp, four-stroke, single-cylinder vertical oil-engine, in which the compression ratio was considerably higher than in existing engines, with a resultant improvement in efficiency, was soon talked about throughout the engineering world.

Petit Pierre, *the first boat to be fitted with a diesel-engine (1903) (MAN Augsburg)*

Frederic Dyckhoff who owned a small engine factory at Bar le Duc, France had been closely following Diesel's progress from 1893 and on 4 April 1894 signed a contract with the inventor. In 1897, on his friend's suggestion, Dyckhoff founded the 'Société Française des Moteurs Diesel', with 1·2 million francs in shares. In 1899 Adrien Bochet of Sautter-Harle & Co., Paris, took out a licence from SF Moteurs Diesel.

The same year Col. Meier, Technical Director of the Diesel Motor Company, built a one-stroke, single-cylinder marine diesel engine – but never got as far as building a full-scale unit.

In 1901 Frederic Dyckhoff built a three-cylinder, downstroke engine developing 15 hp at 600 rpm – **the first to be fitted with a reversible gear** on the Dyckhoff patent. This motor was never used.

Two years later Dr Diesel, Bochet and Dyckhoff teamed-up to produce a more successful marine version. Constructed by Sautter-Harle, the crankcase, which was centrally placed between two opposing cylinders, housed the crankshaft. The valves were positioned so as to reduce the size of the combustion chamber and build up high compression. With a bore 210 mm × stroke 250 mm, the engine developed 25 hp at 360 rpm. In 1903 this was successfully installed in the *Petit-Pierre*, and in October, together with Dyckhoff, Dr Diesel personally test-drove this boat out from her home base at Didier and along the Rhine-Marne canal; he wrote a postcard with a picture of the *Petit-Pierre* to his wife – which can still be read today.

1903 also saw the fitting out at St Petersburg (Russia) of a tank vessel for Messrs Nobel Bros, the great oil distributors, whose immense business employed nearly 60 craft on the River Volga and the Caspian Sea. This vessel, the *Vandal*, was **the first in which the Del Proposto system of transmission was employed on a commercial scale**. Her engines were constructed by the Aktiebolaget Diesels Motorer of Stockholm. They were of the vertical type, and worked on the four-stroke cycle, the crankshaft being direct-coupled to an electric generator which gave current to a motor coupled direct to the prop-shaft. Electrical transmission was used for both ahead and astern movements, and with her three sets of engines aggregating 360 hp, the *Vandal* attained a speed of 7½ knots laden; her dead weight capacity being 800 tons.

Petit Pierre's engine (MAN Augsburg)

In 1905 the Sulzer Brothers made **the first reversible two-stroke diesel engine**, and in 1908 Nobels made **the first reversible four-stroke diesel engine**.

The first sea-going diesel-engined boat was the auxiliary cargo vessel the *Orion*, powered by a Swedish diesel engine developing 60 bhp at 275 rpm. This was in 1907.

In 1890 Herbert Akroyd Stuart (1864–1927), the English engineer/inventor, working in conjunction with Charles Binney, patented and built the world's first 'hot bulb compression-ignition' oil engine, and began manufacturing units at a little factory in Bletchley, Bucks. The manufacturing rights of this engine were soon sold to Richard Hornsby & Sons Ltd of Grantham, who in 1892 started to manufacture the 'Hornsby-Ackroyd Patent Safety Oil Engine' – an instant success, selling in large quantities throughout the world. Claimed by some to predate the pioneering work of Dr Diesel, in 1895 **the first single-cylinder, 8 hp, vertical Hornsby-Ackroyd marine engine** (No. 626) was sold to Robert McFie & Sons of Glasgow – possibly for installation in a boat.

The first diesels to be built in Great Britain were manufactured by Mirrlees of Stockport, in 1897. By 1906, they were making marine engines.

The first diesel-engined vessel to enter the Antarctic was the *Fram*, captained by the Norwegian explorer Ronald Amundsen in 1911.

Between 1903–5, Amundsen had used the 100-ton, cutter-rigged ship, the *Gjøa*, to voyage from Christiania (Oslo) and had succeeded in navigating the north-west passage. *Gjøa* was fitted with an auxiliary horizontal-cylinder, Dan 'hot-bulb' oil engine, installed by Ejnar S. Nielsen. With Amundsen's fame from this expedition went the fame of the Danish 'Dan' motor, nicknamed 'Jumbo'.

Fram, a 103 ft (31 m), three-masted, fore-and-aft schooner originally powered by a 200 ihp reciprocating steam engine, had first been used by Dr Fridtjof Nansen in his Norwegian Arctic Expedition (1893–96), and then on Otto Sverdrup's long wintering Polar expedition in Ellesmere Land. With a speed of 6 knots, *Fram* consumed a bulky 2·8 tons of coal per day.

In 1909, prior to Amundsen's voyage, the steam engine and boiler were removed and a Swedish four-cylinder Polar diesel engine, developing 180 hp at 280 rpm and driving a 5 ft 9 in (1·7 m) diameter propeller, was installed in the extreme afterpart of the lower hold, together with tanks containing 90 tons of oil. At a speed of 4½ knots, *Fram* could now voyage 10000 nautical miles without replenishing her oil supply. *Fram*'s engineer was Knut Sundbeck who had been in on the construction of this engine from the beginning. A 15 hp Norwegian Bolinder oil motor was also installed, to work the capstan.

Amundsen left Christiania (Oslo) in 1910 for the Antarctic and reached the South Pole on 16 December 1911.

By 1911, only eight years after the trials of the *Petit-Pierre*, there were some 150 vessels worldwide which were powered by diesel engines (excluding 115 submarines). This included some 35 tugs, 14 fishing vessels and 16 miscellaneous craft.

During that year, the *Toiler*, built on the Tyne and fitted with a Swedish diesel engine, became **the first diesel-engined craft to cross the Atlantic**.

Despite the brilliant success of his engine, Rudolf Diesel was bitterly disappointed by the failure of his financial speculations in property. He was severely criticised by engineers who claimed that as he had introduced no new theories or techniques he was no *inventor* as such. He was also depressed by headaches, gout, insomnia and fears of heart trouble. In September 1913, Rudolf Diesel committed suicide by drowning himself off the Antwerp-Harwich night steamer. He had, however, outlived both J. J. Etienne Lenoir and Gottlieb Daimler (who had died within five months of each other in 1900) and also Gustave Trouvé (who had died in 1902) to see the first decade of development in motorboating.

2 RACING AND RECORDS

The 100 km race which took place on the Seine in 1900: Titan II *and* Princesse Elizabeth *at Poissy before the start (British Library)*

The first successful motorboat races of the 20th century took place on the Seine at the Paris Universal Exhibition of 1900. Ably organised by Hélice Club President, Gabriel Paillard, on instructions from the Sporting Committee into eight races over a course between Ile St Denis and Bezons Bridge, marked out by yellow buoys. The high-speed race over 7½ miles (12 km), with eight launches competing, saw Marius Dubonnet's *L'Aiglon* ('Eaglet') first over the finishing line with a time of 47 min 15 s, whilst in other races some competitors took 5 hr.

At the Nice Regatta of March 1901 an oak and cedar launch (LOA 33 ft (10 m) × B 5 ft (1·5 m)), built by the engineer Chevreux at Boulogne-sur-Seine, and fitted with a 'Mercédès'-Daimler engine, made a world record of 20 mph (32 km/h). Exactly one year later, engined with a Mercédès-Simplex developing 35 hp at 900 rpm, this launch travelled three times

over a triangular course of a distance of 16 nautical miles in 50 min 7 s, thus clocking a new speed of 22 mph (35·5 km/h). On 18 March, in calm weather, the *Mercedes* travelled from San Remo lighthouse to Nice lighthouse (26 miles (42 km)) in 1 hr 21 min – maintaining a speed of 10 knots throughout the voyage. In 1902 Daimler works adopted Mercédès as the new brand name for their private cars.

In late August 1902, races were held in Arcachon Bay, France, for boats powered by steam, paraffin, petrol and/or electricity. Petrol engines used were the De Dion, Buchet, Couach, Decauville, and Wolverine. **The most successful launch** was the *Trois Etoiles*, belonging to Arcachon Ocean Fisheries and M. Guedon; she measured 30 ft (9 m) and was powered by a twin-cylinder Decauville engine developing 8 hp at 900 rpm, turning a 40 cm diameter prop at the same speed as the engine and consuming 0·9 gallons (4 litres) of petrol per hour. On 26 August *Trois Etoiles* raced reliably for almost 17 hr in a strong north-westerly wind.

The first British firm claiming to design and build a high speed motor-launch was Hart, Harden & Co., of Hampton Wick on the Thames. Designed by A. Harden, *Vitesse* (LOA 34 ft 6 in (10·5 m) × B 4 ft 6 in (1·4 m)) was **the first launch to carry her oak engine bearers the whole length of the hull**, carrying a water-cooled four-cylinder, 12 hp engine, designed by F. C. Blake of Kew Gardens, complete with internal clutch inside the reverse gear. Accommodation was provided for eight persons in wickerwork lounge chairs. In the 1902 season, *Vitesse*, with a speed of 13½ mph (22. km/h), was the fastest motorboat on the Thames.

Her performance inspired a meeting on the afternoon of Thursday, 13 November at the Golden Cross Hotel, Charing Cross, London, of gentlemen interested in the establishment of an association to regulate and encourage motor-launch racing in Great Britain. The word 'racing' was left out of their title – Marine Motoring Association – as a four-word title was considered too cumbersome and restrictive. Naval architect Linton Hope became Hon Sec, and it was decided to form:

1 Dinghy class not exceeding 15 ft (4·5 m)
2 Launch class of 20 ft (6 m) LOA
3 Launch class of 25 ft (7·6 m) LOA
4 Launch class of 30 ft (9·1 m) LOA

A Marine Racing Motorist in 1905

'Motorboating in those days (1905) was a very wet performance and we threw up a tremendous lot of spray, which, if the wind was on one side, blew over us very badly' (S. F. Edge) (Veteran Car Club)

These classes – **the first ever drawn up for the sport in Great Britain** – were to have a minimum beam, freeboard and thickness of planking – and a maximum power of engines. Under Capt. Ernest du Boulay, detailed rules for assessing 'motor power' were only drawn up after all possible information had been collated.

In Spring 1903, following the initiative of the Marine Motoring Association, Sir Boverton Redwood proposed to form a Marine Motor sub-committee of the Automobile Club of Great Britain and Ireland with the object of furthering the sport of marine motoring; immediately following from the formation of this sub-committee, came the generous donation of an International Cup for motorboats by Sir Alfred Harmsworth, proprietor of the *Daily Mail* and many other successful publications.

Very soon after the formation of the Marine Motoring Association, the Columbia Yacht Club (USA) issued a call to all interested yacht clubs to meet and arrange suitable 'rating and time allowance rules' for automobile boat racing. At a fourth and final organisational meeting on 22 April 1903, representatives of 20 clubs attended, and adopted the name American

Why not modernise our tracks so as to lend variety to sport? We fear the suggestion will not hold water.

Cartoon from The Motor *magazine (1904). As Brooklands, the world's first motor-racing track was not built until 1907, the reference is to banked cycle tracks*

Power Boat Association (APBA), set up a constitution, adopted rules and elected officers, with W. H. Ketcham as their founder-President.

France now followed suit with the 'Congress des Bateaux Automobiles', held that same spring at the Yachting Club of France, with Henri Menier in the chair. It was here decided to divide 'automobile boats' into two main classes, mainly racers and cruisers.

The first high-speed American 'auto-boat' was the torpedo-type *Adios*, designed by Leighton of Syracuse in 1903 and credited with some 23 mph (37 km/h) in numerous trials on Lake Onondaga.

Although **the first long-distance motorboat contest of any significance** was a race of 62 miles (100 km) from the Poissy Sailing Club to Meulan, won by Monsieur Senot's Seyler-hulled, 24 hp Otto-engined *Flore*, **the most im-**

portant race of 1903 was the 230-mile (370 km) marathon, organised by *Le Velo* and *Yachting Gazette* from Courbe-Voie (Paris) to Mantes, St Aubin, Rouen, Caudebec, Le Havre and Trouville. 'Paris-to-the-Sea' took place that Autumn, involving 25 cruisers of up to 24 hp and three racers (56 had entered). The race was won by the 35 hp *Mercedes*, owned and driven by Daimler's publicity-minded French agent 'C. L. Charley' (Charles Lehmann); her time totalled 10 hr 26 min 23 s, compared to the eighteenth and last boat to finish with a time of over 25 hr.

The first fatal motorboat racing accident took place at the Poissy meeting. One hour before the start, *Marsoin*, crewed by her builder Perignon and engineer Grosse, was on speed trials when, from a defective carburettor, the boat caught fire and the full fuel tanks went up in flames. Although Perignon swam safely ashore, Grosse drowned.

The most lavish and the most disastrous race ever run was the Algiers–Toulon. Some 120000 francs in prize money and cups by the President of the French Republic, the King of Spain, the Prince of Monaco, etc were set up. Seven competitors presented themselves on 6 May 1905 (including the 72 ft (21·9 m) *Quand-Même*, powered by twin 100 hp Beaudoin motors, and filled up with 550 gallons (2500 litres) of fuel on board). They were escorted by six French, four Italian and four Spanish warships, completing the first leg from Algiers to Port Mahon (220 miles (354 km)) at speeds of from 7·5 to 13·7 mph (12 to 22·1 km/h). The second leg, Port Mahon to Toulon (200 miles (320 km)) was a complete fiasco. After five days' delay due to uncertain weather, the motorboats were started on Friday 13 May. Before long, a freak storm, with 30 ft (10 m) waves, had blown up. *Fiat X* was taken on board a destroyer for safety; *Mercédès CP* was taken in tow, broke loose and sank; *Mercédès-Mercédès* was cut adrift so her warship could save itself; *Malgré-Tout* was smashed to pieces against her destroyer; *Héraclès II* broke away, whilst on tow, with her crew on board, and was only re-located by searchlight. The crew were taken off and she sank. *Camille*, piloted by Madame du Gast who was the last to leave the ship, was abandoned to waves only 50 miles (80 km) from Toulon; *Quand-Même* ran out of petrol, and an attempt was made to tow her. She was finally abandoned to the storm. *Fiat X*, on board a destroyer, reached port safely. *Camille* was re-located several days later by the SS *Tafna* who were unable to take it in tow, therefore it was abandoned to rot in the Mediterranean. There was, however, no loss of life!

In 1910 the British Motor Boat Club inaugurated the 21 ft (6·4 m) Racing Class, perhaps one of **the best class of safe racing motorboats ever developed**. The first of the 21-footers was Fred May's *Defender II*, built by Burgoines of Kingston; powered by a 35 hp Green engine, this boat achieved a speed of 37 knots before World War I, whilst Dr Morton Smart's

Every Spring, between 1904–14, racing took place at Monte Carlo, promoted by Camille Blanc (Société des Bains de Mer) (top). Centre shows the British Napier II *in 1905 at Monaco; the lower illustration shows the German boat* Mercedes *at speed in Monte Carlo harbour*

Angela II, averaged 26·4 knots over a 10-mile (16 km) course. The 1913 Monaco Meeting saw 14 British and three foreign 21-footers (6·4 m) competing. Brooke, Saunders and Hart-Harden were the major builders, using Sunbeam, Austin, Brooke, Wolseley, Vauxhall and Green engines.

The Duke of York's International Gold Trophy was first presented at Torquay in 1924 after a competition between 1½-litre-engined hydroplanes. It was won by Count J. E. de Johnston-Noad in the Aston Martin engined *Miss Betty* at a speed of 28·99 knots. By 1951 the Canadian Art Hatch won the trophy at 60 mph (97 km/h). During this decade, the following have won the trophy:

INTERNATIONAL GOLD TROPHY WINNERS

1924	Count de Johnston-Noad
	W. V. Webber (Sunbeam engine)
1925	Capt. Woolf Barnato
1926	Miss M. B. Carstairs
1927	Mrs James H. Rand Jr
1928	Count de Johnston-Noad
1929	James Talbot Jr and Dr Ralph Snoddy
1930	F. T. Bersuy
1938	S. Mortimer Auerbach
1951	H. A. Hatch
1958	William G. Braden
1959	Harold Bucholtz
1962	C. H. Girard
1963–70	Not contested
1971	Renato Molinari
1972	Bob Spalding
1973	Mike Downard and Tom Posey
1974	Clive Hook and Bill Badsby
1975	Bob Spalding
1976	Hans Pelster
1977	Renato Molinari
1978	Bill Seebold Jr
1979	Bill Seebold Jr

(Top speeds of the competitors in 1978 reached 130 mph (209 km/h))

The first gas-jet propelled boat was the *Eureka* (LOA 110 ft (33·5 m) × B 12 ft (3·6 m)) launched at Brooklyn, USA in 1889. A series of tubes was fitted in the bow, with their muzzles opening under water, and they were divided internally into a number of chambers for the reception of a mixture of gaseous fuel and air. The contents were exploded in rapid succession by means of an electric spark, and the impact of the expanding gases against the surrounding water was sufficient to propel the vessel. *Eureka* was technically described as a Pneumatic Yacht.

The first hydroplane to be powered by an aero-engine driving an immersed propeller was Commodore Garfield A. Wood's *Miss Detroit III*, fitted with a wood-modified, Curtiss 12-cylinder, V-type unit. In 1918 and 1919 *Miss Detroit III* won the US Gold Cup at speeds over 50 mph (80 km/h). Before long, Wood and Carl Fisher formed the Detroit Aero-Marine Engines Company, purchasing 600 Fiat (Italian), 100 Benz (Germany), 200 Mercédès (Germany), 100 Liberty (American) and 50 Beardman (English) aero-units from the US Government. Within a very few years almost every high-powered raceboat in the USA was powered by aero-engines.

The first British boat to be fitted with an aero-engine, driving an immersed propeller was the 28 ft (8·5 m) *Canfly*, built by Harry Breaker of Bowness (Lake Windermere) for Maj. E. H. Pattinson. After World War I, *Canfly* was fitted with a six-cylinder, 7·4 litre Rolls-Royce Hawk aero-engine, developing 85 bhp at 1350 rpm and taken from the RNAS airship, SST3. The 1917 'Hawk' engine was modified by fitting a heavy flywheel in place of the airscrew, a starting handle and modified water pump. *Canfly* had a straight drive with no gearbox and it was essential to turn her round to face into the lake before using the starting handle (ex Rolls-Royce Eagle). To provide more control a Kitchen reversing rudder was fitted in the 1920s but was later discarded as it reduced the boat's speed. At 30 mph (48 km/h), *Canfly* was regularly victorious at the Windermere Motor Boat Racing Club's meetings. She now has the oldest Rolls-Royce aero-engine in working order.

The first hydroplane to be powered by four aero-engines driving twin immersed propellers, was Gar Wood's 32 ft (10 m) *Miss America II*. Fitted with four V-12 modified Grant Liberty units amassing some 1600 hp, *Miss America II* set a new world record of 80·57 mph (129·66 km/h) in 1921.

Thornycroft's Waterlily *(1866), fully restored with
original steam machinery, afloat on Beaulieu River in 1978
(Courtesy Geoff Miles)*

Two steam launches, Esperanza *and* Pierrette, *on the
Thames at Queens Eyot in 1970 (Courtesy Brian Hillesden)*

H. Scott-Paine's Miss Britain III *(1933) (Courtesy Bill Sheaff)*

Sir Malcolm Campbell's Bluebird K4 *(1939) (Courtesy Leo Villa)*

Dick Pope 're-fuelling' the Mullins Rocket Boat in 1929

The first successful rocket-propelled boat was the Mullins Rocket boat, *Dixie Torpedo*, demonstrated on Biscayne Bay in early 1930 for newsreels and the press by Malcolm Pope, when it achieved a speed of 55 mph (102 km/h). It was powered by 40, electrically controlled, rockets fitted at the stern of the boat. Malcolm Pope was the brother of Dick Pope Sr who promoted Cypress Gardens.

The first motorboat to be powered by a turbo-jet engine was Sir Malcolm Campbell's modified Bluebird K4 3 pointer nicknamed 'The Slipper'. Unsuccessful trials were carried out in 1947 and 1948 with a de Havilland Goblin II jet engine, developing 5000 lb thrust.

John Cobb and his team, in front of the turbojet-engined Crusader *(1952) (Peter Leddy)*

The first motorboat to be designed and custom-built around a turbo-jet engine was John Cobb's 31 ft (9·5 m) *Crusader*, powered by a de Havilland Ghost turbo-jet; this craft disintegrated at an estimated 240 mph (386 km/h) on Loch Ness (29 September 1952) with fatal injuries to Cobb.

Donald Campbell steps ashore from Bluebird K7 after setting a World Water Speed Record of 239·07 mph (384·75 km/h) at Coniston (1957) (Hallawell Photos)

A sequence showing the final, fatal loop-the-loop of Donald Campbell's Bluebird K7 over Coniston Water (January 1967) (Popperfoto)

Jean Dupuy (France) racing his Soriano-engined, aluminium powerboat during the 1930s. Observe forward rudder (Antoine Sire)

Evinrude and Elto racing outboard engines developed 60 hp each in 1933 (Maurice Rosenfeld)

Gearle Kuehrl's experimental rig – Chicago 1933 (Maurice Rosenfeld)

The first unofficial outboard race in the USA took place on Lake Pewaukee in 1911.

The first important outboard race took place in Stockholm, Sweden in 1922, involving 75 competitors.

The first 3-mile (5 km) outboard races to be officially contested in the USA took place in 1923 at Oshkosh, Wisconsin, under the aegis of the Mississippi Valley Powerboat Association – and was won by an Elto-Twin at an average 9 mph (14·5 km/h).

The first outboard race to be officially contested in the UK, involving 10 competitors, took place in 1923 on the River Thames at Chelsea under the aegis of the British Motor Boat Club. It was a handicap race and was won by Frank Snoxell, piloting an Elto-engined 16-ft (5 m) narrow river skiff at 5·85 knots.

The first official racing rules and classes for Outboard Detachable Motors were drawn up by the APBA in 1924, to take in a cubic-inch piston displacement of from 0 to over 30, lettered from A to D. In its first competitive appearance at White Lake, Michigan in July 1925, the Johnson 6 hp Big Twin started sweeping the board with speeds of 16·68 mph (26·84 km/h), increasing this to 23·32 mph (37·53 km/h) later that year. After this, Evinrude, Elto, Johnson, Lockwood and Caille all started developing increasingly powerful racing versions of their engines. Before long, the APBA had established Class F for 50 to 60 cu in engines, then Class X for non-stock motors over 60 cu in or with supercharger. By 1929, racing had become so significant to these manufacturers that the National Outboard Association (NOA) was formed, both to adjudicate over the sport and to try and maintain relationships with the sales of stock outboards, led by James L. Mulroy. In 1933, the $7\frac{1}{2}$ cu in Class M (the 'Racing Midgets') was introduced for women and teenagers to participate: intercollegiate and inter-scholastic competitions now blossomed. Membership of the NOA increased from 4980 in 1929 to 7662 in 1938, whilst crowds from 10000 to 30000 could often be seen watching outboard contests. **The first organised outboard marathon** was held in August 1926 over 71 miles (114 km) – New York–Bear

'A slight prang!' Chicago 1932 (Antoine Sire)

With 4 Packard aero-engines, totalling 7500 hp, Miss America X *achieved 125 mph (200 km/h) in 1932 (Maurice Rosenfeld)*

The stern-engined Californian *competed in the 1930 APBA Gold Cup, attaining speeds around 60 mph (95 km/h) (Maurice Rosenfeld)*

Horace Tennes competing on Lake Worth (Palm Beach), powered by a 4-60 factory Evinrude; he won 6 out of 8 races (Maurice Rosenfeld)

Twin Rolls-Royce 'R' aero-engines, totalling 4700 hp, powered Miss England III *in 1932 (Maurice Rosenfeld)*

Mountain–New York. The winner, Vic Withstandley, completed the course in 4 hr 46 min in a 6 hp Johnson Big Twin-engined 16-ft (5 m) hydroplane. After this marathon racing became popular. **The most famous outboard marathon** was the 125-mile (201 km) Albany–New York, which was contested from 1928–41, 1947–53 and 1963–72.

Thanks to racing, the Department of Commerce estimated that outboard production in the USA increased from 24 628 units in 1925, to 58 456 in 1929, to 130 000 by 1939. Until its merger with the Outboard Motors Corporation, Johnson maintained the lead with their racing engines.

In sharp contrast – Bill Muncey, piloting Atlas Van Lines *at 160 mph (250 km/h) plus in 1977 (Tony Hogg)*

The outboard section of the British Motor Boat Club was formed in 1927, and **the first contest under its new rules** took place on the Thames that June, with the C Class winner achieving a speed of 20·6 mph (33·1 km/h).

The first crossing of the English Channel in an outboard, home-designed 12-footer (3·7 m) was made in 1927 by W. T. Fry using a Johnson. He made the crossing from Dover to Calais in 1 hr 34 min. At an outboard race meeting held at the Welsh Harp Lake, Hendon in July 1928, there were 77 entries. The Duchess of York (now the Queen Mother) presented her own trophy to H. J. P. Bomford, winner of the race for C Class boats at 30·71 mph (49·42 km/h) with his 466 cc Evinrude-engined See hydroplane. Long-distance races held in the UK during 1928 included a 50-mile (80 km) race off Brighton and a 100-mile (160 km) race on the River Bann in Northern Ireland, won at 29·51 mph (47·49 km/h). At the end of 1928 a syndicate known as Motor Boat Speedways Ltd acquired a lake at Rickmansworth to hold outboard races on a commercial basis. All outboard racing rigs had to be registered with the Marine Motoring Association (MMA), and by the end of the 1928 season, 206 applications for registrations had been received.

The first two-way crossing of the English Channel was made by the Hon. Mrs Victor Bruce in her Elto-powered hydroplane, *Mosquito*, on 8 September 1928; Mrs Bruce took 1 hr 47 min. By early 1929, manufacturers estimated that there were about 1200 outboard motorboats in the UK and the British Outboard Racing Club was founded by the Count Johnston Noad, a wealthy racing motorboatist.

The most unfortunate outboard race during this period was the Dover–Calais–Dover contest of June 1929: only two or three of the 36 boats competing succeeded in reaching the French coast; most of the fleet were put out of action by damage to hull or engine and some competitors became hopelessly lost. There was no loss of life, all competitors finally being picked up.

By 1930, nearly two dozen outboard clubs were in operation in the British Isles and by the end of the 1930 racing season, 679 applications for registrations had been received by the MMA.

The same year a National Utility Dinghy Class was established by the MMA and a 100-mile (160 km) race was specially organised for the *Yachting World* trophy for National Utility dinghies and runabouts. The first race for this trophy, at Poole Harbour in May 1930, was won by Viscount Kingsborough at 22·77 mph (36·64 km/h), and in 1931 the race was won by the Italian Count Salvi at 29·02 mph (46·70 km/h). The National Utility Dinghy Class was given international status in 1933.

The most successful British hydroplanes in this class were built by Percy See of Fareham. In Official Measured Mile trials in October 1935, Roy Fedden averaged 35·22 mph (56·68 km/h) on Lake Windermere in a 1000 cc 'X' Class See runabout.

Several major innovations in specialised racing motorboat design have changed the course of the sport. **The very first racing hydroplanes** were designed and built by Bonnemaison, Le Las and de Lambert. Bonnemaison's *Ricochet-Nautilus* (Ricochet-Rebound) which appeared in 1907 reached speeds of 43 mph (70 km/h). So successful was this design that in 1910 at Monaco there was *Richochet XV* racing. W. H. Fauber took out several patents in 1908 on multi-stepped Vee-hydroplanes, having experimented with his Antoinette-engined prototype along the River Seine at Nanterre. The first British hydroplane race took place in May 1909, under the British Motor Boat Club (BMBC), at Lowestoft, between the *Dollydo II* and *Baby Hydro*. *Dollydo II*, powered by a twin-cylinder 13 hp Boulton & Paul engine, won at 17 knots. Later that year, Sam Saunders' hydroplane *Columbine*, based on Saunders patents, won 14 firsts and two seconds out of 18 starts at BMBC meetings, whilst the 360 hp *Pioneer* achieved speeds of 40 mph (64 km/h) in 1910. **The first US hydroplane**, *Baby Reliance I*, built in 1912 by Chris Smith, achieved speeds of 50 mph (80 km/h) before she flipped. *Baby Reliance II* and *III* turned US powerboat racing rules 'head-over-heels'.

The Ventnor three-point hydroplane was developed by Adolph E. Apel, of the Ventnor Boat Works, Atlantic City during the mid 1930s. A concave bottom was employed and instead of the usual step, two-stepped sponsons or stabilisers

Dollydo II, *winner of the first British hydroplane race (1909) (Boulton & Paul Ltd, Norwich)*

were arranged on each side of the hull. When the boat was planing forward, part of its concave bottom was entirely clear of the water – and with a Lycoming engine of only 175 hp output, a speed of 60 mph (96 km/h) could be reached with an 18 ft (5·5 m) boat.

It was the Italian boatbuilder, Angelo Molinari, who developed **the first outboard-engined tunnel-hull racing motorboat** in 1955. It dispensed with the aft-planing step and the propeller merely acted to give balancing lift.

In 1968 James Beard built an offshore racing catamaran in Guernsey and successfully raced it with Clive Curtis. Following requests for further craft, Beard and Curtis formed Cougar Marine at the Netley Abbey Boatyard, Hampshire, England. (The cougar is a puma, or American panther – a type of wild cat(amaran)!) In 1969 Cougar built **the first twin-engined offshore 'cat'**, *Volare II*, with stepped, picklefork sponsons and flaps at the stern of the tunnel. In 1970, the *Miss Cougar* circuit 'cat' also incorporated for the first time the picklefork, stepped sponsons with stern flaps. Both these prototypes, developed too hastily, were not successful; it was only since 1975 that the picklefork, stepped sponson and stern flaps were re-adapted for both circuit and offshore racing craft, and is now commonplace. In Spring 1978, Ken Cassir's Mercruiser-engined Cougar-cat, *Yellowdrama III* achieved a new World Class I Offshore Record Speed of 92·17

mph (148·33 km/h), a tribute to the advantages of seaworthy cat design.

The highest offshore race speed attained by 1969 was 73·1 mph (117·6 km/h) by Don Aronow (USA) in his 32 ft (10 m) *The Cigarette* powered by two 475 hp Mercruiser engines over 214 miles (344 km) at Viareggio, Italy on 20 July.

The fastest average speed set by an offshore powerboat during an inshore race on 30 June 1973 is 93·1 mph (149·8 km/h) by *Aeromarine II*, an ultra lightweight Bertram-Memco 36 ft (11 m), powered by twin Kiekhaefer aeromarine 468s (totalling 1200 hp). She was driven by Lazar 'Sonny' Kay (Lakeside Yachting Club, Cleveland) and Tom Kipp in the 63 mile (101 km) CLOPRA 'Firecracker 50' on a fairly calm Lake Erie (normally the toughest, roughest of the Great Lakes). An aircraft also clocked them at 104+ mph (167+ km/h) during the race.

The first drag boat to attain 200 mph (321 km/h) was Sam Kurtovich's *Crisis* which attained 200·44 mph (322·57 km/h) in California during October 1969 at the end of a one-way run down the Oakland Marine Stadium. *Climax* has since been reported to have attained 205·19 mph (330·22 km/h).

The longest and hardest powerboat race ever staged was the Port Richborough London to Monte Carlo Marathon Offshore International

Bronze Medal: Monte Carlo Meeting 1913–14   *Bronze Medal: Monte Carlo Meeting 1913–14*

British International (or Harmsworth) Trophy (1903)   *Duke of York's International Gold Trophy (1924)*

APBA Gold Cup (1904)   *Canon Formula One European Powerboat Championship (1978)*   *Beaverbrook Trophy (1961)*

event. The race extended over 2947 miles (4742 km) in 14 stages: London–Southampton–Brest–La Rochelle–Bilbao–La Coruna–Oporto–Cascais (Lisbon)–Portimao–Marbella–Almeria–Alicante–Barcelona–La Grande Motte–Monte Carlo. Organised by John Chitty, Commodore of the Offshore Powerboat Club of Great Britain and also the RYA, some 19 contestants took the Starting Flag from HRH Princess Margaret on 10 June 1972. BP produced over 100000 gallons (454610 litres) of high octane petroleum diesel oil and lubricants.

The first powerboat to arrive at Monte Carlo on the 25 June was Ralph Hilton's 32 ft (19·7 m), Shead-designed, Souter-built *HTS* (GB) powered by twin 250 hp Ford Sabre engines, and driven by Mike Bellamy, Eddie Chater and Jim Brooker in 71 hr 35 min 56 s (average 41·15 mph (66·24 km/h)), overall victors by nearly 9 hr. Only five other powerboats completed all stages. Of the total 111 trophies and £16225 prize money that was presented, *HTS* took away £6900 and 29 trophies, including the coveted Prince Rainier Gold Challenge Trophy, presented to Bellamy by Princess Grace of Monaco.

The *Daily Telegraph* and BP Round Britain event was inaugurated on 26 July 1969 at Portsmouth with 1403 miles (2257 km) in ten stages west – about England, Wales and across North Scotland via the Caledonian Canal. The 1969 race (26 July–7 August) was won by *Avenger Too* (Timo Makinen, Alan Pascoe Watson and Brian Hendicott) in 39 hr 9 min 37·7 s. Of the 42 starters, 24 finished.

Over the past 70 years women have occasionally tackled the sport of powerboat racing. **The first British lady motorboat racing driver** was Dorothy Levitt who raced S. F. Edge's *Napier* in 1903. **The first US woman powerboat driver** was Ethel Salisbury Hanley who piloted *Ethel III* in the 1911 Mississippi Valley Powerboat Regatta and went on to pilot seven subsequent *Ethel* powerboats which were built for her. **The first European woman powerboat driver** was France's Camille du Gast ('L'Amazone') whose 43-footer (13 m) CVG-engined *Camille* was the last to retire during a Mediterranean storm in the 500-mile (805 km) Algiers–Toulon marathon motor-launch race of 1905.

In the 1920s/early 1930s, Marion Barbara Carstairs ('Betty'), the Standard Oil millionair-

ess and brave tomboy, graduated from long-distance cruiser racing in her yacht *Sonia* to racing at 40 mph (64 km/h) for the Duke of York's Trophy in her 1½-litre Sunbeam-engined hydroplanes (*Newg* and *Leumas*). She then survived the 90 mph (145 km/h) plus ordeal of the Harmsworth Trophy races in her privately-sponsored series of four multi-aero-engined 30 ft (9 m) hydroplanes (*Estelle*) costing £30000 apiece. She then moved on to a quadruple-aero-engined 78 ft (24 m) juggernaut called *Jack Stripes*, designed and built to cross the Atlantic Ocean, but never used for this purpose.

In America, Mrs J. W. ('Fingy') Connors, the young wife of a well-known Buffalo publisher and politician, is estimated to have won 64 contests during the early 1920s in her 500 hp Liberty-engined *Miss Okeechobee*. Helen Hentschel of Flushing, NY and Loretta ('Sunkist Kid') Turnbull of Monravia, California, became outboard-engined championesses during the late 1920s, whilst in the UK the Hon. Mrs Victor Bruce became the first person to make a two-way crossing of the English Channel in her Elto-powered hydroplane *Mosquito* (1928), while in 1929 Mrs Bruce completed 694 nautical miles in 24 out of 36 hr of motorboat driving, sponsored by Hubert Scott-Paine of the British Power Boat Company (see p. 129).

During the 1950s Grace Walker of Australia won a number of championship contests in her Jaguar XK140-engined *Diane* three-pointer. Fiona, Countess of Arran, and Lady Violet Aitken have been powerboat racing since the mid-1960s. Graduating from her *Badger* circuit boats on 21 October 1971, the 53-year-old Countess drove her offshore powerboat, *Highland Fling*, for a Class III world record of 85·63 mph (137·80 km/h) in a hailstorm and despite fuel trouble on the back-up run. She has since raced the Lorne Campbell-designed *Skean-Dhu* ('Dagger') and *Ceal-na-Mara* ('Song of the Sea').

In 1977 America's Betty Cook, 54 years old, piloting the *Scarab Kaama*, won the World Offshore Power Boat Championship at Key West, Florida – this was **the finest achievement by a woman driver in the history of the sport**.

As an outboard-engined racing driver, **Carlo Casalini** of Italy raced for the first time on Lake Maggiore on 15 August 1926 and for the last time on 23 September 1973, at the age of 62 years. During this period, Casalini took part in 447 competitions and was still holding 20-year-old international outboard records as late as 1973, for 2-Hour Class OD with a Mercury-engined Molinari hull.

Ernie Nunn of Australia raced his grandfather's three-cylinder displacement boat in 1918, aged 12; by 1939, driving a single-step Margaret hydro-powered by a V8 Ford, Nunn won the NSW Open Championship. Post war, Nunn's Ferrari-powered *Wasp* hydroplanes achieved 84 championship and speed record certificates, including the coveted E. C. Griffith Cup (four times), the NSW Open Championship (11 times) and the Bridge/Bridge (six times). In 1978, aged 72, Ernie Nunn was still acting as mechanic whilst his grandson Steve Turvey drove the 21 ft (6·5 m) *Wasp* hydro, powered by twin 4½-litre Ferraris in tandem.

The UK offshore powerboat driver, Tim Powell, competed in his first race at Miami in 1962; he has since raced in England, the USA, France, Italy, Spain, North Africa, East/West Germany, the Bahamas, Argentina, Uruguay, Sweden, Brazil and Yugoslavia. Powell has estimated that at an average of 12 races per year, with an average 200 miles (322 km) per race, he has travelled some 24000 miles (38 625 km) in excess of 60 mph (97 km/h). In 1977 the *Limit-Up* team of Mike Doxford/Tim Powell competed in 21 races in nine different countries, using two offshore powerboats.

'Like father, like son' in motorboat racing and record-breaking must include Sir Malcolm Campbell (Bluebirds 1936–48) and his son Donald (Bluebird K7 1955–67); Gar Wood Sr (1911–33 *Miss America*'s) and his son Gar Wood Jr (1932–39); Sir Max Aitken (1961–76) and his son Maxwell (1960–); Sir Tom Sopwith (1912–13, *Maple Leaf IV*) and his son Tommy (1961–76, *Tramontana, Telstar, Miss Enfield*, etc); Angelo Molinari (1950–64) and his son Renato (1964–). 'Like grandfather, like son, like grandson' may be applied to Mawdsley Brooke (1905–14, *Baby*), Jack Brooke (1921–28, *Poo* and *Bulldog*) and Tom Percival (1960–); and also to Bill H. Seebold Sr (1932–58), Bill E. Seebold Jr (1952–) and Mike Seebold (1972–). As yet there is no fourth-generation powerboat racing driver!

Renato Molinari was born in February 1946 at Como. Renato's father, Angelo Molinari, began to construct motorboats in 1949, and by 1955 had developed the world's first prototype tunnel-hulled/catamaran powerboat, achieving a speed of 50 mph (80 km/h) on Lake Como. At this time Angelo was racing with Cesare Scotti, his nephew. When Angelo stopped racing, Renato took over, his first contest being in Rome in 1964. His first international victory was the Paris Six Hours in 1966, co-driven with his cousin Cesare Scotti, and won because their 'cat' was far faster than the conventional three-pointer boats. Renato has since won nine World Championships, 14 European Championships – including the Paris Six Hour (four times), Havasu (twice), Berlin (three times), Parker, USA (twice) and Pavia–Venezia (twice). He also holds 11 world records.

Kenneth Peter Warby MBE (b 1939) is not only **the first Australian to create a world speed record in Australia**, but is also the first man to design, build and drive his 27 ft (8·24 m) boat, the Westinghouse J34 turbo-jet-engined *Spirit of Australia* through both the 300 mph (480 km/h) and the 310 mph (500 km/h) barriers simultaneously on the waters of Blowering Dam, NSW. He achieved this on 8 October 1978 when he created a new two-way average of 317·186 mph (510·452 km/h) – thus establishing the biggest ever speed increase (28·59 mph (45·98 km/h)) made by a world water speed record breaker on the previous mark.

Chevalier Leopoldo Alfonso Villa OBE (1899–1979) as Chief Engineer to Sir Malcolm Campbell and his son Donald Campbell worked on and supervised their aero-engined *Bluebirds* for some eleven world water speed records between 1937 and 1964. He also rode as racing mechanic to Donald Campbell in the 1950 Oltranza Cup race on Lake Garda when, after Leo had changed 24 sparking plugs on their Rolls-Royce 'R' aero-engine in a record 2½ min, they won at a lap speed of 98·99 mph (159·31 km/h). From Donald's death in 1967 until Leo's death in 1979, he was technically **the fastest man on British waters** having survived a 170 mph (275 km/h) crash with that same Bluebird on Coniston Water in the autumn of the same year.

BRITISH MOTORBOATING CLUBS
(in chronological sequence)

Marine Motoring Association (Founded 1902. Linton C. Hope (Hon. Sec.). Defunct by 1959; replaced by the British Powerboating Union. (Founded in 1961 by Cyril Benstead); replaced by the RYA in 1964.

Nore Yacht Club (Founded 1902).

Norfolk Automobile and Launch Club (Founded 1903).

British Motor Boat Club (BMBC; founded 1904) 1st Commodore Admiral Sir William Kennedy KCB; permitted to fly the Blue Ensign. Merged with the Royal Motor Yacht Club in 1933.

Royal Motor Yacht Club. Founded 1905 as the Marine Motoring Section of the Automobile Club of Great Britain and Ireland (today RAC); 1st Commodore Dr (later Sir) Boverton Redwood. Admiralty Warrant to wear the Blue Ensign of His Majesty's Fleet in 1906; became the Royal Motor Yacht Club in 1910. Floating Clubhouse *Enchantress* until 1915; Floating Clubhouse *Florinda*, Poole Quay 1933–35; Hythe Pier 1920–40; since 1936 at Sandbanks, Poole, Dorset.

Royal Scottish Motor Yacht Club (Founded 1906).

Sussex Motor Yacht Club (Founded 1907) 1st Commodore Fred May 1907–51). Founded the London–Cowes race; guardians of the Britannia Trophy.

Cambridge Motor Boat Club (Founded 1911).

Windermere Motor Boat Racing Club (Founded 1925). 1st Commodore E. H. Pattinson; Waterhead Trophy. Windermere International Grand Prix.

British Outboard Racing Club (Founded 1929) 1st Commodore Lord Louis Mountbatten. Duchess of York's Trophy.

Thames Motor Yacht Club (Founded in 1930 as the Thames Motor Cruising Club) 1st Commodore E. W. West.

Oulton Broad Motor Boat Club (Founded 1936) 1st Commodore E. M. Treglown. Became Lowestoft & Oulton Broad Motor Boat Club in 1946. Daily Mirror Trophy Race.

Lancashire Powerboat Racing Club. (Founded 1936).

London Motor Boat Racing Club (Founded 1956) 1st Commodore Cyril F. Benstead.

Cotswold Motor Boat Racing Club (Founded 1958) 1st Commodore Len Bliss.

South Staffs Hydroplane & Speedboat Club (Founded 1958) 1st Commodore Eric Platt. Became the Chasewater Powerboat Club in 1960. Atlantis Trophy.

Offshore Powerboat Club of Great Britain (Founded 1966) 1st Commodore John Chitty.

United Kingdom Offshore Boating Association (Founded in 1962) President N. G. Ramseyer. 1st Commodore Ray Bulman.

UNION INTERNATIONALE MOTONAUTIQUE (UIM)

The International Association of Automobile Yachting (AIYA) was founded in 1907 with Vice-Admiral Aschenborn as its first President. The founders were the Marine Motoring Association (MMA), the Motor Yacht Club de Belgique, the Ostend Yacht Club, the Nederlandse Motorboot Club, the Svenska Motorboot Club and the Motor Yacht Club of Germany. The AIYA governed racing was directed by a Central Committee whose President and site changed each year. Such a system was doomed to failure; on the outbreak of World War I in 1914, the President of the Association was Dr Busley of Berlin. After the Armistice in 1918, President and Archives had disappeared.

In May 1922 Dr (later Sir) Morton Smart (Commodore of the British Motor Boat Club (BMBC) and Vice-President of the MMA) and John Ward, an Irishman emigrated to Belgium who spoke perfect French, wrote a letter advocating the re-establishment of an international controlling body for racing and the adoption of one or more international restricted classes. Copies of this letter were distributed to the

Meeting of the Permanent Committee of the IMYU (April 1926). Left to right: *Boutry, Bray, Fair, Borromeo, Massieu, Bauer, Pierrard, Teupken, Bernard, Bouriez, Huybreghs, Pauwaert and Tattersall*

world Press, and all published in the same week; they invited 16 nations and self-governing states to send representatives to a meeting in Brussels. On 27–29 September 1922, Belgium, Spain, France, Great Britain, Monaco, Norway, Netherlands and Sweden were represented. Members decided that the social 'seat' would have to be permanent and established in a small country. Belgium was chosen for her central position, and the first President of the International Motor Yachting Union was a Belgian called Mr A. Pierrard, an engineer in the Belgian Navy, with John Ward as secretary. Ward died unfortunately in May 1925 and was replaced by Mr Maurice Pauwaert.

At the beginning, the role of the Union began by internationalising three English classes: the 30-footer (9 m) class, the 1½-litre class and the 3-litre class, and then also by the establishment of the first ruling for international tonnage for cabin cruisers, a ruling modified some dozens of times and forerunner of the rules for cabin cruisers so cherished by competitors of deep sea races, badly named 'offshore' races.

In 1923 race rules, class rules, contest rules and rules for world records were revised. Originally the promoters had suggested the named 'Union Internationale de Yachting Automobile de course' and its English equivalent 'International Motor Yacht Racing Union' (IMYU) to make it depend on the international authority organising sailing races, whose seat was in London and whose influence was felt for a long time even in the rules of the Union of Automobile Yachting.

The words 'de course' (racing) were taken from the title on demand of the Dutch delegates who thought that for the most important reasons, the Union should not only concern itself with racing, but also with cruisers and pleasure craft. In this change the Netherland authorities were most fair and far-sighted.

The first statutes of the Union were those of the old Association and these statutes remained strong until 31 December 1923. Finally it was decided to copy the Sailing Union and create, for example, a 'Permanent Committee', comprising a President, two vice-Presidents, five members and a Secretary. In 1924 the statutes were revised, article by article.

Originally the Permanent Committee had nine members and had a reunion every year, and did not cease growing in number until its abolition in 1971.

In 1924, it received Royal recognition: King Albert I offered a prize for the 12-litre class, which had just been created. The same year Germany was re-admitted to the IMYU. This same year the IMYU was faced with its first litigation: a conflict arose between two Dutch associations, the Koninklijke Nederlandshe Motorboot Club, the original national authority, and the Dutch pleasure-boating federation, the dynamic Koninklijke Verbonden Nederlandshe Watersport Vereenigingen. After many exchanges, it was decided that the Koninklijke Nederlandshe Motorboot Club should keep its authority. In 1924 also, the first sporting calendar for International Motor Boating was issued and saw some 15 international race meetings. In 1926 there were only nine, whilst 1928 had ten contests.

In 1925, Poland and the Yachtsmen's Association of America were admitted as members.

Outboards were classed in 1926, with as cylinders the 250, 350 and 500 cc, whilst the 1000 cc were admitted two years later in 1928. From this moment, the term 'outboard' replaced the words 'detachable motor'.

The Yacht Club Argentino was admitted in 1927 and Ireland in 1928, and at the General Assembly of 1928, two delegates from the Royal Scottish Motor Yacht Club were refused admission because the Union did not then accept devolutionists!

In 1929, the rules for the John Ward Trophy were organised. Also in 1929 the IMYU did not recognise the statute English mile. For the first time a distinction was made between stock and unlimited engines, and records of speed, distance, hour, 5, 10 and 15 nautical miles were recognised.

The telegram code word for the IMYU is 'Alleluia'. This is because at the end of one of their meetings, the secretary, in order to hasten the closure of the meeting, said 'Allez l'UIYA, il est temps d'aller dejeuner'. The members were so struck by the idea that they adopted it for their telegrams.

In 1930 Norway, Austria, Lithuania, Finland, Portugal, Spain, Switzerland and Czechoslovakia rejoined the ranks. In 1931 it was Australia's turn and in 1932 Canada. In 1933 Czechoslovakia and Ireland dropped out.

World War II interrupted the sport and it was only in September 1945 that the first restrained General Assembly met in Brussels and became the UIM. On 12 September 1945, Mr Alfred ('Freddy') Buysse was named as President of the UIM, succeeding A. Pierrard who died in December 1944.

In 1954 the Yachtsmen's Association of American handed over national authority to the American Power Boat Association (APBA) and the UIM recognised as world records, all records established or bettered in the APBA Class. It was also decided that timing of speed records over 124 mph (200 km/h) should be to the 100th of a second.

The first record ever to be homologated international by the IMYU was established in 1923 by the French pilot Canivet in an unlimited hydroglider at 75 mph (120 km/h). This record is still held for its Class. By 1939, 200 records had been homologated; by 1956 some 500, and by 1972 some 2250, whilst by 1977 some 2500 records had been homologated by the UIM. The Union currently comprises 44 member countries.

ROLL OF HONOUR

The following is a list of names of those who have successfully lived – and some of whom have died – for the sport of motorboat racing:

Fred Alter, Ward Angelly, Adolph Apel, Don Aronow, Art Ashbury, S. Mortimer Auerberbach, Bill Badsey, Vincenzo Balestieri, James Beard, A. Becchi, Dick Bertram, Carlo Bonomi, Maurice E. Bothner, Len Britnell, Mawdsley and Jack Brooke, Norman Buckley, Alf Bullen, Bill Cantrell, Giulio Carcano, Lewis Carlisle, Count Carlo Casalini, L. Casanova, Gian Franco Castiglione, Achille Castoldi, George Coleman, Doug Creech, Red Crise, Sam H. Crooks, John Crouse, Aldo Dacco, Dapp, E. T. Bedford Davie, Giulio de Angelis, Victor Despujols, André Dieckx, Horace and Delphine Dodge, R. Stanley Dollar Jr, Kaye E. Don, Michael Doxford, Dean Draper, Marius Dubonnet, Roy Duby, Jean Dupuy, Tom d'Eath, S. F. Edge, Hu Entrop, Dr Hugo Etchegoin, Walter Everett, Colin D. Fair, Tony Fahey, Clinton Ferguson, Norman Fletcher,

Edsell Ford, Danny Foster, Trevor Fox, Charles and Jimmy Gardner, Sam Griffith, A. Guillard, Joel Halpern, Dan Hanbury, Charles Harrison, Art Hatch, E. Hedges, Bob Hering, John Hill, Ronny Hoare, Howard Hollingsworth, G. Holt, Albert Hoy, J. E. Hutton, Harry Hyams, Haruo Ishikaura, 'Pop' and Fred Jacoby, Jeremy James, P. and Didier Jouseaume, Dieter König, Herr Kreuger, Hermann Leiven, Renato 'Sonny' Levi, Odell Lewis, Guy Lombardo, Forrest Lundy, Ken Mackenzie, Robert C. Magoon, Oscar Martin, Bob May, Fred May, Len Melly, Herb Mendelson, Nino Mereghetti, John Merryfield, Fred Miles, Ernie Millot, Angelo and Renato Molinari, Giorgio Mondadori, Monnier, Lord Montagu of Beaulieu, Moreau, Fred Mulkey, Bill Muncey, Ron Musson, Hub Myers, Kenjiro and Masaaki Nakamura, Dick Neal, Tony Needell, Count J. E. Johnston-Noad, Bob Nordskog, H. C. Notley, Ernie Nunn, Louis Nuta, G. Parodi, Hans Pelster, Tom Percival, John Pertwee, Attilio Petroni, Dick and Malcolm Pope, Tim Powell, Gordon Pratt, Ray Pregenzer, Don Pruett, Bobby Rautboard, Jack Regas, John Reid, George Reis, Roy Ridgell, Noel Robbins, Conte Theo Rossi di Montelera, Lionel de Rothschild, Vittorio Rustici, Sandy Satullo, Art Sauerberg; Dr Emil Savundra; Paul Sawyer, Jack Schafer, Lee Schoenith, Bill Schumacher, Vic Scott, Cesare Scotti, Mulford Scull, Bill Seebold Sr, Jr and III, Ezio Selva, Bill Shakespeare, Don Shead, Eugenio Silvani, Sirois, Mira Slovak, Dr Ralph Snoddy, Sir Tom and Teb Sopwith, Keith Sorensen, Pedro Soriano, Len Southwood, Bob Spalding, Mario Speluzzi, Bill Stead, C. Stefanoni, Lars Ström, Yutaka Sugihara, Joe Taggart, Bill Tenney, Chuck Thompson, Joel Thorne, Tom Thornycroft, Peter Thorneywork, Peter Twiss, Tommy Tyson, Maurice Vasseur, J. van Blerck, W. K. Vanderbilt, Cees van der Velden, F. Venturi, Mario Verga, Walter Vieser, Frank Vincent, Lord Howard de Walden, Gerry Waldman, Ken Warby, Duke of Westminster, D. Whitfield, Bud Wiget, Tony Williams, Don Wilson, Harold Wilson, Jackie Wilson, Bill Wishnick, Garfield A. Wood, George Wood and Phil Wood, Jim Wynne, Kevin Wyld, Erwin Zimmerman.

S. F. Edge (GB 1902–06)

Duke of Westminster (GB 1909–12) (RTHPL)

E. T. Bedford Davie, Fred Jacoby, Dean Draper (USA)

Dick Neal (USA)

George C. Reis (USA)

Count Theo Rossi (Italy)

Charles Harrison (GB)

H. C. Notley (GB)

Gar Wood and Orlin Johnson (USA)

H. Scott-Paine (GB)

Betty Carstairs and Malcolm Campbell (GB) (RTHPL)

Guy Lombardo (USA)

Stan Sayres (USA)

John Cobb (GB)

Mario Verga (Italy)

Donald Campbell and Leo Villa (GB)

Tommy Sopwith
(GB 1960s)

Tim Powell and Michael Doxford (GB 1960s/1970s)

Bill Muncey
(USA 1950s–1970s)

Bill Seebold Sr, Bell Seebold Jr and
Mike Seebold (USA 1940s–1970s)

Bob Spalding and Tom Percival
(GB 1960s/1970s)

Renato and Angelo Molinari
(Italy 1960s/1970s)

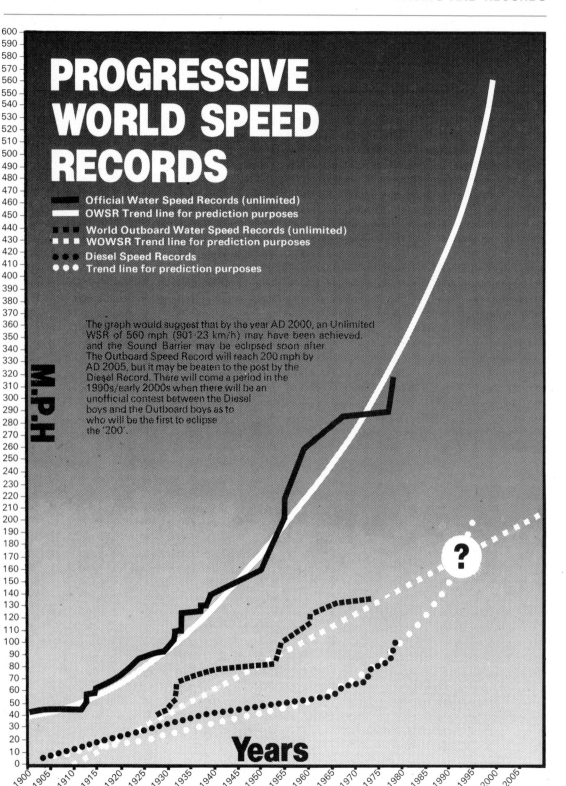

PROGRESSIVE WORLD SPEED RECORDS

■ Official Water Speed Records (unlimited)
▬ OWSR Trend line for prediction purposes
■■■ World Outboard Water Speed Records (unlimited)
▪▪▪ WOWSR Trend line for prediction purposes
●●● Diesel Speed Records
●●● Trend line for prediction purposes

The graph would suggest that by the year AD 2000, an Unlimited WSR of 560 mph (901·23 km/h) may have been achieved, and the Sound Barrier may be eclipsed soon after. The Outboard Speed Record will reach 200 mph by AD 2005, but it may be beaten to the post by the Diesel Record. There will come a period in the 1990s/early 2000s when there will be an unofficial contest between the Diesel boys and the Outboard boys as to who will be the first to eclipse the '200'.

M.P.H

Years

BRITISH INTERNATIONAL (OR HARMSWORTH) TROPHY FOR MOTOR BOATS

				Speeds	
Year	Nationality	Boat	Venue	mph	km/h
1903	England	Napier I	Queenstown, Ireland	19·53	31·43
1904	France	Trefle-A-Quatre	Solent, England	26·63	42·86
1905	England	Napier II	Arachon, France	26·03	41·89
1906	England	Yarrow-Napier	Solent, England	15·48	24·91
1907	USA	Dixie I	Solent, England	31·78	51·14
1908	USA	Dixie II	Huntington Bay, NY	31·35	50·45
1910	USA	Dixie III	Huntington Bay, NY	36·04	58·00
1911	USA	Dixie IV	Huntington Bay, NY	40·28	64·82
1912	England	Maple Leaf IV	Huntington Bay, NY	43·18	69·49
1913	England	Maple Leaf IV	Osborne Bay, England	57·45	92·46
1920	USA	Miss America I	Osborne Bay, England	61·51	98·99
1921	USA	Miss America II	Detroit River	59·75	96·16
1926	USA	Miss America V	Detroit River	61·118	98·359
1928	USA	Miss America VII	Detroit River	59·325	95·474
1929	USA	Miss America VIII	Detroit River	75·287	121·163
1930	USA	Miss America IX	Detroit River	77·233	124·294
1931	USA	Miss America VIII	Detroit River	85·861	138·180
1932	USA	Miss America X	Lake St Clair	78·489	126·315
1933	USA	Miss America X	St Clair River	86·939	139·915
1949	USA	Skip-A-Long	Detroit River	94·285	151·737
1950	USA	Slo-Mo-Shun IV	Detroit River	100·680	162·029
1956	USA	Shanty I	Detroit River	89·750	144·439
1959	Canada	Miss Supertest III	Detroit River	99·789	160·595
1960	Canada	Miss Supertest III	Lake Ontario, Canada	115·483	185·852
1961	Canada	Miss Supertest III	Lake Ontario, Canada	98·218	158·066

After a lapse of some 15 years, the rules of this Trophy were re-written and it became known as

THE HARMSWORTH BRITISH & COMMONWEALTH TROPHY FOR MOTOR BOATS

1977	England	Limit-Up	Michael Doxford and Tim Powell
1978	England	Limit-Up	Michael Doxford and Tim Powell

This trophy was originally presented by Sir Alfred Harmsworth (Lord Northcliffe).

The greatest number of wins has been achieved by Commodore Garfield A. Wood with eight (1920–21, 1926, 1928, 1929, 1930, 1931, 1932, and 1933). **The only boat to win three times** (1959, 1960 and 1961) is *Miss Supertest III*, owned by James G. Thompson (Canada). In the 1931 contest, an estimated 500 000 spectators watched three boats racing round the course.

THE AMERICAN POWER BOAT ASSOCIATION GOLD CHALLENGE CUP

Year	Pilot	Boat	Venue	Average speeds (mph)	(km/h)
1904	C. C. Riotte	*Standard*	New York	23·6	38·0
1904	Willis S. Kilmer	*Vingt-et-un II*	New York	25·3	40·7
1905	J. M. Wainwright	*Chip*	St Lawrence River	15·9	25·6
1906	J. M. Wainwright	*Chip II*	St Lawrence River	20·6	33·1
1907	J. M. Wainwright	*Chip II*	St Lawrence River	20·8	33·5
1908	E. J. Schroeder	*Dixie II*	St Lawrence River	30·9	49·7
1909	E. J. Schroeder	*Dixie II*	St Lawrence River	32·9	52·9
1910	F. K. Burnham	*Dixie III*	St Lawrence River	33·6	54·0
1911	J. H. Hayden	*Mit II*	St Lawrence River	36·1	58·1
1912	Alfred G. Miles	*P.D.Q. II*	St Lawrence River	44·5	71·6
1913	Casimir S. Mankowski	*Ankle Deep*	St Lawrence River	50·49	81·25
1914	Robert Edgren	*Baby Speed Demon II*	Lake George	48·5	78·0
1915	J. Milot-J. Beebe	*Miss Detroit*	Long Island Sound	49·7	80·0
1916	Bernard Smith	*Miss Minneapolis*	Detroit	36·8	59·2
1917	Gar Wood	*Miss Detroit II*	Minneapolis	56·5	90·9
1918	Gar Wood	*Miss Detroit III*	Detroit	52·1	83·8
1919	Gar Wood	*Miss Detroit III*	Detroit	56·3	90·6
1920	Gar Wood	*Miss America*	Detroit	70·0	112·6
1921	Gar Wood	*Miss America*	Detroit	56·5	90·9
1922	Jesse G. Vincent	*Packard-Chris-Craft*	Detroit	40·6	65·3
1923	Caleb Bragg	*Packard-Chris-Craft*	Detroit	44·4	71·5
1924	Caleb Bragg	*Baby Bootlegger*	Detroit	46·4	74·7
1925	Caleb Bragg	*Baby Bootlegger*	Long Island Sound	48·4	77·9
1926	George H. Townsend	*Greenwich Folly*	Long Island Sound	49·22	79·21
1927	George H. Townsend	*Greenwich Folly*	Long Island Sound	50·99	82·06
1928	No competition				
1929	Richard F. Hoyt	*Imp*	Red Bank, NJ	50·489	81·254
1930	Victor Kliesrath	*Hotsy Totsy*	Red Bank, NJ	56·05	90·20
1931	Victor Kliesrath	*Hotsy Totsy*	Montauk, NJ	54·92	88·39
1932	Bill Horn	*Delphine IV*	Montauk, NJ	59·21	95·29
1933	George Reis	*El Lagarto*	Detroit	60·866	97·795
1934	George Reis	*El Lagarto*	Lake George	58·06	93·44
1935	George Reis	*El Lagarto*	Lake George	57·582	92·669
1936	Bennett Hill	*Impshi*	Lake George	47·12	75·83
1937	Clell Perry	*Notre Dame*	Detroit	68·645	110·473
1938	Rossi di Montelera	*Alagi*	Detroit	66·08	106·34
1939	Z. G. Simmons Jr	*My Sin*	Detroit	67·05	107·90
1940	Sidney Allen	*Hotsy Totsy III*	Long Island Sound	51·316	82·585
1941	Z. G. Simmons Jr	*My Sin*	Red Bank, NJ	52·509	84·505
1942–45	No competition				
1946	Guy Lombardo	*Tempo VI*	Detroit	70·878	114·067
1947	Danny Foster	*Miss Peps V*	Jamaica Bay, New York City	57·02	91·76
1948	Danny Foster	*Miss Great Lakes*	Detroit	52·89	85·12
1949	Bill Cantrell	*My Sweetie*	Detroit	78·645	126·567
1950	Ted Jones	*Slo-Mo-Shun IV*	Detroit	80·892	130·183
1951	Lou Fageol	*Slo-Mun-Shun V*	Seattle	91·766	147·683
1952	R. Stanley Dollar	*Slo-Mun-Shun IV*	Seattle	84·355	135·765
1953	J. Taggart Lou Fageol	*Slow-Mo-Shun IV*	Seattle	95·268	153·319

Year	Pilot	Boat	Venue	Average speeds (mph)	(km/h)
1954	Lou Fageol	*Slo-Mo-Shun V*	Seattle	99·784	160·587
1955	Lee Schoenith	*Gale V*	Seattle	100·954	162·470
1956	Bill Muncey	*Miss Thriftway*	Detroit	100·906	162·392
1957	Bill Muncey	*Miss Thriftway*	Seattle	109·828	176·751
1958	Jack Regas	*Hawaii Kai III*	Seattle	108·734	174·990
1959	Bill Stead	*Maverick*	Seattle	104·033	167·425
1960	No competition				
1961	Bill Muncey	*Miss Century 21*	Lake Pyramid, Nevada	99·676	160·413
1962	Bill Muncey	*Miss Century 21*	Seattle	100·102	161·098
1963	Ron Musson	*Miss Bardahl*	Detroit	114·650	184·511
1964	Ron Musson	*Miss Bardahl*	Detroit	108·104	173·976
1965	Ron Musson	*Miss Bardahl*	Seattle	110·655	178·082
1966	Miro Slovak	*Tahoe Miss*	Detroit	97·861	157·492
1967	Bill Schumacher	*Miss Bardahl*	Seattle	104·691	168·484
1968	Bill Schumacher	*Miss Bardahl*	Detroit	—	—
1969	Bill Sterett	*Miss Budweiser*	San Diego, California	103·587	166·707
1970	Dean Chenoweth	*Miss Budweiser*	San Diego, California	101·848	163·908
1971	Jim McCormick	*Miss Madison*	Madison, Indiana	101·522	163·384
1972	Bill Muncey	*Atlas Van Lines*	Detroit	103·547	166·643
1973	Dean Chenoweth	*Miss Budweiser*	Tri-Cities, Washington	104·046	167·446
1974	George Henley	*Pay'N Pak*	Seattle	112·056	180·337
1975	George Henley	*Pay'N Pak*	Tri-Cities, Washington	113·350	182·419
1976	Tom d'Eath	*Miss US*	Detroit	108·021	173·843
1977	Bill Muncey	*Atlas Van Lines*	Tri-Cities, Washington	114·849	184·832
1978	Bill Muncey	*Atlas Van Lines*	Owensboro, Kentucky	103·974	167·330

The Gold Cup has been won a record six times by Bill Muncey (b 1929), and was won four times by Garfield A. Wood. The only boat to win four times was Stan S. Sayres' *Slo-Mo-Shun IV*, whilst George Reis scored the hat-trick in his *El Lagarto*. In 1963 the record lap speed for this race was 114·650 mph (184·511 km/h) by Ron Musson in *Miss Bardahl*. In 1977 the lap speed stood at 128·338 mph (206·539 km/h) by Bill Muncey in *Atlas Van Lines* for a $2\frac{1}{2}$-mile lap.

MONACO RACES (April)

The Prince Albert 1st of Monaco Cup (Awarded for the best times for the Standing Mile and Flying Kilometre)

Championship of the Sea (200 km)

Year	Boat	Combined time for mile/km	Year	Boat	Combined time for km
1904	*Trefle-a-Quatre-Feuilles*		1906	*Delahaye*	4 hr 40 min 12 s
1905	*Le Dubonnet*	3 min 38$\frac{4}{5}$ s	1907	*Panhard-Tellier*	3 hr 33 min 4 s
1906	*Fiat XIII*	3 min 36$\frac{4}{5}$ s	1908	*Panhard-Levassor*	3 hr 45 min 2 s
1907	*Panhard-Tellier*	3 min 26$\frac{1}{5}$ s	1909	*Chantecler*	4 hr 45 min 58 s
1908	*Panhard-Levassor*	3 min 3 s	1910	*Cocorico*	4 hr 22 min 35 s
1909	*Duc*	2 min 45$\frac{2}{5}$ s	1911	*Lurssen-Damiler*	4 hr 45 min 17 s
1910	*Brasier-Despujols*	2 min 20$\frac{4}{5}$ s	1912	*Mais-je-vais-piquer X*	3 hr 32 min 39 s
1911·	(No race)		1913	*Sigma IV*	3 hr 33 min 28 s
1912	*Motocratie*	2 min 46$\frac{1}{5}$ s	1914	(No race)	
1913	*Santos-Despujols*	2 min 27$\frac{4}{5}$ s			
1914	(No race)				

RAID PAVIA–VENEZIA
(432 km)

Year	Engine/Hull	Pilot	Time	Average speed mph	km/h
1929	Elto/Picchiotti	Ettore Negri	11 hr 26 min 23 s	22·2	35·7
1930	Isotta Fraschini/SIAI	Franco Mazzotti	8 hr 10 min 35 s	31·4	50·6
1931	Isotta Fraschini/SIAI	Franco Mazzotti	6 hr 52 min 54 s	38·3	61·7
1932	Fiat/SIAI	Attilio Biseo	5 hr 27 min 26 s	47·2	75·9
1933	Isotta Fraschini/SIAI	Theo Rossi	6 hr 37 min 54 s	40·6	65·4
1934	Farina/SIAI	Theo Rossi	5 hr 44 min 8 s	46·9	75·5
1935	Isotta Fraschini/SIAI	Theo Rossi	5 hr 1 m 50 s	53·5	86·1
1936	Isotta Fraschini/SIAI	Theo Rossi	4 hr 45 min 2 s	56·6	91·1
1937	Alfa Romeo/SIAI	Goffredo Gorini	4 hr 47 min 32 s	56·2	90·4
1938	Alfa Romeo/SIAI	Goffredo Gorini	4 hr 11 min 28 s	64·2	103·3
1939	Alfa Romeo/Gorini	Goffredo Gorini	4 hr 19 min 16 s	62·3	100·2
1952	Lancia/Cranchi	Carlo Toselli	6 hr 22 min 49 s	42·7	68·8
1953	BPM/Abbate	Renzo Rivolta	5 hr 41 min 29 s	47·3	76·1
1954	BPM/Abbate	Augusto Cometti	3 hr 28 min 4 s	77·6	124·9
1955	BPM/Abbate	Augusto Cometti	4 hr 11 min 10 s	60·4	97·2
1956	Mercury/Cantarelli	Gianni Goitre	5 hr 18 min 49 s	45·0	72·4
1957	BPM/Timossi	Augusto Cometti	2 hr 57 min 38 s	85·4	137·5
1958	BPM/Timossi	Tarcisio Marega	3 hr 10 min 28 s	79·7	128·2
1959	BPM/Timossi	Augusto Cometti	2 hr 29 min 46 s	100·6	161·9
1960	BPM/Timossi	Augusto Cometti	2 hr 52 min 16 s	88·1	141·8
1961	Chevrolet/Celli	Dino Celli	3 hr 29 min 40 s	72·4	116·5
1962	Mercury/Molinari	Gianfranco Dogliogli	4 hr 57 min 59 s	50·9	81·9
1963	BPM/Timossi	Augusto Cometti	2 hr 26 min 45 s	99·3	159·8
1964	Alfa Romeo/San Marco	Leopoldo Casanova	3 hr 35 min 19 s	67·8	109·2
1965	Alfa Romeo/Popoli	Leopoldo Casanova	2 hr 57 min 39 s	81·8	131·7
1966	BPM/Celli	Ermanno Marchisio	3 hr 39 min 33 s	66·2	106·5
1967	BPM/Molinari L	Renzo Faroppa	2 hr 46 min 23 s	87·4	140·6
1968	Alfa Romeo/Molinari	Guido Caimi	2 hr 51 min 17 s	84·9	136·6
1969	Mercury/Molinari A	Carlo Rasini	2 hr 47 min 12 s	86·9	139·9
1970	BPM/Timossi	Roberto Brunelli	2 hr 40 min 22 s	90·7	145·9
1971	BPM/Timossi	Roberto Brunelli	2 hr 22 min 7 s	102·3	164·7
1972	BPM/Timossi	Roberto Brunelli	2 hr 27 min 11 s	98·7	158·9
1973	Mercury/Molinari A	Renato Molinari	2 hr 30 min 10 s	96·7	155·6
1974	BPM/Timossi	Antonio Petrobelli	2 hr 20 min 41 s	103·3	166·3
1975	Mercruiser/Molinari	Giuseppe Colnaghi	2 hr 33 min 12 s	93·2	150·0
1976	Mercruiser/Clerici	Giuseppe Colnaghi	2 hr 31 min 27 s	94·3	151·7
1977	BPM/Molinari A	Annibale Beltrame	2 hr 16 min 7 s	104·9	168·8
1978	Mercury/Molinari A	Renato Molinari	2 hr 14 min 42 s	117·7	189·4

The greatest number of starters for this race has been 152, with 120 finishing the race, which starts down the River Po and finishes across the lagoon of Venice. In the early 1930s the Po was full of treacherous shallows, hence hydrogliders were successful. After 1955, the Po was excavated and a system of buoys was organised. The organising club of Pavia offers the Montelera Cup to the highest speed from Revere (railbridge) to Pontelagoscuro (railbridge) – a distance of 55 km. Augusto Cometti's record of 178·582 km/h (in 1963) was beaten by Renato Molinari in 1978.

THE PARIS SIX HOURS RACE

Organised by Jean Noel Bladinaire, President of the Yacht Moteur Club de France (YMCF – the oldest motorboating club in France, created in 1907), to publicly test the speedboats on display at the Paris Nautical Salon, alongside the River Seine.

Year	Pilot/co-pilot	Class	mph	km
1955	Guyard R. (France)	585 sport	175·164	281·900
1956	Desfilles (France)	585 util.	177·840	286·207
1957	Brunet (France)	R.02 sport	227·439	366·028
1958	Caldéac/Bonnett (France)	C1 util.	213·522	343·631
1959	Millon R. (France)	R.02 sport	219·200	352·769
1960	Kirié/Viry (France)	XU 1.200	245·364	394·875
1961	Colombé/Fauré (France)	XU	243·947	392·594
1962	De Biasi/Prat (Morocco)	XC	264·193	425·177
1963	Melly/Merryfield (GB)	XT	276·647	445·220
1964	Melly/Merryfield (GB)	XC	281·846	453·588
1965	Guyard/Monier (France)	R.1	286·146	460·508
1966	Molinari R./Scotti (Italy)	ON	293·427	472·225
1967	Rasini/Rasini (Italy)	ON	327·938	527·765
1968	Leonardi/Molinari R. (Italy)	ON	381·421	613·838
1969	Molinari R./Pellolio (Italy)	ON	405·775	653·032
1970	Sanders/Posey (USA)	ON	438·574	705·817
1971	Pellolio/Donard (Italy/USA)	ON	464·136	746·955
1972	Molinari R./Hering (Italy/USA)	ON	522·906	841·535
1973	Sanders/Schumacher (USA)	ON	455·051	732·334
1974	Van der Velden/Seebold B. (Holland/USA)	ON	383	616
1975	Jousseaume/Jousseaume (France)	ON	458·5	737·9
1976	Percival/Spalding (GB)	OZ	514	827
1977	Percival/Spalding (GB)	OZ	505·24	813·10
1978	Spalding/Seebold M. (GB/USA)	OZ	546·1	878·9

MIAMI–NASSAU OFFSHORE POWERBOAT RACE
(184 miles (296 km))

Year	Pilot	Boat	Time
1956	Sam Griffith (USA)	Doodles II	9 hr 20 min
1957	Sam Griffith (USA)	Doodles III	10 hr 42 min
1958	Gordon Hoover (USA)	Crystaliner	8 hr 4 min
1959	(No race)		
1960	Sam Griffith (USA)	Moppie	8 hr
1961	Sam Griffith (USA)	Glass Moppie	4 hr 20 min
1962	John Bakos (USA)	Aokone	3 hr 42 min
1963	Odell Lewis (USA)	Mono Lou	3 hr 30 min
1964	Harold Abbott (USA)	Rum-Runner	4 hr 55 min
1965	Don Aronow (USA)	Donzi 007	3 hr 19 min
1966	Jim Wynne (USA)	Ghost Rider	3 hr 51 min
1967	Allan Brown (USA)	Donzy Baby	3 hr 18 min
1968	Mel Riggs (USA)	Mona Lou III	3 hr 12 min
1969	Don Aronow (USA)	The Cigarette	2 hr 50 min
1970	Vincenzo Balestieri (Italy)	Black Tornado	2 hr 30 min
1971	Tom Gentry (USA)	Innerspace	2 hr 31 min
1972	Bob Magoon (USA)	Aeromarine III	3 hr 5 min
1973	Carlo Bonomi (Italy)	Dry Martini	2 hr 39 min
1974	Billy Martin (USA)	Bounty Hunter	2 hr 36 min
1975	Rocky Aoki (USA)	Benihana Special	2 hr 24 min
1976	(No race)		

DAILY EXPRESS INTERNATIONAL COWES–TORQUAY OFFSHORE POWERBOAT RACE
(200 miles)

Year	Starters/ Finishers	Boat	Engines	Pilot	Nationality	Average speed mph	km/h
1961	38/9	Thunderbolt	2 Crusader	Tommy Sopwith	GB	25	40
1962	48/15	Tramontana	2 Isotta	Jeffrey Quill	GB	37	60
1963	54/28	A'Speranzella	2 Dearborn	Renato Levi	Italy	41	66
1964	58/39	Surfrider	2 Daytona	Charles Gardner	GB	49	79
1965	59/27	Brave Moppie	2 Detroit diesels	Dick Bertram	USA	39	63
1966	50/18	Ghost Rider	2 Daytona	Jim Wynne	USA	41	66
1967	70/39	Surfury	2 Daytona	Charles Gardner	GB	53	85
*1968	67/23	Telstar	1 Daytona	Tommy Sopwith	GB	38	61
1969	75/41	The Cigarette	2 Mercruiser	Don Aronow	USA	66·7	107·3
1970	68/32	Miss Enfield 2	2 Mercruiser	Tommy Sopwith	GB	58·5	94·1
1971	54/11	Lady Nara	2 Mercruiser	Ronny Bonelli	Italy	39	63
1972	54/27	Aeromarine IX	2 Mercury	Carlo Bonomi	Italy	55	88
1973	56/20	Unowot	2 Kiekaefer Aeromarine	Don Shead	GB	62	100
1974	32/15	Dry Martini	2 Kiekaefer Aeromarine	Carlo Bonomi	Italy	66·9	107·7
1975	38/17	Uno Embassy	2 Kiekaefer Aeromarine	Don Shead	GB	72·86	117·26
1976	35/19	I Like It Too	2 Chevrolet	Charles Gill	GB	69·9	112·5
1977	26/13	Yellowdrama III	2 McLaren/ Chevrolet	Ken Cassir	GB	75·13	120·91
1978	34/10	Kaama	2 Mercury	Betty Cook	USA	77·42	124·59

* The race was extended as the Cowes–Torquay–Cowes.

Originally instituted by Sir Max Aitken, then Chairman of Beaverbrook Newspapers, to promote a fast, safe, good sea-going cruiser with specifications for head-room and numbers of bunks according to the length of the boat; it has since developed into a high-speed offshore powerboat race. For many years the gas-turbined HMS *Brave Borderer* led the rolling start off the Royal Yacht Squadron Line at Cowes, with the race usually taking finishing competitors over 3 hr. The only man to win this race three times has been Tommy Sopwith in 1961, 1968 and 1970. The most number of boats to compete in any one year were 75, in 1969. The roughest race was in 1971, when competitors battled through a Force 8 gale off Portland Bill. The only fatality occurred in 1976 when Alf Bontoft was thrown out of *Blitz* and died later from injuries. The smallest boat to finish high up in the field was E. Fattorini's *Big Ed Too* (a 21 ft (6·4 m) Avenger, powered by twin Mercury 100 hp outboards), normally raced in Class IIIE, up-rated to Class II for this event; in 1970, co-driven by her owner and Vic Jenkinson, *Big Ed Too* finished 10th overall. In 1971, this same boat competed in eleven Class III races, winning eight of them and becoming the smallest boat to win the Bolinger Goblet. Sir Max Aitken himself competed from 1962–75. In 1969 Sir Max's son, the Hon Maxwell Aitken (then 17 years old) competed in his father's race. In 1970, Sir Max and his son competed together in his father's race. In 1970 Sir Max and his son competed in *Gypsy Girl*, whilst Lady Violet Aitken and her 16-year-old daughter, the Hon Laura Aitken, took the wheel of *Fiducia*. The four members of the Aitken family competed again in 1972 – the ladies in *Ford Express*, the Hon Maxwell in *Fino*, and Sir Max in *Gypsy Girl*.

AROUND LONG ISLAND MARATHON (USA)

Year	Boat	Engines	Pilot	Distance mile	km	Time
1961	31 ft *Bertram*	2 Chrysler	Sam Griffith	264	425	6 hr 22 min
1962	17 ft *Eltro*	2 Mercury	Augie Nigl	264	425	7 hr 16 min
1963	18 ft 6 in *Glastron*	1 Mercruiser	Ray Attwood	264	425	5 hr 37 min
1964	25 ft *Bertram*	2 Mercruiser	Odell Lewis	264	425	5 hr 6 min
1965	20 ft *Owens*	1 Mercruiser	Stan Humes	264	425	7 hr 45 min

HENNESSY LONG ISLAND MARATHON

Year	Boat	Engines	Pilot	Distance mile	km	Time
1966	28 ft *Donzi*	2 Holman & Moody	Alan Brown	253	407	4 hr 42 min
1967	31 ft *Thunderbird*	1 Mercruiser	Dick Genth	253	407	5 hr 23 min

HENNESSY NEW YORK GRAND PRIX

Year	Boat	Engines	Pilot	Distance mile	km	Time
1968	31 ft *Bertram*	2 Mercruiser	Bill Sirois	253	407	3 hr 59 min
1969	32 ft *Bertram*	2 Mercruiser	Pete Rittmaster	222·5	358·1	4 hr 38 min

HENNESSY GRAND PRIX

Year	Boat	Engines	Pilot	Distance mile	km	Time
1970	32 ft *Cary*	4 Mercury	Bob Magoon	—	—	4 hr 12 min
1971	32 ft *Cigarette*	2 Mercruiser	Bob Magoon	181·3	291·8	2 hr 56 min
1972	36 ft *Cigarette*	2 Mercruiser	Sandy Satullo	181·3	291·8	2 hr 31 min
1973	36 ft *Cigarette*	2 Kiekhaefer	Bob Magoon	181·3	291·8	2 hr 28 min
1974	36 ft *Cigarette*	2 Mercruiser	Art Norris	180·1	289·8	2 hr 29 min

BENIHANA GRAND PRIX

Year	Boat	Engines	Pilot	Distance mile	km	Time
1975	44 ft *Miller-Saccente*	2 Mercruiser	Jon Varese	179·9	289·5	3 hr 14 min
1976	40 ft *Cigarette*	2 Mercruiser	Bob Magoon	200	322	2 hr 33 min
1977	38 ft *Cobra*	2 Mercruiser	Joel Halpern	200	322	2 hr 46 min
1978	39 ft *Cigarette/Halter*	2 Mercruiser	Billy Martin	178	286	2 hr 8 min 37 s

The Benihana Grand Prix is currently sponsored by Rocky H. Aoki, a former Olympic wrestler and president of Benihana of Tokyo Inc., an American-based Japanese steak restaurant chain, incorporating hibachi table cooking. The overall winner receives a 200-year-old plus bronze Japanese urn as the Trophy. In 1977, 65 entries and 55 boats took the starter's flag.

WORLD OFFSHORE CHAMPIONSHIP –
SAM GRIFFITH TROPHY

Year	Pilot	Points
1966	Jim Wynne (USA)	36
1967	Don Aronow (USA)	41
1968	V. Balestrieri (Italy)	51
1969	Don Aronow (USA)	60
1970	V. Balestrieri (Italy)	51
1971	William Wishnick (USA)	75
1972	Bobby Rautbord (USA)	70
1973	Carlo Bonomi (Italy)	62
1974	Carlo Bonomi (Italy)	64
1975	Wallace Franz (Brazil)	74
1976	Tom Gentry (USA)	⎫ Fought over one
1977	Betty Cook (USA)	⎬ offshore race instead of on
1978	Francesco Cosentino (Italy)	⎭ points system

EUROPEAN OFFSHORE CHAMPIONSHIP
(CLASS I)

Year	Pilot
1973	Carlo Bonomi (Italy)
1974	Giorgio de Angelis (Italy)
1975	Carlo Bonomi (Italy)
1976	Giorgio de Angelis (Italy)
1977	Michael Doxford (GB)
1978	Francesco Cosentino (Italy)

WORLD OZ-CLASS CIRCUIT
CHAMPIONSHIP

Year	Pilot
1975	Billy Seebold (USA)
1976	Reggie Fountain (USA)
1977	Earl Bentz (USA)
1978	Billy Seebold (USA)

WORLD ON-CLASS CIRCUIT
CHAMPIONSHIP

Year	Pilot
1973	Renato Molinari (Italy)
1974	Cees Van der Velden (Holland)
1975	Cees Van der Velden (Holland)
1976	Renato Molinari (Italy)
1977	Billy Seebold (USA)
1978	Erwin Zimmerman

UNLIMITED – SPEED (UNOFFICIAL)

Boat	Hull	Engine	Owner	Country	Pilot	Venue	Date	mph	km/h
Mercedes	Linton Hope	Daimler		France		Nice	Mar 1902	22·36	35·98
Napier	Seyler	Napier	S. F. Edge	GB	Campbell Muir	Cork Harbour	12 Jul 1903	24·9	40·1
Trèfle-à-Quatre	Seyler	Brasier	Henri Brasier	France	M. Thery	Monaco	11 Apr 1904	25·1	40·4
Trèfle-à-Quatre	Crane	Richard-Brasier	Henri Brasier	France	M. Thery	Monaco	1 Apr 1904	26·65	42·89
Challenger		Simplex	Smith and Mabley	USA	Proctor Smith	Palm Beach, Flo.	Feb 1905	29·3	47·2
Napier II	Yarrow	Napier	S. F. Edge	GB	Tucker	River Thames	1905	29·93	48·17
Dubonnet	Tellier	2 Delahayes	Marius Dubonnet	France	Marius Dubonnet	Juvissy	11 Jun 1905	33·82	54·43
Legro-Hotchkiss	Legro	Hotchkiss		France		River Seine	1 Feb 1906	34·17	54·99
Dixie II	Crane	Crane	Crane-Whitman	USA	Clinton Crane	Bayonne, NJ	1908	36·6	58·9
Ursula	Saunders	2 Wolseleys	Duke of Westminster	GB	Noel M. Robbins	Monaco	Apr 1910	43·6	70·2
Dixie IV	Tams, Lemoine, Crane	2 Crane-Whitmans	'Dixie Syndicate'	USA	Fred K. Burnham	Huntingdon Bay	Sep 1911	45·21	72·76
Maple Leaf IV	Saunders	2 Austins	Sir E. Mackay Edgar	GB	Tom Sopwith	Solent	Jul 1912	46·51	74·85
Santos-Despujols			Victor Despujols	France	Victor Despujols	Monaco	Apr 1914	59·964	96·503
Miss Minneapolis	C. C. Smith		C. C. Smith	USA	C. C. Smith	Putin Bay, Ohio	1915	66·66	107·28
Hydrodome IV	C. Baldwin	2 Liberty Aeros	A. Graham Bell	Canada	Casey Baldwin	Beinn Bhreagh	9 Sep 1919	70·86	114·04
Miss America	C. C. Smith	2 Smith Twin Six	Gar Wood	USA	Gar Wood	Lake George	18 Sep 1920	77·89	125·35
Miss America II	C. C. Smith	4 Smith Twin Six	Gar Wood	USA	George Wood		1921	80·57	129·66
Farman Hydroglider	Farman	Hispano-Suiza	Maurice Farman	France	Jules Fischer	River Seine	9 Nov 1924	85·56	137·69

After this, world records were homologated by the IMYU (UIM) at Brussels

Boat	Hull	Engine	Owner	Country	Pilot	Venue	Date	mph	km/h
Miss America VII	Gar Wood	2 Packards	Gar Wood	USA	George Wood	Detroit	4 Sep 1928	92·834	149·402
Miss America VII	Gar Wood	2 Packards	Gar Wood	USA	Gar Wood	Indian Creek, Miami	25 Mar 1929	93·12	149·86
Miss England II	Saunders	2 Rolls-Royce Aero	Lord Wakefield	GB	Sir H. O. D. Segrave	Lake Windermere	13 Jun 1930	98·76	158·94
Miss America IX	Gar Wood	2 Packards	Gar Wood	USA	Gar Wood	Indian Creek	1931	102·16	164·41
Miss England II	Saunders	2 Rolls-Royce Aero	Lord Wakefield	GB	Kaye E. Don	River Parana	2 Apr 1931	103·49	166·55
Miss England II	Saunders	2 Rolls-Royce Aero	Lord Wakefield	GB	Kaye E. Don	Lake Garda	9 Jul 1931	110·223	177·387
Miss America IX	Gar Wood	2 Packards	Gar Wood	USA	Gar Wood	Indian Creek	5 Feb 1932	111·712	179·783
Miss England III	Thornycroft	2 Rolls-Royce Aero	Lord Wakefield	GB	Kaye E. Don	Loch Lomond	18 Jul 1932	117·43	188·98
Miss England III	Thornycroft	2 Rolls-Royce Aero	Lord Wakefield	GB	Kay E. Don	Loch Lomond	18 Jul 1932	119·81	192·81
Miss America X	Gar Wood	4 Packards	Gar Wood	USA	Gar Wood	Revier Canal	20 Sep 1932	124·91	201·02
Bluebird K3	Cooper	Rolls-Royce	Sir M. D. Campbell	GB	Sir M. D. Campbell	Lake Maggiore	1 Sept 1937	126·33	203·31
Bluebird K3	Saunders-Roe	Rolls-Royce	Sir M. D. Campbell	GB	Sir M. D. Campbell	Lake Maggiore	2 Sep 1937	129·5	208·4
Bluebird K3	Saunders-Roe	Rolls-Royce	Sir M. D. Campbell	GB	Sir M. D. Campbell	Lake Hallwyl	17 Sep 1938	130·94	210·73
Bluebird K4	Vospers	Rolls-Royce	Sir M. D. Campbell	GB	Sir M. D. Campbell	Coniston Water	19 Aug 1939	141·74	228·10
Slo-Mo-Shun IV	Jensen	Allison	S. C. Sayres	USA	Stan C. Sayres	Lake Washington	26 Jun 1950	160·32	258·01
Slo-Mo-Shun IV	Jensen	Allison	S. C. Sayres	USA	Stan C. Sayres	Lake Washington	7 Jul 1952	178·497	287·263
Bluebird K7	Norris	Metropolitan-Vickers 'Beryl'	D. M. Campbell	GB	D. M. Campbell	Ullswater	23 Jul 1955	202·32	325·60
Bluebird K7	Norris	Metropolitan-Vickers 'Beryl'	D. M. Campbell	GB	D. M. Campbell	Lake Mead, USA	16 Nov 1955	216·2	347·9
Bluebird K7	Norris	Metropolitan-Vickers 'Beryl'	D. M. Campbell	GB	D. M. Campbell	Coniston Water	20 Sep 1956	225·63	363·12
Bluebird K7	Norris	Metropolitan-Vickers 'Beryl'	D. M. Campbell	GB	D. M. Campbell	Coniston Water	7 Nov 1957	239·07	384·75
Bluebird K7	Norris	Metropolitan-Vickers 'Beryl'	D. M. Campbell	GB	D. M. Campbell	Coniston Water	Sep 1958	248·62	400·12
Bluebird K7	Norris	Metropolitan-Vickers 'Beryl'	D. M. Campbell	GB	D. M. Campbell	Coniston Water	14 May 1959	260·35	418·99
Bluebird K7	Norris	Metropolitan-Vickers 'Beryl'	D. M. Campbell	GB	D. M. Campbell	Lake Dumbleyung	31 Dec 1964	276·30	444·66
Hustler	Hallett	J46 Westinghouse	Lee A. Taylor	USA	Lee A. Taylor Jr	Lake Guntersville	30 Jun 1967	285·21	459·00
Spirit of Australia	Warby/Fink	J34 Westinghouse	Ken Warby	Australia	Ken Warby	Blowering Dam	20 Nov 1977	288·60	464·45
Spirit of Australia	Warby/Fink	J34 Westinghouse	Ken Warby	Australia	Ken Warby	Blowering Dam	8 Oct 1978	317·186	510·461

SPEED

Boat	Hull	Engine	Country	Owner	Pilot	Venue	Date	mph	km/h
Unlimited One Hour,									
Motoscafo	Baglietto	Isotta-Fraschini	Italy	Regia Masura	Lieut. E. Silvani	Lake Maggiore	23 Dec 1937	54·55	87·79
Motoscafo	Baglietto	Isotta-Fraschini	Italy	Regia Masura	Lieut. E. Silvani	Lake Maggiore	6 Feb 1938	55·75	89·71
Matthea VII	Staeves	Jaguar	Germany	Ch. von Mayenburg	Charles von Mayenburg	Austria	8 Sep 1954	64·028	103·043
Miss Windermere III	Henderson	Jaguar	GB	N. H. Buckley	N. H. Buckley	Lake Windermere	17 Sep 1956	79·660	128·200
Unlimited Three Hours									
Motoscafo 163	Baglietto	Isotta-Fraschini	Italy	Regia Masura	Lieut. E. Silvani	Lake Maggiore	23 Dec 1937	52·52	84·51
Motoscafo 163	Baglietto	Isotta-Fraschini 1000 hp	Italy	Regia Masura	Lieut. E. Silvani	Lake Maggiore	6 Feb 1938	55·01	88·54
Miss Windermere IV	Borwicks	Jaguar	GB	N. H. Buckley	N. H. Buckley	Lake Windermere	25 Apr 1966	75·96	122·23
Unlimited Six Hours									
Motoscafo	Baglietto	Isotta-Fraschini	Italy		Lieut. E. Silvani	Lake Maggiore	6 Feb 1938	53·45	86·02
Unlimited Nine Hours									
Motoscafo	Baglietto	Isotta-Fraschini	Italy		Lieut. E. Silvani	Lake Maggiore	6 Feb 1938	52·62	84·69
Unlimited Twelve Hours									
Motoscafo	Baglietto	Isotta-Fraschini	Italy		Lieut. E. Silvani	Lake Maggiore	6 Feb 1938	51·75	83·27
Unlimited Three Miles									
Miss Bardahl	Jones	Rolls-Royce	USA	Ole Bardahl	Ron Musson		3 Oct 1965	117·13	188·50
Unlimited Five Miles									
Slo-Mo-Shun IV	Jensen	Allison	USA	S. C. Sayres	Lou Fageol		8 Dec 1957	111·742	179·831
Unlimited Fifteen Miles									
Miss Bardahl	Jones	Rolls-Royce	USA	Ole Bardahl	Ron Musson		3 Oct 1965	116·08	186·81
Unlimited Distance									
Dream Girl III	Chris-Craft	Chrysler	GB	A. Bray	A. Bray	Poole Harbour	21 Sep 1934	36·55	58·82
Beluga			France	J. Schoëller	J. Schoëller		15 Dec 1934	49·83	80·20
Long Tom		BPM	Italy		Fr. Gilberti		7 Dec 1961	53·34	85·84
Sonia I		BPM	Italy		Eng. Molinari		21 Dec 1968	77·69	125·00

WEIGHT
(900 Kilos)

Boat	Hull	Engine	Owner	Country	Pilot	Venue	Date	mph	km/h
				Speed					
Niniette VI	Bugatti	Bugatti		Belgium	Maurice Vasseur		27 Nov 1937	83·160	133·833
Asso	Baglietto	Isotta-Fraschini		Italy	Guido Cattaneo		24 Nov 1938	93·59	150·62
Keeno	Kirby	Ford		USA	Chuck Powell		9 Nov 1951	97·494	156·901
Moschettiere III	Selva	BPM		Italy	Elzio Selva		10 Dec 1952	121·00	194·73
Laura Iᵃ	Abbate	Alfa Romeo		Italy	Mario Verga	Lake Iseo	29 Jan 1953	125·67	202·25
Laura Iᵃ	Abbate	Alfa Romeo		Italy	Mario Verga	Lake Iseo	15 Feb 1953	140·73	226·49
Arno XI	Timossi	Ferrari	Achille Castoldi	Italy	Achille Castoldi	Lake Iseo	15 Oct 1953	150·19	241·71
				One Hour					
Pantera	Felbunelli	BPM		Italy	F. Venturi	Berlin	5 Dec 1937	43·75	70·40
Tempo	Engelbrecht	Auto Union	Auto Union	Germany	Hans Stuck		Jun 1939	51·13	82·27
Miss Windermere II	Ventnor	Jaguar	N. H. Buckley	GB	N. H. Buckley	Lake Windermere	9 Oct 1950	55·55	89·40
Angelica	Abbate	Ferrari		Italy	V. Oggioni		3 Nov 1953	72·00	115·87
Mathea VII	Staeves	Jaguar		W. Germany	Charles von Mayenburg		1 Jul 1954	76·151	122·553
Mathea VII	Staeves	Jaguar		W. Germany	Charles von Mayenburg		7 Jul 1956	81·26	130·77
Miss Windermere III	Henderson	Jaguar		GB	N. H. Buckley	Lake Windermere	23 Jun 1958	89·08	143·36
				Three Hours					
Blue Ace	Barrus Seahawk	Lycoming	E. P. Barrus	GB	H. C. Notley	Poole Harbour	20 Mar 1937	33·32	53·62
Pantera	Felbunelli	BPM		Italy	Franco Venturi		24 May 1937	37·94	61·06
L-28	Taroni	BPM		Italy	C. R. Clerici		26 Oct 1937	41·42	66·66
Miss Windermere II	Ventnor	Jaguar XK 120	N. H. Buckley	GB	N. H. Buckley	Lake Windermere	9 Oct 1950	51·58	83·00
Nercio 2	Molinari	Maserati		Italy	Alfredo Prandoni		21 Dec 1968	62·09	99·93
				Six Hours					
Blue Ace	Barrus Seahawk	Lycoming	E. P. Barrus	GB	H. C. Notley	Poole Harbour	20 Mar 1937	30·85	49·65
Nercio 2	Molinari	Maserati		Italy	Alfredo Prandoni		21 Dec 1968	32·22	51·86
				Nine Hours					
Blue Ace	Barrus Seahawk	Lycoming	E. P. Barrus	GB	H. C. Notley	Poole Harbour	20 Mar 1937	29·65	47·72
				Twelve Hours					
Blue Ace	Barrus Seahawk	Lycoming	E. P. Barrus	GB	H. C. Notley	Poole Harbour	20 Mar 1937	29·22	47·02
				Distance					
Maca II	Riva	BPM 140	N. H. Buckley	Italy	V. Roncoroni		12 Apr 1938	59·93	96·45
Miss Windermere II	Ventnor	Jaguar		GB	N. H. Buckley	Lake Windermere	9 Oct 1950	63·49	102·17
Arno XI	Timossi	Ferrari	Achille Castoldi	Italy	Achille Castoldi	Lake Iseo	15 Oct 1953	101·85	163·91

THE UNLIMITED OUTBOARD SPEED RECORD

Boat	Engine	Country	Pilot	Venue	Date	mph	km/h
Spirit of Peoria	Elto Quad	USA	Eldon Travis	Peoria	29 Sep 1928	41·75	67·19
—	Johnson	USA	Clinton Ferguson	—	1929	47·32	76·19
—	Laros	Italy	Passarin	—	1929	48·00	77·30
—	Johnson	USA	Clinton Ferguson	—	1929	48·37	77·89
Spirit of Peoria	Johnson	USA	Clinton Ferguson	Peoria	1929	49·45	79·63
—	Elto	USA	Ray Preganzer	—	28 Jul 1930	49·72	80·01
Mariella IV	Laros	Italy	Aldo Dacco	Lake Garda	19 Oct 1930	50·77	81·61
—	Elto	USA	Ray Preganzer	—	1930	51·62	83·12
Non Sequitur III	Elto	GB	Charles H. Harrison	River Medina, Isle of Wight	20 Dec 1930	51·98	83·65
—	Laros	Italy	Aldo Dacco	Lake Garda	5 Apr 1931	52·64	84·66
—	Johnson	USA	Dick Neal	—	1931	52·98	85·31
Folgore 'F39'	Laros	Italy	Aldo Dacco	Lake Garda	17 Jun 1931	54·00	87·20
'F-13'	Elto	USA	Hal Myers	Middletown	14 Sep 1931	54·83	88·33
—	Johnson	USA	Dick Neal	—	3 Oct 1931	55·37	89·16
Non Sequitur X	Elto	GB	Charles H. Harrison	River Medina	19 Dec 1931	55·56	89·42
—	Johnson	USA	Tom Estlick	California	17 Oct 1931	56·71	91·23
'F-54'	Soriano	France	Soriano	Maisons Laffitte	16 Jul 1932	59·47	95·69
'Y'	Dupuy	France	Jean Dupuy	River Seine	18 Oct 1934	65·21	104·95
'Y'	Dupuy	France	Jean Dupuy	River Seine	12 Jul 1936	74·39	119·71
'Y'	Draper	USA	E. T. Bedford Davie	Green Pond, NJ	16 Oct 1937	77·75	125·11
'Y'	Draper	USA	E. T. Bedford Davie	Green Pond, NJ	17 Oct 1937	78·12	125·69
Massimo	Soriano/Lecco	Italy	Massimo Leto di Priolo	Idroscalo (Milan)	26 Sep 1953	83·473	134·337
'RX-3'	Mercury	USA	Hu Entrop	Lake Washington	7 Jun 1958	107·82	173·64
Starflite Too	Evinrude	USA	Hu Entrop	Lake Havasu	3 May 1960	114·65	184·51
—	Mercury	USA	Burt Ross	Lake Washington	5 May 1960	115·54	185·92
Starflite III	Evinrude	USA	Hu Entrop	Lake Havasu	6 Sep 1960	122·98	197·92
Starflite IV	Evinrude	USA	Gerry E. Walin	Lake Havasu	7 Mar 1966	131·05	210·90
Twistercraft II	Mercury	USA	James F. Merten	Fox River, Wisconsin	8 Aug 1973	136·381	219·484

DIESEL

Boat	Hull	Engine	Owner	Country	Pilot and crew	Date	mph	km/h
Speed								
Lüzssen 32	Wescz	Daimler-Benz	Kriegsmarine	Germany	G. Lüzssen	7 Aug 1939	42·33	68·12
Brave Moppie	Bertram	Phillips 66/2	R. Bertram	USA	R. Bertram	10 May 1965	57·66	92·79
Merry-go-Round	R. Levi	2 Cummins	Sir Max Aitken	GB	Sir Max Aitken	13 Mar 1966	60·21	96·90
Lätmej fä dansa	Boghammer	Daytona	Tage Boghammer	Sweden	Pia Boghammer	16 Oct 1966	61·12	98·36
Maltese Magnum	Magnum	Daytona	Donald Aronow	USA	Donald Aronow	27 Dec 1967	64·47	103·75
HTS II		Ford Sabres	Mike Bellamy	GB	Mike Bellamy	19 Oct 1972	68·86	110·82
	Abbate	Perkins	Perkins	Italy	Livio Macchia	26 Nov 1972	78·36	126·10
	Abbate	Fiat AIFO	Abbate	Italy	Tullio Abbate	1977	87·38	140·62
	F.B. Marine	VM3·5	Buzzi	Italy	Fabio Buzzi	7 Oct 1978	103·01	165·88
One Hour								
		Perkins		France	Gilbert Vizy	11 Nov 1959	32·52	52·33
	Allied Marine	General Motors	W. L. McKnight	USA	John F. Manson	25 Mar 1962	34·63	55·73
	Allied Marine	General Motors	W. L. McKnight	USA	John F. Manson	12 Aug 1962	39·90	64·21
Crusader Diesel	Rayson	Crusader	Fred Alter	USA	Fred Alter	8 Jan 1966	42·67	68·67
	Abbate	Perkins	Perkins	Italy	Livio Macchia	Apr 1977	47·59	76·59
	F.B. Marine	VM3·5	Buzzi	Italy	Fabio Buzzi	7 Oct 1978	79·60	128·18
Three Hours								
	Allied Marine	General Motors	W. L. McKnight	USA	J. F. Manson	25 Mar 1962	34·70	55·84
	Allied Marine	General Motors	W. L. McKnight	USA	J. F. Manson	12 Aug 1962	39·93	64·26
Crusader Diesel	Rayson	Crusader	Fred Alter	USA	Fred Alter	8 Jan 1966	44·78	72·06
Long Distance								
	Abbate	Perkins	Perkins	Italy	Livio Macchia	Apr 1970	47·80	76·92

AERIAL PROPELLER

Boat	Hull	Engine	Country	Pilot	Date	mph	km/h
Unlimited Speed							
Marcel Besson	Besson	Hispano-Suiza 350	France	Pierre Canivet	22 Dec 1923	65·09	104·75
Farman	Farman	Lorraine-Dietrich 450	France	Jules Fischer	9 Nov 1924	85·56	137·69
900 Kg Speed							
Giovinezza 32	Saiman	Fiat	Italy	F. Venturi	Jul 1939	49·62	79·86
Giovinezza 32	Saiman	Fiat	Italy	F. Venturi	24 Jul 1939	57·57	92·65
G2		Alfa-Romeo	Italy	G. Gorini	6 Aug 1939	75·62	121·69
1200 Kg Speed							
G3	Centro Sp.	XRA	Italy	G. Gorini	6 Aug 1939	91·22	146·81
G3	C. Spezium	XRA	Italy	F. Venturi	19 Aug 1951	96·86	155·88
900 Kg Distance							
Giovinezza 32	Saiman	Fiat	Italy	E. Lazzaroni	12 Jul 1939	41·38	66·59
Giovinezza 32	Saiman	Fiat	Italy	E. Lazzaroni	24 Jul 1939	43·30	69·69
Unlimited Distance							
Ardea	SIAI	Isotta-Fraschini	Italy	Conte Theo Rossi	14 Jan 1934	50·51	81·28
Ardea	SIAI	Isotta-Fraschini	Italy	Conte Theo Rossi	24 Jan 1934	60·59	97·52

3 CRUISING AND LONG DISTANCE

One of the first British records for small-class off-shore cruising was claimed by the Mitcham Motor Company, Wandle Works, Mitcham, Surrey. On 25 September 1901, Mr A. McWan-ken, his wife and a friend climbed into their 14 ft (4 m) 1½ hp Mitcham motor-dinghy and from Ventnor, Isle of Wight they motored 73 miles (117 km) round the island. Deducting the stop at Cowes and stoppages to clear weeds their total running time was 8 hr 40 min, and their motor consumed 1½ gallons (7 litres) of petrol. By 1903, Mitcham Motors had moved down to Cowes – some 250 motors having been installed in auxiliary craft. The company did not survive World War I.

The first motor-auxiliary to cross the Atlantic Ocean was the 38 ft (11·6 m) *Abiel Abbot Low*, fitted with a 10 hp engine and sponsored by the New York Kerosene Company. Commanded by the 40-year-old Capt. William C. Newman, and crewed by Newman's 16-year-old son, the boat was loaded with 800 gallons (3640 litres) of kerosene, 200 gallons (900 litres) of fresh drinking water, and enough food for 60 days. The *Abiel Abbot Low* left New York on 9 July 1902. In the face of Atlantic gales, the nauseating fumes of kerosene, and severe fatigue from 45 hr or more on watch, Newman and son eventually arrived at Falmouth on 14 August – a journey of some 36 days covering 3100 miles (5000 km). For their troubles they were paid $5000 by Mr A. A. Low, President of the Kerosene Oil Engine Company.

In March 1903, there were 41 motor-launch owners on Lloyds Register of Shipping.

The 38 ft (11·6 m) Abiel Abbot Low, *first motorboat to cross the Atlantic Ocean (Osborne Studios Ltd)*

Captain William C. Newman and son Edward, the morning after their arrival in Falmouth (1902) (Osborne Studios Ltd)

Napier Major *departing for the Shetland Isles (April 1905) (Veteran Car Club)*

The first motorboat to be pressed into the service of a burglar was in June 1903. A sum of £50 was stolen from a tradesman's safe at Blyth, Northumberland, and the thieves escaped on a petrol-engined lugger belonging to a Mr Foster. A fortnight later the lugger was discovered at Esbjerg, Denmark – after a journey of some 400 miles (645 km) across the North Sea!

The first long-distance British motor-cruiser was S. F. Edge's *Napier Major* (LOA 45 ft (13·7 m) × B 9 ft 6 in (2·9 m) × D 5 ft 6 in (6·4 m), powered by a four-cylinder, 20 hp Napier engine. On 29 April 1905, manned by a crew of four, *Napier Major* left the Thames and reached Lerwick, Shetland Isles after a 750-mile (1200 km) journey, completed in seven days. She had one run of 660 miles (1060 km), only stopped by stormy weather. Returning home along the East Coast, this motor-cruiser called in at the principle ports to exchange information on the exact

requirements of the fishing industry as regards auxiliary motor power.

In June 1906 *Napier Major*, skippered by an Australian Walter E. Herman, took 50 days to circumnavigate the British Isles – a distance of 2125 miles (3420 km). It was then described as **'one of the most remarkable voyages ever made by a motor-propelled boat'**.

In June 1907 James Gordon Bennett, a member of the New York Yacht Club, offered a cup and $1000 for a 699-mile (1125 km) cruiser race from New York to Bermuda, described as **the longest race on record**. Messrs Eben Stevens and James Craig's 65 hp-engined *Ailsa Craig* (LOA 59 ft 10 in (18·2 m) × B 10 ft 1 in (30·5 m) × D 4 ft (1·2 m)) made the run from Norton's Point, Coney Island to a point off St David's Head, Bermuda in 64 hr 49 min. Her average speed was 10·34 knots. There were nine other contestants.

In the summer and autumn of 1907, the *Beaver*, a 35 ft (10·7 m) motor-cruiser (built at Limehouse, London, to the designs of Linton Hope, and powered by a 16 hp Dan paraffin motor constructed by the Jorgensen Motor Works of Copenhagen) travelled a distance of some 6850 miles (11000 km) across the water-ways and canals of Europe. Crewed by three Americans – Dr Henry ('Hank') Cottrell Rowland (the owner), Sanford B. Pomeroy (an artist) and A. N. Ranney – the *Beaver*, patriotic-ally flying the American flag, voyaged from London across the Channel to Le Havre and on to Paris, Marne, Strasbourg, Mainz, Frankfurt and the Danube. After 1500 miles (2400 km) along the winding Danube, the *Beaver* reached Sulina in Roumania – **the first motorboat to be seen in those parts**. But by this time the steering gear had been damaged and the Dan engine was diminishing in reliability. The journey came to an end on 23 September 1907 during a freak storm on the Black Sea and luckily her crew were able to beach the *Beaver* near Darbox on the Turkish Coast.

In 1908, H. C. Rowland, as the author of two other books (*In the Shadow* and *The Wanderers*), wrote up their experiences in a book entitled *Across Europe in a Motor Boat*, published by D. Appleton & Co., NY.

In 1928, Harry Greening drove his *Rainbow VII* 735 miles (1183 km) in 720 min (12 hr), all stops included. They had to take on 180 gallons (680 litres) of gasoline every 180 miles (290 km) and this was done in just under 45 s. **This record remained unbeaten for over three decades.**

The first time the North Sea was crossed by an open motorboat was in 1929. Using a 144 hp Thornycroft, Lieut.-Col. Stewart and his wife, Gwenda, left Aberdeen at 4.45 p.m. on 30 June and arrived at Sola, 10 miles (16 km) from Stavanger in Norway, at 6.30 p.m. on 1 July (ap-proximately 400 miles (650 km) in 25 hr at an average speed of 16 mph (26 km/h).

The outstanding event in motor-cruiser passage races took place in 1938 when a fleet raced over a 225-mile (360 km) course, Poole–Cherbourg–Havre–Poole.

A notable event in the 'Pavillion d'Or' series was the Liege gathering of 1939 when 86 motor-yachts and cruisers were reviewed by King Leopold of the Belgians. The complete entry list totalled about 100, from five nations.

Motorcruisers during the Thames rally to celebrate the Jubilee of King George V in 1935 (Motor Boat & Yachting)

Howard Hollingsworth, of the London store of 'Bourne and Hollingsworth', motor-cruising on the Norfolk Broads in the 1930s.

The first motor-driven craft to arrive in India was a 40 ft (12 m) Taylor-Bates river-launch, fitted with a four-cylinder, 25 hp Filtz marine motor, capable of 10 mph (16 km/h), with a seating capacity of ten. It was sent out by the P & O SS *Sardinia* in April 1903, delivery being given to the Nawab of Dacca on the Hooghly River.

Although there are vague reports of a 17 ft (5 m) motor tender called the *Comcimbo* dated to 1870, **the first definite report of a Norwegian motorboat** dates to 1880 when Paul Henning Irgens installed his heavy oil engine in a fishing smack. **The first mass-produced Norwegian engine** was the 'Eureka' of H. P. Andresen in Kristiana (Oslo) in 1902–3, followed by Gullowsen's single-cylinder 5 to 6 hp 'Grei' motor and Haldorsen's single-cylinder 3 to 4 hp unit constructed in Rubbestadnesset in 1903–4. In 1905, 12 motorboats were registered in the Royal Norwegian Yacht Club (RNYC), but by 1909 this number had risen to 54 registered motorboats – particularly due to Alf G. Nielsen's newly-established 'A/S Maritim' boatyard. **The first RNYC motorboat race** took place on 14 September 1907, involving 13 craft, including the successful 15 hp Fay & Bowen engined *Dux* belonging to Fr Johannessen. In 1917, Alf Nielsen's 100 hp van Blerck engined hydroplane, *Aase IV*, reached 37 knots racing in Stockholm. **One of the most prominent Norwegian boatbuilding yards** was 'A/S Maritim', employing such talented engineers as Rich G. Furuholmen. Another famous designer was Bjarne Aas.

The first Japanese motorboat was designed as a 24 ft (7 m) displacement hull by Shozo Ikushima, built by the Ishikawazima Ship Building Co. in 1910 and installed with a 10 to 12 hp Waterman engine, to travel at 13 mph (21 km/h). Boatyards which came to specialise in motorboats were the Sumida-Gawa, the Tsushima, the Noguchi and the Yokohama yards. In 1928 the 20 ft (6 m), 200 hp *Miss Sumida* hydroplane became **the first Japanese speedboat to achieve 50 mph** (80 km/h). Haruo Ishikawa built **Japan's first outboard-engined boat**, whilst **the first Japanese outboard engines** were the 'Amagi' and the 'Kinuta'. On 26 July 1931, 41 Japanese outboard boats competed over 5 miles (8 km) of the Sumida River, while in 1932 the first 34·9 mile (56·1 km) marathon race was held. The only Japanese offshore race is for the Atami Ocean Cup and it has seen as many as 180 contestants take part.

The first motorboats to navigate the Blue Nile from Shafartak to Sirba, some 270 miles (435 km), were part of the British Army's Great Abbai Expedition of 1968, commanded by Lieut.-Col. J. N. Blashford-Snell MBE, RE. Four Royal Engineer Aluminium Assault Boats, powered by 40 hp Johnson outboards (*Kitchener*, *Wingate*, *Standford* and *Cheeseman*) rode some pretty ferocious rapids in August of that year.

In addition, *Stanford* made **the first ever upstream journey from Shafartak to the Bascillo river junction** on the Blue Nile in September 1968. Capt. J. F. W. Wilsey, Devon & Dorset Regiment, was in command and the helmsman was R. Wright, Warrant Officer 2, Royal Engineers, with Sgt J. Huckstep, Royal Engineers and Lieut. Telahoon Makonnen, Imperial Ethiopian Navy, as crew. Two small Royal Engineer recce boats with 9½ hp Johnson outboards were **the first powered craft to run the river from the Portuguese Bridge to Shafartak** in September 1968. They were the 'gunboats' involved in the battles at the Tammi River and further downstream.

The Zaire River was first navigated by motor-driven craft from Bukama in the province of Shaba to Banana on the Atlantic coast (with the exception of a short stretch of a few miles near the Inga Dam complex in North West Zaire, where craft had to be portaged). The total distance was around 2400 miles (3860 km). The

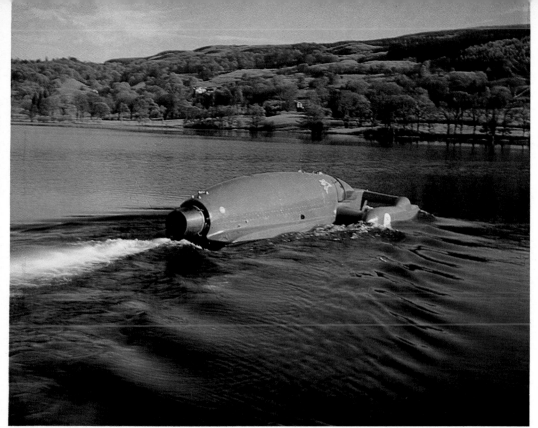

Donald Campbell's Bluebird K7 (1955–67) (Courtesy Leo Villa)

Ken Warby's Spirit of Australia (1977) (Australian High Commission)

*Madame du Gast's rescue during the disastrous 1905
Algiers–Toulon race*

*'30 Years On': Donald Campbell and the Hon. Greville
Howard in a vintage, 1½-litre-engined hydroplane in 1958.
(Courtesy Leo Villa)*

Capt. G. E. T. Eyston in his 1½-litre Aston Martin-engined
Miss Olga, *competing in the 1926 Duke of York's Trophy*

Spectacular start of the Cowes–Torquay–Cowes offshore powerboat race on 27 August 1978. 25 started. 10 arrived back at Cowes (Steve Powell/All Sport)

The Shead-designed, aluminium Alitalia Due, *piloted by Francesco Cosentino to 2nd place in the Cowes–Torquay–Cowes race, 1978. Four months later, Cosentino became World Offshore Champion (Steve Powell/All Sport)*

Line-up for the Embassy Grand Prix, Bristol Docks, June 1978. Right to left: *Percival, Van der Velden, Spalding, Seebold, Molinari, etc (Steve Powell/All Sport)*

The 1949, Harmsworth Trophy contender, Miss Canada IV, fully restored at Detroit, Michigan in the late 1970s (Courtesy Harold and Chuck Mistele)

One of the three 37 ft (11·3 m) outboard-engined inflatables navigating the Zaire River in 1974–5

craft used were three 37 ft (11 m) giant inflatables, powered by twin 40 hp Mercury outboards (*La Vision, Barclays Bank, David Gestetner*), and Avon S400s 14 ft (4 m) inflatables, powered by 40 hp Johnson or 40 hp Mercury outboards.

In addition, two Hamilton 18 ft (5·5 m) water-jet craft, with 220 hp Ford engines (piloted by Jon Hamilton of New Zealand and Ralph Brown of USA) were **the first powered craft to navigate from Kinshasha to Inga over the Livingstone Falls**.

The first time that a motor-driven craft successfully navigated the rivers of British Columbia (Canada) from Yukon to Point Roberts, USA (some 2800 miles (4500 km)), was the 'Headless Valley' Expedition of 1971. Three Royal Scots Greys Corporals, under the command of Capt. Sir Ranulph T. W. Fiennes Bt FRGS, used two 16 ft (4·9 m) RFD inflatables and a Dunlop C136 inflatable, powered by 40 hp Evinrudes. After an 800-mile (1290 km) return journey to Virginia Falls, via Headless Valley, the expedition headed south-east to Vancouver by way of some 1500 miles (2410 km) of vastly differing rivers – including the Fraser River, with its notorious rapids and magnificent canyons. The most furious rapids that year were the Bridge River Rapids, stretching for 20 miles (32 km) along the

Moran Canyon. The outboard engines were sometimes refuelled in transit, and had to run for up to 10 hr at a stretch.

In August 1958, Col. James F. Calvert, commanding the US Navy's third nuclear submarine *Skate*, wished to locate the Ice Station Alpha (drifting several miles a day in the neighbourhood of the North Pole). Having established an approximate position by radio, Col. Calvert used his sonar to 'home-in' on the sound of Alpha's Johnson outboard-engined dory, motoring up and down a small lake. *Skate* immediately surfaced at the correct location of the station. This demonstrated that nuclear submarines could support bases in the so-called 'area of inaccessibility'.

In 1961, **Michel de Hemptinne** (b 1931) made his first long-distance voyage in an outboard-engined inflatable by returning from Turkey to Belgium, via the Aegean islands and canals.

In July/August 1973, de Hemptinne commanded a crew with two Zodiac Mark V inflatables (*Ulysse* and *Ras-le-Bol*), powered by 65 hp Johnson outboards on a relay journey of 880 miles (1416 km) across the stormy waters between the North Atlantic and the Arctic Ocean. Starting from Reykjavik (Iceland), they made

Miami–New York Record-Holder, pulling into New York, piloted by Dr Robert C. Magoon (Courtesy of Mercury Marine)

15-hour legs to the Vestmanna Isles, to Hofn, to the Faeroe Islands, to Lerwick (Shetland Isles) and finally to Bergen (Norway).

In July 1977, de Hemptinne commanded a seven-crew expedition, using two 19 ft (5·8 m) Zodiac Mark V inflatables (*Berani* and *Selamat*), powered by 70 hp Johnson outboards, to hop from Singapore to Darwin, via the Indonesian Isles. Their longest leg (200 miles (322 km)) was from Babar to Melville, but the whole journey totalled some 4970 miles (8000 km).

On 15 January 1970, Jacques Meunier, Jacques Chabat and Pierre Machat set out from Ciudad Bolivari, Venezuela, with a Zodiac Mark III inflatable boat, powered by a 25 hp Johnson engine, with the ambition of covering the three main water areas of South America: the Orinoco, the Amazon and the Rio de Plata. Using some 700 gallons (3200 litres) of petrol, after a water marathon of over 5280 miles (8500 km), the expedition arrived at Buenos Aires on 11 July, having crossed Venezuela, Columbia, Brazil, Bolivia, Paraguay and Argentina, and survived the Orinoco Rapids, the Casquiare Canal and two storms on the Rio Negro.

As a tribute, salute and thanks to Her Majesty the Queen for the first 25 years of her reign on 1 June 1977 a river pageant was organised on the Thames which included dumb barges, HM revenue cutters, lifeboats, a motor-torpedo boat, 16 motor-launches, 15 motor-yachts and 28 motor-tugs, not to mention passenger vessels, steam launches, steam yachts, pilot vessels, etc. This unprecedented armada of some 140 small craft proceeded from Blackwall Reach to Cherry Garden Pier. This ceremony was followed by the largest firework display ever to be staged in the heart of London.

Miami to New York motorboat record. In 1922, Gar Wood piloted his 50 ft (15·2 m) twin-Liberty aero-engined express cruiser, *Baby Gar*, from Miami to New York (1257 miles (2023 km)) in 47 hr 15 min. In 1962 Sam Griffith lowered that record to 38 hr 33 min in his 31 ft (9·5 m) Bertram *Blue Moppie*. Two years later, Capt. Charles F. Johnson, driving a 1500 hp 41 ft (12·5 m) Daytona Marine Special, further reduced that time to 31 hr 27 min. **The fastest time yet made from Miami to New York** is 22 hr 41 min (average 55·4 mph (89·1 km/h)) by Miami eye-surgeon Dr Robert Magoon in a twin 500 hp V-8 Mercruiser sterndrive, 40 ft (12·2 m) Cigarette hull, on 3 July 1974. The boat was equipped with aircraft landing lights, whilst 'Doc' wore a helmet-mounted transceiver for sea-to-air communication. He was presented with the Charles F. Chapman Trophy.

New Orleans to St Louis motorboat record. The 90½ hr record established in 1870 for this 1027-mile (1653 km) stretch of the Mississippi by the *Robert E. Lee* paddle-steamer, remained unbeaten until 1929 when Dr Louis Leroy of Memphis broke the *Lee*'s record by 2 hr 59 min to become the first holder of the Challenge Trophy presented by Edward C. Koenig to encourage competition to lower the record. Despite approximately 1000 attempts, only those shown in the Table have succeeded in winning the Koenig Trophy.

Bill Tedford, a Pulaski county treasurer, was 60 years old when he became **the first pilot to win the Koenig Trophy three times**, in his 17 ft (5·2 m) catamaran, powered by two 135 hp Evinrude outboard motors. To make the distance in 24 hr a racer would have to average 42·79 mph (68·86 km/h).

Fort Lauderdale (Florida) to Mystic (Connecticut). The first 73 ft (22·3 m) aluminium luxury motor-yacht to be built by Chris-Craft was the *Kirkline*, owned by Fred J. Kirk. Powered by twin 655 hp 12-cylinder turbo-charged General Motors V-71 diesels, the *Kirkline* covered, on her maiden voyage, the 1300 miles (2090 km) from Fort Lauderdale to Mystic in 50 hr 10 min at an average 22 knots. This beat the 54-hr mark set by Dick Bertram in 1969 in his 56 ft (17·1 m) cruiser, *Envoy*. Kirk, who had owned 11 Chris-Craft motorboats since 1956, commented that he could have made the run in 42 hr if he hadn't stopped more than 8 hr for routine maintenance and fuel.

On 26 May 1978 Betty Cook, piloting a 29 ft (8·8 m) Scarab hull, powered by twin 200 hp V-6 Mercury Black Max outboards, became **the first powerboat driver to complete the 580-mile (935 km) run down the Gulf of California, East of the Baja Peninsula, from San Felipe to Lapaz in one day** (12 hr 45 min) running at 50 mph (80 km) approximately.

In 1978 Jack Atkinson and Gene Howard achieved an NOA world record by taking their Mercury 1750-engined Hurst B-175 Bass Boat from Long Island (New York) to Tavares (Florida) in 46 hr 15 min at an average speed of 29·924 mph (48·158 km/h). The event was known as 'Operation Sea-run'.

The first British legal description of the motor-boat appeared in the Merchant Shipping Act of 1894 where paragraph 743 reads:

WINNERS OF THE KOENIG TROPHY

Boat	Owner	Date	Time
Bogie	Dr Louis Leroy	25 Jul 1929	87 hr 30 min
Evinrude II	G. F. Schomiller	28 Sep 1931	79 hr 46 min
Mark Twain	Roy F. Smith	5 Jul 1953	79 hr 12 min
Cisco	F. G. Brukrath	8 Oct 1953	61 hr 22 min
Huckleberry Finn	Lee Sawyer	15 Aug 1954	56 hr 56 min
Loetscher Special	Ray Loetscher	5 Aug 1955	52 hr 53 min
Rambler	Roy Cullum	24 Jun 1956	47 hr 20 min
Robert E. Lee III	Bill Tedford	22 Jul 1956	41 hr 57 min
Huckleberry Finn	Lee Sawyer	25 Aug 1956	39 hr 41 min
Rambler II	Roy Cullum	13 Jul 1957	31 hr 11 min
Robert E. Lee IV	Bill Tedford	23 Jul 1964	29 hr 22 min
Micro Lube	Lou Cooley	7 Jul 1968	29 hr 5 min
Robert E. Lee VI	Bill Tedford	23 Jul 1972	26 hr 50 min

'Any provisions of this Act applying to steamers or steamships shall apply to ships propelled by electricity or other mechanical power with such modifications as the Board of Trade may prescribe for the purpose of adaptation.'

Under the Thames Conservancy Act of 1894, as amended by the Port of London Act of 1908, bye-laws were laid down regulating 'both the construction and navigation of petrol motor-launches plying the Thames above Teddington Lock to Cricklade in Wiltshire, on the Isis and on the Kennet as far as the common landing places in Reading'. Under these bye-laws, petrol is taken as defined by the Petroleum Acts of 1871 and 1879. **A petrol motor-launch** is any vessel in which motive power is supplied by petrol, whether such petrol is used in an internal combustion engine or for the generation of steam, or otherwise, but the expression does not include a petrol motor-launch having no petrol on board when being towed. The word covers any person controlling the boat whether lawfully or not.'

ENSIGNS

In 1707 the Red Ensign of His Majesty's Fleet was set apart as the particular flag of the British Merchant Vessel. Yachts and similar vessels used solely for pleasure and not for profit are, by the terms of the Merchant Shipping Acts of 1894, etc, defined as merchantmen – hence entitled to wear the Red Ensign. The Admiralty also conceded the privilege to certain yacht clubs to use a special ensign – either the White or Blue Ensigns of HM Fleet, or the Blue or Red Ensigns emblazoned (defaced) with the device of a yacht club. Such rights are transferable to selected members of the club. An official list of Blue and Red Ensigns, defaced and emblazoned, may be found in the Navy Lists.

LLOYDS REGISTER OF SHIPPING

In 1688 Edward Lloyd kept a coffee-house in Tower Street, London; this coffee-house was also a popular meeting place for underwriters – those who would accept insurance on ships for the payment of a premium (by writing their signatures one under another on a policy). Over the years, Lloyd's coffee-house became recognised by seekers of insurance cover as the most likely place where a number of underwriters could be found. Among the men who conducted their business, the need was felt for some guide to the ships available. In 1760 a group of underwriters issued a Register, the first known edition of which appeared in 1764. The symbol 'A1' denoting the highest class of ship was introduced in 1775. In 1834, after some rivalry with shipowners, issue of the Register was placed under the control of a society to be known as Lloyd's Register of British & Foreign Shipping (British and Foreign later deleted) and for the first time standard rules for shipbuilding were issued.

INSURANCE

The Standard Marine Policy – otherwise known as the 'Lloyds Form', was drawn up in 1779; the motorboat policy was introduced in the 1930s.

The Aberdeen-based Barnet motor-lifeboat, Emma Constance *in 1926*

LIFEBOATS

In 1854, the National Institution for the Preservation of Life from Shipwreck was re-established as the Royal National Lifeboat Institution (RNLI).

The first steam-powered lifeboat was the 50 ft (15·2 m) *Duke of Northumberland* which was built, in 1889, around the principle of water-jet propulsion. Screw propulsion was not then favoured owing to the dangers of damage to the screw by wreckage, moreover the paddle-wheel system had never seemed very practical for smaller steamboats. The steel-built *Duke* achieved 9·17 knots on the Measured Mile on the Thames, powered by a horizontal steam engine with Thornycroft boiler. R. & H. Green built the second boat, *City of Glasgow*, in 1893. Her machinery was made by John Penn & Son, with a 200 ihp engine, again placed nearly horizontally – with a horizontal crankshaft, but having a vertical turbine on each end. Operationally this arrangement was not satisfactory, and after

only seven years on duty at Harwich, the *City of Glasgow* was sold out of commission in 1901. The *Queen*, as the third steamboat in the RNLI's power fleet was wholly built by J. I. Thornycroft of Chiswick – again using a horizontal turbine layout compound engine of 198 ihp, driving a 2 ft 6 in (0·8 m) diameter turbine.

Steam lifeboats were not ideally suited to the RNLI's work because they needed a full-time crew of Chief Engineer, Assistant Engineer and two firemen, instead of a part-time volunteer crew. The steamer had to be kept afloat at all times and not in the boathouse as was usual. Full steam could be raised in 20–25 min, but when bad weather approached the fire was lit, keeping the boiler warm. The boat could then be ready for sea in 15 min.

The development of the protected screw-prop in naval gunboats, whereby the screw is placed in a tunnel-shaped cavity, made it possible for later boats to dispense with the turbine-jet arrangement.

The RNLI had three steam-propelled, screw-driven lifeboats: *James Stevens No. 3* (1898),

James Stevens No. 4 (1899) and the second *City of Glasgow* (1901).

The first tragedy associated with steam lifeboats occurred on 11 April 1900. The *James Stevens No. 4*, stationed at Padstow in North Cornwall, when outward-bound, with a hard west-north-west wind blowing was struck by a huge wave rolling up on her port-quarter. The sea broke as it struck her, and she turned over. She became a complete wreck and was washed up on the rocks. Of those on board eight were drowned, including her four engine-room staff.

The first rescue made under steam was undertaken by the *Duke of Northumberland* on 22 February 1908. She had just returned from giving help to a disabled steamer when she received news that another ship, the *Harold*, was in danger, drifting with the tide towards the rockbound shore of Anglesey, between the North and South Stacks.

The wind was at hurricane force at the time, and the *Harold* had come to anchor close under the cliffs, but in seas so violent that it was at first impossible for the lifeboat to get near her. Helped by the slackening tide, the coxswain, after two hours of intricate manoeuvring, at last succeeded in getting a line across, by means of which seven were saved. A huge sea then washed the *Duke* right alongside the *Harold*, and the remaining two men were able to jump to safety.

By the end of her active 30 years' service, the *Duke of Northumberland* had saved some 295 lives.

The first British motor-lifeboat was the converted pulling/sailing self-righting 38-footer (11·6 m), *J. McConnell Hussy*, previously stationed at Folkestone, Kent. In early 1904, this vessel was installed with a two-cylinder, two-stroke Fay & Bowen petrol motor, developing about 9 hp, supplied by the Mitcham Motor Co. and installed by Capt. Ernest du Boulay of Thellusson & Co. The motor was encased in a watertight, copper-lined mahogany cover. Capacity in the petrol tanks was sufficient for a run of over 10 hr; the engine could be restarted immediately after the self-righting manoeuvre. In her trials the *J. McConnell Hussy* reached 6 knots with the engine running at 450 rpm. After modifications had been completed, she was sent

to Tynemouth in Northumberland. Here an army officer, Capt. H. E. Burton, was well known for his interest in lifeboating. At first the Northumbrian crew, who like most seamen regarded major changes with suspicion, would have nothing to do with a petrol motor-lifeboat. Burton therefore got together a volunteer crew, drawn from his own men, soldiers one and all, and before long the Burton team had made a successful rescue, without local help. Then the old crew agreed to return, only on condition that Burton would remain in charge of the station and take responsibility of the petrol engine.

At almost exactly the same time, the Société des Hospitaliers Sauveteurs Bretons, at La Rochelle, were putting **the first French motor-lifeboat**, the 34·5 ft (10·5 m) *Docteur Jules Baisnée*, powered by a 12 hp engine, through her trials. This lifeboat first saw service at the Portshall lifeboat station, off Brest, in 1905.

The first American motor-lifeboat was the US Life Saving Service's 27 hp self-righter, *Dreadnought*, also launched in 1904.

As a result of the technical success of the *J. McConnell Hussy*, three other RNLI lifeboats were converted. The Newhaven 38 ft (11·6 m) self-righter was equipped with a 24 hp Thornycroft motor, while the 43 ft (13·1 m) Ramsgate self-righter was fitted with a 30 hp Tylor and the 43 ft (13·1 m) Walton on the Naze boat was equipped with a 32 hp Blake motor.

The first custom-built, as opposed to converted, motor-lifeboat was the 42 ft (12·8 m) self-righter, *John A. Hay*, which went into service at Stromness in 1908.

By 1912, there were 17 motor-fitted boats on station in the British Isles. The new construction, although it could not be completely standardised, was mainly of large G. L. Watson-type boats, 43 ft (13·1 m) by 12 ft 6 in (3·8 m), which were given 50 hp Tylor motors. The Tylor engine had emerged very successfully from trials, and within the next few years all motor-lifeboats of large size either had 60 or 40 hp Tylor engines, the smaller, self-righters being given one of 35 hp, which was found adequate for a speed of about 7½ knots. By this time the USA led the field with over 100 such craft in service, but of these, 39 were known as motor-surfboats, and even the largest was only 36 ft (11 m), equipped with a six-cylinder, four-cycle Holmes auto-marine engine. The Germans had four motor-lifeboats, France and the Netherlands three apiece, and there was a solitary example in Spain.

The first RNLI lifeboat to be fitted with diesel engines was the Yarmouth, Isle of Wight, *Hearts of Oak*, in 1934.

In 1940 some 19 RNLI lifeboats went to Dunkirk. This was **the largest number of lifeboats used on one rescue attempt**. They rescued some 323 troops off the beach. During the operation, two coxswains won Distinguished Service Medals: Coxswain Primrose of Ramsgate and Coxswain Parker of Margate. The Hythe lifeboat was lost.

When the new Arbroath lifeboat, the *Duke of Montrose*, reached her station on 28 June 1957, the RNLI had replaced half its fleet of lifeboats since the war ended in 1945. The Arbroath lifeboat was the 87th to be built since the end of the war, at a total cost of £1 750 000. The RNLI complement was then 155 motor-lifeboats and one pulling boat for harbour use. Of these motor-lifeboats, 62 were 46-footers (14 m) of the Watson-type. In addition there were some 20 retired motor-lifeboats in the Reserve Fleet and one pulling/sailing boat.

In 1954 Lieut.-Cdr C. H. Harcourt-Smith RN and a crew of four, took a 25-year-old converted 61-ft (18·6 m) Barnett lifeboat, formerly *Princess Mary*, re-named *Aries*, with twin six-cylinder Foden FD6 diesels, totalling 210 bhp, across the Atlantic Ocean from Kingston-on-Thames to Kingston-on-Hudson; the journey took 33 days. The return journey back across 3000 miles (4830 km), took 18 days. During the total 80 days elapsed since her departure, *Aries* covered well over 8000 miles (12 875 km).

The first 37 ft (11·3 m) motor-lifeboat designed by the RNLI Surveyor, R. A. Oakley, was built by William Osborne Ltd of Littlehampton in 1958. She followed a model by Saunders-Roe for extended tank tests at Cowes. The self-righting process was reduced down to 6 s by the speedy transfer of most of the 1½ tons of water ballast into a righting tank on the port

side, via two rectangular pipes. Engines were twin Perkins PM4 diesels. Trials were so successful that before long the Oakley-type was the standard design.

A 48 ft 6 in (14·8 m) Oakley-type was first introduced in 1963 and was the first RNLI boat to be fitted with radar; she was the *Earl and Countess Howe* of Yarmouth, Isle of Wight, fitted with a prototype Decca 202.

The first RNLI inflatable inshore rescue boat (IRB) went out on service from Aberystwyth in June 1963 to rescue three people and a dog. By 1968 1500 people had been rescued by IRB's – a figure which has increased to over 4500 recently. Fifty of these 15½ ft (4·7 m) RFD (see p. 169) boats, powered by 40 hp outboard engines were equipped with VHF radio telephones in 1969.

Between 1968 and 1978, there were never less than 244 offshore and inshore RNLI lifeboats in operation. At the end of 1977 the RNLI had some 134 offshore lifeboats – as well as a relief fleet of 32 offshore lifeboats. The largest offshore lifeboat was a relief 50 ft (15·2 m) Thames Class boat carrying out station duties in Falmouth. Then there were 13 different types: Clyde (70 ft (21·3 m)), Arun (54 ft (16·5 m) and 56 ft (17·1 m)), Barnett (52 ft (15·8 m)), Solent (48½ ft (14·8 m)), Oakley (48¼ ft (14·8 m)), Watson (46–47 ft (14–14·3 m)), Waveney (44 ft (13·4 m)), Watson (41 and 42 ft (12·5 and 12·8 m)), Beach (37 and 42 ft (11·3 and 12·8 m)), Keith Nelson GRP (40 ft (12·2 m)), Rother (37½ ft (11·4 m)), Oakley (37 ft (11·3 m)) and Liverpool (35 ft (10·7 m)).

There are also 127 inshore lifeboats and a relief fleet of 25 inshore lifeboats, which for the most part are inflatables, although there are some 24 rigid inflatables.

During 1977, offshore lifeboats saved some 527 lives, whilst inshore lifeboats saved some 601 lives. Lives saved in the period from the foundation of the Institution on 4 March 1824 to 31 December 1977 totalled 103 258. Lives saved since 1909 and the beginnings of the motorised fleet, totalled 54 634.

The lifeboatman with the longest record of service with the RNLI was Coxswain Henry C. Blogg of Cromer who joined the service when he was 18 years old (in 1894) and left when he was 71. He was 53 years as a member of the crew. During that time the Cromer lifeboats went out 387 times and rescued 873 people. No other lifeboatman won so many medals for gallantry. His lifeboat was the 46 ft (14 m) *H. F. Bailey III*.

The engineer with the longest record of service with the RNLI is George Harrison, BEM of Lytham. He became a mechanic in 1939 and is still serving, having completed 39 years of service.

The motor-lifeboat which had the longest record of service with the Institution was the ON 808 *Mary Anne Hepworth* on station at Whitby from 1938 to 1975. The ON 761 *Charles Cooper Henderson* was stationed at Dungeness from 1933 to 1957, and in the relief fleet until 1975.

MOTOR FISHING VESSELS

The first British-built iron steam-powered, screw-driven fishing trawler was the 93 ft (28·4 m), 35 hp Hull-built *Zodiac* (GY 828) of 1881; she was followed within months by the Grimsby-built *Aries* (G 832). The third steam-engined trawler to be built that year was the 35 hp *Pioneer*; she was built by J. Shuttleworth of Hull for J. Sellars of Scarborough. All three vessels carried a complete set of sails.

Hull's first purpose-built steam fishing vessel is claimed to be the iron 100-footer (30·5 m) *Irrawaddy*, laid down at George Beeching's Hull yard as a steam trawler, and launched into service in 1885 with a 45 hp engine.

In 1887 there were 448 sail-powered fishing smacks and 38 steamers at Hull, and 815 sail-powered fishing smacks and 15 steam trawlers at Grimsby. By 1903 the Hull fishing fleet of 413 trawlers and drifters was entirely steam-powered, whilst at Grimsby there were only 34 sailing smacks left and 475 steam trawlers. This totalled 888 steam-powered fishing vessels.

P. Jorgensen's machine factory in Copenhagen produced the first 'Dan' motors, designed and built by J. C. Larsen as a four-stroke 'hot bulb' oil engine in 1894. The first boat to be fitted with a Dan engine was the fishing vessel *Francisca Helene*, owned by the Houmøller Brothers of Frederickshaven. This was **the first motor auxiliary fishing vessel in the world**. By 1900, some 1000

Scandinavian fishing vessels had been fitted with this auxiliary motor, nicknamed 'Jumbo' because of its horizontal cylinder.

The first British Lowestoft fishing drifter to be fitted with an auxiliary engine was the *Pioneer* (LOA 67 ft (20·4 m) × B 17 ft 3 in (5·25 m) × D 7 ft (2·1 m)). She was fitted with a 35 bhp four-cylinder four-stroke American 'Globe' motor (manufactured by the Pennsylvania Iron Works, Philadelphia) by Arthur F. Evans in 1901. *Pioneer* was a fully-rigged sailing drifter complete with steam capstand. Her Westmacott carburettor enabled the Globe engine to burn either petrol or paraffin – giving a speed of 7 knots on petrol and 6¾ knots on paraffin. Her original Edison batteries proved unsuitable for the work, so accumulators and a magneto generator were finally installed.

In 1905 Cdr Mansfield Cumming RN was sent by the Scottish Fisheries Board on a tour of inspection through Holland, Denmark, Norway and Sweden, and on his advice a new *Fifie* drifter (LOA 72 ft (21·9 m) × B 21 ft (6·4 m) × D 8 ft (2·4 m)) was purchased and fitted with a 25 bhp Dan motor, imported from Copenhagen.

The second motor-drifter to be built, in 1906 by H. Reynolds, at Lowestoft was the *Thankful* (LOA 73 ft (22·2 m) × B 17 ft 6 in (5·3 m) × D 8 ft 2 in (2·5 m)). She was fitted with a two-cylinder, 86 hp Brauer and Betts engine, driving a 42 in three-bladed Meissner propeller. Although gross tonnage was 56½, trial speeds reached 8 knots. But to compete with a steam drifter at this time, a petrol engine of some 200 hp was required, with little or no saving in weight over equivalent steam machinery. The petrol-engined capstans also did not prove themselves as efficient as their steam-powered equivalent.

In 1905 the Thames Yacht Building Co. Ltd of Greenhithe, Kent built their first 85 ft (26 m) auxiliary motor-trawler, *Ibis III*, to the designs of Linton C. Hope. In 1908, Thames Yachts adapted the 50 ft (15·2 m) Irish long-liner and drifter, *Ovoca*, to a 20 bhp motor for the Fisheries Department of the Board of Agriculture for Ireland. In 1909, the company built the auxiliary steel herring drifter, *Pioneer II*, for Crown Prince Leopold of the Belgians for use at the Ostend School of Fishing. By 1911, some several dozen British fishing craft had been fitted with auxiliary internal combustion engines.

In 1911, hot-bulb engines were adapted for the Japanese fishing fleets. By early 1920, low-speed diesel engines were first introduced, but by the end of that year there were some 5600 Japanese motor-fishing boats.

During World War I, nearly 800 Humberside fishing vessels were called up for Naval service. The Trawler Reserve (founded 1911) was a division of the Royal Naval Reserve. The first units were formed at Grimsby and Aberdeen and by September 1914 250 steam trawlers had been armed with 1 lb guns and minesweeping gear – many more had soon been adapted. They were often commanded by their peacetime skipper and crewmen as members of the Royal Naval Reserve. Many trawlers were lost in this cause. Between 1922 and 1928 Hull built 86 new steam trawlers.

The first British motor-trawler in Grimsby was called the *Beardmore* (LOA 115 ft (35 m) × B 21·4 ft (6·5 m) × D 12·4 ft (3·8 m)) which was built in 1921 to be powered by a three-cylinder, 375 bhp Beardmore diesel engine. This vessel, with mechanical clutch-driven trawl-winch from the engine, was owned by Messrs J. S. Doig Ltd of Grimsby. Before long the Beardmore engine had been replaced by a four-cylinder, 350 hp Bolinder engine and the vessel was re-named the *Lillias*, working from Milford Haven.

In 1934, the *Lillias* was purchased by the Chantier Dubigeon in Nantes, where the Bolinder engine was replaced by a five-cylinder 500 bhp Sulzer diesel engine, the fish hold was insulated, and the trawl-winch given a speed changing device powered by an auxiliary 75 hp Renault diesel lorry engine coupled directly to an electric generator.

The first fully-powered motor-drifter to join the Lowestoft fleet was the *Veracity*. She was built in 1926 by S. Richards & Co. to prove the advantages of the diesel engine for fishing vessels. Powered by a 200 hp Deutz diesel, she was of similar size to contemporary wooden steam drifters (LOA 82 ft (25 m) × B 18 ft 6 in (5·6 m) × D 9 ft (2·7 m)). In the early 1930s her owner/builders, S. Richards & Co., ran into severe

J.A.P. was the first motor-drifter-trawler at Lowestoft (1931)

financial difficulties and *Veracity* was laid-up and eventually sold to an expedition engaged in treasure-hunting in the Cocos Islands, off Costa Rica and made the passage out under her own power. The expedition failed to find treasure through lack of funds and *Veracity* was sold to South Americans who employed her on the Amazon with a native crew. She was eventually lost on the Orinoco when run down by a large river steamer.

In 1927 Japan built their **first deep sea diesel trawlers**, including the *Kushiro-Maru* (LOA 135 ft 4 in (41·3 m) × B 24 ft (7·3 m) × D 13 ft 5 in (4·1 m)), powered by a 550 hp engine.

By 1930, Hull had 301 steamers and Grimsby 506. By the end of 1931 some 85 fishing vessels in the UK were fitted with heavy oil engines.

The first motor-drifter-trawler at Lowestoft, *JAP*, was built in 1931 by S. Richards & Co. for W. H. Podd & Co. who had pioneered the fitting of motors into sailing trawlers. Unusually for a fishing vessel, she was fitted with twin screws, driven by Allen engines totalling 140 hp. For the first two years of her life, she worked as a drifter, but thereafter worked as a trawler. Re-engined in 1966, she foundered near the Smith's Knoll in February 1967 after springing a leak.

In 1932, S. Richards & Co. ran into financial difficulties and a rescue operation was mounted by Mr W. F. Cockrell of the East Anglian Ice and Cold Storage Co. A new company, Richards Ironworks Ltd, was formed and plans drawn up for a 75 ft (23 m) steel motor-trawler, powered by a 150 bhp Ruston & Hornsby diesel. Mr Cockrell placed an order for 12 of these vessels, which became known as the *Ala* Class, after the lead vessel *Ala*. Only seven ships were actually built, the remaining five being cancelled on the outbreak of war in 1939. One of the seven, *Eta*, was a war loss being mined while fishing near the Outer Gabbard in January 1940. *Ala* was sold to G. D. Claridge in 1945, followed by the remaining five vessels in 1947. *Ala* was resold in 1947 to the Indian Government, subsequently being transferred to the Pakistan Government, and finally being reported in 1968 as 'no longer navigable'. The other five vessels continued fishing for the Colne group of companies until 1970 when two, *Rewga* and *Celita*, were scrapped; the three survivors, *Willa*, *Gula* and *Rotha*, were converted into oil rig safety vessels, and are still afloat in service.

By March 1933, some 238 fishing vessels in the UK were fitted with heavy oil engines, varying in power from 25 to 60 hp, of which about 100 were deep sea diesel trawlers. In 1933 the total number of craft engaged in fishing in the UK comprised 2948 steam trawlers and drifters, 5259 motor-craft (most auxiliary paraffin engines) and 3756 sail-powered craft. Grand total: 11 963. Over 50 000 people were employed in the actual catching of fish in the UK at that time. In 1933 Japan was already operating 28 diesel-engined trawlers.

The first North Sea diesel motor-trawler built for the Grimsby fishing fleet was the *British Columbia* (LOA 100 ft (30·5 m) × B 21 ft (6·4 m) × D 11 ft (3·3 m)), built in 1934 of steel by Richards Ironworks Ltd in Lowestoft and powered by a six-cylinder 310 bhp Ruston Hornsby diesel. *British Columbia* was **the first British trawler to be fitted with an electric winch**; this was powered by a 75 bhp Ruston auxiliary connected to a Laurence-Scott electric generator, built in Norwich. The winch had a hauling speed of 200 ft (61 m) per minute and carried 400 fathoms of line on each drum. A 14 hp Lister engine coupled with a 3 kW Laurence-Scott

generator and clutch gave electric light and floodlighting on the deck. *British Columbia* was launched in March 1935 from Lowestoft. Otherwise, the Grimsby fishing fleet comprised some 400 steam trawlers.

The second Grimsby diesel-engined trawler was the *British Columbia*'s sister ship the *British Guiana*, built by Messrs Cochrane & Sons Ltd, Selby and powered by a Ruston diesel engine. Under very adverse weather conditions on the River Humber, the *British Guiana* achieved a speed of 10·192 knots, and left Grimsby on her maiden voyage to the North Sea fishing grounds in late October 1936.

The first conversion from steam to diesel propulsion of a fishing vessel in the Lowestoft fleet took place in 1935. The 1905 *Togo* was converted by L. B. S. Engineering Co. to a three-cylinder 200 hp Mirrlees, Bickerton & Day diesel. While this engine was being assembled in the Mirrlees factory at Stockport, *Togo*'s future chief engineer, Edward Henry Carr, was at the works to see the engine constructed; Mr Carr served continuously in *Togo* for 22 years, until his death in October 1956 at the age of 58; in his 22 years as *Togo*'s chief engineer he only missed one trip, and that was through a family bereavement. *Togo* survived until 1964; although laid-up for a time at the end of her career, she was not towed to the breakers, but made her last passage under her own power, and even acted as a tug, towing the engineless hulk of the motor-trawler *Tobago* (damaged earlier in the year while ashore near the harbour entrance) to the breakers-yard at Queensborough.

Of the 385 Scottish fishing vessels available for fishing at the outbreak of World War II, 209 had been built before 1914, and 169 between 1914 and 1921. Of the 277 English drifters available for fishing at that time, 101 were built before 1914 and 115 between 1914 and 1921. The bulk of the herring taken round the coast of Great Britain in 1938 was accounted for by a fleet of about 700 steam drifters and 300 motor-boats. In 1939 there were 700 steam trawlers and drifters registered on the Humber; the last stronghold of steam applied to shipping were the twin Humber fishing ports of Grimsby and Hull.

The first oil-burning steam-engined trawler in Hull was the *St John*, built in 1946.

The first fishing vessel in the world to be fitted with full radio, radar and echometer equipment as well as **the first oil-fired steam-engined trawler to be built post-war for Grimsby** was the *Rinovia III* (LOA 170 ft (51·8 m) × B 29·5 ft (9 m) and D 14·3 ft (4·4 m)), ordered in August 1945 and ready for regular fishing trips from February 1948. *Rinovia III*, built by Cochranes of Selby, was equipped with a Kelvin-Hughes radar, of $\frac{3}{4}$ to 27 miles (1 to 43 km) range, two echometers, two logs and the first 'trans-Arctic' radio-set ever installed on ship, covering all wavebands. A loudspeaker system was fitted through the trawler for her 28-man crew, under the command of P. Adelsteinsson of the Rinovia Steam Fishing Co.

All new vessels built for the Lowestoft fishing fleet during 1945–61 were motor-vessels, the last steam fishing vessel built for the port being *Merbreeze* in 1931. The number of steam vessels declined steadily, although a number of second-hand vessels did join the fleet; the decline was hastened by the White Fish Authority's (WFA) 'scrap and build' scheme, whereby one new vessel could be built with the aid of a generous WFA grant, if two old vessels were scrapped; other vessels were converted from steam to diesel power, while, with the decline in the herring fishery, many steam drifters were withdrawn without replacement at the end of their working lives.

The first motor fishing vessel to develop the method of stern-fishing and filleting and quick-freezing at sea was the converted Black Swan Class steam-propelled frigate *Fairfree*; she was on trials from 1948.

The first modern factory stern trawler to be custom-built in 1953 by John Lewis and Son of Aberdeen for Chr Salvesen of Leith was the 270 ft (80 m) *Fairtry*. The Fairtry method was soon copied in the Soviet Union in its 'Pushkin' class, 277 ft (84·5 m) shelter-deck stern-ramp trawlers, of which 24 were built in West Germany between 1954 and 1956. By 1970 there were about 900 freezer trawlers and factory trawlers of over 1000 tons in the world's fishing fleets, of which 400 belonged to the USSR, 125 to Japan, 75 to Spain, 50 to West Germany, 40 to France, and 40 to Britain. Salvesen's built two more large British factory trawlers in the late 1950s, *Fairtry II* and *Fairtry III*, but the general adoption of shelter-deck stern-ramp trawlers

Rinovia, *the first fishing vessel in the world to be fitted with full radio, radar and echometer equipment (1948) (RNLI)*

was not introduced into the British distant-water fleet until the early 1960s. The first of these out of Hull was the 240 ft (73 m) *Lord Nelson*, built at Bremerhaven in 1961; she could only freeze a portion of her catch. The first Hull stern trawler capable of freezing the whole of her catch was the 245 ft (74·6 m) *Junella*, built in 1962 for J. Marr & Son, the largest privately owned unit in the UK fishing industry. Norway's first factory stern trawler was the 200 ft (61 m) *Longva*, built in Aalesund in 1962.

The first British middle-water transom-stern trawler to be powered by diesel-electric engines was Storgram Ltd's *Atlantic Seal* (LOA 115 ft (35·1 m) × B 26½ ft (8·1 m) × D 14½ ft (4·4 m)), built at the Union Dockyard of J. S. Doig of Grimsby for starboard-side trawling only. Powered by three diesel-electric engines of 440 bhp each, *Atlantic Seal* was launched in July 1960 and achieved a speed of 11 knots.

At the end of 1976, the UK fishing fleet comprised 344 deep sea vessels (80 ft (28·4 m) and over in length) and 2000 inshore and herring vessels of between 40 and 79·9 ft (12·2 and 24·3 m) in length. In addition there were over 4000 smaller vessels, although many of these did not fish regularly. The deep sea fleet operated mainly from Hull, Grimsby, Aberdeen, Lowestoft, Leith, Fleetwood and Peterhead. At this period in the UK, there were some 18 600 full-time fishermen and about 4900 part-timers: of which about 12 000 full-time and 5000 part-time were employed on inshore craft.

By May 1977, the GY and H-numbered Humberside fleets, restricted from freezer fishing off Iceland in 1973 and wet-fish distant-water fishing in 1976, had dwindled to some 303 inshore/offshore vessels. Of these, some 78 operated from Hull and 225 from Grimsby. Of these, 102 were seiners under 100 ft (30·5 m), 65 were distant-water wetfish trawlers over 100 ft (30·5 m) and 43 were distant-water freezer trawlers over 100 ft (30·5 m). Some distant-water vessels have been laid-up and may never fish again.

The last steam fishing vessels at Lowestoft were withdrawn in 1961; in the trawling fleet, the last

steamer was the *Cairo*, built in 1902 at Beverley, which was sold to breakers. The last steam drifter was *Lizzie West*, a wooden vessel built at Buckie in 1930; she was sold to Peterhead owners for use as a stationary net-tanning vessel, in which role she served for a few years more, until, with major boiler repairs required, she was dismantled and her hull towed out of the harbour, beached and abandoned. Since 1961, Lowestoft's fishing fleet has been entirely diesel-powered.

At the time of writing, a fleet of 60 Lowestoft trawlers fishes the North Sea grounds, and the port ranks as the fifth fishing port in the UK.

The last coal-fired steamer, Sir Thomas Robinson's *Athenian* (GY 357), went out of service in 1963 after 44 years of service. But by 1977, Humberside's last 50 oil-fired steam trawlers had been scrapped, the last oil-fired steam 'sidewinder' being Boyd's *Arctic Ranger* (H 155), built in 1957, withdrawn in 1976.

Possibly the last Hull distant-water trawler to be built was the *Junella* (II) in 1976 – a stern freezer for J. Marr & Son.

The first experiments with the construction of motor fishing vessels in fgrp were made by Scott Bader with Maritime Industries of Cape Town, South Africa from 1959. With no previous examples, a series of 17 ft (5·1 m) flat section hard chine V-bottom outboard-engined boats were sold cheaply to the local fishermen of Cape Peninsula, South Africa. From the lessons learnt, several 30 ft (9·1 m) single-crew craft, powered by a 56 hp diesel engine, were followed by two 63 ft (19·2 m) stern trawlers, one twin-screw 340 hp and the other single-screw 250 hp. Some 19, 74 ft (22·5 m) 350 hp pilchard catchers followed, one of which made a successful test voyage of over 5000 miles (8000 km) from Cape Town to St Helena, to Luanda to Walvis, and back to Cape Town. In 1965, seven 83 ft (25·3 m) fgrp seiners were ordered, the first of which was launched in May 1966 as the **then largest deep sea commercial vessel in the world to be built entirely of reinforced plastics**. By 1968 construction was underway for a 146 ft (44·5 m) trawler. Since then, an increasing number of motor fishing vessels, worldwide, have been moulded in fgrp (see p. 157).

TUGS

In 1839, the *Robert F. Stockton*, fitted with an Ericsson double-screw propeller was built by Messrs Laird of Birkenhead. She carried out successful trials on the Thames in the same year, towing four coal barges between Southwark and Waterloo Bridges. The forward prop was driven at 44·1 rpm and the aft at 49 rpm.

The major development of the coal-fired steam tug took place between 1850 and 1910. The first steam collier for William Cory & Son Ltd (established 1838) was the *John Bowers* which did the return trip between London and the North-East in 120 hr in 1852. *William Cory I* (nicknamed 'Dirty Billy') came into service in 1857. It was soon reckoned that one steam collier could do as much work in a year as 15 sailing colliers.

The Liverpool Screw Towing & Lighterage Company, founded in 1877, put paid to the old-fashioned paddle-tugs, with its series of 'Cock Tugs', for which some 23 types of cock were named (*Woodcock*, *Peacock*, *Weathercock*, *Game Cock*, etc), of which the first was *Bantam Cock* (LOA 68 ft (20·7 m) × B 12 ft (3·7 m) × D 6 ft (1·8 m)), built in Preston in 1878, and powered by compound machinery.

The first tug to go into service with the Alexandra Towing Company Ltd was the 88-ton iron-built *Flying Breeze*, built in 1874 at Port Glasgow for the Clyde Tug Company as the *Clyde*, then sold to the Clyde Shipping Co. in 1881, and then to George Bell Cowl of Liverpool in 1882, then to the Alexandra Towing Company in 1887. *Flying Breeze* was broken up at Garston in 1903.

The first tugs to be given the 'Sun' name were *Sunrise* and *Sunshine*, introduced by W. H. J. Alexander & Co. Ltd in 1899. In 1909, *Sun II* and *Sun III* were the first of a long series of 'numbered' Suns. The latest 'Sun' tug, *Sun XXVII*, was launched from J. Pollock & Sons yard, Faversham on 10 July 1968. Her Mirrlees oil engine developed 2100 bhp to give a bollard pull of 22 tons. Full fire-fighting equipment was fitted.

In 1861 a typical Thames barge-handling tug was the *Swan* (LOA 57 ft 9 in (17·6 m) × B 9 ft 6 in (2·9 m) × D 6 ft (1·8 m)), built of iron with wood sheathing and deck, and powered by a single-cylinder steam engine of 40 ihp with iron boiler consuming 4 lb of coal per hour. In 1907, a typical Thames barge-handling tug was the *Diligence* (LOA 77 ft 8 in (23·7 m) × B 18 ft (5·5 m) × D 9 ft 6 in (2·9 m)), built in steel 20 in frame spacing and powered by a compound steam engine of 250 ihp with steel boiler consuming only 1·75 lb of coal.

The world's first motor-barge was the 98 ft (30 m) steel-hulled *l'Idée*, powered by a 40 hp Simplex motor, modified by Delamare-Deboutteville and Malandin; the reversible prop turned at between 170 and 260 rpm. On Sunday 10 June 1894, *l'Idée*'s trials were carried out on the Tancarville Canal, from Le Havre, France. Despite five or six bridges on the canal, the barge moved at 6 mph (10 km/h) with 80 tons of ballast on board. Some weeks later, *l'Idée* again voyaged to Tancarville (72 miles (116 km)) there and back, with 145 tons of ballast at an improved speed of 7·1 mph (11·5 km/h).

The 127-ton Alexandra Towing Company tug *Sandon* was built in 1902 and sank in the Mersey after a collision with the steamer *Sobo* (January 1906), being salvaged, then sinking again after a collision with the steam packet *Wicklow*, in September 1914. Re-named *Huskisson* after salvage, she went to Portus/Lamey in 1934 and was re-named *Baltic*; thence to Cooper of Belfast where she was re-named *Ridgway*; thence to Aberdeen Steam Tug Co. in 1955, being finally broken up at Vlaardingen in 1961.

The first motor chain-haulage tug ever constructed was designed by Linton C. Hope and built by his Thames Yacht Building Co. Ltd in 1907. She measured LOA 30 ft (9·1 m) × B 7 ft 8 in (2·3 m) × D 2 ft 2½ in (0·7 m) and was fitted with a 16 bhp motor developing 450 rpm, geared down to a gipsy wheel running at 57 rpm.

At the end of 1911, there were some 22 Russian diesel-engined tugs on the Volga and Caspian, three diesel tugs in Germany and 10 in other countries. The offshore tug, *Vesuvio*, delivered in 1911, measured LOA 42 ft 6 in (13 m) × B 11 ft 6 in (3·5 m) × D 4 ft 4 in (1·3 m) and was powered by a German MAN Nurnberg two-stroke, direct-drive diesel engine developing 80 hp at 320 rpm.

The diesel-engined offshore-tug, Vesuvio *was delivered to Italy in 1911 (MAN Augsburg)*

In 1940, there were approximately 250 coal-fired steam tugs on the River Thames and 100 semi-diesel and diesel tugs. Only one new steam tug had been delivered to the Thames in 1936, two in 1937, none in 1938 or 1939, and one in 1940 – and of these, all save one were delivered to coal-towing companies. It wasn't a very good advertisement to tow barges filled with coal, with a diesel-engined tug!

The last Thames tug to be built as a steamer was the *Pinklake* (LOA 71·3 ft (21·7 m)×B 24·5 ft (7·5 m)×D 10 ft 6 in (3·2 m)), constructed in 1943 for River Lighterage – now belonging to Everards, who re-named her the *R. A. Everard* and installed a 900 hp Lister Blackstone diesel engine in January 1961.

The very last coal-fired steam tug on the Thames was the Hull-built *Pretoria*, owned by W. J. R. Whitehair of Seething Lane. She worked on the French canals during World War I and was a hospital barge in World War II. She finished life as a ballast carrier from the lower Thames reaches up to London. *Pretoria*'s coal consumption was 4 tons per month, working night and day; she was known to have towed 20 barges in still water conditions. Her last skipper was John W. Jackson, first apprenticed to the Thames in 1921.

The first Thames steam tugs to be converted to diesel in the late 1920s were H. Lane's *Orient*, built in 1894, operating from Cherry Garden Pier, and converted by J. T. Stratford at Wool-

wich; the *Tayna* of Gayflee and the *Churchill* (ex-*Mary Blake*, ex-*Denton*) of R. G. Odell.

The oldest custom-built working tug is the *Khurda* of J. P. Knight (1930), powered by a 300 hp Atlas Polar engine.

The first hot-bulb diesel tug on the River Thames was the *Grove Place* of 1919, belonging to Humphrey & Grey Lighterage Co.

The *Tudor Rose* and the *Vange* (later *Lads Spearing*) were both built as 375 bhp diesel tugs in 1936 for a Dutch company, whilst **the first medium-Thames custom-built British diesel-tug** was the *Hurricane* built in 1938, powered by a 600 hp Sulzer diesel; this engine was replaced by a Lister engine in 1969.

The worst inshore tug disaster occurred in 1929 when William Cory Ltd's *Royalist* was run down by a ship at Woolwich and some three or four men were drowned.

During the 1930 Dunkirk Evacuation, some four tugs lifted out 3164 troops.

The tug design to which the most number of craft were built was the Tug Invasion Duty (TID) Class, of which some 182 were pre-fabricated using hard-chine, all-welded steel hulls by Dunstons of Hessle, during the early part of World War II. Some were coal-burners and others oil-burners, all powered by twin compound steam engines. The 'tiddlers' or 'tid-tugs'

Britannia, *built in 1893, is the oldest converted diesel tug still working the Thames and Medway (A. T. Freeman)*

were largely used by the Inland Water Transport Division of the Royal Engineers, although some went across the Channel to Normandy, Antwerp and even out to the Middle and Far East.

Naval paddle-tugs. Seven of these were built in the 1950s (LOA 157¼ ft (48m) × B 30 ft (9·1 m) × D 10 ft (3 m) 60 ft (18·3 m) across paddle-boxes). They are very large diesel-electric tugs with side-wheel paddles, driven by four engines via electric motors and chain-drive transmission systems – to handle aircraft carriers. Two have recently been withdrawn, but the remainder are still stationed at various naval dockyards.

The first motor-tug to be custom-built for service on the River Mersey (Liverpool) was the Liverpool Screw Towing and Lighterage Company's *Heath Cock*, built by Cammell, Laird & Co. Ltd and launched in December 1957. *Heath Cock* (LOA 102 ft 2 in (31·1 m) × B 26 ft 2 in (8 m) × D 10 ft (3 m)) was powered by Ruston & Hornsby oil engines developing 1088 bhp, driving a single screw.

In 1960 there were some 83 tugs operating on the River Mersey, of which only fifteen were diesel-powered. All Mersey tugs were single-screw steamers of which 19 were post-war built. The last steam tugs built for Liverpool were seven vessels of the 'North' Class, built between 1956 and 1959: *North Beach, North Buoy, North End, North Light, North Quay, North Rock, North Wall.*

The first motor-tug in the Alexandra Towing Company's fleet was the *North Isle* (LOA 103 ft (31·4 m) × B 26½ ft (8·1 m) × D 10 ft 2 in (3·1 m)) and 205 gross tons), launched in November 1958 from W. J. Yarwood & Sons Ltd, Northwich and completed in April 1959. *North Isle* was powered by a Crossley oil engine of 1350 bhp. The second sister motor-tug was the *North Loch*.

In February 1959, an offshore diesel tug, the *Hawkstone*, set off from Shellhaven, Canvy and coming round from Sheerness met with a snowstorm and gale; her six-man crew was lost, unaccounted for by the following morning, although the tug was salvaged and refloated soon after. This was **the worst offshore tug disaster since World War II**.

In 1960, of the 47 tugs operating on the Manchester Ship Canal between Manchester and Eastham, 16 post-war built tugs were twin-screw diesel. The policy of building fairly large (150 tons) twin-screw motor-tugs persists. The present canal fleet comprises 12 tugs for ship-handling plus a small number of dredging support tugs of about 30 tons.

Only two or three literage tugs were built during the 1960s. In 1964, James W. Cook built the *Touchstone* for Cory Lighterage (LOA 75 ft (22·9 m) × B 18 ft 10 in (6·1 m) × D 9 ft 1 in (2·7 m)). She was powered by a Lister Blackstone diesel developing 528 bhp at 600 rpm. She incorporated the modern wheelbox design and was all-welded in steel with her bow and stern protected by rubber fenders. **The last conventional tug to be built for the river** was Thames & General's 77-gross-ton *General 8* of 1966, powered by a 1000 bhp Mirrlees National Diesel.

Present-day Mersey tug fleets are controlled by only two companies – Alexandra Towing Company and Rea Towing Company Ltd – with 17 and 9 vessels each, respectively. Lighterage work supported by tugs on the Mersey is almost non-existent.

The longest surviving tug, originally built for the Alexandra Towing Company, was the single-screw *Langton* (LOA 92 ft (28 m) × B 20 ft 1 in (6 m) × D 11 ft 3 in (3·4 m)) delivered in 1892 from S. McKnight's yard in Ayr. She was powered by compound steam engines of 600 ihp, built by Muir and Houston. In 1909 *Langton* was sold to J. T. Baley of Newcastle. After war service in the Eastern Mediterranean (1914–19) she returned safely and in due course became a unit of the Lawson-Baley fleet. The BBC used the *Langton* in 1954 to carry television equipment for a film about the whaling factory ships refitting in the Tyne. In 1955 she passed to the Blyth Tug Company Ltd. When she was scrapped at Gateshead in 1962, *Langton* had completed some **71 years of service**. Her bell was presented to Mr Eric Johnson, superintendent of the British Leprosy Relief Association, for use in the settlement at Kumi, Uganda.

The oldest converted diesel tug still working the Thames and Medway is the *Britannia* (LOA 68 ft 6 in (20·9 m) × B 15 ft 6 in (4·7 m) × D 8 ft 9 in (2·7 m)) of Greenhithe Lighterage. Weighing some 62 gross tons, she was built at Gainsborough in 1893 as one of three coke-fired 60 ihp steam tugs, together with the *George Livesey* and the *T. B. Heathorn*. Soft iron plates left over from HMS *Thunderer*, the last battleship to be built on the River Thames, were used

in her construction. She first saw service in 1894 under the South Metropolitan Gas Co. and was known as the *Partnership*. Her name changed to *Britannia* and she was converted to a 350 hp National R4 AUM7 oil engine in 1956. She is at present completing her 86th year of service, proving the old adage that 'old tugs never die, they simply fade away'!

The second oldest converted tug is the *Union*, built in 1894 for Union Lighterage, converted by R. G. Odell, her new owners, in 1950 to a 300 hp Widdop diesel engine. She is at present working in the Channel Islands. Her skipper, until 1973, was G. Stevens.

One of the most recent types of tug is the 'E' Class, of which the *Edengarth, Eskgarth, Exegarth* and *Eyegarth* are stationed at Milford Haven, whilst the *Brigadier* and *Strongbow* are at Glasgow. *Edengarth* (LOA 122 ft (37·2 m) × B 33 ft 6 in (10·3 m) × D 16 ft (4·9 m) and 380 gross tons) was built in 1976–77 by Richards of Gt Yarmouth and powered to travel at 14 knots by a Ruston Paxman diesel engine developing 3520 bhp at 900 rpm – with controllable pitch propeller and Kort propulsion single-steering nozzle. She is fitted with radar, radiotelephony, VHF radio, echo-sounder and has a crew of eight.

A number of harbour tugs in use today, or under construction, are fitted with **the Voith-Schneider propulsion unit** mounted under the forward portion of the hull. This arrangement allows the tow hook to be situated well aft, thus eliminating the common hazard of capsizing, should a tow get out of control. The Port of London operates four Voith-Schneider 'water tractors' – *Platoon, Placard, Plankton* and *Plasma*. The Forth Ports Authority are taking delivery of a third and the Admiralty have about 15.

The Schottle rudder-propeller was first developed in the late 1940s in Germany (see p. 204) and is again fitted under the forward part of the tug. An example of this is the *Lashette* (LOA 79½ ft (24·3 m) × B 28 ft (8·5 m) × D 8½ ft (2·6 m)), fitted with twin Schottel rudder-propellers, each driven by a 365 hp Caterpillar diesel engine to a speed of 8 knots. *Lashette* was built by Crescent Shipping of Rochester in 1972 and soon fol-

37·2 m Edengarth, *built in 1976–7 for Cory Ship Towage Ltd, is one of the 'E' Class motor tugs, along with* Eskgarth, Exegarth *and* Eyegarth *(A. T. Freeman)*

lowed by *Grey Lash* in 1974, both intended for barge work on the Thames and Medway. *Greatham Cross* and *Skelton Cross* of Tees Towing Ltd are shiphandling vessels of this type and are due to be joined by a third similar tug.

In 1978 the Port of London Authority's records listed just over 100 tugs on the Thames, ranging from the large ocean-going type down to small local vessels.

MOTOR NARROWBOATS

The first wholly artificial major navigation canal in the UK was the Bridgewater Canal, dug in 1759–61, under the auspices of Francis Duke of Bridgewater. Thereafter followed a canal-building boom throughout the UK, which lasted until the 1830s where canal barges, or narrowboats, were towed by horses along a path running parallel to the canal. Such boats, in general, measured LOA 70 ft × B 7 ft × D 3 ft 6 in.

The longest-surviving canal boat from that era was the *Duchess Countess* (early 19th century), which during the Victorian era ran a passenger-carrying commuter service between Stockton Heath (near Warrington) to Manchester. Owned by the Bridgewater Canal Company, she had right of way and bore on her bows a great S-shaped knife which gaily cut the tow ropes of other boats which, through inexperience, did not make way for her at once. Although later carrying merely cattle, poultry and parcels the service of *Duchess Countess* only lapsed in 1915 through lack of crew. She sank in the early 1920s, was salvaged in 1933 and became a houseboat on the Welsh section of the Shropshire Union Canal. She was last heard of in the early 1950s, estimated at being at least 140 years old.

Duchess Countess, the longest surviving canal-boat, survived in one form or another for 140 years (Hugh McKnight)

The first steam-powered boat to work on the canals was the *Charlotte Dundas* (see p. 6).

The earliest steam-powered narrowboat was the wood-hulled *Dart* of 1864, owned by the Grand Junction Canal Company. The cargo space was reduced to 39 ft (12 m) by the steam machinery, although towing speeds increased.

The most spectacular canal boat accident occurred on Friday, 2 October 1874 on the Regents Canal, when 5 tons of blasting gunpowder carried by *Tilbury*, one of five barges towed by a steam tug, were ignited by a spark from the tug's funnel and exploded, and demolished Macclesfield Bridge. A section of *Tilbury*'s keel fell on the roof of a house 300 yd (270 m) away – and penetrated the basement. Miraculously no one was hurt, although steam-tug Capt. John Edwards was temporarily stunned!

The uniquely designed steam launch *Dragon Fly* was conceived by her wealthy owner, canal boat company director H. R. de Salis (together with Mr G. Davis of St Helens Works, Abingdon) for the detailed inspection of the variously sized English canals. Her 59 ft (18 m) length related to the 'short barge' locks of the Leeds to Liverpool Canal, whilst her 6 ft 8 in (2 m) beam was chosen to fit the 7 ft (2 m) narrow canal locks. Her draught was 2 ft 6 in (0·8 m), and she was built in steel. During the period of 11 years leading up to 1904, H. R. de Salis travelled an estimated 14000 miles (22500 km) on the inland waterways of England and Wales, using *Dragon Fly* and her two namesake successors.

H. R. de Salis's Dragon Fly, *built in 1893, was 59 ft (18 m) LOA with 6 ft 8 in (2·03 m) Beam for specific navigational reasons (Hugh McKnight)*

Fellows, Morton & Clayton steam-driven narrowboat, Baron *seen on the Grand Union Canal shortly after she was built in 1898* (*Hugh McKnight*)

During the first decade of the 20th century, canal boat owners made efforts to improve powered narrowboats. In 1905, the *Duchess*, an ex-steamer of 1881 belonging to Fellows, Morton & Clayton of Birmingham, was converted to a Thornycroft gas motor. Induction pipes connected to a 'producer' burning anthracite, erected a jet of steam beneath the grate, and from a mixture of gas and steam, the plant developed about 30 hp at 300 rpm, with a two-thirds reduction in fuel consumption; a twin-cylinder petrol engine ran the main machinery at 100 rpm to start it firing. *Duchess* was then described as **the first motor-driven narrowboat**. In January 1906, to demonstrate reliability, she made a publicity tour of the canals, covering many hundreds of miles.

In 1907, an ex-steam narrowboat belonging to Fellows, Morton & Clayton, called the *Vulcan*, was converted to a Crossley **suction-gas** engine, then in 1911 to a Bolinder semi-diesel engine.

On 17 August 1907, 50 interested gentlemen took part in a run between Kings Norton and Tardibigge in the **paraffin-engined** *Progress*, designed and built by Edward Tailby of Birmingham.

The last motor canal boats to carry passenger-commuters were run between Aston, Birmingham and the works of the Dunlop Rubber Company at Fort Dunlop for Dunlop employees from August 1919 until May 1920.

The last steam narrowboat built for Fellows, Morton & Clayton (FMC) was the *Dutius* of 1923, converted to diesel power in August 1924. The **first motor narrowboat custom-built** was the *Linda* in 1912. The FMC *steam* narrowboat fleet was converted to diesel power mainly between 1924 and 1926, although **their very last conversion** took place in 1932. The *Cactus*, built and finished in May 1935, was their 100th motor narrowboat. Bolinder semi-diesels were used in most cases. By World War II, the FMC fleet of 140 narrowboats was fully motorised.

Between 1935 and 1937, beginning with the *George*, the Grand Union Canal Carrying Company (GUCCC) fitted two-cylinder, $18\frac{1}{2}$ hp National oil engines to their fleet of 186 narrowboats, the majority of which were being custom-built during this period by Harland and Wolfe, Yarwoods, and Walkers boatbuilding yards.

The longest time that a man might spend on the canals, in a working role, could be 70 years, depending on his fitness: from a 5-year-old child helping with the locks to a 75-year-old man.

With nationalisation on 1 January 1948, many commercial fleets on broad and narrow waterways were transferred to the predecessors of British Waterways – including the narrowboats worked by FMC and GUCCC – although a number of smaller operators continued under private enterprise. In 1953 British Waterways owned 25 tugs, 47 powered barges, 199 motor narrowboats, 315 butties and 197 dumb craft. During 1964 British Waterways narrowboats were officially phased out – although in February 1969 the Board was still running four pairs. Narrowboats in private hands available for carrying number about 143, excluding dayboats. In 1978 there were a small number of enthusiastic narrowboat-owners still carrying 'commercially', eg lime juice in barrels was still being conveyed from Brentford on the Thames up to Roses at Boxtall, near Hemel Hempstead, as regular traffic.

MOTOR PILOT VESSELS

The pilot launch *Vigia* (LOA 41 ft 2 in (12·5 m) × B 12 ft (3·7 m) × D 3 ft (0·9 m)), owned by Trinity House, was moulded in fgrp by Halmatic Ltd in 1965 and fitted with twin Cummings diesel engines to give her a working speed of 18

knots. By May 1978 she had 'steamed' a total of 295 000 miles (474 750 km) (the equivalent of twelve times round the world) in all conditions from calm to Force 9, Beaufort Scale. *Vigia* is currently steaming about 16 000 miles (25 700 km) per year.

CUSTOMS AND EXCISE VESSELS

The English, Scottish and Irish Customs and Excise each had their own fleet of sailing cruisers or revenue cutters. In time of war, the Admiralty used to take them over, to act as Navy despatch boats. In 1816 they were all transferred to the Admiralty and in 1822–24 were transferred back to the Consolidated Board of Customs for the UK.

The first Customs steamer was the *Vulcan* (325 tons), built at Cowes by Thomas White & Son in 1834 and launched that October. Powered by a 140 hp steam engine, *Vulcan* had been stationed at South Wales and Dartmouth, before being introduced into the service at Largs in 1844. She was paid off in May 1849. The second Customs steamer was the *Argus* (1854).

Pilot Launch Vigia, *built 1965 (Halmatic Ltd)*

HM Customs Steam Launch, Lively, *built 1908 (HMSO)*

In the Coastguard Service Act (1856), the protection of the Revenue afloat was placed under the Admiralty once more and the only cruiser left to the Customs was the *Vigilant*, which was substituted for steam in 1866.

The steamer *Vigilant* (the sixth vessel of that name) was built at Poplar in 1865. She was 82 tons, and measured LOA 80 ft (24·4 m) × B 15 ft (4·6 m) and a 69 ft (21·1 m) keel. Her twin 30 hp engines gave her a speed of 10·7 knots. Stationed at Gravesend and patrolling the Thames Estuary to Nore and back, *Vigilant* was also used to take the Commissioners on their tours of the Out-Ports. When sold out of 35 years of service in 1901, *Vigilant* was **the longest-serving Customs vessel afloat**.

From 1856 until 1872, the only other craft under the Customs were rowboats. In 1873 the Customs tried the experiment of substituting custom-built steam launches (at first built on Admiralty specifications). **The first Customs steam launch** was the *Fly*, built by Yarrow & Hedley of Poplar. *Fly* (LOA 33 ft (10·1 m) × B 7 ft 4 in (2·2 m) × D 3 ft 10 in (1·2 m)) had a speed of 7 knots and was first used on 28 May 1873.

By 1902, there were 20 steam launches in service, varying in size and engine power, according to the amount of work to be performed and the tidal conditions of the ports at which they were stationed. **The longest serving steam launch** was the *Hotspur*, built by Cox & Co. of Falmouth in 1897. She had a tonnage of 40, a 70 hp steam engine and a speed of 8 knots. Stationed at North Shields, *Hotspur* was sold in 1933.

In 1899 The Department experimented with a ¾ hp motor-launch driven by paraffin; built by Vosper & Co. of Portsmouth, the *Gnat* (LOA 24 ft (7·3 m) × B 6 ft (1·8 m) × D 2 ft 6 in (0·8 m)) was **the first Customs motor-launch**. By 1905 after six years of continuous service, *Gnat*'s paraffin motor had worked itself out although the hull was still sound – so a 6½ hp Thornycroft petrol engine was installed in its place. Experience with this new engine having come fully up to expectations, the Board of Customs decided to provide, where circumstances permitted, motor-propelled boats in place of steam launches. The *Nimble* was built in 1905 by Clare Lallow & Co., Cowes. Her 7 bhp American motor gave her a speed of 7 knots. Fitted with new engines (a Kelvin) in 1919 and 1924,

Nimble was sold out of 30 years of service in 1935. She was **the longest serving customs vessel afloat**.

1907 saw the setting up of a special branch of the Waterguard Service, called the Launch Service, specially to man these launches. By the end of World War I, there were 24 steam launches and 17 motorboats (mostly named after birds – *Curlew*, *Hawk*, *Swallow*, etc). By 1921, the complement of vessels in the Department was one steam cruiser (the seventh *Vigilant*), 22 steam launches, 16 motor-launches and two sailing cutters fitted with auxiliary motors. Steam launches were still being built in the 1920s, and the last one was built in 1937.

The first diesel-engined Customs vessel was the *Stork*, originally built in 1926 by Vosper & Co., Portsmouth as a petrol-engined boat and converted to Thornycroft diesel engines in 1933.

The first purpose-built diesel-engined vessels in the Department were the 11-ton *Alert* and *Puffin*, built by Gregson & Co. in 1938 and installed with a 70 hp diesel to give a speed of 8¾ knots. By 1943, there were 10 steam, 23 petrol and 10 diesel vessels.

In 1974, the Department decided that the Revenue Cutter Service should return. They purchased two 72 ft (21·9 m) Harbour Defence motor-launches, powered by twin diesel engines developing approx 150 hp each, from the Admiralty. Capable of 1000 miles (1600 km) at 12 knots and 2000 miles (3200 km) at 10 knots, these were converted into the Revenue Cutters, *Valient* and *Vincent*, to support the *Vigilant*.

It was not until 1962 that a fourth vessel was added to the Service as the *Venturous*, 90 ft (27·4 m), twin-screw craft capable of 1000 miles (1600 km) at 15 knots. The *Valient* was withdrawn in 1965 and in the same year *Vigilant* was replaced. In 1967 *Vincent* was withdrawn and replaced by a new *Valient* (LOA 81 ft 2 in (24·7 m) × B 16 ft (4·9 m) × D 5 ft 7 in (1·7 m)), constructed by Richard Dunston Ltd, Thorne and powered by twin six-cylinder Davey Paxman diesels, developing 615 bhp at 1380 rpm. She went into commission from March 1968, and was based at Plymouth.

The next new vessel arrived in December 1975 when *Gazelle* was introduced as a special Harbour Patrol Vessel. In 1976, two new fast 65 ft

HM Customs Cutter Challenge, *a 64 ft (19·5 m) Tracker Mk 2, built by Fairey Marine. Her sister ship,* Champion, *was launched June 1978 (HMSO)*

(19·8 m) Patrol Vessels, Tracker Mark 1's moulded in fgrp by Fairey Marine of Hamble and each powered by twin 645 bhp General Motors diesel engines, to give a cruising speed of 20 knots and a maximum 25 knots, were commissioned as *Active* and *Alert*. An improved version, the Tracker Mark 2 (LOA 64 ft (19·5 m) × B 19 ft (5·8 m) × D 6 ft (1·8 m)) was developed and the *Challenge* (1977) and *Champion* (1978) were commissioned as Her Majesty's Revenue Cutters. By 1978, there were six Customs Cutters and 18 Customs launches based around the Thames and South Coast, as well as 19 small 21-footers (6·4 m), four outboard-engined 13-footers (3·9 m) and four outboard-engined dinghies. A 108 ft (33 m) Customs Cruiser was due for 1979.

SMUGGLING

In 1924 the rum-runner 'Big Bill' Dwyer, operating on the stretch of Atlantic coastboard known as Rum Row, equipped 18 speedboats with aero-engines to beat the Government's 36 ft (10·9 m) and 75 ft (22·9 m) Coastguard patrol boats. These speedboats measured LOA 65 ft

(19·8 m) × B 15 ft (4·6 m) × D 4½ ft (1·4 m) and were triple-screwed, engined with army-surplus Liberty aero-units of 450 hp each, fed from a 1000-gallon (4546 litre) gasoline tank. Their engine-room hatch was made of bullet-proof steel, armour plating surrounded the engine-room, whilst the pilot house was steel with bullet-proof glass some 1¼ in (32 mm) thick. Cruising speed of 20 knots could be boosted to 50 knots for sprint escapes.

Roy Olmstead, 'The Major', whose rum-running activities were masterminded in code-form on Seattle's first radio station, KFOX, in the guise of children's bedtime stories during 1925, also ran a fleet of high-speed motorboats.

For a long time **the fastest rum-running motorboat** was the 65 ft (19·8 m) *Rex*, capable of at least 45 mph (72 km/h). In 1924 the American Power Boat Association's (APBA) Gold Cup contest at Detroit was won by Caleb S. Bragg's beautiful Wright marine-engined craft, 27 ft (8·2 m) *Baby Bootlegger* ('liquor-smuggler'), at an average speed of 46 mph (74 km/h). She repeated this in 1925, powered by twin Packards at 48 mph (77 km/h). It is interesting to note that Coastguards patrolled the course during the second race!

From 31 March 1928 to 1 April 1929, 55 rum-running vessels had been seized in New York waters. Some of these boats had been collected as many as four times, having been libelled, sold by the US Government and somehow repeatedly come into rum-runner ownership.

In May 1928, after a chase of 3½ hr during which shots were fired by the crew of Coastguard patrol boat 2313, a 45 ft (13·7 m) speedboat, laden with 1926 bottles of champagne, cordials, brandy and whisky, valued at $20000, was captured in the Rahway River, New Jersey. The crew of the rum boat, said to be one of the fastest ever captured, escaped by jamming their craft into a mud-bank and wading ashore. The speedboat was said to be worth $10000.

During June 1928, 30 alleged rum-running vessels were arrested on the US/Canadian border.

Machine guns were first used by rum-runners and Coastguards from June 1929.

In 1933 the 'fresh fish' rum-running motor-boats were built to outwit the Government 'dry' armada. Two of these were built in utter secrecy in an old shed on Long Island. They were 60 ft

Contraband cargo from seized motorboat K-10193, captured by 75 ft (22·8 m) patrol boat C.G. 128 on 30 Dec 1929 in New York harbour (US Coast Guard)

(18·3 m) long with a 12 ft (3·7 m) beam, and two Liberty aero-engines gave a speed of 35 knots empty and 25 knots laden. Their holds were divided by watertight bulkheads into five compartments to hold 75 cases each, and each had a trapdoor in its bottom, just in case.

The most famous immediate post-war case of smuggling concerned a war-surplus Royal Naval harbour patrol launch called *Dawn Approach*. During 1949 and 1950, some 100000 Swiss watches were smuggled across the Channel and hidden in the main transverse bulkhead between the saloon and the engine-room. *Dawn Approach*'s owner was intercepted by HM Customs & Excise on 21 February 1951 and was subsequently imprisoned.

In the September/October 1952 issue of the *Lilliput Magazine*, a short story by Nicholas Montserrat, dealing with the brandy and nylon smuggling escapades of *MBG 1087*, was published as 'The Ship That Died of Shame'. The film rights of this story were sold in February 1954, and in 1955 a film version of 'The Ship That Died of Shame', made at Ealing Studios and starring Richard Attenborough, George Baker and Virginia McKenna, went out on general release. Montserrat's short story was subsequently re-published in book form by Cassell Ltd in 1959, and is still in print in paperback form.

On 6 August 1964 a motor-fishing boat called the *Anne Lyn*, having rendezvoused with another vessel the night before, docked at the Shaldon side of the Teign estuary in Devon in an attempt to smuggle in some 74000 duty-free cigarettes and 268 bottles of spirits (mainly whisky). Her owners were, however, intercepted by Waterguard Officers on the beach and charged with evasion of duty contrary to Section 304 of the Customs & Excise Act.

The biggest seizure of drugs (up to June 1978) was made on 2 May 1978 when more than half a ton of Cannabis Resin was found in onyx-veneered tables in a Cardiff warehouse. The drugs were valued at over £1 million. The tables had arrived at Liverpool on a ship from Pakistan, transhipped to Manchester and then by rail to be stored in the warehouse in Cardiff.

FIRE-FIGHTING VESSELS

During the 18th and 19th centuries, London grew to be the largest port in the world, with docks, wharves, and warehouses lining the Thames, presenting special fire-fighting problems. The easiest way to reach a riverside incendiary was via the river, using the river water to extinguish the flames.

London's earliest fireboats were seen about 1760. These were manually operated land fire-engines, mounted on barge-like vessels which had to be rowed to a fire. As many as 90 to 120 men at a time were needed to work the pumps and each man was paid one shilling for the first hour, six pence for each subsequent hour and as much free beer as they could drink. The enormous quantities of beer they consumed added substantially to the cost of maintaining the float. A further problem was encountered in ferrying replacement pumpers between the shore and float.

In 1835, an inventor named John Braithwaite, who invented the land steam fire-engine, submitted plans for a floating steam fire-engine to Superintendent James Braidwood of the London Fire Engine Establishment. His ideas were at first rejected and the potential of steam power was overlooked – but some months later, when the pumpers stopped work several times to demand more beer, Braidwood experimented with steam-driven engines in two floats. It was

Fire Float and Tug at Cherry Garden Pier, SE London (1902). These composite craft were introduced in 1877 and replaced by fire boats from 1900 (London Fire Brigade)

intended that they should be propelled by the thrust of their own jets of water over the stern, but the experiment was thought unsuccessful, and tugs were used to tow the floats to fires. The saving in men, wages and beer money was nonetheless large.

In 1855, Braidwood had **the first ever self-propelled floating steam fire-engine built** to special designs. At the great fire at Cotton's Wharf, Tooley Street, Southwark in 1861, the new floating engine was soon steamed to the incident and her crew waited for an hour and a half after their arrival for sufficient water pressure to use their branches. But after 2 hr, by 7 p.m. on that June evening, the tremendous heat being generated by the fire was scorching both the woodwork of the firefloats and the faces of the men on board. Walking down one of the narrow streets from Tooley Street to the waterside to investigate, Braidwood was buried under a falling wall and killed instantly.

Despite the losses at the Tooley Street fire and the London Fire Engine Establishment's opposition to large riverside warehouses, they were still being built in large numbers. It was a major disadvantage of the first steam-driven vessels that they required so much draught that they could not operate at many riverside fires. The Metropolitan Fire Brigade in 1866 took over a steam-driven fireboat from the London Fire Engine Establishment, but it was of little practical use. Capt. (later Sir) Eyre Massey Shaw, the first Chief Officer, reverted to putting a steam pump on a raft or shallow barge which was towed into position by a tug, but the tugs also drew as much as 9 ft (2·7 m) of water.

By 1896–97, the Brigade's river service could boast five river stations, eight steam tugs, 13 barges, 12 skiffs and nine barges with fixed steam pumps; 17 full-time watermen were then employed as pilots, working different hours from the foreman and not entitled to a pension.

Ex-Naval Officer, Capt. Lionel de Latour Wells, on becoming Chief Officer in 1896, cut the river service drastically, replacing tugs and barges with **the first practicable steam-driven fireboats**, built on similar lines to the river gunboats. The first of these craft was the *Alpha II*, built by G. Napier & Sons of Southampton, with twin screws and separate pumping machinery, driven by coal-fired boilers. Brought into service at Blackfriars station in 1900, and having a draught of less than 2 ft (0·6 m), *Alpha II* was powerful enough to navigate the river at all stages of the tide. She stayed in service until 1935. Also at that time two rafts were maintained at Battersea which could be propelled by jets of water projected by their fire pumps over the stern; at Deptford there was a tug fitted with fire pumps, while at Cherry Garden Pier, Bermondsey, a tug was maintained with two rafts with steam engines aboard.

The cost of *Alpha II* (£6300) had caused the Fire Brigade Committee some concern, but the total bill for a second steam fireboat, the *Beta II* (again named after a letter in the Greek alphabet) in 1906, was even heavier, for nearly £11000 went to Forrest & Co. and Shand Mason who supplied the pumps. Nevertheless, two more fireboats were ordered in 1909: the *Gamma II*, built by John I. Thornycroft & Co., with fast running paraffin motors and turbine pumps, and commissioned in 1911; and the *Delta II* with

three, slow-running Kromhaut paraffin engines developing 56 hp each and three Hatfield reciprocating pumps, delivering 500 gallons (2270 litres) of water per minute, commissioned in 1913. These vessels were stationed at Battersea, Blackfriars and Rotherhithe and were manned by firemen. The pilots, however, were licensed watermen who worked different hours of duty, were paid at different rates from firemen, and were without pension rights. They took no part in fire-fighting, and their only responsibility was handling their craft. It was claimed in 1913 that the men on duty were able to get away with their craft in 3 to 6 min.

One of the greatest of many big riverside fires was the incendiary at Concordia Wharf, Poplar, East London on 7 January 1924. The wharf was stored with many bales of crude rubber and the fire was fanned by a strong wind. A force of 30 motor-pumps, nearly 250 firemen, the four fireboats (*Alpha*, *Beta*, *Gamma*, *Delta*), seven motor escapes and ladders, and five motor-tenders and motor-lorries were assembled to fight the fire.

Fireboat *Beta III* was commissioned in February 1926. Driven by two Gardner paraffin engines developing 110 hp each, she was fitted with two Merryweather centrifugal pumps, delivering 2000 gallons (9100 litres) of water per minute.

The London Fire Brigade's first diesel-engined fireboat was the all-steel-hulled *Massey Shaw*, designed to be able to pass under all the Thames bridges in the London County Council area at any state of the tide as well as to navigate narrow and shallow canals; her design was evolved from tank-model tests carried out at the National Physical Laboratory at Teddington, so as to keep a minimum wash at a maximum 12 knots. Built by J. S. White & Co. of Cowes in 1935, *Massey Shaw* was 78 ft (23·7 m) long, powered by twin eight-cylinder Gleniffer diesel engines developing 160 bhp each. Her worth was first demonstrated in full at the Colonial Wharf fire on 25 September 1935 when the good work of her monitor, capable of discharging 2800 gallons (12700 litres) of water per minute at 250 lb per sq in with a $3\frac{1}{2}$ in nozzle, was mainly responsible for saving an adjoining warehouse containing stock worth an estimated £60000.

Massey Shaw, *London Fire Brigade's first diesel-engined fireboat (1935) (London Fire Brigade)*

A smaller, faster fireboat, the triple-skinned hard chine *James Braidwood* (LOA 45 ft (13·7 m) × D 3 ft 6 in (1·1 m)), capable of 20 knots by the 330 bhp from her three petrol engines, was delivered to the Brigade in 1939 to replace *Gamma II*. The wing engines each drove a turbine-type fire pump, with a capacity of 750 gallons (3410 litres) per minute at 100 lb per sq in.

The outbreak of war in 1939 restored the importance of the river fire service from its decline over the past 40 years. The *Gamma II* was brought back into service as a fireboat. The *Atash Kush*, a purpose-built fireboat destined for service in the Persian Gulf, was hired and a small number of twin-engined motorboats were fitted with emergency pumping units and brought into service at temporary stations which were opened up and down river.

Massey Shaw became one of the fleet of 'Little Ships' at the evacuation of Dunkirk in 1940. With a volunteer amateur pilot on board she made three trips to Dunkirk, bringing 96 men back on board and transferring 500 others to larger vessels. It is believed that she was the last of the small boats to leave Dunkirk Harbour.

It was not until later the same year that the fire service found itself in the front line. During the 'Blitz' the river service was invaluable in dealing with many of the dock and wharf fires. The water mains were, in fact, bombed many times during the 'Blitz' and water from the river was often relayed well inland. In an effort to ensure supplies for fire-fighting, a system of emergency water mains was laid down in the streets. These mains were merely cast-iron pipes bolted together and connected to pumps which had been installed on London's bridges to relay water from the river.

The worth of the river service was recognised when, following nationalisation of the fire services in 1941, it became a separate command known as the 'River Thames Formation', with its own Commander and staff. Larger craft, to cover the lower reaches of the river, were requisitioned and fitted with emergency pumps.

In 1943 three purpose-built fireboats, 52 ft (15·8 m) long of shallow draft with a speed of 10 knots, and each carrying four heavy emergency pumping units with a total output between them of about 3600 gallons (16 365 litres) per minute, were built in wood. These were the first of the famous 'Jewel' Class of fireboat – *Amethyst*, *Diamond* and *Sapphire*. Many vessels of this class were delivered by men of the River Thames Formation during the summer of 1943 to places such as Newcastle, Middlesborough, Hull, Cardiff, Plymouth, Southampton and Portsmouth.

Possibly the largest fireboat built during World War II was the 134 ft (41 m) *Fire Fighter*, commissioned into the New York Fire Department. Her four centrifugal pumps were capable of delivering 22 000 gallons per minute (gpm) at 150 lb. She had nine monitors, the bow monitor delivering 6500 gmp at 150 lb.

With the end of the war, and the re-constitution of the London Fire Brigade, it was decided to reorganise the permanent establishment which had included 13 pilots for the river service who had been licensed watermen and freemen of the river by virtue of their membership of the Amalgamated Society of Watermen and Lightermen of the River Thames. In 1948 it was laid down that the wartime practice of firemen acting as coxswains under the direction of brigade officers should be continued.

In 1954, 1956 and 1957, the Jewel Class fireboats went out of commission. South Wharf fire station, Bermondsey, was closed in 1956, and only two river stations, at Lambeth and Woolwich, remained.

To replace the wartime fireboats and the *James Braidwood*, the welded-steel *Firebrace* (LOA 65 ft (19·8 m) × B 13·75 ft (4·2 m) × D 3 ft 8 in (1·1 m)) was built by Saunders-Roe (Anglesey) Ltd and installed with twin Dorman 6QA diesels, each developing 228 to 230 bhp at 1900 rpm – for a speed of 11½ knots. Her two pumping sets could deliver 2160 gallons (9820 litres) per minute at 80 lb.

In 1966 the *Fireflair* (LOA 66 ft (20·1 m) × B 16 ft (4·9 m) × D 4 ft 6 in (1·4 m)), formerly with the Kent and Essex fire brigades, was transferred to London Fire Brigade for the training of members of the Auxiliary Fire Service. Her twin Foden diesels, totalling 200 bhp, give her a maximum of 10 knots.

The London Fire Brigade's latest craft are the 45-footers (13·7 m), *Firehawk* and *Fireswift*, built in fgrp and installed with Perkins turbocharged diesels to achieve a speed of 17½ to 18 knots.

Possibly the largest fireboat in the world is the *Alexander Grantham* of Hong Kong harbour. Built by the Hong Kong and Whampoa Dock Co. Ltd in 1953, this vessel is 352 gross tons, measuring LOA 127 ft 9¾ in (39 m) × B 29 ft (8·8 m) × D 10½ ft (3·2 m). Powered by two Paxman 12 RPH marine diesels developing 400 bhp at 1000 rpm, the *Alexander Grantham* can reach a speed of 11·7 knots with a fuel consumption of 26 gallons (118 litres) of dieseline per hour when fully loaded. Five Merryweather Turbine pumps, powered by three Paxman auxiliary

diesels (400 bhp at 1000 rpm) deliver some 10 000 gallons (37 850 litres) of water per minute, whilst two sets of mechanical foam generator MFG 30 deliver some 7300 gallons (33 185 litres) of foam per minute. Apart from her eight monitors, *Alexander Grantham* is also equipped with hydraulic rescue and water tower with a platform which can be raised 60 ft (18 m) above sea level. A 20 ft (6·1 m) motorboat is carried along for use when it is anchored offshore for rescue work.

During her 26-year career, this fireboat has played a leading role in a diversity of rescue operations, in such incidents as ship fires, aircraft crashes, oil pollution and land fires, the latter by supplying large quantities of sea water through her powerful pumps to the scene of fire. *Alexander Grantham* also escorted the University liner *Seawise* (formerly *Queen Elizabeth*) into Hong Kong harbour for refitting in July 1971 and, half a year later, took part in the battle to save her from tragic destruction. The fire raged for a day and a night before being quenched on this 1031 ft (314 m) long craft.

METROPOLITAN POLICE (THAMES DIVISION) MOTOR-DUTY-BOATS AND LAUNCHES

The first preventative police force in Great Britain was set up as the Marine Police on 2 July 1798 in Wapping High Street. They were equipped with a number of rowing galleys and greatly helped to reduce crime along the River Thames, especially where importation losses were concerned. In 1839, when the separate police services in the London area, excluding the City of London, were amalgamated into the Metropolitan Police, Thames Division came into existence, drawing on the equipment and experience of the old Marine Police, and remaining at High Street, Wapping.

The first steam launch to be taken into service for Senior Officers of the Thames Division was the *Rover* in 1884. This followed the worst disaster ever known on the River Thames. Some six years before, some 600 lives were lost in the disastrous collision between the paddle-steamer *Princess Alice* and the collier *Bywell Castle*. The outcome of the lengthy Board of Trade Enquiry

Alexander Grantham *possibly the largest fireboat in the world, was built in 1953 (Hong Kong Fire Dept.)*

was that the Admiralty recommended that the Thames Division should be supplied with three steam launches – of which the first was the *Rover*. This was capable of 6 knots over the Admiralty Measured Mile, and was purchased secondhand from the Isle of Dogs. She was in operation ahead of a custom-built single-engined teak craft called the *Alert* (LOA 30 ft (9·1 m) × B 6 ft 6 in (1·9 m)), which was soon replaced by the steel-hulled *Chowkidar* ('Night Watchman') which was powered by the *Alert's* former engine.

The largest police launch ever commissioned was the *Watch* (1890) built by Watkins of Bow Creek (LOA 47 ft (14·3 m) × B 9 ft 6 in (2·9 m) × D 5 ft (1·5 m)) which attained a speed of 8¼ knots.

The complement of three launches was made up by the arrival of the *Sir Richard Mayne*. Accompanying her as engineer was George Mitchell, who agreed to remain on Division as **the first Constable-Engineer**.

In 1893, a Daimler motor-launch was supplied on loan to the Thames Division, Wapping by F. R. Simms (see p. 22) and was found to give satisfaction.

While in his first two years on the Thames Division, Mitchell designed and built, at Wapping, one of the first, if not **the first petrol-paraffin engine installed in a boat**, developing 1¼ hp. This was fitted into one of the Division's rowing galleys and used as an assistant craft. Several more rowing galleys were modified to take Mitchell's engines during the early 1900s.

The first motor-duty-boat to be custom-built for the Division was the *Howard*, slightly larger and more robust than the galleys, and designed to proceed above Richmond Lock. Because of a tragic fatality involving one of the Mitchell-converted galleys, it was decided in 1913 that all duty-boats would have to be custom-built. By the end of 1914, all 30 motor-duty-boats in the Division were custom-built. From Wapping up to Staines Bridge, Middlesex, 22-footers (6·7 m) were to be used, whilst 27-footers (8·2 m) were to be used from Wapping down to Dartford Creek, Kent.

The first duty-boat to be installed with a Gardner diesel engine was the 28 ft (8·5 m) Boat Number 14 in June 1926. Between 1930 and 1938 a number of duty-boats were fitted with AEC or Parsons diesel engines. In 1940 the Division

The Watch *(1890), was the largest Thames river police launch ever commissioned (Metropolitan Police)*

*1931: Thames River Police rescue a man at King's Reach, near Waterloo Bridge (*Daily Mail*)*

The first fgrp-moulded motor-duty-boat was Boat Number 11 in 1958 – the mould was built by Watercraft, whilst Tough Bros of Teddington fitted out the installation. By 1968 the fleet of 30 were all fgrp 30-footers (9·1 m), powered by single 105 bhp diesels to attain a speed of 14 to 16 knots. Pye intercom was used. Each of these boats annually performed some 2500 hr of duty.

The most modern motor-duty-boat was assembled in 1977. It is a 34-footer (10·3 m), twin-screw powered by twin 250 bhp Sabre-diesel engines and capable of 27 knots.

Police launches for Senior Officers. The first petrol-paraffin launch was the *Sir Richard Mayne II*, built by J. Samuel Whites in 1910.

During the post-war years, there were three Thornycroft-built launches, engined with twin Perkins 100 hp diesels to run at 24 knots. They were christened the *John Harriott*, the *Patrick Colquhoun* and the *Sir Robert Peel*. The present-day launches were built in fgrp in 1963, engined with twin-screw 144 hp Gardners, and each given the same name as their predecessors.

The keynote to motor-duty-boats has always been reliability and rescue and not speed, but their romantic image has been used by Conan Doyle in 'The Sign of Four', by Sax Romer in

decided to standardise its engines, following experiments made in 1939 with two Osborne-built, Perkins P6-engined boats. By 1941, six new Perkins-engined duty-boats were in operation.

The first duty-boat to be fitted with one way radio telephony was Boat Number 18 in 1931. The first duty-boat to be fitted with two-way Marconi radio telephony went into operation in 1935.

The first and variously-designed cabin-tops were fitted onto the duty-boats at the Wapping Workshops in 1935, officially inspected in 1936. During World War II, during heavy air raids in 1940–41 when frequently most of the City and East End docks were ablaze, Thames Division crews successfully ferried trapped people across the river to safety on the opposite shore. The cabin-tops of the duty-boats were therefore protected from shrapnel by a rubber/wire netting canopy. Also in 1941 the Marconi transmitters were replaced by two-way radio, with telephone-type receivers, powered by charger batteries.

1969: Thames Division Police launches cruising past Tower Bridge

'The Insidious Doctor Fu-Manchu' and by John Buchan in 'The 39 Steps'.

The man longest associated with Thames Division is Mr Fred Byways BEM (Workshop Superintendent). He joined the Civil Staff of the Police in 1927, and joined the Wapping Engineer's Division in 1938. In 1978 he retired from the Division after 45 years of service.

Superintendent Ronald Main holds the longest 20th century record of service with the Thames Division as a policeman. He joined in 1933 and retired in 1971 after 38 years of service.

ST JOHN AMBULANCE VESSELS

The St John Ambulance Transport Division, Guernsey, Channel Islands was operating inflatables for inshore rescue work from the late 1940s. In 1953 it was involved in consultations with the manufacturers of these craft concerning the production of a heavy-duty boat for rescue work, and as a result a 10-man model was introduced to the Department in 1958. The Guernsey Transport Department then played a significant part in the introduction of inshore rescue boats, which went a stage further in the development of the earlier craft and purchased its first powered model, complete with 18 hp outboard motor and trailer, in 1961.

Flying Christine II, *built 1963, is operated by the St John Ambulance Transport Division, Guernsey*

The *Flying Christine II*, built in a Guernsey boatyard, was launched on 6 July 1964 by Lady Colman, wife of the Island's then Lieutenant Governor. The *Flying Christine II* replaced the *Flying Christine*, which was irreparably damaged in harbour during a storm on 10 January 1963. Both launches were built and maintained by voluntary contributions.

As an ambulance motorboat, *Flying Christine II* regularly visits the neighbouring islands to bring sick and injured patients to hospital in Guernsey. These patients are comfortably accommodated in her Neil-Robertson stretcher-cabin which has the appearance of the carpeted interior of a large road ambulance, complete with resuscitator, transfusion bottle and drip-feed apparatus.

With a speed of 20 knots, the *Flying Christine II* is part of the Channel Islands air/sea rescue service, and with her radar, searchlights and flares is able to assist the local Royal National Lifeboat Institution vessels on searches. The legend RESCUE in 17-inch letters on her cabin top, makes *Flying Christine II* very distinctive from the air.

Moored in St Peter Port Harbour, her design is based on the British Power Boat Company's seaplane tenders used during World War II. She is LOA 42 ft (12·8 m) × B 12 ft (3·6 m) × D 3 ft (0·9 m), and is built of double-diagonal teak planking, sheathed in nylon up to the water-line. She is powered by two 125 hp turbo-charged Perkins T6.354 diesel engines.

As a tender to the *Flying Christine II*, the *Gannet* is a 13 ft (4 m) fgrp dory, powered by a 35 hp Mercury outboard to achieve some 20 knots.

The St John Ambulance Brigade River Patrol comprises two outboard-engined dories, *St John 1* and *St John 2*, operating from Reading on the Thames since 1971. These boats are white in colour, carrying the St John Ambulance flag and markings, with the wording 'First – RESCUE – Aid' on each side.

Other inshore rescue vessels, bringing the total to 18, are working in such areas as Rutland Water (Leics), Sussex and Wales. In sharp contrast there are over 580 St John motor-ambulances on the roads of England and N. Ireland.

'The code of **Port Distinguishing Letters** first introduced in the Sea Fisheries Act of 1868, came into effect in 1869. Each letter sequence was accompanied by a number, and the owner was issued with a corresponding certificate; the system is still in operation today.

PORT DISTINGUISHING LETTERS

A	Aberdeen	FR	Fraserburgh	PH	Plymouth
AA	Alloa	FY	Fowey	PL	Peel
AB	Aberystwyth	G	Galway	PN	Preston
AD	Ardrossan	GE	Goole	PT	Port Talbot
AH	Arbroath	GH	Grangemouth	PW	Padstow
AR	Ayr	GK	Greenock	PZ	Penzance
B	Belfast	GN	Granton	R	Ramsgate
BA	Balina	GR	Gloucester	RN	Runcorn
BA	Ballantrae	GU	Guernsey	RO	Rothesay
BCK	Buckie	GW	Glasgow	RR	Rochester
BD	Bideford	GY	Grimsby	RX	Rye
BE	Barnstaple	H	Hull	S	Skibbereen
BF	Banff	HH	Harwich	SA	Swansea
BH	Blyth	HL	Hartlepool	SC	Scilly Isles
BK	Berwick-on-Tweed	IE	Irvine	SD	Sunderland
BL	Bristol	IH	Ipswich	SE	Salcombe
BM	Brixham	INS	Inverness	SH	Scarborough
BN	Boston	J	Jersey	SM	Shoreham
BO	Borrowstoness	K	Kirkwall	SN	Shields, North
BR	Bridgwater	KY	Kirkcaldy	SO	Sligo
BRD	Broadford	L	Limerick	SR	Stranraer
BS	Beaumaris	LA	Llanelly	SS	St Ives
BU	Burntisland	LH	Leith	SSS	Shields, South
BW	Barrow	LI	Littlehampton	ST	Stockton
C	Cork	LK	Lerwick	SU	Southampton
CA	Cardigan	LL	Liverpool	SY	Stornoway
CE	Coleraine	LN	Lynn	T	Tralee
CF	Cardiff	LO	London	TH	Teignmouth
CH	Chester	LR	Lancaster	TN	Troon
CK	Colchester	LT	Lowestoft	TO	Truro
CL	Carlisle	LY	Londonderry	TT	Tarbert
CN	Campbeltown	M	Milford Haven	UL	Ullapool
CO	Caernarvon	ME	Montrose	W	Waterford
CS	Cowes	MH	Middlesbrough	WA	Whitehaven
CT	Castletown	ML	Methil	WD	Wexford
CY	Castle Bay	MN	Maldon	WH	Weymouth
D	Dublin	MR	Manchester	WI	Wisbech
DA	Drogheda	MT	Maryport	WK	Wick
DE	Dundee	N	Newry	WN	Wigtown
DH	Dartmouth	NE	Newcastle	WO	Workington
DK	Dundalk	NN	Newhaven	WT	Westport
DO	Douglas	NS	New Ross	WY	Whitby
DR	Dover	NT	Newport, Monmouth	Y	Youghal
DS	Dumfries	OB	Oban	YH	Yarmouth
E	Exeter	P	Portsmouth		
F	Faversham	PD	Peterhead		
FD	Fleetwood	PE	Poole		
FE	Folkestone	PEH	Perth		
FH	Falmouth	PGW	Port-Glasgow		

5 DEFENCE

By the end of World War I, the Motor Boat Reserve Auxiliary Patrol had more ships and men than the whole of the rest of the Navy. This Reserve was originally urged by, and then commanded by, Surgeon Commander Morton Smart RNVR (pre-war Commodore of the British Motor Boat Club (BMBC)). The Admiralty ordered 550 motor-launches of 80 ft (24·4 m) from America, built by the Electric Boat Company of Connecticut. They came into service in 1916 and were used for harbour defence, anti-submarine work, convoy escort, minesweeping and on occasions, air/sea rescue. It was nothing for one of these vessels to log over 12000 miles (19300 km) during one year of operation.

The first hard-chine motor-torpedo boat ever built was a 60-footer (18·3 m), powered by twin 500 hp Sunbeams and built by Cox and King at Wivenhoe, immediately after World War I.

In 1923 Edward, Prince of Wales, accompanied by Lord Louis Mountbatten, visited the USA on a brief holiday; they soon discovered the delights of speedboating in fast, hard-chine American runabouts. Indeed, Mountbatten bought a 33 ft (10 m) Garwood standard hull powered by a 500 hp war-surplus Liberty aero-engine 'off the shelf' and arranged for it to be shipped over by Robert Kemp of Southampton.

With this first American hard-chine runabout to be imported to England, which he named

British Torpedo Boat No. 75 in 1891; by 1890 Great Britain could boast a fleet of 147 such boats – more than any other country (By permission of the trustees of the Imperial War Museum)

Circuit 'Cat' or UFO? (Steve Powell/All Sport)

The G. L. Watson-designed motor fishing vessel, George Weatherall *(Courtesy Halmatic)*

Superbly finished wood interior of the Edwardian beaver-sterned, river launch Lady Genevieve. *At Peter Freebody and Company, Hurley, Berkshire (Courtesy Peter Freebody)*

The diesel-engined tug, Sun Essex (Courtesy M. J. Gaston)

Sun VIII, *built in 1919 for W. H. J. Alexander Limited. Sold to Belgian shipbreakers 1969 (Courtesy* **M**. *J. Gaston)*

Red Cross inflatables on manoeuvres (Courtesy Zodiac)

A British Coastal Motor Boat (CMB), fitted with depth charges, travelling at 35 knots. CMB's were effective in 1917–20 (By permission of the trustees of the Imperial War Museum)

Shadow II, Lord Louis was determined to prove the superiority of the hard-chine hull over the stepped hydroplane, especially its turning ability, to the senior officers of HMS *Hornet*, at the coastal motorboat base at Gosport.

With a few invited guests on board, he took them out for a 40-knot spin round Portsmouth Harbour, during which he vividly demonstrated the superiority to them by aiming for the jetty and then, at the last moment, putting the wheel hard over and turning away – a manoeuvre he had learnt with practice. Although fully prepared to 'abandon ship' the officers soon realised the turning advantages of the hard-chine boat and at once resolved to adopt this design for their new coastal motorboats.

Before long, *Shadow II* was racing with several other imported Garwood runabouts, such as *TNT*, *Sitnalta* (*Atlantis* backwards) and *Gee-Whizz*, owned by the demonstrative Claude Grahame-White. In July 1925 *Shadow II*, piloted by Lord Louis Mountbatten, won the Sea Mile Trophy at Hythe at an average speed of 47·85 mph (77·01 km/h).

During World War II, some 1953 armament/navigation-equipped motorboats, averaging some 85 ft (26 m) LOA were built inside seven years for the war effort. The armaments and navigational instruments of every one of these vessels were replaced and updated during this period. At its peak, this 'Little Ship Navy' employed some 3000 officers and 22000 men. It is claimed that whilst some 500 enemy vessels were sunk or captured during the 780 to 790 separate enemy actions, only 176 of the following vessels were sunk:

Harbour Defence Motor-Launches: LOA 72 ft (22 m) × B 15 ft (4·6 m). Twin Gardner/Gleniffer or Thornycroft diesels totalling 300 hp; 12 knots/ 2000 miles at 10 knots; from January 1941, 450 built by 25 UK firms.

British Power Boat Company Motor-Gunboats and Motor-Torpedo Boats: LOA 72 ft (22 m) × B 20·5 ft (6·3 m). Triple Packard V-12's totalling 4050 bhp; 40 knots/600 miles at 15 knots. From 1935, 97 motor-torpedo boats and 141 motor-gunboats built at Hythe.

Camper and Nicholson Motor-Gunboats: LOA 117 ft (35·7 m) × B 21 ft (6·4 m). Triple Packard V-12s totalling 3750–4050 bhp; 30 knots/2000 miles at 26 knots. From February 1942, 17 built at Gosport.

Fairmile 'Type A' Motor-Gunboats: LOA 110 ft (33·6 m) × B 17½ ft (5·3 m). Triple Hall Scott V-12

One of 17 Motor Torpedo Boats built by Camper & Nicholsons, during World War II. They were powered by triple supercharged Packard aero-engines (Beken of Cowes Ltd)

engines, totalling 1800 bhp; 25 knots/600 miles at 12 knots. From March 1940, 11 'Type A's' built by ten firms.

Fairmile 'Type B' Motor-Launches: LOA 112 ft (34·1 m) × B 18 ft 3 in (5·5 m). Twin Hall Scott V-12's totalling 1200 bhp; 20 knots/1500 miles at 12 knots. From August 1940, 388 'Type B's' were built in prefabricated parts by 45 firms and 180 built in 12 British colonies.

Fairmile 'Type C' Motor-Gunboats: LOA 110 ft (33·6 m) × B 17 ft 5 in (5·3 m). Triple supercharged Hall Scott's totalling 2700 hp. 27 knots/500 miles at 12 knots. From May 1941, 24 Type C's were built by 13 firms.

Fairmile 'Type D' Motor-Torpedo Boats and Motor-Gunboats: LOA 115 ft (35 m) × B 21 ft 3 in (6·5 m). Quadruple Packards totalling 5000 bhp; 31 knots/1200 miles at 10 knots. **The most heavily armed boats of their kind in the world**, comprising six machine guns, one pom-pom, two depth charges and two torpedo tubes for the motor-gunboat, and two six-pounder automatics, six machine guns, four torpedo tubes and two depth charges for the motor-torpedo boat. From February 1942, 229 'Type D's' were built by 30 firms.

Vosper Motor-Torpedo Boats: LOA 70–73 ft (21·3–22·3 m) × B 19 ft 3 in (5·9 m). Triple Isotta-Fraschini totalling 3600 bhp/Triple Packards totalling 4200 bhp. 39 knots/450 miles at 20 knots. From June 1940, 386 built by Vosper and six UK firms, also produced in USA.

Other craft were built by Thornycroft (10), Whites (35), Elco (120), Higgins (30) and Denny (1).

Of the American Patrol Torpedo boats, some 320 80-footers (24·4 m) were built by Elco and 205 78-footers (23·8 m) by Higgins.

Although there were only 25 German 'schnellboote' (S-boats) at the beginning of 1939, during World War II, some 244 S-boats (average LOA 115 ft (35·1 m)) were built and operated, together with some 325 120 ft (36·6 m) 'Raümboote' (German motor-launches) also saw service.

More than 250 Japanese T-boats (motor-torpedo boats) and over 100 59 ft (18 m) Japanese motor-gunboats were inadequately constructed and built during World War II. At the end of the war, the Japanese introduced the 16–18 ft (4·9–5·5 m) Shinyo suicide motorboats, powered by single or twin automobile engines to give speeds of 30 knots, loaded with 4000 lb of TNT each. The plan was for each kamikaze pilot to aim his warhead at an enemy vessel to blow it up. Over 6000 were built in 1944 for use in the Okinawa campaign but American Patrol Torpedo-boats succeeded in locating their hiding place before they could be used.

The US invasion of the Kerawa Islands in 1945, included the discovery of some 300 Japanese Shinyo suicide boats (Keystone Press)

LANDING CRAFT

From summer 1942 until August 1945 ($2\frac{1}{2}$ years) some 45000 vessels and 56000 amphibians were built using American mass-production methods. During the Normandy landings some 132715 troops were put ashore in 16 hr against some of the most sophisticated defences then known; at Okinawa over 183000 men in 1300 vessels made the last in a succession of major landings by US amphibious forces against determined Japanese resistance.

Among the craft built were:

Landing Craft Personnel (LCP)

The first successful troop-landing craft were built in 1937 by Andrew J. Higgins at the Eureka Tug-Boat Company of New Orleans as the 28 ft (8·5 m) R boat based on a spoonbill-bowed craft, and capable of carrying a platoon. The initial order was for 136 LCP's and the first 50 were delivered to the UK in October 1940; altogether some 2193 of this design were built,

followed by some 2631 LCP (ramped). Hall Scott, Kermath, Gray, Superior, Buda, Chrysler and Palmer petrol or diesel engines, ranging from 115 to 225 hp were used, giving a range of 120 miles (193 km) at between 8 to 11 knots. The LCVP was a development of the LCP and between 1942 and 1945 some 23358 LCVP's were built.

Landing Craft Assault (LCA)

Some 1929 of these were built; by 1944 production from British firms rose to 60 LCA's per month; 371 were lost during the war but many survived to become houseboats with cabins over their well. They were mostly powered by twin Ford V8 engines, marinised by Scripps, Thornycrofts or Parsons.

Landing Craft Mechanised (LCM)

The 44 ft 8 in (13·6 m) × 14 ft (4·3 m) LCM Mk 1, built in steel by Thornycrofts, with twin 60 hp Thornycroft engines, had successful trials in

LCT (Landing Craft Transport) massed for troop transportation during World War II (By permission of the trustees of the Imperial War Museum)

Dunkirk evacuation. Some of the small craft that took part, sailing up the Thames (Imperial War Museum)

February 1940, giving $7\frac{1}{2}$ knots when loaded with the equivalent of a tank. Some 500 LCM Mk 1's were built, many in the Great Western Railway workshops at Swindon and the Southern Railway workshops at Eastleigh and in other metal-working factories. Some 147 LCM Mk 2's (45 ft (13·7 m)) and some 8631 LCM Mk 3's (50 ft (15·3 m)) were built to Andrew Higgins' designs. Some 2718 LCM Mk 6's (56 ft (17 m)) were also built; some 250 British Mk 7's (60 ft 3 in (18·4 m) were being built towards the end of the war.

During World War II, some 10 123 Landing Craft, Rubber Large (LCR(L)s), measuring 16 ft (4·9 m) × 8 ft (2·5 m) and some 8150 Landing Craft, Rubber Small (LCR(S)s) were manufactured for use as tenders or dinghies. A $9\frac{1}{2}$ hp outboard gave the LCR(L) $3\frac{1}{2}$ to $4\frac{1}{2}$ knots, whilst a 6 hp outboard on an LCR(S) gave about the same speed.

Operation Sea Lion, the code name for the German invasion of England, involved some 2000 large river barges which would be towed for most of their Channel crossing by tugs and motorboats. The first wave of 'Sea Lion' was to land from army assault boats and inflatable rafts; about 16 000 men were to man these barges. By August 1940, 500 barges, 400 tugs and 1600 motorboats were ready. Operation Sea Lion was abandoned on 10 October 1940.

On 10 May 1940, Germany invaded Holland, Belgium and Luxembourg. The capitulation of both Dutch and Belgian Armies followed. On 28 May, 'Operation Dynamo' – the evacuation of the British Expeditionary Force was put into action, under the command of Vice-Admiral Sir Bertram Ramsay. It continued until the night of 2–3 June. During this time 'Ramsay's Cockleshell Navy', no less than 848 ships from large to small, of every conceivable description, had evacuated 338 226 men from the beach of Dunkirk, whilst under fire from the *Luftwaffe*, and back to England. Out of those ships, **203 private motorboats** – many of them 16 to 25 ft (4·9 to 7·6 m) cabin cruisers, manned by middle-aged and older skippers, lifted out 5031 troops; seven of these 'little ships' were destroyed by enemy action and 135 lost for other reasons, whilst the number damaged is simply not known.

The first attempt by the Germans to develop a remote-controlled explosive carrying E-boat was code-named *Linsen*; trials proved that at only 35 knots, the craft was too easy to destroy with ship or shore-based guns. *Linsen* was first used in the Normandy Invasion area in June 1944. By the end of 1944, 115 *Linsen* boats had either been destroyed by E-boat patrols, wiped out by fighter bombers or overwhelmed by unfavourable weather. *Tornado* was then developed as two seaplane floats held together by a deck, on top of which was mounted the pulse-jet motor of a V1 missile to push it through the water. A 15500 lb demolition charge was installed on board so that *Tornado* could either be remote-controlled or manned by a pilot, who locked the controls once close to his target and dived overboard in the hope of being picked up by a rescue vessel; but with over 8000 V1 Flying Bombs being launched at the Home Counties in the summer of 1944, V1 motors could not be spared for the further development of this project. Towards the end of the war, the Schlitten (Sledge) hydroplane, powered by a Ford V8 engine, could get up to 65 knots with the same 15500 lb warhead, but the end of the war prevented Schlitten from being put into operation.

The Nazis were involved with motorboat manoeuvres, such as this one in Ostpreusen from 1937

RAF MARINE CRAFT

The earliest RAF motorboats. Altogether 213 marine craft were transferred from the Royal Naval Air Service (RNAS) to the newly formed Royal Air Force (RAF) on 1 April 1918. Of these craft, 190 were motorboats between 16 ft (4·9 m) and 80 ft (24·4 m) in length, the most common being the 35 ft (10·7 m) Brooke Seaplane Tender.

RAF 200, a 37½ ft (11·4 m) seaplane tender built by the British Power Boat Company of Hythe (see p. 129) in 1931, was **the first seaplane tender built specifically for RAF use**. Prior to then, all craft used by the RAF were either of Admiralty design or purchased by the Admiralty.

High Speed Launch 100 (*HSL 100*), built by the British Power Boat Company in 1936, was **the first RAF launch built with open-sea rescue in mind.** It was the fore-runner of 360 HSL's that were to serve in World War II and contribute to the rescue of over 13000 allied and enemy personnel from the seas throughout the world.

The highest number of HSL's of one class built were the 67 ft (20·4 m) Thornycroft Air Sea Rescue Launches. Altogether 104 were built for the RAF.

RAF 1 was a 56 ft (17·1 m) Pinnace, built by Saunders of Cowes. It was on charge in Malta on 21 December 1926. It was sold for £255 in December 1938, *RAF 1* was fitted with two 96 hp Gardner semi-diesel engines.

Squadron Leader G. F. L. Coates DSC, Officer commanding No 27 Air Sea Rescue Unit (Dover) who commanded air sea rescue HSL's working out of Dover was **the first RAF officer to be awarded the DSC in World War II**. His motto was said to be 'Bring 'Em Back Alive'.

HM Air Force Vessel 2769, a 68 ft (20·7 m) Rescue Target Towing Launch commanded by Flight Lieutenant G. E. F. Hubbard RD, RAF was **the first British military vessel to enter an Egyptian port after the Suez War** (1956). *HM AFV 2769* conveyed the bodies of 25 victims of an air disaster when a twin turbo-prop ANTONOV AN 24 of United Arab Air Lines crashed into the sea killing all 40 people on board.

On 1 April 1960 Admiral of the Fleet, Lord Louis Mountbatten, embarked on the Royal Air Force Range Safety Launch (RSL) 1649 at

Aden. This was the first occasion that Lord Louis had flown his Chief of Defence Staff flag at sea.

No 1153 Marine Craft Unit RAF Limassol in Cyprus was awarded the Wilkinson Sword for 1968. The sword was presented at Cutlers Hall, London by Earl Mountbatten. No 1153 MCU won the award after a notable year of rescue work by its launches in the Eastern Mediterranean. This was **the first British Military Motorboat Unit to be awarded the Wilkinson Sword of Peace**.

Group Captain L. R. ('Les') Flower MBE, MM, RAF (retd) was the first motorboat crewman in the RAF to work his way from 'the bottom of the ladder to the top'. Enlisting as airman Motor Boat Crew (MBC) in 1934 he served in the Marine Branch of the RAF until 1970 when he retired as a Group Captain from the post of Director of Marine Craft (RAF). As a Corporal in command of the RAF Seaplane tender at Dunkirk he became the first RAF motorboat coxswain to be awarded the Military Medal; along with other RAF craft he helped to save 500 soldiers from the beaches. In 1952 he became the first RAF Marine Officer to become a graduate of the RAF Staff College.

HM Air Force Vessel 2757, a Mark 2 RAF Rescue Target Towing Launch was presented to the RAF Museum, Hendon when it was withdrawn from service in 1977. It went by sea under its own power from the largest RAF Marine Base at RAF Mountbatten, Plymouth to London Docks where it was lifted out of the water by a heavy-lift crane. It was then transported on a heavy loader by Pickfords Ltd to the RAF Museum through the streets of London early one Sunday morning. It is believed to have been **the biggest motorboat ever to have been moved through the City of London**.

RAF Armoured Target Boats. Believed to be the first manned boats to be used for aerial bombing practice at sea. *RAF A 190* was the first of a fleet of over 30 Armoured Target Boats built for the RAF by the British Power Boat Company Ltd. Fitted with three 100 hp 'Power' marine engines these craft were capable of over 20 knots and could withstand a direct hit from $8\frac{1}{2}$ lb practice bombs dropped from 10000 ft. RAF crews (three to a crew) were paid an extra 6d a day only when on board and acting as a 'target boat'. Some aircraft crews gave the marine craft men a bottle of whisky when they scored a direct hit; although their generosity apparently waned as they got more proficient – while Bomber Command crews became more 'bomb happy'!

One of the fleet of 30 Armoured Target Boats built for the RAF during the early 1930s

Aircraftman T. E. Shaw (formerly 'Lawrence of Arabia') first learned about motorboating in 1929 by repairing, modifying, servicing and driving a Biscayne Bay speedboat, *Biscuit* (formerly owned by Sir Henry Segrave), belonging to Mr and Mrs Sidney-Smith. In 1932 Shaw became involved with developing and testing RAF seaplane tenders and air/sea rescue boats being built at the British Power Boat Company at Hythe (see p. 129), following through with the development of armoured target boats which he himself piloted on 'bomb runs' from April 1933. T. E. Shaw worked from the RAF Marine Aircraft Experimental Station at Felixstowe, travelling to and from several boat building yards. Before he was fatally injured in a motorcycle accident (May 1935) Shaw had been working with Edward Spurr on a totally streamlined lightweight 80 mph (128 km/h) torpedo boat, only one of which, *The Empire Day*, underwent unsuccessful speed trials on Lake Windermere (August 1938).

RED CROSS AMBULANCE BOATS

The first ambulance paddle-steamer was called the *Red Cross* (LOA 105 ft (32 m) × B 16 ft (4·9 m) × D 6 ft 9 in (2·1 m)), built in 1881 for the London Metropolitan Asylums Board and used for the conveyance of infectious cases of disease from the London receiving wharves along the Thames to the hospital ships off Dartford. A silent discharge steam-apparatus prevented noise caused by the safety-valves blowing off steam when the engines were at rest. For'ard of the funnel was for infectious cases, whilst the stern section saloon was designed for the use of patients returning, cured from the hospital ships.

The first Royal Navy 42 ft (12·8 m) ambulance launch was built at the Portsmouth Dockyard in 1883 to take the sick and wounded from the vessels in Portsmouth Harbour to the Naval Hospital at Haslar. With no powerplant, this launch had to be towed by another steam vessel.

The first steam launch to be used abroad by the British Red Cross Society to aid sick and wounded British troops was the *Queen Victoria* which first saw service on an 800-mile (1300 km) stretch of the River Nile between Cairo and Wady Haifa, during the Dervish Rebellion of 1885.

In 1914 four barges with a carrying capacity of 50 patients each, were fitted out by an organisation known as the British Water Ambulance Fund for work on the Seine. When this **Number 1 Ambulance Flotilla**, commanded by Capt. Douglas Hall MP, was disbanded in November 1915 it had carried, in all, 5230

Transfer of a motor ambulance launch from the River Tigris to the River Euphrates in the latter part of World War I

patients from Paris to Rouen and later from Rouen to Le Havre. By 1918, Numbers 2, 3, 4 and 5 Ambulance Flotillas, comprising some 24 barges (LOA 126 ft (38·4 m) × B 16 ft 7 in (5·1 m) × D 7 ft 6 in (2·3 m)), manned by Inland Water Transport medical staff and crew, and towed in pairs by steam tugs, had evacuated some 70 059 casualties away from the Western Front. Because they gave a much smoother ride than either road or rail transport, these specially equipped barges were reserved for head wounds, fractured thighs and injuries to the chest. The average time taken for each daylight journey was some 10½ hr.

In April 1916, wartime units operating on the River Tigris, Mesopotamia had only one petrol-driven private launch, the *Aerial* (so named from its aerial propeller) for the evacuation of serious cases. The Turks recognised this as a hospital launch and refrained from shelling.

From August 1916 until demobilisation on 1 March 1919, an ever-growing fleet of Red Cross ambulance motor-launches in Mesopotamia carried 414 017 sick and wounded and travelled some 683 175 miles (1 099 500 km) on the Rivers Karun, Tigris and Euphrates. The first two converted ambulance motor-launches to be shipped to the River Tigris were the 42½ ft (13 m) *Olinda*, fitted with a 40 hp six-cylinder Napier engine, and the 37 ft (11·3 m) *Alouette*, fitted with a 15 hp Knight-Daimler sleeve-valve engine. The third boat was the converted 45 ft (13·7 m) 40 hp Daimler-engined *Wessex*, which during the first six months of 1916 carried over 15 000 patients alone. The first custom-built ambulance motor-launches were built and engined by John I. Thornycroft & Co. Altogether, some 84 shallow-draught launches went into operation, taking out supplies and bringing back the wounded; they ranged from the 16 ft (4·9 m) De Dion-engined *Jean* (No. 75), up to the 50 ft (15·2 m) 60 hp Parsons-engined *Wardha IV*. Thornycroft, Parsons, Kelvin, Gleniffer, Gardner and Ferro petrol-paraffin engines were largely used. Each launch, painted white with three red crosses painted on each side, was equipped with thick double canvas awnings and strong towing posts, fore and aft. Despite malfunction due to inexperienced misuse, these launches were efficiently maintained at the British Red Cross Society's repair depot at Basrah.

The Red Cross River Hospital Ship *Nabha* (LOA 150 ft (45·7 m) × B 30 ft (9·1 m) × D 3 ft (0·9 m)) was built in England for special service on the Tigris, and sent out in sections to Bombay, where she was put together again under the supervision of Red Cross engineers. Powered by her twin 150 hp Thornycroft paraffin engines, *Nabha* journeyed from Bombay to Basra at an average 8 mph (13 km/h). She arrived at Basra on 23 May 1917. In June and July she made two complete round trips between Basrah and Baghdad – 2000 miles (3200 km) in all. By demobilisation on 1 March 1919, *Nabha* had travelled 12 338 miles (19 856 km) in Mesopotamia, carried 27 233 sick and wounded, and distributed 10 740 blocks of ice for refrigeration, each weighing 30 lb.

6 INTERFACE

AMPHIBIOUS CRAFT

The first known amphibious vehicle was designed in 1588 by the Italian, Agostino Ramelli, as a military fighting car which could be drawn by horses on the land and moved through the water by man-powered winches and paddle-wheels.

The first powered vehicle to travel on both land and water was the *Orukter Amphibolos* (Amphibian Digger), designed and built in 1805 by the American inventor Oliver Evans to dredge the Philadelphia Docks. The 30 ft (9·1 m) flat-bottomed boat was powered by a single-cylinder steam engine (bore 15 in × stroke 19 in) with 20 in boiler, and could either be coupled to a wooden-wheeled waggon or fitted with a stern paddle-wheel. On 13 July 1905, *Orukter Amphibolos* travelled for $1\frac{1}{2}$ miles (2·4 km) to the Schuykill River, then at high tide she paddle-steamed up-river to Philadelphia where another wooden-wheeled waggon was coupled to her for the journey to the city's Central Square. Evans was paid £1000 when the dredging had been completed.

In the 1880s, Capt. J. B. Eads, the American engineer, proposed a plan for a ship railway across the Tehuantepec in Central America, but it was not until 1895 that **the first amphibious passenger train went into public service**. This was

Orukter Amphibolos (1805) with its designer/builder/ driver, Oliver Evans (Inset) (Science Museum, London)

1897 advertisement for 'The Swan', the first amphibious passenger train (Mary Evans Picture Library)

the *Amfibiebadden Swanen* ('Amphibious Boat Swan'), which ran on water-rails-water between Farum and Fredericksdal, via Fiskebaek, north of Copenhagen, Denmark. The *Swan* (LOA 46 ft (14 m) × B 9½ ft (2·9 m) × D 3½ ft (1 m)) was originally designed by a Swede named Magnell and constructed by Ljunggreen of Christians-bad, Sweden to be driven by either a screw-propeller or to run on two pairs of wheels, some 18 in apart. The 900 ft (275 m) railway section was built by F. A. Velschow of Copenhagen. By 1897, after two summer seasons, with half a dozen trips per day, some 40000 people had journeyed in this amphibian.

The first amphibian vehicle to combine a motor-car with a motor-launch was built and tested by the French engineer, Fournier, in Paris and on the Seine in 1905–6.

Successful attempts to develop alternating and watertight drives for floatable motorcars and wheeled motorboats include: *The Ravillier* (1907), *Waterland I* (1908), Jean Rech's *Schwimmwagen* (1909), William Mazzei's *Hydrometer* (1915).

In October 1918, a Mark IX, large 27-ton supply tank, with a carrying capacity of 54 men, became the first British amphibian tank, when it successfully crossed a stretch of water at the Brent Reservoir (Welsh Harp), North London. By 1922, the 7-ton Light Infantry Tank, with a top land speed of 30 mph (48 km/h) and water speed of 1½ mph (2·4 km/h), was developed.

In 1923, the American J. Walter Christie's convertible track/wheels amphibian Type M tank was tested by the US Army and Marine Corps across the Hudson and Potomac rivers. A six-cylinder 120 hp engine drove twin screw-propellers. Six of the Christie amphibians saw service in China in 1927.

The *Voran* amphibian of 1929, commissioned by the German Admiralty, was a 22·3 ft (6·8 m) fishery patrol cruiser, installed with a four-cylinder, 40 bhp Opel engine for use on the marshy North Sea coastline. Land speed was 15 mph (24 km/h) and water speed was 7 mph (11 km/h).

The Vickers-Carden Lloyd A.4 amphibious light tank, weighing 3·35 tons and powered by a 50 hp Meadows-engine, was developed for the British Army in 1931 by Vickers Armstrong.

With a crew of two, the A4 amphibian was fitted with a ·303 in Vickers machine-gun. Its land speed was 20 mph (32 km/h) and water speed 3·7 mph (6 km/h). Eight A.4's were sold to Russia who subsequently pushed it into quantity production as the T-37 or Vickers-Russkij.

In 1932, 24-year-old German mechanic Hans Trippel began work on an amphibious version of the twin-cylinder Opel 2½-litre Kapitan, nick-named the 'Land/Water Zeppelin', with two gearboxes for wheels and stern propeller. In 1934 Trippel was given a research grant by Gen. Becker of the German Weaponry Establish-ment to develop his vehicle for military use. Trippel's SG4, centrally powered by a four-cylinder 45 bhp engine had a top land speed of 40 mph (64 km/h) and water speed of 4½ knots. In 1935 Trippel developed the SG6 with retract-able propeller at his new Homburg factory on the Saar. Between 1937 and 1944, **some 1000 SG6 amphibious vehicles** were constructed for the Army, by which time the power unit had been changed from a four-cylinder Adler motor to a six-cylinder Opel unit. In 1937 Trippel attempted to market a pleasure version SK8, improved to SK9, but these only sold in small numbers. Between 1940 and 1942, 350 Trippel amphibians were produced at the former Bugatti racing-car factory in Molsheim. During 1943 the V8 Tatra-engined SG7 was developed as an armoured, tank-identifying amphibian – the twin-prop 'Schildkrote' (Tortoise) E3.

The first 150 amphibious Volkswagen, Type 128 designated Schwimmwagen, were built largely from Type 82 VW staff car parts by Porsche in 1940, to replace the many side-car motorcycles in German motorised formations. Type 138 was drawn out but never built, but during 1941, the four-cylinder Type 166 proved a greater success and between 1942 and 1944, some 14625 pressed-steel amphibious Schwimm-wagen Type 166's were manufactured at the Wolsburg plant; many of them were used for reconnaissance purposes in Russia.

The first successful LVT had been constructed in 1937 as a 7·8 ton amphibious tracked vehicle evolved by Donald Roebling for rescue work in the swamp areas of Florida. In 1940, the US Marine Corps ordered their first 100 military versions from Roebling. LVT1, known as the

A column of DUKWs after delivering supplies during an exercise; 21000 were built (By permission of the trustees of the Imperial War Museum)

'Alligator', was built by the Food Machinery Corporation and supplied to the First Amphibious Tractor Battalion in late 1941. LVT2 was a sheet metal, improved version supplied to the US Army, whilst LVTA2 was an armour-plate version, first used in the Pacific in February 1944. LVTA4 was fitted with an open-top turret. The LVT4 was first used in June 1944. Altogether, some 18620 LVT or 'Water Buffalo' were built up to the end of World War II. By that time the Marine Corps alone had nine LVT battalions and three LVTA battalions operating in the Pacific. The British version of the LVT, known as the *Neptune*, was built by the Nuffield Organisation.

In 1941 Division 12 of the US National Research and Development Council developed **their first amphibious jeep** largely from a $\frac{1}{4}$ ton General Purpose Truck. With a land speed of 50 mph (80 km/h) and a water speed of 5 mph (8 km/h), some 7000 amphibious jeeps were built during World War II.

In May 1942, Roderick Stephens of Sparkman & Stephens Inc, naval architects, teamed up with the Studebaker Corporation to produce a multi-purpose rubber track-laying vehicle called the *Weasel*, designated T-15, later standardised as M-28, and capable of travelling through mud, swamp, soft sand and thick snow. The field-test-improved T-24/M-29 went into production on 30 August 1943. Altogether over 4000 Weasels were ordered. The amphibious adaptation of the Weasel, the M-29C, equipped with buoyancy cells, skirts, rudders, etc was capable of a land speed of 36 mph (58 km/h) and a water speed of 4 mph (6·4 km/h). Production of the M-29C began on 25 May 1944, and by May 1945 some 19619 amphibious Weasels had been ordered.

In April 1942, Sparkman & Stephens teamed up with General Motors Corporation Truck and Coach Division to convert the US Army's $2\frac{1}{2}$-ton truck into a cargo/armament-carrying amphibian, to be called the **DUKW** (D = the year 1942; U = utility; K = front-wheel drive and W = two rear-driving axles). On its first water tests on 3 June 1942, the prototype DUKW carried 63 people, crew included, at $5\frac{1}{2}$ mph (8·9 km/h). Although greeted with initial coolness, by December the DUKW had proved itself in trials in front of 86 top-ranking officials of both the US Army and Navy. By 15 August 1945, over 21000 DUKWs had been produced for 76 US DUKW companies of 50 DUKWs, each manned by approximately 13000 US Army and Marine Corps, trained by six special schools, one of which was in Mumbles, Wales (UK).

DUKW's top land speed was 50 mph (80 km/h) and water speed 5 knots; it could carry 10 tons on the water and 4 tons on the land. It was fitted with a centrifugal bilge pump, operating from the propeller, with a capacity of 260 gallons (1180 litres) per minute, and a cockpit-controlled variable tyre pressure.

In 1945, the Penguin amphibian vehicle, a shallow draught, lightweight sled, powered by an aero-engine, was designed by Dr Arthur B. Cleaves in conjunction with the Acorn Assembly and Naval Training Detachment at Port Hueneme on the Californian coast. Penguin was to transport land troops, ammunition and supplies across the extremely shallow waters of broad tidal flats on the Chinese coast. This vessel, developed from all the intensive know-how of World War II, was never put into production.

At Morris Motors, Alec Issigonis (later of Mini motorcar fame) produced the *Gosling*, a baby landing craft for the Signal Corps on which a two-cycle Villiers outboard motor drove both rear wheels or a screw-propeller.

Half Safe, **the first converted amphibious jeep to cross 2000 miles (3218 km) of the North Atlantic Ocean**, was modified, developed and driven by Australian-born Ben Carlin, accompanied by his wife Elinore. After four years of false starts, setbacks and tribulations, the Carlins left Halifax Nova Scotia on 19 July 1950 with some 735 gallons (3340 litres) of petrol on board and on tow in a streamlined tank. After stopping at San Miguel (Azores Islands), Madeira and the Canary Islands they eventually reached Cape Juby (Africa), some six months later. Motoring across the desert of French Morocco, the Carlins crossed the Straits of Gibraltar, motored across Spain, Portugal, France, Belgium, Holland, Germany, Denmark, Sweden, then retraced their steps to Calais, crossed the English Channel and motored to London. They were last heard of, planning to continue their amphibious journey round the world in 1953 . . .

The first amphibious vehicle to make use of fgrp construction was the Swedish Allskog Aquacar of 1955 which had a stepped 'V' hull and could seat five passengers.

Possibly the best-known modern amphibian was Hans Trippel's prototype Alligator, being unveiled at the 1959 Geneva Salon and reaching production as the **Amphicar** two years later. This rear-engined, twin-screw convertible with syncromesh gearbox was powered by a 43 bhp British Triumph Herald car engine. By 1965, some 3000 Amphicars were produced of which half were exported to the USA. But the Amphicar's doors were not watertight and it failed to pass exhaust emission regulations. By 1968 it had ceased to be marketed or built.

The first air jet-propelled amphibious car was a £9000 private four-wheel drive vehicle, designed by the mechanic engineer Herrtwich for wealthy textile magnate Karl Mayer in 1976, so that he could get to his island home on the Rhine with the minimum of bother. It was powered by a 2-litre 100 hp Opel Rekord engine to give a top land speed of 75 mph (120 km/h) and a water speed of 6–9 mph (10–15 km/h).

HYDROGLIDERS

Both Forlanini and Crocco/Ricaldoni hydrofoil craft of 1906–7 were powered by aerial propellers, but one of the first non-hydrofoil vessels to be driven by an aerial propeller was the semi-inflatable *No. 18* trimaran, designed and piloted by the famous French aviator, Santos Dumont, in trials on the Seine at Neuilly, during the latter part of 1907. After initial experiments with a 50 hp engine driving a two-bladed propeller, a 100 hp Antoinette engine was coupled with a three-bladed tractor propeller.

Early hydrogliders, despite their advantages for navigation in weed-infested or shallow waters, were initially thought of as weird hybrids. In 1911 the French airman M. Pavaud's 20 ft (6·1 m) Saunders-built 50 hp Gnôme-engined craft was variously described as an 'aeroscaphe', 'motoscaphe', 'Aero motorboat', 'hydro-aeroplane', 'aero-hydroplane', 'aero-quat' and 'skimmer with aerial propeller'!

This tri-maran with aerial propeller was designed and driven by celebrated French aviator Santos-Dumont in 1907 (Mary Evans Picture Library)

The first racing between hydrogliders took place at the Monaco Meeting of 1912.

In 1914 the Blackburn Aeroplane Company Ltd fitted one of their 8 hp Alpha engines, complete with a four-bladed aerial propeller outfit, at the stern of a 53 ft (16·2 m) pleasure launch which was in service for passenger hire on a lake at Leeds.

In 1920 the Englishman W. Miller Metcalf built the *Amphiglyder*, aerially propelled by a three-cylinder radial engine driving a tractro airscrew, capable of 60 mph (96 km/h) on the land and convertible to a twin-float hydroplane in under 30 min.

In 1921 Alfred A. Gassner, an Austrian aeronautical-engineer, designed a 40 ft (12·2 m), twin 300 hp Daimler-engined hydroglider for Charles McDaniel of Vienna. Used on the Danube between Vienna and Budapest, the Gassner hydroglider had a carrying capacity of 35 passengers. The cabin top was of aerofoil section to assist 'lift'.

On 21 December 1923, aeroplane pilot Pierre Canivet piloted the Marcel Besson marginal-draught hydroglider, powered by a water-cooled 300 hp Hispano-Suiza engine, driving a 7 ft 6 in (2·3 m) Chauvière propeller, to a new european record of 75·22 mph (121·05 km/h) along the River Seine. Not only was this the first record to be officially homologated by the fledgling International Motor Yacht Racing Union (IMYU), but was also a publicity stunt to launch the sporting version of the Besson hydroglider at 90 000 Fr.

On 10 November 1924, aeroplane pilot Jules Fischer piloted a hydroglider, manufactured by H. & M. Farman, powered by a 450 hp Lorraine Dietrich engine and driving a trestle-mounted, four-bladed propeller to a new record average of 87·392 mph (140·643 km/h) for six runs on the Seine between Sartrouville and Maisons-Lafitte. Again this was a publicity stunt for the marketing of two smaller versions of Farman-built hydrogliders: the 190 hp Renault aero-engine limousine, capable of carrying 10 passengers at almost 60 mph (96 km/h), and the Passe-Partout, powered with a 10 hp Anzani motor giving a speed of 13–16 mph (21–26 km/h); with

Alfa-Romeo-engined Italian hydroglider in Venice in the 1930s

a draught of only 4 in. The Passe-Partout was designed to carry five passengers or about 1000 lb of cargo. Another manufacturer of hydrogliders was Dumond-Galvin.

After visiting the European hydroglider yards and riding in their craft, the American automotive engineer Henry Lowe Brownback returned to the Brownback Motor Laboratories in Cincinnati and after several prototypes, succeeded in developing **the first large American passenger-carrying hydroglider**. This was powered by two 450 hp Liberty aero-engines, one driving a tractor propeller while the other turned a pusher wheel. There were seats for 30, arranged exactly similar to a bus, with 'Gents' and 'Ladies' toilets at the stern. The first Brownback hydroglider was scheduled to go into operation between Cincinnati and St Louis in May 1928 – as the first of a fleet.

During the 1930s a number of hydrogliders competed in the Pavia-Venezia race – these were built by the SIAI aircraft factory and powered by either Isotta Fraschini or nine-cylinder Alfa Romeo rotary engines achieving maximum speeds of between 60 and 80 mph (100 and 130 km/h) towards the end of the decade.

The most famous British hydroglider designer/ builder/driver was W. F. W. ('Wallie') Davies (1891–1972). On 25 July 1932, Wallie Davies and his brother-in-law, Sid Bray, became **the first to take a motor-vessel on the treacherous upstream journey of the River Severn from Bewdley to the Welsh Bridge at Shrewsbury**. They were piloting the D7, powered by a secondhand Austin Seven engine. In 1934, a small Davies hydroglider was exhibited at the Car and Boat Show, Olympia, one of which was sold to a Brazilian businessman. In 1937 the 90 hp D16 reached 50 mph (80 km/h), whilst in 1938 the D17 Severn Star, a 40 ft (12·2 m) hydroglider fitted with a Ford V8 engine, successfully met the 7 ft (2·1 m) high waves of the Severn bore at Newnham and also successfully crossed the Bristol Channel. In 1948, Davies Hydrogliders of Dudley were offering a 28 ft (8·5 m) catamaran, powered by a twin-

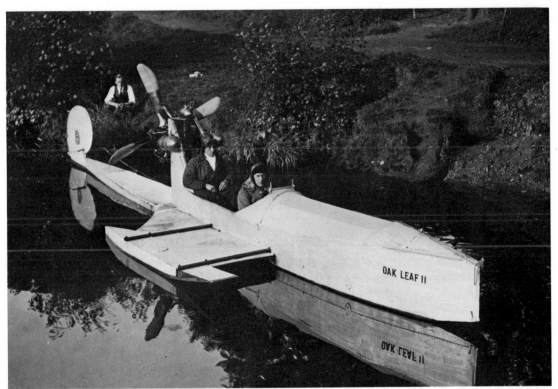

W. F. W. Davies, British hydroglider pioneer, with his brother-in-law Sid Bray with his first boat, Oak Leaf II *(1922), on the River Severn (RTHPL)*

cylinder 3 hp air-cooled Norman engine, belt-driving a pusher propeller at the stern of the cockpit. A speed of 10½ knots with one person on board was reduced to 8¾ knots for a crew of two. In October 1950, the D22 100 hp Lapwing hydroglider achieved a new 450 kg speed record of 51·4 mph (82·7 km/h) against the 4 mph (6 km/h) current. Davies' (now 71 years old) last hydroglider D24 cabin cruiser was exhibited at the first Birmingham Boat Show of 1962.

René Cousinet continued the development of hydrogliders, from 1944–45, by building a 16-passenger, 50-knot hydroglider in Rio de Janeiro, Brazil and powering it with a 500 hp Hispano aero-engine; this was an exact replica of the one Cousinet had built on the Seine in 1930, but was destroyed by fire. Back in France, in 1948, Cousinet resumed his activities at Meudon and in 1951 produced **the world's first (Turbomeca) jet-propelled hydroglider**. In 1952 he built the H80, a 26 ft (7·9 m) six-passenger hydroglider with light metals, and powered it with a 190 hp Mathis aero-engine, to give a

speed of 34 knots. He then built a 24-passenger, 47 ft (14·3 m) light alloy hydroglider to be powered by a 500 hp Hispano engine.

Since the late 1950s the aerial propulsion concept has been adapted for hovercraft of all sizes (see p. 124) and there are no new hydrogliders being built.

HYDROFOILS

In 1861 Thomas Moy, an Englishman, made trials with a boat on the Surrey Canal, which linked Rotherhithe and Camberwell, for the purpose of aerodynamic research – in his own words, 'water flight'. His boat, fitted with three planes on its underside, was **the first hydrofoil vessel**.

After almost a decade of design work, Prof. Enrico Forlanini of Milan, tested a hydrofoil boat, in 1905, and his work on the craft of this type continued for some years thereafter with the application of seaplanes in mind. A marine craft of 1·65 tons was demonstrated on Lakes Maggiore and Garda in 1906. It lifted clear of the water and reached a speed of 38 knots, using a 75 hp engine, driving two enormous metal air propellers, one pushing and the other pulling. Stable in small waves, it made smoothwater trials and avoided such waves. Thus he was the inventor of the ladder foil system and his was **the first successful manned hydrofoil to fly with the hull clear over the water**.

In 1906–7, Forlanini had been handicapped by an unsatisfactory engine and, after the formation of a sponsor company 'Leonardo da Vinci', the Professor tested a steam-engined hydrofoil during 1908 and 1909. This engine proved reliable, and although giving only 25 hp it propelled the boat, which weighed over a ton, at about 30 mph (48 km/h). During 1910 Forlanini was experimenting with a two-ton craft having very accurately made steel foils and designed for a carrying capacity of two to four persons. A 100 hp engine gave a speed of 45 mph (72 km/h).

Forlanini's inability to overcome the buffeting ride over waves, despite an increasingly complex arrangement of foils, ultimately led Forlanini to abandon his project.

In 1907, to test air propellers for his airship designs, Arturo Crocco and O. Ricaldini tested a 26 ft (7·9 m) hydrofoil, powered by a 100 hp Clement-Bayard engine driving two aerial propellers astern of midships, across Lake Bracciano at a speed of 50 mph (80 km/h). It had adjustable frames carrying submerged steel foils mounted at stem and stern. Although Crocco wrote a pamphlet that year, concluding that the hydrofoil could be applied for sport and on rivers and calm lakes, he too abandoned the task of a seaworthy hydrofoil.

America's first powered hydrofoil craft was constructed and tested by Peter Cooper Hewitt, inventor of the mercury vapour lamp, during 1907. From its light mahogany hull a rigid rectangular framework of steel tubing was projected. This framework carried the engine, whilst sheet-steel foils were attached to projections from its lower extremities. At a weight of 2500 lb, a speed of 30 mph (48 km/h) was readily attained.

The first hydrofoil to create a world water speed record of 70·86 mph (114·03 km/h) was the 60 ft (18·3 m) *Hydrodome IV*, piloted by Casey Baldwin across a lake in Nova Scotia (September 1919). Aerially propelled by twin 350 hp Liberty aero-engines, this was the fourth prototype to be designed and built for telephone inventor Alexander Graham Bell. It was cigar-shaped with two sets of hydrofoil ladders forward and one aft. Two of Bell's Hydrodomes were supplied to the Royal Navy in the 1920s. Soon after their delivery they were put through high-speed towing tests off Spithead in a heavy gale. Their structures were not designed to withstand the sea state and the two craft fell apart under stress.

The first practical usable hydrofoil craft was painstakingly developed by Baron Hanns von Schertel, after nine years of trials with no less than eight boats. It was von Schertel's aim to develop a foil system which could safely be applied for commercial or military rough water purposes. At first the Baron used an obsolete air-cooled three-cylinder aircraft engine, then powerful outboard engines, and finally the light

Baron Hanns von Schertel, hydrofoil pioneer with one of his experimental craft in the 1930s

Freccia d'Oro, *the first commercial passenger hydrofoil on regular service on Lake Maggiore (1953)*

American boat motors to patiently tackle the problems of submergence depth, roll, pitch and directional stability, as well as the rudder and propulsion characteristics.

Finally, in 1936, a craft with the new invented foil system (a surf-piercing V-foil configuration in a tandem arrangement, with front and rear foils differently shaped) made long trips on the Rhine. It performed so well in waves that the 'Köln-Düsseldorfer Rheindampfschiffahrt' decided to order the first passenger hydrofoil boat for regular service on the Rhine. Gotthard Sachsenberg, owner of the Gebrüder Sachsenberg shipyard at Dessau-Rosslau and Hamburg-Harburg, concluded a contract with von Schertel for the Schertel-Sachsenberg Schnellboots-Konsortium. This company, which was under the technical management of Prof. G. Weinblum, possessed a team of very highly qualified engineers. Fifteen different types of boat, of various sizes, were developed. All underwent trial testing and some of them were subjected to extensive research experiments. Model tests were undertaken at the yard's own facilities, the Hamburger Schiffbau Versuchsanstatt, and at the circulating water channel of the Technische Hochschule in Berlin.

In the autumn of 1939, the Konsortium completed a 2·8 ton experimental craft for demonstration purposes. It might well have been this design that was to be used on the Rhine River Passenger boat, but World War II meant that a delegation of high-ranking officers from the German Navy were so impressed by the performance of this hydrofoil, particularly in the Baltic, that both the Navy and Army made orders for military hydrofoils.

Hence the first successful German Naval hydrofoil craft to be built as the *VS6*, constructed between June 1940 and 1941 when it went on test runs, achieving speeds up to 47·5 knots compared to the 30-knot top speed of a minelayer. *VS6* was 51 ft 7⅝ in (15·74 m) long and was powered by twin Hispano-Suiza gasoline engines, developing a total 1560 hp. After lengthy trials and modifications to the foil system on both the River Elbe and the Baltic, *VS6* was about to be commissioned as a Red Cross supply boat when Germany was defeated.

One month after starting the construction of *VS6*, a series of six smaller boats were laid on the stocks. Intended for coastal surveillance, these 39 ft 2 in (11·96 m) TS craft, each powered by a single Lorraine-Dietrich 12EB gas engine, attained speeds of nearly 40 knots – in the hands of the Russians (!) who occupied Dessau-Rosslau just after the craft had completed its trials.

The world's largest hydrofoil vessel for two decades was the *VS8* (80-ton) hydrofoil transporter. The keel of this 105 ft (32 m) craft was laid in 1941, but due to delays the *VS8* was not launched until 1943. Even then the two supercharged 20-cylinder Mercédès-Benz diesel engines (total output: 5000 hp) which should have given it a speed of 45 knots, were not forthcoming, and the normal engines totalling only 3660 bhp could only give *VS8* a speed of 37 knots against waves up to 6 ft (1·8 m). Although this hydrofoil was capable of carrying a 20-ton army tank and ammunition, in 1944 *VS8* was stranded in a storm due to a number of incidents following the failure of both engines.

On 29 May 1952 Supramar was founded on a hotel lawn on the shores of Lake Lucerne by the Schertel-Sachsenberg Konsortium and the Kredit-und-Verwaltungs bank, Zug. The legacy left to Supramar by the Konsortium was in the form of **the world's first passenger hydrofoil**, the *PT 10*. She was a 9-ton boat with a seating capacity of 28 passengers. Powered by a 500 hp Mercédès-Benz diesel engine located in the stern of the vessel.

Soon after her first demonstrations on Lake Lucerne, in 1953, two public companies, the Navigazione Lago Maggiore and the Ticino Railway, decided to charter this boat for passenger service between the Swiss and Italian part of Lago Maggiore under the technical management of Supramar. Thus **the first scheduled hydrofoil boat service** in the history of shipping was inaugurated on 16 May 1953. Today more than 100 passenger vessels are operating in all parts of the world with still the same foil system.

The first Supramar licensee to start building and exporting hydrofoils was Carlo Rodriguez of the Cantiere Navale Rodriguez Shipyard at Messina, Sicily. This was the 32-ton PT20, *Freccia del Sole*, with seats for 75 passengers. By 1956, *Freccia del Sole* had completed several demonstration runs along the Italian coast and a round trip of 1600 nautical miles from Italy to Greece. She proved her seaworthiness on many occasions and in waves up to 13 ft (4 m) high. Built in accordance with all safety regulations, PT20 was **the first hydrofoil to receive class certification**. In August 1956 Rodriguez started a shipping company called Aliscafi and the company's first scheduled service was inaugurated in that same month between Messina and Reggio di Calabria – 22 trips daily.

Three years later, in 1959, the 63-ton PT50 became **the first hydrofoil to receive classification for coastal sea operation**. Also in 1959, the PT27 became **the world's first hydrofoil for offshore oil drilling rigs service**.

In 1959, test runs were made with **the first gas-turbined-engined amphibious hydrofoil** – the *Flying Dukw*, a version of the World War II *Dukw* (see p. 115). The craft was developed by Lycoming, under contract to the US Army Ordnance Corps. Foils raised its speed on water from 6 to 35 mph (9 to 56 km/h).

In 1961, with sufficient data accumulated by the US Navy to suggest a successful configuration for ⊥-shaped fully-submerged foils at high speed, an accelerated research and development programme was initiated. **The first really practical military vessel** was the Patrol Craft Hydrofoil (PCH)-1 *High Point*, designed by the Bureau of Ships and constructed by the Boeing Aircraft Company as a hydrofoil subchaser. This sleek 116 ft (35·4 m) vessel has been used as a research and test vehicle since its delivery to the Navy in 1963; *High Point* has reached some 57·5 mph (92·6 km/h), powered by two Rolls-Royce gas-turbines, driving four propellers.

The world's largest hydrofoil is the US Navy's 320-ton AG(EH)-1 *Plainview* with a length of 210 ft (65 m). Propulsion is supplied by two General Electric gas-turbines of 14000 bhp each. *Plainview* made its test runs in 1967 at 40 knots.

The world's largest seagoing passenger hydrofoil, since 1968, is the Supramar *PTS 150* with 165-ton displacement and a length of 125 ft (38 m).

The world's fastest hydrofoil vessel is the Boeing turbofan-engined *FRESH-1*, a 59 ft (18 m), 16·5 ton twin-hulled aluminium and steel craft, which created a speed of 96·7 mph (155·6 km/h) on Seattle's Puget Sound in 1963, the year it began operation. *FRESH-1* was constructed so that different types of foils could be mounted on it in different arrangements and the problems of cavitation at high speed be overcome. Her fan-jet engine was capable of 18000 lb thrust.

The first hydrofoil built by Boeing to prove the feasibility of the water-jet propulsion system was the 20 ft (6·1 m) 2·6-ton *Little Squirt*. A 520 gas-turbine-driven pump squirted water over its stern at 3500 gallons (15910 litres) per minute, propelling the boat at 56·4 mph (90·7 km/h).

The first Naval hydrofoil to use water-jets was the Patrol Gunboat Hydrofoil-2 (PGH-2) *Tucumcari*, 74·6 ft (22·7 m) long, 57·5-ton aluminium craft with steel struts and foils capable of high-speed turns. Launched in 1967, *Tucumcari*'s 3200 hp gas-turbine driven water-jet powered her at over 57·9 mph (92·6 km/h) in

Vietnamese combat waters and also in European waters. A 40 mm gun was mounted forward and an 80 mm mortar astern; twin 20 mm automatic cannons were positioned on each side of the bridge. *Tucumcari* ran aground in the Caribbean in autumn 1972 and was subsequently decommissioned.

The first passenger hydrofoil to use water-jets was the 929 *Jetfoil 010*, the first of which was launched in March 1974. Weighing 106 tons, this 90 ft (27·4 m) long aluminium craft, powered by two 3780 bhp Allison 501-K20A gas-turbines with two Rocketdyne R-20 water-jet pumps, has a carrying capacity of 250 to 400 passengers. It went on its first foil-borne flight on 16 July 1974, proving its ability to cruise in 12 ft (3·7 m) waves at 51·8 mph (83·3 km/h), while giving its occupants a smooth ride.

Hong Kong has been a key area of hydrofoil activity for many years. Nineteen surface-piercing hydrofoils were providing service between Hong Kong and Macao, a Portuguese province, 36 nautical miles to the west across the Chinese waters of the Pearl River estuary. More than five million passengers travel this route annually, about three million by hydrofoil.

The first Jetfoil to enter commercial service, *Madeira*, was put into operation here by the Far East Hydrofoil Co. Ltd on 25 April 1975. A second craft, *Santa Maria* was introduced in August of the same year. Configured to carry

260 passengers each, the two Jetfoils had carried 1 to 1½ million passengers by October 1975.

For a quarter of a century the only passenger transportation between the islands of Hawaii was by air. In June 1975, Pacific Sea Transportation Co. Ltd, introduced Jetfoil service. By October of that year, three Jetfoils, the *Kamehameha*, *Kalakaua* and *Kuhio* were in service between Oahu (Honolulu) and Kaui, Maui and the big island of Hawaii. This operation was discontinued in January 1978 and the three Jetfoils were purchased by Far East Hydrofoil to go into service in February 1978.

The first Jetfoil passenger service to operate in North America began in September 1976 with the *Flying Princess* travelling between Seattle (Washington) and Victoria, BC, Canada. By November, with the British Columbia Steamship Co. providing marketing and facilities, 18 500 passengers had been carried.

The first Jetfoil service in Japan was introduced on 1 May 1977 by Sado Kisen Kaisha, with the *Okesa* providing six trips per day between Sado Island and Niigata City on the north-west side of Honshu.

The first Jetfoil service in Europe was introduced on 1 June 1977 by P. & O. Ferries, one of the world's largest shipping companies. A round trip service between St Katherine's Dock, Central London and Zeebrugge, Belgium was

Flying Princess *on trials in Seattle, USA (1977) (Boeing Marine Systems)*

provided by the *Flying Princess*. Prior to entering service, this Jetfoil carried out 65 demonstrations in 52 days in six different countries in Northern Europe; in all, she travelled over 7000 miles (11 265 km) with a 100 per cent dispatch reliability from 30 different ports-of-call. About 2700 representatives of industry, governments, military and press participated. The highlight of the adventure was the 260 nautical mile non-stop foil-borne crossing of the North Sea from Stavangar (Norway) to Aberdeen (Scotland) in 6 hr and 11 min. Possibly **the most lavish publicity venture ever mounted for the promotion of any new form of transport**.

By 7 August 1977, the Boeing Jetfoil fleet had attained 100 million passenger miles in service. Over the next ten years, Boeing expects to sell as many as 200 Jetfoils.

There are an estimated 1000 hydrofoils plying the inland waterways of the Soviet Union as well as 150 others in use in Europe and Asia.

To date, a hydrofoil has never crossed the Atlantic, and there has never been a hydrofoil race.

HOVERCRAFT
Air-Cushion Vehicles (ACV)

The principle of creating a cushion of air between the bottom of a boat and the surface of the water was patented by Sir John Thornycroft in 1877; among the few craft which were constructed on the principle of an air-trapped cushion was the Hickman Sea Sled built in some numbers in the USA during the early 1920s.

In 1953, Christopher Cockerell, an electronics engineer with a small commercial boat-building interest, developed model boats with fixed sidewalls and hinged doors at the ends with air pumped into the centre for 'lubrication'. This was followed in 1954 by fixed sidewalls with water curtains sealing the ends, substituted by air curtains. In December 1955, Cockerell applied for his first British patent covering lift by means of peripheral annular jets. During 1957, the Ministry of Supply (R. A. Shaw in particular) approached Saunders-Roe who accepted a contract to undertake a feasibility study and to do model tests. With their experience of building seaplane and hydrofoils, a SARO team headed by Richard Stanton-Jones, the Chief Aerodynamicist, enthusiastically pursued the hovercraft principle. Cockerell had meanwhile approached the National Research and Development Corporation (NRDC) – and through them a subsidiary company, known as Hovercraft Development Ltd, was set up in January 1958, with Cockerell as Technical Director.

The first manned hovercraft was the *SR.N1* constructed by SARO for the NRDC. Given the registration mark G-12-4, the craft was completed on 28 May 1959 and made its maiden flight (and first public hover) on 11 June of the

1953: Christopher Cockerell experimenting with the concept of the Air Cushion Vehicle (Hovercraft Development Ltd)

same year. Initially *SR.N1* weighed about 3½ tons and was limited to a speed of 25 knots. It was unable to overcome waves greater than 1½ ft (0·5 m) or solid obstacles of more than about 9 in. Later the craft was modified. Weighing almost 7 tons and fitted with other engines, plus a flexible skirt, *SR.N1* could attain speeds of 60 knots plus.

The first hovercraft crossing of the English Channel was performed on 25 July 1959 with the *SR.N1* hovercraft to mark the 50th Anniversary of the Blériot aeroplane flight from Calais to Dover. *SR.N1* made the same journey from France to England with three persons: Cdr Peter Lamb, John Chaplin and Christopher Cockerell. The latter acted as 'mobile ballast' and sat outside of the craft's cockpit for the journey.

The first rescue by a hovercraft was made on 17 July 1963 by research hovercraft *D.1-001*, operated by Hovercraft Development Ltd of Hythe. During test runs in Southampton Water the craft encountered two young men whose sailing dinghy had capsized and they were in difficulties. Despite the shallow water at the spot, the hovercraft moved in and picked up the two boys, Nigel Plaisted and David Riley.

The first hovercraft races were held on 14 March 1964 at Lake Burley, Griffin, Canberra in Australia. Twelve craft entered, 11 arrived and 10 took part; only five finished the course which measured ¾ mile (1·2 km) in length; other events were held over a 1½-mile (2·4 km) course. The winner was Allen Hawkins.

The first European hovercraft races were held on 18 June 1966 at Apethorpe Hall, Northants. Twelve craft attended the event, won by Dan Reece with *HA.1*.

The first light hovercraft to cross the English Channel was *Cyclone 2*, piloted by Nigel Beale on 22 August 1972. The journey achieved with this craft – basically a 1–2 seater – was from Hoverlloyd's Hoverport at Pegwell Bay (Ramsgate) to a point about 2 miles (3·2 km) south of Calais Hoverport. This route measured about 34 nautical miles and took *Cyclone 2* about 2 hr 20 min.

SR.N2 (LOA 64½ ft (19·6 m) × B 29½ ft (9 m)), 27 tons, was used from January 1962 to develop the swivelling pylon mounted propeller control system (originally used on hydrogliders) and the integrated lift/propulsion system using quadruple Nimbus engines totalling 3600 hp. *SR.N2*, with two crew and 70-passenger capacity, was capable of 75 knots. *SR.N2* was used on passenger services in the Solent and the Bristol Channel, also making an historic crossing of the Lachine Rapids on the St Lawrence River.

During the 1961–63 period, Vickers, Denn, HDL and Britten-Norman each developed research and experimental hovercraft. The formation of the British Hovercraft Corporation in 1966 merged the Westland, Vickers and NRDC interests into a single company.

The first flexible skirts were developed by Latimer-Needham in 1962. This enabled the British Hovercraft Corporation to lay down the world's first production-line of hovercraft in 1964. This was the 7-ton *SR.N5*, known as the Warden Class, which was followed in 1965 by a stretched version known as the Winchester Class. By 1968, some 45 craft had been produced and were in operation throughout the world. Indeed one of them had become **the first hovercraft to go through the rapids of the Amazon River, South America**.

The 165-ton 'soft wall' *SR.N4*, with a capacity 254 passengers and 30 cars, to be known as the

SR.N4 Mk 3 ('Super 4') entering Dover Harbour (July 1978) (British Hovercraft Corp.)

Mountbatten Class, was **the first truly open-water passenger/car ferry capable of all-year-round services** over sea routes where wave heights of 8 to 12 ft (2·5 to 3·5 m) could be encountered. *SR.N4* was powered by four Rolls-Royce 'Marine Proteus' gas turbines of 3400 hp, each driving a variable pitch propeller mounted on a pylon. Interconnected with the propellers were four centrifugal fans for delivering cushion air.

The largest hovercraft in terms of loaded weight is the British Rail Hovercraft Ltd SR.N4 Mk 3 craft, *The Princess Anne*. It is the largest hovercraft in commercial service and weighs 300 tons. It began service (as a Mk 3 craft) in July 1978 after being modified from an earlier version of the SR.N4 design. Its other dimensions are: LOA 185 ft (56·4 m) × B 92 ft (28 m).

Another large hovercraft is the *Sea Pearl*, a Hovertransporter of 750 tons loaded weight. This differs a great deal from the SR.N4 Mk 3 because the *Sea Pearl* is designed to carry very large and heavy loads – perhaps weighing up to 100 tons each – at slow speed. Empty, the *Sea Pearl* weighs 500 tons, and it can carry 250 tons. It can be towed at 7 knots and is currently based in the Middle East where it is used from time to time to move large, indivisible sections of plant. It was built in 1974 and was designed to carry large steel sections from Abu Dhabi to Das Island in the Gulf.

The fastest hovercraft. The world record for speed with a hovercraft over water is presently held by the US research hovercraft, SES-100B. This test craft, designed on the sidewall principle and thus unable to operate over land, achieved a speed of 104 mph (168 km/h) on a run in St Andrews Bay, near Panama City, Florida on 2 April 1977. The same craft was used to fire an SM-1 medium range guided missile on 8 April 1976 while travelling at a speed of 70 mph (113 km/h) in the Gulf of Mexico.

Speeds of more than 70 knots have been reached with craft of the SR.N4 type but these are not needed for commercial passenger service on the English Channel ferry routes.

High speeds have been achieved by some fully amphibious hovercraft of British construction over ice. However, details of these and overland performance are difficult to establish because of the military nature of these particular craft.

The highest hovercraft is a solid sidewall HM.2 Mk 3 hovercraft, Serial No. 324. It is operated on Lake Titicaca at a height of about 12 500 ft (3810 m) above sea level. This craft was recently joined by a second craft of the same type and both are employed on tourist services on the Lake.

In global terms there is much evidence to suggest that **the longest recorded journey undertaken by any hovercraft was that of the 1969 Trans-African Expedition** using SR.N6-018. This hovercraft travelled about 5000 miles (8000 km) along the Senegal, Niger, Chari and Ubangi rivers in Western Africa and made a trip across Lake Chad. There have been similar expeditions proposed but none have been mounted that approach this distance. Other small hovercraft have also undertaken fairly long journeys of 300–400 miles (480–650 km) but most of these are unrecognised trips.

The 1968 Amazonas expedition using SR.N6-024, travelled about 2000 miles (3200 km) along the Amazon and Orinoco rivers, and after the African expedition is probably the longest single journey.

The most active organisation for recreational hovercraft is the Hoverclub of Great Britain (1000 members plus), established in 1966. Currently, British members own more than 200 craft, and regular national race meetings held at venues in England and Wales attract up to 50 craft at a time. Sites feature 1-mile circuits of land and water (sometimes land and liquid mud!); a typical craft, 10 to 12 ft (3 to 3·7 m) long and 6 to 7 ft (1·8 to 2 m) wide and rectangular in platform, has an obstacle clearance of 8–10 in. Lift engines varied in output between $3\frac{1}{2}$ hp and 15 bhp, usually using converted motorcycle engines. Reliability is now very high and some of the competition craft can achieve speeds of 60 mph (95 km/h) over land and water.

The Hoverclubs of America and Japan are very active and there are smaller hoverclubs in Sweden, France, West Germany, Italy and Trinidad, as well as New Zealand and Australia.

7 BOATBUILDERS

Merk, *the original Andrews Greyhound launch of 1912, alongside the* Victorine Merrend *slipper-stern launch, built by Andrews in 1961 (Prof. L. Hudson)*

ANDREWS

John and Frederick Andrews were taught boat-building by Ned Andrews of Maidenhead on Thames when the latter was running his hire fleet of electric launches. In 1912, when John Andrews was 19 years old, he designed and built a 25 ft (7·6 m) flat-bottomed river motor-launch with a sloping or slipper-stern, powered by a twin-cylinder copper-jacketed Watermota inboard engine, complete with reversing propeller. Selling it to Sir Arthur Whitten-Brown (of Alcock and Brown Transatlantic fame) this very first slipper-stern launch was named the *Merk* after Brown's Mercédès motorcar.

Purchasing Thames Meadow at Bourne End in 1925 and building a new boatbuilding yard there, it was not long before John Andrews

'Greyhound' launches had become a familiar sight – not only on the Thames, but also in France on the canals, in Venice, on the River Nile and even down the Penang. From 25-footers (7·6 m), to 30-footers (9·1 m), ultimately half a select dozen 50-footers (15·2 m) were built (including *Knight Errant*, *Maid of Kent*, and *Leisure*) – all of which were of shallow-V hull bottom with one-piece mahogany sides and powered by six-cylinder Gray engines of Morris 'Navigator', 'Commodore' or 'Vedette' engines. So popular did this marque become that during one year the Bourne End yard was turning out as many as 20 to 25 slipper-stern launches. The more deluxe versions were fitted with wicker-work chairs, leather convertible tops, car head-lamps, car dashboard (walnut facia) and car steering wheels. Among the celebrities who owned a slipper-stern were the Maharajah of Jodhpur, Austin Seven racing driver Eric Gordon England, Louis Renault of French motorcar fame, comedian Max Miller, Benny Hill, the Beverly Sisters, and TV compere Michael Parkinson. Louis Renault sank his in the Seine when the Germans entered Paris, to stop it falling into their hands; the boat was recovered after the war and put back into service little the worse for submersion.

Andrews built an estimated 400 slipper-stern launches, many of which are today becoming collectors' pieces, with their woodwork being brought back to its former varnished elegance. At the same time, Andrews at Bourne End are running a hire-cruiser fleet under the *Sun* name (*Sun Tan*, *Sunglow*, *Sun Squaw*, etc.).

W. BATES & SON LTD

Established by James C. Taylor and William B. Bates at the turn of the century to build steam-boats on the River Thames at Chertsey Wharf, Surrey. During the Edwardian era, the company changed over to motorised river launches, pro-gressing to coastal motorboats and Admiralty motor-pinnaces of various sizes during World War I. Len Bates joined the yard in the early 1920s, having served an engineering apprentice-ship with Drummonds in Guildford. During the 1920s, James Taylor & Bates Ltd installed Gardner, Parsons and Brooke engines into their river launches and motor-cruisers, noted for their elegant lines, stemming from the blue-prints of the artistic William Bates; some ultra deluxe motorboats were constructed for the fabulously wealthy Indian Rajahs and Mahara-jahs. In 1934, after a bitter argument, the Taylor-Bates partnership came to an end, Taylor leaving to set up his new boatbuilding yard at Shoreham, whilst W. Bates & Son was now formed at Chertsey.

During World War II, as an Admiralty shipyard, Bates built air/sea rescue vessels, sea-plane tenders, marine target towers and harbour launches for the Forces.

Post-war, Len Bates designed a round-bilge Chrysler-engined 25 ft (7·6 m) motor-cruiser, along the lines of the American Richardson, which began to sell extremely well for £200 to £300 under the tradename Star Craft, and put a stop to the importation of expensive American motor-cruisers. As **the first popular post-war British-built motor-cruiser** between 1946 and 1976, some 150 wood-built Star Craft (between 25 ft (7·6 m) and 47 ft (14·3 m) in length) have been built, then sold or hired-out at the Chertsey Yard. At the 1979 Boat Show, Bates were offer-ing the 'Astral 810 Sport' with twin diesels.

W. Bates & Son's Star Craft at Chertsey: 33 ft (10 m) Camelia IV, *30 ft (9·1 m)* Sulynna *and 25 ft (7·6 m)* Cintra *in 1957–58 (Motor Boat & Yachting)*

BERTHON BOAT COMPANY LTD

Wooden boats have been built on the site of this Lymington yard since Roman times. In 1819 Thomas Inman bought the yard and turned it into **the first known large pleasure and racing yacht yard in Britain**. In 1877 the Berthon Boat Company Ltd was founded by the Rev. E. L. Berton (a clerk in Holy orders, simply because he was the tenth son), a peer of the realm (Lord Dunsany), an MP, an Army officer and three solicitors, to build boats and 'other floating machines'. Their yard in Romsey flourished, building 7 ft (2·1 m) portable folding boats (the fore-runner in convenience of the inflatable dinghy). In 1917 H. G. May bought the Berthon Boat Company and in 1918 the Lymington Shipyard, and the Mays carry on the family business today. A number of large motor-cruisers were built at this yard between 1926 and 1935, among them the 25-ton, 54 ft (16·5 m) *Nefertari* for £2472 and the 55-ton *Onward* of 1934, as well as a number of 40 to 45 ft (12·2 to 13·7 m) auxiliary cutters down to a 16 ft (4·9 m) fast motor-launch for the Hon. Peter Beatty.

During the war the Berthon built some 223 vessels including some motor-torpedo boats and harbour defence motor-launches.

In 1959 the Berthon built a 53 ft (16·2 m) motor-yacht, designed by Arthur Robb, for Lord Craigmyle as a tender for the America's Cup Challenge Races. During the 1960s the yard was turning out motor-sailers, such as the 60 ft (18·3 m) *Eskasoni*, built for Col. John MacKeen of Halifax, Nova Scotia.

THE BRITISH POWER BOAT COMPANY (BPBC)

In 1927 Hubert Scott-Paine, the wealthy aeronautical/seaplane designer/entrepreneur, joined forces with the wealthy Noel van Raalte to purchase a small, neglected shipyard at Hythe, beside Southampton Waters, from Robert Kemp for £5000. His aim: to bring success and pride back to British motorboat/marine engine-building, and to promote the hard-chine hull for defence purposes.

Although in the early 1920s this 36-year-old Sussex man had raced a Beardmore aero-engined craft called *Tiddly-Winks* and also achieved recent success with the 30 ft (9·1 m) Saunders-built six-cylinder 250 hp Siddeley-Puma-engined *Panther I, II* and *III*, he and van Raalte began by offering first 13 ft (4 m) and then 16 ft (4·9 m) clinker-built outboard-engined dinghies. During the 1927–28 Season, the *Panther I* won nine first prizes and two seconds in the eleven races for which S-P had entered her, and Scottie was able to sell several Puma-Class boats to a passenger-carrying service at Brighton Pier. By this time he had also begun construction of assembly-line techniques and by the end of 1928, outboard dinghies were being exported from the Hythe yard.

With design assistance from Fred Cooper (see p. 147) the embryo BPBC built several 12–14 ft (3·7–4·3 m) boats, powered by marinised Riley motorcar engines fitted at their stern, known as the 'Puppy Dog' Class. In 1929, from Fred Cooper's elaborate design work, the Hythe yard built the revolutionary 26 ft (8 m) single-stepper, *Miss England I*, whose 900 hp Napier Lion aero-engine turned a single propeller at an unheard-of 6500 rpm – Scott-Paine also helped Segrave to race this 90 mph (145 km/h) speedboat during that season. By the end of 1929, the BPBC was equipped with multi-frames, jigged and patterned ensuring replica construction, and the first fast motor-cruisers were built. In 1930, Scott-Paine won the Detroit News Trophy in his 20 ft (6 m) aerodynamically streamlined single-seater hydroplane, *Miss Britain I*, at 40 mph (65 km) powered by a standard 120 hp US Scripps engine, to comply with the $5\frac{1}{2}$ litre Class regulations; but by this time, he had already bought up and was modernising the Meadows Motor Company to produce 100 hp 'Power' marine engines, for the hulls, being replica-produced at Hythe.

By the summer of 1931, after two years of negotiations, Scott-Paine was successful in persuading the Air Ministry to commission some 16 $37\frac{1}{2}$ ft (11·4 m) seaplane tenders for the RAF. By the beginning of August, six of these boats were nearing completion when the old, timber-built premises of BPBC were rased to the ground in an accidental fire, and two years of work was destroyed in two hours. But within two months, Scott-Paine and his 300 employees had rebuilt a new, ultra-modern and totally fireproof yard with concrete, steel and corrugated iron; there was even a custom-built canteen – possibly the

Baron Louis Empain's 60 mph (96 km/h), £5000 runabout, Blue Peter *(Bill Sheaff)*

first in the UK. The construction of the RAF boats was recommenced and the original delivery dates were kept, alongside the marketing of a 16 ft (4·9 m) 8–28 hp utility speedboat, the *'Power' Sea Trump*, which was the first high-speed boat to be used by the Royal Navy, on loan from the RAF.

In 1933, Scott-Paine not only designed and built the revolutionary 1375 hp Napier Lion aero-engined *Miss Britain III*, which became **the first single-engined hydroplane to achieve an official 100·132 mph (161·147 km/h) in the offshore conditions** of the Solent, but also built *Blue Peter*, a special 27½ ft (8·4 m) runabout, capable of achieving over 60 mph (96 km/h) from her 500 hp Power Sea Lion engine, for which Baron Louis Empain paid £5000. At the same time, the BPBC was offering some 15 different types of motorboat ranging from 15 to 37½ ft (4·6–11·4 m), named *Sea Ace, Sea King, Sea Queen, Sea Jack, Sea Trump* (after a pack of cards), and also *Sea Emperor, Sea Monarch, Sea Rover, Sea Swift, Sea Swallow*, etc. These boats were installed with 'Power' engines developing from 8–28 hp, 12–48 hp, 100–110 hp and 500 hp. The 37½ ft (11·4 m) pleasure motorboat was but a modified version of a series of armoured target boats built that year for the RAF, and powered by three 100 hp engines driving three propellers to give a maximum speed of 24 knots.

In 1934, the first direct order placed by the Admiralty with the BPBC was for a triple-engined Admiral's motor-barge (LOA 45 ft (13·7 m) × B 9½ ft (2·9 m) × D 2⅓ ft (0·7 m)) for the Commander-in-Chief, Devonport, to replace the outdated, expensively maintained steam launch still in use. The company also built a batch of 25 ft (7·6 m) fast motor cabin cruisers for destroyers, a 35 ft (10·7 m) twin-engined seaplane tender and a 45 ft (13·7 m) triple-engined picket boat. After profound discussion, only made more immediate by the Abyssinian crisis of 1935, in 1936 six Scott-Paine-designed 60 ft (18·3 m) motor-torpedo boats, each powered by three 500 hp Power Sea Lion engines, were built at Hythe, designated the PV4's; during the latter part of 1936 and 1937, another 18 of these vessels were built. These were **the first fleets of High-Speed Motor-Torpedo Boats to go into service with the British Admiralty.** Also by 1937, BPBC had completed some 64 motor-vessels for airlines between England, Africa and Australia, including some 30 Imperial Airways police tugs, and a fast 45 ft (13·7 m) Air Route patrol boat with a range of over 900 miles (1450 km). Early in 1938, the company received a contract from the Air Ministry for 32 boats – 25 38-footers (11·6 m) and the remainder, 64-footers (19·5 m). Late that year the first six motor-torpedo boats went to the Mediterranean, via a stormy Bay of

Biscay, under their own power – the then **longest journey undertaken by high-speed boats**; by this time, a 60-footer (18·3 m) had also been modified into the express cruiser *Kalan* for Lord Strathcona.

By the end of 1938, assisted by a design team headed by George Selman, Scott-Paine had successfully developed, at his own cost, a 70 ft (21·3 m) motor-torpedo boat, powered by three Rolls-Royce Power Merlin engines, developing a total 3000 hp and giving the boat a speed of over 50 mph (80 km/h). Although other Navies bought this larger version in large numbers, the British Admiralty were not interested and in September 1939 Scott-Paine left Hythe with his motor-torpedo boat for America, where a building licence had soon been sold to the Electric Launch Company, who began to build the 70-footer (21·3 m) as the PT9, eventually extending its length to 77 ft (23·5 m) and then 80 ft (24·4 m). Meanwhile, by 1942–43, Scott-Paine had built up from scratch the Canadian Power Boat Company Ltd in Montreal, where triple Packard marinised aero-engines, developing 1250 hp, were installed in Canadian motor-torpedo boats, air/sea rescue boats and armoured target boats built on an improved assembly-line system by some 1400 Canadian employees, with one boat being produced per week. Simultaneously in England, the first 72 ft (22 m) 'Whaleback' motor-gunboat was successfully designed by George Selman and built at Hythe by the BPBC, followed by another nine motor-gunboats, followed by a further 69, each fitted with three imported Packard marine units. The output of Scott-Paine's British and American companies was notably prodigious.

The biggest boat that the British company ever built was the *Long Range*, a 110 ft (33·5 m) air/sea rescue boat, with a wooden hull of 30 ft (9·1 m) beam which was to be powered by four Bristol Hercules aero-engines, totalling 6600 hp to give a speed of 45 knots. £100 000 of development work went into this prototype, but the end of the war put a stop to her completion, and post-war her hull was sold-off as a houseboat for £700!

In 1945, refusing to return to peacetime commercial and pleasure motorboat-building, Scott-Paine as sole director closed down the Canadian and British Power Boat Companies that he had spearheaded, and retired to Greenwich, Connecticut where, after a series of severe strokes, he died in 1954, aged only 63 years old.

CAMPER & NICHOLSONS

It was towards the end of the 18th century, definitely after 1782, that Benjamin Nicholson became an apprentice at Mr Camper's boatyard in Gosport. When Camper died without issue, the yard went under the sole ownership of the Nicholson family, whilst retaining the name Camper & Nicholsons (hereafter referred to as 'C & N'). From building Royal Naval pinnaces, C & N became increasingly involved with pleasure yachts, but because of their berth limitations, tended to have their designs realised locally, whilst completing the yachts' trimmings in their own yard.

One of the first private steam yachts recorded in the 1890s, was Mr Whittaker's *Angela*, whose interior was fitted out with rich panelling and tapestries. Day Summers steam machinery with coal-fired boiler was installed.

In 1903, *Romola*, a 65-ton, 75 ft (22·8 m) private yacht built for Capt. Sanderson, was initially fitted with steam then subsequently with a Thornycroft paraffin engine; the modification allowed for additional sleeping cabins in place of the boiler forward of amidships.

In 1908, SY *Sagitta* (LOA 211 ft (64·3 m)), 756 tons, was designed and built for the Duc de Valency. Featuring a clipper-cut water stem, *Sagitta* proved to be one of the finest sea-going yachts of her time and served in both world wars.

The last true steam yacht was the 234 ft (71·3 m), 900-ton *Marynthea*, built in 1911 for H. J. Mason. Her hull and steam machinery were built by Thornycroft, whilst her design and luxurious fitting-out were by C & N. Subsequently re-named *Emerald*, then *Conqueror*, during her lengthy career, amongst her owners were the late Mr Gordon Selfridge and Sir Hugo Cunliffe Owen.

The first power yacht to be equipped with diesel engines was the 165 ft (50·3 m) *Pioneer* of 400 tons. Designed and built by C & N for American millionaire Parry Singer, *Pioneer* was originally constructed with the engine exhaust being carried up inside the mast, although later on a funnel was added. (With her diesel engines having provided exceptional long-distance patrolling capacities during World War I, *Pioneer* was subsequently purchased by the Crown Agents for the Colonies, and after an extensive re-fit, became the Governor's yacht in the Fiji Islands.) She was eventually scuppered by the authorities.

Aware of their building limitations, towards the end of the 1914–18 war, C & N purchased larger yard facilities, including sizeable berths and slipways where vessels of up to 265 ft (80·7 m) LOA could be constructed. **One of the largest motor-yachts** to be built at the new yard was the MY *Ara*, commissioned in 1917 by M. Irwin Hériot. Of 870 tons, she was 213 ft (65 m) long. As *Ara* neared completion M. Hériot loaned her to his Government, who equipped her with two equivalent 6 in guns. Following Armistice, *Ara* was purchased by the fabulously wealthy W. K. Vanderbilt, thoroughly improved, then taken on a worldwide cruise, Miami to Miami, during which Vanderbilt indulged in his hobby of studying tropical fish.

Throughout this period and during the following decades, much of the design work was carried out by a team headed by the brilliant Charles Nicholson and realised by some of the finest craftsmen families in England.

In 1922, MY *Sona* was built for Lord Dunraven; *Sona*'s smoking-room incorporated an open wood-burning stove and from the time of her commissioning, the logs of *lignum vitae* for the stove were specially cut and supplied by C & N. She was powered by a twin-screw oil engine, manufactured by Vickers Petters Ltd of Ipswich (see p. 183).

In 1926, C & N built *Alastor*, the first in a series of successive yachts which were to be commissioned from them by the aviation magnate, Sir Tom Sopwith. In 1937, *Philante I* was built for Sopwith. Of 1629 tons, LOA 273 ft (83·2 m), she was **the largest twin-screw diesel steel motor-yacht built during that period in Great Britain**, and was equipped with the most magnificent and luxurious accommodation. One of the most striking aspects was her internal staircase with its 'barley sugar twist', the balustrading being both left- and right-handed. Panelled in matching American walnut, the lounge itself was set off by four display alcoves in each corner, and in order to achieve the de-

Sir Tom Sopwith's Philante *(built 1937), the then largest twin-screw diesel, steel, luxury motor yacht in Great Britain (Beken of Cowes Ltd)*

sired 'domed-cabinet' effect, the top of the alcoves was fitted with beaten copper, prior to fixing the walnut veneer to match the rest of the panelling. A unique collection of quartz *objets d'art* were displayed within these alcoves. *Philante I* is still considered by C & N to be one of the most remarkable boats they ever created. Following Government requisition for wartime work, she was bought and completely re-fitted by donations from the Norwegian people as a gift for King Haakon VII, to demonstrate their appreciation for his most principled wartime leadership. She was re-named *Norge* and became the Royal Yacht. A further five *Philante*'s have since been commissioned by the Sopwith family.

During World War II, C & N built in excess of 900 vessels of a defence type as part of the war effort, including seventeen 117 ft (35·7 m) C & N Motor-Torpedo Boats, each powered by triple Packard aero-engines.

Post-war, C & N retained their almost unique ability to fit out lavish and luxurious interiors for their motor-yachts. On board *Chambelle IV*, the dining-room was panelled in teak, featuring 1100 ft (335 m) of in-laid gold strip! The *Beatrice of Bolivia* incorporated exquisite mahogany panelling inlaid with ivory strips of 3 and 7 mm width! These are just two examples.

C & N launched their first fgrp family motor-yacht in the early 1970s: the 75 ft (22·9 m) *Lady Galaderiel*. Today they are still producing some of the most sophisticated and beautifully appointed yachts to be launched at a British yard – either in welded steel, laminated wood or fgrp, from 75–135 ft (22·9–41·1 m). They also hold the Royal Warrant as yacht builders to HM the Queen.

The longest serving employee with Camper & Nicholsons is Mr Wally West, who began his 14-year apprenticeship with the company on 10 March 1924. By 1939 he was a charge-hand of the shipwrights, and at present is projects manager. His stated reason for 55 years' service was the friendliness of the Nicholson family fostering a happy atmosphere at the yard.

CHRIS-CRAFT

During the 1870s, whilst helping out his black-smith father at Algonac, Michigan (USA), the teenage Christopher Columbus Smith began carving short, broad, flat duck decoys. This gave him the idea of making a boat hull of the same shape, which would ride through the water more swiftly. From 1881 Chris Smith and his brother Henry built the fastest skiffs, rowboats and sailboats on the local St Clair River. From the mid 1890s, Smith began to power his boats with simple gasoline engines, capable of 9 mph (15 km/h), and by 1906 he had purchased some van Blerck engines and progressed to a 26 ft (7·9 m) inboard capable of nearly 20 mph (32 km/h). At the 1910 New York Boat Show, Smith exhibited a 29 ft (8·8 m) *Queen Reliance* with a price tag of $100 per mile speed – or 35 mph (56 km/h). In 1911 the Smith-Ryan Boat Co. built three 150 hp Sterling-engined single-step hydroplanes, called *Baby Reliance*. *Baby Reliance III* clocked a race speed of 53·7 mph (86·4 km/h) as the then fastest boat in the USA. In 1913, on John Ryan's bankruptcy, Smith broke away and with his four sons formed the C. C. Smith Boat & Engineering Company. In

Christopher Columbus Smith, founder of Chris-Craft (1861–1939)

1915, financed by the Miss Detroit Powerboat Association, Smith built the 250 hp Sterling-engined *Miss Detroit I* which captured the American Power Boat Association Gold Cup and was bought by the wealthy Gar Wood. Backed by Wood, Smith now built two further Miss Detroit hydroplanes, and in 1920 the Liberty aero-engined *Miss America I* with which Gar Wood won the Harmsworth Trophy and achieved speeds over 75 mph (120 km/h).

By this time, Smith had purchased large quantities of war-surplus aero-engines, especially the Curtis OX-5 'Jenny' engine, which enabled the company to keep the price of its runabouts competitively low. When these engines ran out, they installed Packard, Chrysler and Kermath engines, until 1925 when they built their own – and one of the first – V8 marine engines, developing 250 hp. Apart from satisfied customers – Charlie Chaplin, Vincent Astor, Walter Chrysler and Harvey Firestone – even the legendary Al Capone used a fleet of Smith's runabouts for his rum-running escapades of Prohibition days. In 1930 the company became known as the 'Chris-Craft' Corporation (a tradename originally coined by Chris Smith's son, Hamilton, in 1922 and destined for several decades to become a worldwide household synonym for the word motorboat) and was the first boatbuilding company to design and construct machines and jigs for the mass-production of motorboats. Before long, the Corporation was geared up to build 1000 wood boats a year, ranging in size from $15\frac{1}{2}$ to 48 ft (4·7 to 14·6 m), divided mainly into three styles – runabouts, cruisers and utility boats, not to mention the occasional elegant motor-yacht; all boats were double-planked in mahogany. Distribution was throughout the world by 250 dealers (the English agent was Arthur Bray Ltd). In 1939, the year that Christopher Columbus Smith ('The Dean of American Standardised Boatbuilding') died, his Corporation was offering some 115 different models for sale.

During World War II, Chris-Craft produced up to 14000 military landing craft and the three major plants at Algonac, Cadillac and Holland (Michigan) all received 'E' awards for excellence by the Army and Navy.

The first Chris-Craft boats to be fitted with fgrp trimmings were the 18 and 21 ft (5·5 and 6·4 m) Cobra series, featuring fgrp deck and golden fin, marketed from 1955. In 1957 Chris-Craft moved its administrative offices to Pompano Beach, Florida and later became the major subsidiary of the NAFI Corporation and changed its name to Chris-Craft Industries. The first all-fgrp Chris-Craft runabout was the 19 ft (5·8 m) Silver Arrow, marketed in 1959. The first all-fgrp Chris-Craft motor-cruiser was launched in 1964. Today, Chris-Craft produces motorboats, largely in aluminium, from 17 to 74 ft (5·2 to 22·6 m). It is estimated that since 1894 some 100000 Chris-Craft motorboats have been built and sold.

FLETCHER

When he entered a Mercury '28'-powerboat for his first race as a hobby in 1959, Norman Fletcher was professionally designing and marketing model aircraft and boats in a small shop in West Bromwich, Staffordshire, England. The following year he decided to build his own small sportsboat, incorporating a revolutionary lapstrake design, which enabled him to compete on equal footing against powerboats with much greater engine capacity.

In 1964, using their model-making experience for forming shapes and producing a good 'finish', Fletcher Marine developed the lapstrake/fgrp 12 ft (3·7 m) runabout called the Arrow 120 ('Fletcher' means 'Arrow-maker'). That same year, together with Lionel Vizor as navigator, Norman Fletcher raced his *White Tornado*, a standard Arrow 140 production boat, powered by a 50 hp Mercury, to win the first Class III Championships with a spectacular 1800 points out of a possible 2000 – as against the

Norman Fletcher, after winning the 1964 Southend Festival Race, pictured with Lionel Viser in White Tornado *(a Fletcher Arrow 140) (Mike Peters)*

runner-up's 880 points. From 1965 onwards, always testing their designs under the most severe conditions on the Welsh coast, and racing standard models for publicity, Fletcher began to forge ahead with the deep-V design for 14-footers (4·3 m), and ultimately 17-footers (5·2 m). The late 1960s saw the rise of British and European waterski racing, and Fletcher power-boats towed winning skiers to victory on many occasions, becoming renowned for their sea-worthiness in testing Channel conditions. Variously named *Arrow Man, Arrowbolt, Arrowflyt, Arrowsport, Arrowstreak, Arrowbeau,* by this time the prolific Fletcher output was distributed worldwide from a larger factory at Burntwood, Staffordshire. Never ever having built a hull in wood, by the mid-1970s, over 25000 Fletcher motorboats had been moulded. In 1976, Fletcher Marine adopted the new tradename of 'Zingaro', a word used round the Mediterranean coasts for 'Gypsy'; the first Zingaro was the *Flying Bridge,* followed in 1977 by the *Zingaro Express* and the *Zingaro Sedan,* all three of which were 26 ft (8 m) in length. The *Zingaro Sprint* was first exhibited at the 1979 Boat Show.

In May 1978 a 28 hp Yamaha outboard-engined, 13 ft (4 m) 'Arrowsprint 129' made the first recorded clockwise 1798-mile (2890 km) circumnavigation of Britain in 13 days. The boat was accompanied by Yamaha-engined *Arrowflyte* and *Arrowsport* and also by a *Zingaro Express.* This is **the first circumnavigation of Britain by a boat of this size**.

In June 1978, tests were performed on **the first British Kevlar-built motorboat**, which was a 175hp Mercury-engined Arrowshaft 25 Class II powerboat (see p. 174).

GLASTRON

In 1956, Robert R. Hammond, formerly general manager of the fgrp division of a Dallas-based boat company, launched Standard Glass Products with 4000 sq ft of rented space in Austin, Texas; he was backed by 11 associates to $22000 and began with three employees, one of whom was a designer called Mel Whitley. 1957, the first production year saw an output of some 900 units of only one model – the 15 ft (4·6 m) Fireflite, offered in three colours. The name Glastron was coined in 1960 by Bob Hammond's wife and

Robert R. Hammond (left) with Glastron designer, Mel Whitley

combines 'glas' for fgrp and 'tron' as a reference to modern-day technology. In 1962 Glastron was one of the inboard/outboard pioneers with the first Volvo-Penta engines installed, whilst at the same time introducing the first deep-V aqua-lift hulls to small pleasure boats. Hammond personally tested his products by racing them. By 1965, Glastron had won more than 50 national race victories including the 1962 Salton Sea '500', the 1962, 1963, and 1964 265-mile (426 km) Long Island Marathon, the 1963 and 1964 Hudson River Marathon, the 1965 Orange Bowl six-hour Regatta, etc. In 1967 Glastron introduced three new 'Swinger' models of open-bow design. By 1969 the company had 800 employees and supplied boats to 1200 dealers in 50 states and 38 foreign countries through 29 distributors; licensees also built Glastron boats in GB, Spain, Finland, Trinidad, South Africa and Australia. The 1970s saw an ever-increasing output, together with the introduction of the Aqua-Lift II Tri-Hull, the Walk-Through Windshield and the SSV hull – all developed by a design team headed by Mel Whitley. By 1978, with 1400 employees in a huge plant in north-west Austin, with their Spanish-based **largest pleasure boat plant in Europe** and several other factories, Glastron were producing an average of 70 boats per day and could offer 43 different models ranging from 15 ft (4·6 m) runabouts and bassboats to 27 ft (8·2 m) cruisers; this made the company **the world's largest manufacturer of small fgrp boats**. Their **most popular selling model** has been the T-166, 15 ft (4·6 m) Sportster.

Henley Regatta (July 1921): The Prince of Wales (later King Edward VIII) is seated in Magician's *prow, wearing the straw boater (Geo Bushell & Son)*

HOBBS & SONS LTD OF HENLEY

Established by H. E. ('Harry') Hobbs in 1870 at Wharf Lane, Henley-on-Thames, and helped by his sons Bill, Arthur, Fred, Frank, Ernest and Bert (apart from their five sisters). During the late 19th century the Hobbs family hired out punts and rowing skiffs and also served as a charging station for electric launches. The Company of Hobbs & Sons Ltd was registered in 1902 when the Mill Meadows site was taken over and a boatyard constructed. Hobbs bought up and stationed themselves at East & Co. of Shiplake in 1907, Ellis & Co. of Goring in 1908 and the S. E. Saunders Ltd, Springfield Works at Goring in 1911. The first petrol-driven launch to be owned by Hobbs was the *Sunstar*. In 1914, following the tunnel-stern design set by S. E. Saunders Ltd with his *Consuta*, Hobbs built the *Enchantress* (LOA 49 ft (15 m) × B 7 ft (2·1 m) × D 2 ft (0·6 m)), powered by a Sunbeam Straight Eight engine for 20 knot speeds, and to be used as an Umpire's launch at Henley Royal Regatta. In 1920, Hobbs brothers also took on the task of pile-driving for the Henley Regatta and in 1921 they built a second Umpire Launch,

Magician, powered by a six-cylinder Sunbeam, followed in 1928 by the four-cylinder Wolseley-engined *Amaryllis*.

When the **Oxford *v* Cambridge Varsity Boat Race was broadcast for the first time** in 1927, the transmitter was specially built for the broadcast. The *Magician* was hired and four points along the river were selected as reception points. The range of the transmitter on the launch was so uncertain and so limited that the commentary was picked up by each point in turn as the *Magician* came within range. Two masts were erected on the launch with a horizontal aerial slung between them. The gear on board weighed about a 1000 lb; the gentlemen on board also weighed a good deal – there were four engineers, two commentators, a pilot, a ship's engineer and a BBC programme representative. At that time, and for many years afterwards, those on the launch had no idea whether the commentary was being picked up and broadcast success-fully. As the launch passed the receiving points along the river, visual signals were exchanged between the engineers aboard and those on the roofs of buildings at the reception points.

Scaled-down private versions of these elegant

Vosper MTB 102 (built 1938) restored and currently maintained by the 1st Blofield & Brundall Sea Scout Group, Norfolk (Courtesy Brian Ollington)

HMS Cutlass, HMS Sabre and HMS Scimitar, 100 ft (30·5 m) Fast Training Boats (40 knots) with twelve-crew compliment, in manoeuvres off the South Coast (RN photo)

The Fighting Temeraire *tugged to her last berth to be broken up, 1838, by J. W. M. Turner (National Gallery)*

Capt. Sir Ranulph T-W-Fiennes Bt. during the first ever hovercraft ascent of the White Nile in 1969 (Courtesy Capt. Fiennes)

and highly popular river launches, were the Arethusa, the Elsie, the Thelma and the Gorka.

The £4000 Bosporous, built in 1953 to exactly the same design and quality as her sister launches, is reported to have been paid for by William Morris (Lord Nuffield) and installed with a 100 hp Austin Skipper engine developing 3500 rpm; simultaneously the Enchantress, Magician and Amaryllis were re-engined with Austin Skippers. Since then these famous launches have always been present at the Varsity Boat Race, Henley Royal Regatta and several other Thames festivities.

In 1958, Hobbs & Sons began their hire cruiser fleet with the 24 ft (7·3 m) Girl Pat and Girl Jean, followed by Girl Marian, Girl Vanessa, Girl Ravena, Girl Nicola, and finally, Girl Lutena in 1968.

MORGAN GILES

In 1920 F. C. Morgan Giles took over the derelict Mansfield yard near the mouth of the River Teign, Devon and began designing and building yachts, using local labour. During the inter-war years, the Morgan Giles yard became famous for finely built yachts, including the Hibernia IV, built for King Alfonso of Spain. In 1938, the yard was entrusted with repair work for the Admiralty and shortly afterwards awarded contracts for new building. By the end of World War II, vessels constructed by the 150-strong company included some 50 pinnaces, 8 motor-torpedo boats and 4 harbour defence motor-launches. In 1942, the Carissima, one of the largest yachts built in Teignmouth since the turn of the century, was registered for a local owner.

In 1957, after consultation with George Selman (formerly of British Power Boat Company), Cdr C. F. Parsons, J. Collier and R. Shorland of Morgan Giles designed one of the first monohedron-hulled motor-cruisers to be seen in the UK. The first 35-footer (10·7 m), powered by twin 120 hp Volvo Penta inboards was called the Monaco cruiser, delivered to a Mr Oppenheim in Monaco. Between 1957 and 1969, some 80 to 90 'Monaco cruisers' were timber-built at the Teignmouth yard using Canadian rock elm 'hoop' framing and a water-tight skin of seraya plywood panels.

Starting with three 27-footers (8·2 m) and six 35-footers (10·7 m), the yard progressed to a 36-footer (11 m), initially installing twin Perkins S6 diesels, but progressing to twin Rootes-Lister two-stroke TS3's developing 110 bhp. Altogether some 35 to 40 of this size were built in the Monaco Class. Powered by General Motors and Caterpillar diesels, 42-footers (12·8 m) developing 270 bhp, followed. Powered by 200 hp Caterpillars, 48-footers (14·6 m), reached some 34 knots, and were built alongside a number of 52-footers (15·8 m), powered by either triple TS3 engines or twin General Motors developing 250 bhp each. The quality of these hulls was kept to the pre-war standards set by Morgan Giles.

The first 'Monaco' cruiser, built by Morgan Giles in 1957 (Cdr C. F. Parsons)

In 1963 the yard also built a 75 ft (22·9 m) fast patrol boat, the *Gay Charger*, for the Navy.

In 1966 the Teignmouth yard got into financial difficulties and was taken over by Thomas Roberts of Westminster. When current Chairman John Roberts who had ploughed a lot of money into the firm was killed in a car crash in 1968, his executors decided to close down the Teignmouth yard.

But in 1968, Morgan Giles had set up a second yard at Warsash, whence they built some 50 fgrp canal boats for the Inland Waterways – the largest LOA 45 ft (13·7 m) × B 6 ft (1·8 m). This yard was also sold in 1976.

Today the name of Morgan Giles continues at Rushton in Northamptonshire, where hydraulic transmissions are manufactured for marine craft.

WILLIAM OSBORNE LTD

William Osborne Sr (1880–1931) served his apprenticeship with the Motor Supply Company in Piccadilly, London, and formed his own company to custom-build motorcar bodies in 1912, moving to premises in Long Acre. By this time he was a member of both the Royal Motor Yacht Club and the Sussex Motor Yacht Club, and he raced a Buick-engined Saunders 21-footer (6·4 m) called *Frigidy Pedibus* ('Cold Feet').

After World War I, Osborne moved down to

Ma Joie, first motor-cruiser ever built by William Osborne Ltd (1919)

the River Arun at Littlehampton, West Sussex and with some of his motor craftsmen, together with local long-established boatbuilding families, built their first 40 ft (12·2 m) motor-cruiser to a Cox & King design, which was towed up to London by steam tractor and exhibited at the 1920 Motor Show at Olympia. This was soon sold and named *Ma Joie*, and during the rest of the year, 'William Osborne Ltd, Motor Yacht Builders and Motor Body Builders' constructed two 60-footers (18·3 m) (*Ma Joie II* and *Bonne Chance*). A boost to business came when Osborne built some 12 racing boats, powered by marinised Buick tractor-engines for the Sussex Motor Yacht Club. By this time, the 19-year-old William Osborne Jr was serving his apprenticeship in his father's drawing office. The Motor Body Building side was dropped in 1924 and the Johnson outboard-engined Osborne Speedcraft was marketed. Osborne Sr raced his own craft, *Miss Littlehampton*, at the major race meetings of the late 1920s. In 1930, although dying of cancer, Osborne saw the construction of his first Everyman motor-cruiser. During the next few years some six of these were built, together with a number of express motor-cruisers, powered by American four-cylinder 100 to 200 hp Scripps engines.

During World War II, Osbornes expanded their premises to build one Fairmile 'A', six 'B', one 'C' and 17 'D' type gunboats. Also as an Admiralty broadside slipway, they serviced 160 ft (48·8 m) steel tank-landing craft.

During the 1940s, Osbornes began to build for the RNLI and must take credit for building every wood prototype lifeboat to RNLI architects' designs ever since. In total they have built over 50 conventional lifeboats, including such well-known classes as the Watson 47 and the Oakley 37. Also, in 1945 the first of six 41 ft (12·5 m) Morris Commodore-engined cruisers were produced, named by William Osborne after the *Eagle*, and soon followed by the *Kestrel*, the *Swallow*, the *Swift*, the *Falcon*, and other motor-cruisers named after birds. The 20 ft (6·1 m) Snipe-Class aluminium cruiser was first built in 1951. **The largest boat ever built at Osbornes** was in 1963; it was called the *Blue Leopard* (LOA 111 ft 6 in (34 m) × B 19 ft (5·8 m) × D 9 ft 6 in (2·9 m)), powered by two Rolls-Royce diesel engines and capable of 15 knots either under power or sail alone.

Osbornes changed over to frgp boatbuilding techniques in the late 1960s with the *King Swift*, of which some 30 have been built. They are currently building diesel-powered inboard rigid inflatable boats (see p. 170).

The longest-serving employee with Osbornes was boatbuilder Leonard Ross, who started with the company in 1919 and left in 1977 after 58 years of service.

RAMPART BOAT WORKS

It was founded in 1919 by G. A. Desty (1885–1946) at Bitterne Manor, Southampton, site of the old Roman settlement – hence the name Rampart. After a decade of building sailing dinghies and small launches, when H. G. Desty joined his father's yard in 1927, plans were put in motion to build their first 30 ft (9·1 m) motor-cruiser, the *Teal*, powered by a Thornycroft DB2 engine. Rampart sea-going motor-cruisers, pine-built and powered by either Thornycroft or Gray marine engines, sold for £495 in the 1930s. One of these cruisers was built for the film-stars Douglas Fairbanks Jr and Gertrude Lawrence. Boats were built to stock and not only to commissions. In 1978 this yard was still building motor-cruisers using the old-fashioned methods of all-wood construction.

J. SAMUEL WHITE

Thomas White and family were building sailing ships at Broadstairs, Kent from the first half of the 17th century, progressing to steam launches from the 1840s, by which time the business had been established for almost 40 years at Cowes, Isle of Wight. John Samuel White became involved with the family business from 1860. Yard Number 1 on the J. S. White list is dated to 1864 and was a steam-engined 'lifeboat' for the Ottoman (Turkish) Navy. During the next two decades J. S. White were building torpedo boats, installed with either Ballis or Maudslay or Penn reciprocating steam engines, until 1889 when they began to build their own engines. From 1897 the White-Foster water-tube boiler achieved high praise from progressive engineers for its efficiency. Whites was one of the first firms to take a licence for the Parsons-type marine steam turbine.

The first motorboat built at Whites was a 30 ft (9·1 m) launch for Messrs Whitehead in 1904; she did not even qualify for a separate Yard Number and was given 1183 B. Four years and 64 steamboats later, Yard Number 1247 was a 60 ft (18·3 m) steel Harbour Launch for the British Admiralty, powered by a Mirlees diesel engine. Yard Number 1260 was a 36 ft (11 m) motor-canoe called *Firefly* for the Crown agents. White also began to build petrol and subsequently diesel-engined lifeboats. Small motor-craft were always to take second place to the construction of naval ships, destroyers, etc at J. W. Whites, although a fair number of motor-yachts and motor-cruisers were built during the inter-war years.

In 1926 Whites built the first Motor Landing Craft, to the designs of Mr Fleming of the Fleming lifeboat. Birmabright alloy was used and a powerplant of twin 120 hp Chryslers made a terrifying noise when propelling the hull!

In the mid-1930s, Whites built a small single-screw hydrofoil and impressed by its possibilities, boldly decided to construct a hydrofoil motor-torpedo boat. The £51 000 triple-engined *MTB 101* was lost three years after construction when one of the foil struts collapsed. Whites' designer during the inter-war years was George Carey. During this period they also built some 36 16-footer (4·9 m) Ford V8-engined motor-launches for use on destroyers.

During World War II, 25 destroyers, including the first all-welded hull, and over 300 other small type craft were built for the Royal Navy.

Shipbuilding was discontinued in 1965 for economic reasons and the yard at East Cowes sold to the British Hovercraft Corporation. Since then the company has concentrated on the manufacture of heavy industrial turbines and compressors – being re-named Elliott Turbo-machinery Ltd from April 1977.

S. E. SAUNDERS LTD

Founded in the 1830s by Moses Saunders at Streatley on Thames (Berks) to build and repair weirs and locks, they progressed to building fine skiffs and punts under his son, Cornelius

Saunders. By 1880 Samuel Edgar Saunders (1856–1933) of Streatley and Goring had built his first steam launch, *Thistle*, following very soon with some electric launches. During the 1890s the Saunders' Springfield Works built a number of steam, electric and Daimler launches, including *Hera*, *Maritana*, *Mariposa* and an electric pinnace for HM Yacht *Victoria and Albert*. The Saunders Patent Launch Building Syndicate, formed by Saunders and a group of local craftsmen on the success of their Consuta system (see p. 154), now began building both petrol and paraffin-engined launches. As these building techniques had much to offer to sea-going motorboats, in 1901 Sam Saunders and a nucleus of craftsmen moved down to Cowes, Isle of Wight to establish a second boatbuilding yard. During the next few years Saunders-built motorboats ranged from the *Rattler* (LOA 75 ft (22·9 m) × B 12 ft (3·7 m) × D 3½ ft (1·1 m)), powered by two 60 hp Gardner paraffin engines, and in 1905 claimed as **the largest British motor-boat**; down to the 80 hp 40-footer (12 m) *Napier* racing launch, capable of a speed of 23 knots. On the expiration of the Syndicate in 1906, Sam Saunders started on his own again at the Columbine Yard, East Cowes, Isle of Wight. In 1908, S. E. Saunders Ltd was formed, with a part interest held by the Wolseley Tool and Motor Car Company.

Up to 1914 the yard turned out some of the most famous and successful racing motorboats of that era. The 49 ft (14·9 m) 720 hp twin-Wolseley-engined *Ursula* (1909) became **the first displacement motorboat to reach 35 knots**. The 40 ft (12·2 m) *Pioneer* (1910) became **the first single-engined hydroplane to attain 40 knots**. The 40 ft (12·2 m), 360 hp Austin-engined *Maple Leaf IV* became **the first multi-step hydroplane to reach 50 mph (80 km/h)**. The Wolseley-engined *Angela II* (1913) became **the most successful racer in the British Motor Boat Club 21 ft (6·4 m) Class**. In 1912, Saunders built the *Bat Boat*, **the first amphibian flying boat in Europe**. Apart from building **the first motorboat for the British Admiralty**, and receiving a Royal Warrant as launch-builder to HM King George V, Sam Saunders also started building lifeboats for the RNLI (by the early 1930s no fewer than 45 motor and pulling/sailing lifeboats had gone into service).

During World War I, Saunders expanded considerably to build 210 Avro biplanes, 80 Short seaplanes, 24 NT2B flying-boats, 100 F2A flying-boats, several F5 flying-boats, 8 gondolas for airships, 416 sets of aeroplane and seaplane parts (equal to 200 completed machines), 116 flying-boat hulls, 389 seaplane floats and over 100 000 ft (30 500 m) of Consuta plywood.

A post-war slump in aircraft orders saw a return to high-speed racing motorboat construction, including the Puma-Class express launch. In 1928 S. E. Saunders Ltd was taken over by a syndicate and became Saunders-Roe Ltd ('Saro'). Apart from the *Miss England II* hydroplane and Sir Malcolm Campbell's first *Bluebird*

Launching a racing motorboat from Sam Saunders' yard on the Isle of Wight (1904) (Veteran Car Club)

Sam Saunders held a Royal Warrant as Launch-Builder to HM King George V, with whom he is seen here

hydroplane, from now on the company became totally involved with aircraft.

This Bain-designed boat was built in 1939 and christened Jennifer-Ann

JAMES A. SILVER (ROSNEATH)

Boatbuilding at Rosneath on the Gare Loch, NW of Glasgow (Scotland) was initiated by Mr McLean in the early 1890s, continued by Mr Davidson in 1900, and by Jimmy Silver, the son of a local businessman from 1903–12. Under the last-named, the yard became known as James A. Silver. In 1912 this small yard was taken over by a syndicate and John Bain came as Yard Manager. After World War I, Bain began his Maple Leaf-type of hard-chine 25 to 30 ft (7·6 to 9·1 m) motor-cruisers. During 1926 Bain built a large ketch and in 1928–29 a larger schooner, which gained the yard a reputation in both the sailing and motor-cruising world.

The early 1930s saw the appearance of the 30 ft (9·1 m) 'Silverette' type motor-cruiser fitted with Morris Navigator (and later Commodore) petrol engines. John Bain, now a well-known motor-cruiser designer became the first man to introduce the self-drive type of motor-cruiser. It was a novel experience in 1932 to come down, step aboard one's yacht, press a self-starter and control everything from the wheelhouse. Silver Productions now ranged from a 12 ft (3·7 m) motor-dinghy, to 22 ft (6·7 m) Stuart-engined auxiliary yacht, to a twin 38 hp Gardner diesel-engined 56 ft (17·1 m) motor-yacht. By 1937, after expansion, some six slip-ways were in full-time operation. To attract skilled labour to a somewhat outback area, Bain even built a block of eight modern flats, following up with another block of four houses a couple of years later, by which time the international famous yard of James A. Silver (Rosneath) was building both refrigeration/cargo-type motor-vessels, as well as the 'Brown Owl Class' of yacht, for which 52 ft (15·8 m) was a popular length.

During World War II, the yard expanded further to build motor-torpedo boats and Fairmile gunboats of from 100 to 120 ft (30 to 37 m) length, as well as harbour launches, naval cutters and dinghies. Post-war, John Bain branched out again with the world-famous 'Ormadale' class of yacht, as well as many other famous luxury motor-yachts up to 80 ft (24·4 m) long. In 1957, Bain sold the yard to another syndicate of which John Boyd became Managing Director, and during the next decade the yard stepped up its boatbuilding activities to both steel and timber boats from 96 to 112 ft (29·3 to 34·1 m) LOA.

In 1969–70 the firm went into voluntary liquidation and it was not until June 1977 that the old yard was officially re-opened as D. M. Russell Marine (Rosneath) Ltd, Mr Russell's ambition being to restore the yard to its pre-war glory. In conjunction with G. L. Watson (Naval Architects), a 35 ft (10·7 m) fgrp motor-sailer of the traditional Scottish fishing boat type, with superstructure, deck and interior in wood, was launched in January 1978 and sold immediately.

8 BOAT SHOWS

The Monaco Motor Launch Exhibition was held annually from 1904–14, when 100 to 140 boats were exhibited and demonstrated by racing (RTHPL)

The first Trade Exhibition to include a section for motorboats was the 1902 Paris Automobile Salon where there was a Marine Motor Section. In 1903 the Thames Boating Trades Association Ltd organised a Boating Exhibition at Earls Court and amongst those exhibiting were Vosper & Co. (today part of the Vosper-Thornycroft group). In February 1905 some 180 000 sq. ft of Olympia was devoted to a motorboat section as part of the Automobile Exhibition, held under the auspices of the Society of Motor Manufacturers and Traders. There were 29 'Constructors and Launch Motor Makers' in addition to those showing accessories, and 22 boats were displayed. During that year there were, for the first time, special motorboat sections at the Brussels Automobile Salon, the Crystal Palace Automobile Exhibition, the Berlin Automobile

Fiat motorboat at the New York Boat Show 1904

Salon, the Monaco Motor Boat Race Meeting, the Copenhagen Automobile Exhibition – whilst **the first US National Boat Show was held in New York** at the old Madison Square Garden.

During the March 1907 Commercial Motor Show in England, a motorboat Section saw 35 exhibitors and 29 boats, including one steamer. Until 1953 the Boat Show always formed part of the London Motor Show – whether this was held in the Agricultural Halls (Islington), then at Olympia (Kensington) and finally at the Earls Court Exhibition Hall. In 1953 the demand for space at the Motor Show from the motor manufacturers, made it impossible for the boat section to expand and the Ship and Boat Builders' National Federation decided to organise a separate Boat Show at the Empire Hall Olympia on 30 December 1954. In 1955 National Boat Shows Ltd was formed, with the sponsorship of the *Daily Express* (Beaverbrook Newspapers) to operate and run the show. In 1955 some 120 851 people visited the 45 exhibitors at this Show. In 1960, the Boat Show moved to the much larger Exhibition Building at Earls Court. In 1972 a record number of 338 451 people visited the Show. In 1974 there were a record 466 exhibitors and in 1977 there were a record 17 011 foreign visitors. Since 1966 features in the Olympic Swimming Pool at Earls Court have included Old Amsterdam (1966), Inland Waterways (1967), Malta (1968), Ireland (1969), France

Marine Section of a Pre-War London Motor Show (Motor Boat & Yachting)

The 1979 London International Boat Show at Earls Court (Motor Boat & Yachting)

(1970), Hong Kong (1971), Cowes (1972), Spain (1973), Bahamas (1974), Quay Haven (1975), Aquitaine, France (1976), Brighton Marina (1977), Scotland (1978) and the Royal Navy (1979).

The third US Boat Show was held in February 1907 and the fourth in December 1907! Until 1915, the US National Motor Boat Show was held in the Old Madison Square Garden. In 1916 it moved to Kingsbridge Armoury, Bronx, NY. In 1957 it moved into its new and present home, the New York Coliseum. Until May 1965 the exposition was known as the National Motor Boat Show – since then, just the Boat Show.

The oldest 'pure' Boat Show in Europe started in Stockholm, Sweden in 1933. In 1978 some 140 000 visitors saw 500 boats at the Stockholm Boat Show.

The Ship & Boat Builders National Federation (SBBNF) was founded on 24 September 1913 as 'The Boat and Yacht Builders and Proprietors and Allied Trades Protection Association Ltd', a company limited by guarantee; of its nine Presidents, including boatbuilders such as Maynard, Salter and Bates, N. W. Prangnell had the longest 15-year term of office. In 1942 it became necessary to add the negotiation of wage rates and conditions and the Ship & Boat Building Employers' National Federation was formed. Then in 1947 a merger of the Ship & Boatbuilders Association and the Ship and Boatbuilding Employers' National Federation saw the establishment of the present-day SBBNF, which has to date had 22 Presidents. In 1957 the yacht agents and brokers formed their own Association, as did the chandlery and retail traders in 1959 (Marine Trades Association) and again the engine makers in 1960 (Marine Engine & Equipment Manufacturers Association).

The National Association of Engine & Boat Manufacturers (USA) was founded in 1904; today its membership totals 350 firms.

9 DESIGNERS

Fred Cooper (designer), with Kaye Don, Lord Wakefield of Hythe ('Castrol'), Arthur Bray and Fred May (RTHPL)

FRED COOPER (1898–1972)

Prevented from following through his childhood ambition of becoming an aeroplane designer, Cooper attended the Portman House Academy. During World War I, he was a sub-lieutenant in the RNVR. After serving a post-war apprenticeship with Thornycroft at Basingstoke, Cooper learnt perfectionism in boatbuilding design and construction from Sidney E. Porter, chief draughtsman at S. E. Saunders Ltd. In 1925 he assisted in the design of Miss Betty Carstairs' 1½-litre-engined hydroplane *Newg*, which was so successful in the following two racing seasons. In 1928–29 he also worked out the designs of the Napier Lion-engined single-step hydroplane

Miss England I, but was so embittered at Scott-Paine's claiming that he had designed Segrave's 90 mph (145 km/h) racer, that he resigned from British powerboats and set up as a free-lance, based in the New Forest. Among his designs during the 1930s period were the 100 mph (160 km/h) Rolls-Royce-engined *Miss England II*, piloted to a world water speed record on Lake Windermere in 1930, Aldo Dacco's 55 mph (88 km/h) world outboard record holder of 1931, Sir Malcolm Campbell's first Rolls-Royce-engined 130 mph (210 km/h) *Bluebird* (with Reid Railton) of 1936, and a 1937 Cadet-Class Riley-engined racer, built by Vospers with its cockpit resembling those of the racing cars of the period.

Sir Henry Segrave on board the Cooper-designed Miss England II *on Lake Windermere (June 1930)*

Just before the war Cooper was managing and designing for the Berthon Boat Co. at Lymington. He submitted a design to the Admiralty for *Celerity* as the combat answer to the German E-boat, but no interest was shown. However, in 1941, Cooper joined the Fairmile design team and was largely responsible for the inception and development of **the most powerful petrol-engined motor-gunboat** built in Britain and one of **the most expensive light craft produced during the war** – the *Fairmile F*, powered by four Bristol Hercules engines developing 1650 bhp and attaining a speed of 36 knots on trials in 1943, despite her 100 tons displacement. The *Fairmile F* was never commissioned. Post-war, apart from advising Len Bates on the prototype design of his Star-Craft motor-cruiser (see p. 128), Cooper worked for a time at the Cornubia Yard, East Cowes. He was a great friend of Uffa Fox.

LAURENT GILES

Qualified naval architect/engineer Jack Laurent Giles was 26 years old when he retired in 1927 from Camper & Nicholsons to set up practice in partnership with George Gill, and shortly afterwards with Humphrey Barton. As a keen ocean racing yachtsman, it was not long before the very distinctive 'Giles look', incorporating

classical ideas for yacht interiors, was already well-known to the world of sail by the early 1930s. Messrs Giles and Gill also worked together to design one or two very elegant motorboats based on the idea of low displacement hulls, rather than planing-types.

Aetea, *designed by Jack Laurent Giles* (inset) *in the 1960s*

During World War II, Giles saw service with the Small Boats Division of the Admiralty, designing a 75 ft (22·9 m) Harbour Defence Motor-Launch, before he went out to Washington DC and became involved with wooden aircraft construction.

Re-starting Laurent Giles & Partners in 1947, this extremely artistic but disciplined mathematician designed the *Myth of Malham*, undoubtedly the outstanding ocean racing yacht of the post-war period up to 1960, by which time the firm reigned supreme as the most fashionable yacht designers in Italy. At the same time, starting with the 70 ft (21·3 m) *Woodpecker of Poole*, he recommended design on a number of motor-yachts which were to range from 40 to 112 ft (12·2–34·1 m).

Increasingly dissatisfied with the Royal Ocean Racing Club Rating Rule, then in force, he began to develop the motor-sailer, the sailing hull with a powerful auxiliary engine, beginning with the *Taylor-Trusty* built by James Taylor of Shoreham and culminating in his masterpiece, the 112 ft (34·1 m) *Blue Leopard* (see p. 140) which broke through the old barrier of 1·5√L both under power and sail. Jack Giles' versa-

tility encompassed designs for wood, steel, and aluminium (see p. 164), all of which bear the hallmark of his aesthetic profiles and deck structures.

In 1968 Jack Giles went into hospital for a serious operation, and died of cancer in February 1969. His firm passed into the control of the existing directors. Just before his death, the maestro had made his first venture into fgrp production boats with the *Centaur*, a small bilge keel yacht, of which Westerly Marine have now produced over 1800 copies. In 1976 the Laurent Giles designed motor-cruiser, the Fastnet 27, went into fgrp construction.

ARTHUR E. HAGG

Arthur Hagg was born in Brighton in 1888 and educated in Bournemouth. His first employment was with the Bath Cabinet Makers Co. where he learnt furniture and interior design, subsequently moving to London to work for Maple & Co. On the outbreak of war (1914), Hagg joined the Aircraft Manufacturing Company, Hendon. In 1918 he became a founder member of the de Havilland Aircraft Company as Assistant Chief Designer and Director. During this period, Hagg ordered a 42-footer (12·8 m), of his own design, to be called *Sylph*, from the Walton Yacht & Launch Works, but when he learnt that this company was in danger of going bankrupt, Hagg purchased the yard so that his motorboat could be completed. During the inter-war years, a line of fast, aerodynamically-designed motor-yachts were built, including Hagg's own yachts, *Waltona I* and *Waltona II*, both of which won many prizes in the London–Cowes races organised by the Royal Motor Yacht Club. On the outbreak of war, Arthur Hagg left de Havillands and devoted his entire attention to running the boatyard which was rapidly enlarged and became the parent firm for a number of yards engaged on the manufacture of air/sea rescue craft. At the end of the war, Hagg sold his Walton Yacht & Launch Works and reverted to aircraft design as Technical and Design Director of Airspeed Ltd, a subsidiary of de Havillands. He retired from the aircraft industry in 1949, aged 61 years, but continued to design motor-yachts in a private capacity. These

47 ft (14·3 m) fishing cruiser Taro *designed by A. E. Hagg (inset) and built by Thornycrofts of Southampton*

included Tom Delaney's *Delanare* 60-footer (18·3 m), Steve Macey's *Spirit of Ecstasy* and Maj. J. G. Abraham's second *Rosabelle* (designed in 1959 when Hagg was 71 years old); the *Rosabelle* (LOA 63 ft (19·2 m) × B 14 ft (4·3 m) × D 4½ ft (1·4 m)) was powered by twin 230 bhp Rolls-Royce diesel engines and attained speeds of 16 to 17 knots in calm weather.

Although previous Hagg-designed boats were often built using a single diagonal layer of mahogany planking, overlaid with marine plywood, this septuagenarian designer now tackled the fgrp medium with a 37-footer (11·3 m), six of which were moulded by the Dorset Lake Shipyard and a 42-footer (12·8 m), six of which were moulded by Tylers Boatyard.

Arthur Hagg always aimed to provide a seaworthy cruiser, never top heavy, but rather more sylph-like, sleek and agile. In this, his training and experience as an aircraft designer was always an advantage.

At the time of writing, Mr Hagg is alive and in his 91st year, living in Bournemouth, and possibly **the oldest-living motorboat designer in the world**.

LINTON CHORLEY HOPE

Little is known of this British pioneer of motorboat design. He was practising as a designer of vessels, particularly yachts, from 1887. In October 1893, he became both designer and managing director of the Thames Yachtbuilding Company Ltd of Greenhithe, Kent. By 1896, resident in Greenhithe, Linton Hope had designed over 40 yachts from 60 tons and over, down to small raters, besides other vessels. In 1902 he was a founder-member of the Marine Motoring Association. By 1904 he had established a new company at Adelphi House in the Strand, London WC called 'Linton Hope & Co. Specialists on Motor Boats', designing seagoing launches such as the 25 ft (7·6 m) *Cornubia*, several 40 ft (12·2 m) motor-racing launches including *Napier I*, the 34 ft (10·4 m) cabin launch called *La Coquette*, up to a 53-ton auxiliary schooner, *Mollihawk II*. The 1920 *Transactions* of the Royal Institute of Naval Architects listed Hope as a Major in the RAF, living at 14 Queen's Road, Kingston Hill, Surrey.

The Shead-designed Miss Embassy. Inset: *Don Shead*

DON SHEAD

Donovan ('Don') Shead was born in Birmingham in May 1936, the son of a mechanical engineer. After attending the Birmingham College of Technology, he worked for a time for a company called 'Automatic Doors'. He first started racing small hydroplanes in the late 1950s, and competed in the inaugural Cowes–Torquay race of 1961, in a boat which broke down – *Blue Marlin*. His first offshore victory came in the 1966 Wills International Race, with the Levi-designed *Delta 28*. He began designing boats in 1967 with the 21 ft (6·4 m) *Avenger*, which won the National Class III Championship with 20 victories. Tommy Sopwith drove his Shead-designed 26 ft (7·9 m) single-engined *Telstar* to the 1968 Cowes–Torquay–Cowes. The successful *Miss Enfield II*, UNO, and the gas-turbined *Miss Embassy* followed. Shead's ambition was always to design a boat capable of a good seaworthy average, rather than its ultimate top speed. In 1977, 56-year-old UIM President, Francesco Cosentino, commissioned Shead to design an identical pair of 38 ft (11·6 m) aluminium hulls to be built in Viareggio, Italy: *Alitalia Uno* and *Alitalia Due*. These boats won four UIM races between them in their first year of combat; *Alitalia Uno* won the 1978 World Offshore Powerboat Championship at Mar del Plata, Argentina in the face of 6 to 10 ft (1·8 to 3 m) waves, when only six boats finished. Apart from racing boats, Shead has also designed high speed luxury yachts – such as Tommy Sopwith's 92 ft (28 m) *Philante VI* – for the USA, Argentina, Saudi Arabia, Singapore, Greece, Italy, Spain and the UK. At the time of going to press, he is involved with his most ambitious project to date – a 90 ft (27·4 m) aluminium motor-yacht, its drive incorporating two MTU diesels, a Lycoming gas turbine and water-jet propulsion – to be capable of 40 knots; the yacht is commissioned by a Head of State; hitherto unnamed!

G. L. WATSON & CO. LTD

Founded in Glasgow by George Lennox Watson in 1873, designing large luxury sailing yachts and steam-powered auxiliaries – such as the 278 ft (84·7 m) *Margarita*, launched in 1896 and from 1900–9 owned by King Leopold of the Belgians. On his death, at the age of 53, G. L. Watson had designed some 400 craft and lived to see the dawn of the motorboat. He was succeeded by J. R. Barnett, consulting naval architect to the RNLI – whose 61 ft (18·6 m) and 52 ft (15·8 m) motor-lifeboats carried his name. In 1945, the company first became involved with the development of an experimental 65 ft (19·8 m) motor fishing vessel for the Herring Board. Barnett was succeeded by William Smart, who was joined in 1958 by Allen McLachlan. The building of the Watson-designed *Spey* class motor sailer yachts by Jones Shipyard Ltd of Buckie, Banffshire in the early 1960s, led to the purpose-building of motor-vessels for white fish and herring trawling. Beginning with the 80 ft (24·4 m) *Shemara* in November 1964, G. L. Watson soon became known as extremely pro-gressive designers of motor fishing vessels. Using the advantages of fgrp moulding to the full, Allen McLachlan's ragged chine form for offshore powerboats was soon adapted for 25 to 42 ft (7·6 to 12·8 m) fast lobster boats, which in turn evolved into the Poseidon-Class of fgrp moulded fishing vessels. From the fishing boat type of hull form, Allen McLachlan ingeniously developed the 75 ft (22·9 m) wooden MY *Brittina III*, built of wood in 1967–68 by Einar Johansson in Sweden for a private owner, who from May 1968 to Sept 1969 cruised *Brittina III* some 17 000 miles (27 350 km) without incident.

The first 'Arun' class of 52 ft (15·8 m) self-righting lifeboat, built in wood by William Osborne (see p. 140) in 1971, was a G. L. Watson design, whilst the ragged-chine 19 knot, 18½ ft (5·6 m) inshore rescue boats have been called the McLachlan Class. By the 1970s the Tyler/Watson ragged chine fgrp Poseidon-design had been adapted for pilot cutters and for the 'Viscount Class' of luxury motor-yacht, whilst the 50 to 54 ft (15·2 to 16·5 m) fgrp Watson/Halmatic standard fishing boat hull was also adapted for marine research vessels.

10 CONSTRUCTION METHODS

WOOD

The following woods have been used in the construction of motorboats: ash, cedar, deal, elm, larch, lignum vitae, mahogany, oak, pine, rosewood, spruce, teak, and walnut.

There are two quite distinct systems of planking a boat, namely the clench or clinker system, and the carvel system. The clench system consists of lapping the bottom edge of each plank over the one below it. In the carvel system each plank, after being, if necessary, steam-bent into shape, is very carefully planed along the edge to make a perfect fit with the neighbouring plank, the two surfaces simply butting together, and the planks being through-fastened to the timbers.

The oldest known plank-built boats in Europe are the three Ferriby boats (carbon-dated at 1500 BC Bronze Age), discovered and excavated from the mud of the River Humber's main channel (North Ferriby, Yorkshire) between 1937 and 1963, by E. V. and C. W. Wright. One of these, of 43·5 ft (13·1 m) LOA, has a flat bottom comprised of three massive oak planks curving upwards, and side planks curved round to meet them – their 'lashed' construction method, incorporating flexible yew withy stitches and cleats, is almost unique.

The earliest dug-out-based 'clinker-built' wood boat so far found in Northern Europe is the Bjorke boat, 23·5 ft (7·2 m) long, dated from AD 100. It is a dug-out with two planks added, one each side, clinker style, fastened with iron rivets. The Nydam oak boat, discovered in Jutland (South Denmark) and dated to AD 300, was built of broad, 50 ft (15·2 m) planks, five each side, one overlapping the other.

The boats built by the Saxons and Vikings were clinker-built with their planks overlapping in one way or another. The Gredstedbro boat (AD 600–650) had eight narrow planks each side, 'tree-nailed' with wooden pins. A boat found in Kvalsun (West Norway) and dated to AD 700, had been built of 50 ft (15·2 m) long narrow oak planks, secured to upper strakes with tree-nails and iron spikes.

The only method of building wooden boats until the 14/15th century was the 'shell' system of edge-joined construction, whereby a skin of planks, fastened together at their edges, was strengthened by frames shaped and inserted later. However, **the greatest change in the history of boatbuilding technique** came about in the late Medieval period, with the non-edged joined boat, whereby a frame based on the skeleton was built up, and then planks fastened together around that skeleton. Boats were built in this way for the next five centuries.

The first use of mahogany wood in shipbuilding was made by Hernan Cortés, the Spanish conquistador, in 1521. The first record of its importation into Britain refers to Jamaican 'magogany' which arrived during Christmas 1699–1700. The Lancastrian furniture-maker, Richard Gillow, was using both mahogany and teak in his workshop in the early 1700s, and it is likely that ship's fittings thereafter used mahogany.

Before the coming of steam power and construction in iron, which ended the desperate need for timber for naval and mercantile needs, suitable sources of supply were found in widely differing parts of the world. By 1811, African teak from the Cape Colony was in use, and, during the next decade, mahogany from British

Honduras and Cuba, and teak from the Bombay region were also obtaining recognition as a shipbuilding timber equal to British oak and elm. HMS *Cornwallis* (LOA 177 ft (54 m)) was **one of the first ships to be built of teak** in the Bombay Dockyard; she was launched in May 1813.

There have been well-known timber importers and merchants used by the motorboat-building industry in previous decades. J. Williams & Son (Colliers Wood, London) were known as **The Boatbuilder's Timber Merchants**. Other companies were M. & J. Reuben Ltd (Essex Wharf, London E16), William Oliver Ltd, W. W. Howard, Taylor of Wroxham, John Sadd of Malden, and a number of others.

In terms of fine wood for boatbuilding, **the finest oak** has come from England, **the finest mahogany** has come from Cuba and Spain, followed by Honduras and the Philippines. **The finest teak** has been Burmese, followed by Indian teak. Canadian rock elm has proved good for engine bearers and stringers, whilst the best of cedars is the Western Red Cedar. Of pines, Oregon and pitch pines are good.

Timber prices have depended on availability, on quality, on hardness, etc. In terms of length, there are 'shorts' (under 6 ft (1·8 m)) and 'longs' (over 6 ft (1·8 m)). In terms of widths, there are strips (up to 6 in (15 cm)) and boards (over 6 in (15 cm)). Because it is harder to find long boards, the price escalates considerably after the 6 ft 6 in demarcation. Prices, quoted by the cube (or cu ft), concern 8 ft (2·4 m) × 8 in (20 cm)), or 12 ft (3·6 m) × 12 in (30 cm) × 1 in (2·5 cm) thick, or 24 ft (7·3 m) × 6 in (15 cm) × 1 in (2·5 cm) thick. The following table shows the rise in prices of three major boatbuilding hardwoods, price per cube:

	1930s	1960s	1970s
Honduras Mahogany	8–10s (40–50p)	24–29s (£1.20–1.45)	£11–14
Teak	14s (70p)	84–98s (£4.20–4.90)	£15–28
Oak	1–2s (5–10p)	5–40s (25p–£2.00)	£10–25

The most superb pieces of wood are well-remembered, long after the motorboat has been built: such as a Honduras mahogany board

(2 in (5 cm) thick × 5 ft (1·5 m) wide × 25 ft (7·6 m) long; straight at the edges) seen on one of Williams' lorries in the early 1930s. In the 1960s, on request, a 45 ft (13·7 m) mahogany log was located, with the greatest of difficulty, and then abandoned, simply because there was no longer a sawing machine left in the country, capable of cutting that sort of length.

PLYWOOD

The first all-plywood boat, a 12 ft (3·7 m) fishing skiff, was built in 1934 of resin-bonded plywood, supplied by the Harbor Plywood Corporation of America.

Plywood is, however, a form of veneer, and the headpiece of a bedstead found in the tomb of Iouya and Touya, the grandparents of the Ancient Egyptian, Tutankhamen, was veneered with laburnum wood, the glue having lasted some 35 centuries. A sarcophagus from a royal tomb of the Third Dynasty has sides which consist of six layers of wood securely glued together.

The master cabinet makers of the 18th/19th century realised that by taking a number of thin sheets of wood and glueing them together with the grain of adjacent sheets at right-angles to each other, much greater strengths could be obtained in both directions. With the advent of the rotary cutter in the 1890s, 3-ply boards of exceptional size and strength were developed.

The practice of building a skin of a number of thicknesses of wood by sewing them together was first developed by the boatbuilder Samuel Edgar Saunders of Goring-on-Thames in the early 1890s. Finding that there were then no reliable glues to hold a plywood-system together during long periods of immersion in either fresh or salt-water, Saunders succeeded in patenting a 3-ply double-diagonal/longitudinal sandwich system of thick solutioned wood skins and waterproof canvas, sewn together with annealed brass or copper wire (64th gauge thickness).

In 1896 there was a public outcry against the large wash at Henley Regatta, set up by the umpire's launch then in use. The Regatta Committee made enquiries for a launch which, whilst capable of 25 mph (40 km/h), should produce

Sam Saunders' early steam-powered cabin cruiser Mariposa, *built 1898, was constructed on the Consuta system*

little or no wash. One of Saunders' customers, Mr Chilton, offered to have a launch built to suit these conditions. Thus *Consuta* ('Sewn Together') (LOA 51 ft (15·5 m) × B 7½ ft (2·3 m) × D 2 ft (0·6 m)) was built with a special anti-weed/debris 'tunnel stern'. Given a triple expansion steam engine and boiler by Des Vignes of Teddington, *Consuta* reached 27½ mph (44·3 km/h) on the Measured Mile, with complete absence of wash. Seven years later, having officiated at seven Regattas and travelled some 8000 miles, *Consuta*'s hull was as good as ever.

By this time, Saunders had formed his Patent Launch Building Syndicate and all his boats were constructed on the 'sewn system'. Hand-sewing was slow, so he and his daughter, Ethel, next adapted large sewing machines so that several thickness of plywood could be sewn together quickly and easily.

Final testimony to the system is that *Consuta*'s hull is still afloat in 1979, having been twice re-engined with a six-cylinder Vickers Wolseley engine, then with a six-cylinder Gray Marine engine. As late as the early 1950s, she was being used at Varsity Boat Races on the Thames.

During World War I, aircraft factories required considerable quantities of thin birch plywood, and the dependable development of the plywood industry and waterproof glues, kept pace with that of the aeroplane.

The first suggestion that phenol-formaldehyde could be used as wood adhesive was made, about 1912, by Dr Bakeland, who gave his name to the moulded products known as Bakelite. Some experimental work followed and in 1918 a thin sheet of paper, impregnated with resin, made its appearance. It was not until 1930 that a resin film was produced in Germany in a form suitable for commercial application in plywood mills. But before long, this costly item had been replaced by various types of water-resistant bonding materials, to be used in boatbuilding.

By 1940, **the first lengths of reliable waterproof plywood** had been developed. During the war, in the USA, certain craft of the motor-torpedo class were constructed entirely of plywood, each side being composed of a single sheet prefabricated to size. In the UK, the Service departments tackled the scarcity of timber by manufacturing plywood in continuous lengths. A vast programme of assault landing craft was built on this principle, using panels of 40 ft (12·2 m) and over. Just after the war, the USA began to manufacture 50 ft (15·2 m) long, 9 ft (2·7 m) wide lengths of plywood for the boatbuilding industry.

The first plywood-hulled boat to be 'hot-moulded' was the RYA National One Design

Showing the autoclave for hot-moulding a hull (Fairey Marine)

Class, 12 ft (3·7 m) sailing dinghy, *Firefly*, designed by Uffa Fox and Charles Currey and built by Fairey Marine Ltd on the Hamble, as a subdivision of Fairey Aviation Company. Immediately after the war, Sir Richard Fairey, a keen and famous yachtsman, conceived the idea of producing high-class hulls at a reasonable price by using modern moulding methods to bring boating within the reach of the average man; thus a boatyard, manned by a nucleus of craftsmen trained in the techniques of plywood aircraft production (on such aircraft as the Mosquito), begun to turn out standard types of craft in large numbers.

The technique of hot-moulding involved the construction of a semi-solid mould, accurately fashioned to the internal shape of the hull sitting on a base plate. Skins of mahogany or Agba plywood were layered up diagonally on the mould, each skin being secured to the one below by a synthetic, waterproof, fungus-proof and bacterial-proof adhesive, applied to the planking by glue-spreading machines and hand-stapled into position. Staples securing the final skin were removed after curing. After fitting a rubber bag over the whole assembly to ensure good vacuum, the complete assembly was wheeled into the autoclave where steam heat up to 100°C, and an additional pressure of 45 lb per sq in, making a total pressure of about 60 lb, was applied. Initial curing took approx 30 min, but after removal from the mould, hulls were left for a week or more for final curing before being trimmed and worked upon.

Among the standard types produced up to 1955, were a general purpose motor-launch, and the *Flatfish*, a tunnel stern motor-launch – both were 16½ ft (5·1 m) LOA. By 1959, Fairey Marine production stood at 1000 boats per annum, including the 26 ft (8 m) *Atalanta* motor-sailer.

The success of hot-moulding, soon made Fairey Marine **the largest boatbuilders in Europe**, and possibly the third largest in the world, in terms of numbers built and types available: Swordsman 33, Atalanta 31, Fisherman 27, Cinderella 15, Huntsman and Huntress were just some of the standard motorboat hulls which contributed towards a total of 13 500 hulls 'hot-moulded' by the mid 1960s. One of these moulds went in and out of the autoclave some 700 times!

Huntsman and *Huntress* powerboats, with their deep V hull-form conceived by designer Ray Hunt of Boston, Massachusetts (USA) and powered by Perkins diesel engines, competed in every one of the first ten Daily Express International Offshore Powerboat races from Cowes to Torquay. In 1962, for example, a Huntsman came sixth overall in a race so gruelling that only 14 out of 46 starters finished the course – a good test of the hot-mould technique.

Fairey ultimately went over from hot-moulded hulls to glass reinforced plastic techniques, with the standard Spearfish twin-diesel motor-cruiser.

FIBREGLASS REINFORCED PLASTIC (fgrp)

The first small plastic craft were developed in 1876 when George Waters of Troy, NY made laminated paper rowing shells, bonded in layers with shellac (a refined, melted form of seed-lac obtained from resinous deposit secreted by insects on certain trees).

Glass-fibre reinforced plastic boats could only be produced after the marriage of two developments: unsaturated polyester resin, and continuous glass-fibre filaments.

In 1847, Herr Berzelius produced a chemical reaction which formed a resinous mass called polyglyceryltartrate. **The very first, if somewhat brittle, plastic** was Parkesine, a thermoplastic material produced from nitro-cellulose, camphor and alcohol by Alexander Parkes of Birmingham and originally manufactured by the Parkesine Company at Hackney Wick, London in 1866. An almost exactly similar thermoplastic was patented by John Wesley Hyatt of Albany, NY in 1869 and given the name Celluloid.

Herr Vorlander (1894), Mr W. J. Smith (1901) and Herr Kienle (1927) made successful chemical advances in polyester resin technology. By 1932, the UK electrical industry was researching polyester resins for its insulation properties. 1942 saw the introduction of the first unsaturated low-pressure polyester resin (called CR39), noted for its mouldable qualities.

As far back as 1370 BC, from the XVIIIth Dynasty of Ancient Egypt, 5-in high glass vases were constructed by making a 'male' mould out of mud, then laying thin molten glass canes round the outside and 'trailing-in' canes of a different colour. Once the glass had cooled, the mud was carefully chipped away, leaving the polychrome vase; several of these polychrome vases, as well as a glass fish, were discovered at the remains of Tell-el-amarna, Akhenaton's capital city.

Fibrous glass was first commercially produced in the early 1930s, the culmination of many attempts to make pliable glass. In 1931, the Owens Illinois Glass Company, then the large bottle makers in the world, had embarked on research to discover what use they might make out of glass. As they did not intend invading either the flat glass or the door-knob markets, they experimented and came up with the glass block which could be lighted from behind. Next came glass wool, made by drawing fibres of melted glass out of a battery of furnace-openings by shooting a flow of steam past each opening, as an aspirator; these glass fibres matted and fell as a resilient pad on a conveyor-belt.

During the remaining 1930s a great deal of glass-fibre cloth was manufactured by the Owens-Corning Fiberglas Corp. for the business of heat and cold insulation. Corporation President, Harold Boeschenstein, and his brilliant Vice-President, James Alter, were responsible for getting the word fiberglass (as it was then spelt) accepted into *Websters Dictionary*.

On the introduction of radar to aircraft during World War II, the need arose for protective coverings over the scanning apparatus which would give a minimum of hindrance to radar transmission and reception. As aircraft performance increased, most materials of the correct electric characteristics no longer had sufficient structural strength. It was from then on that the first polyester resin-impregnated glass-fibre – an electrically acceptable combination – 'radomes' was built.

In February 1945, Lieut.-Col. Henry S. Thorne, commanding the New York region of the Army's Air Technical Service Command, announced that a successful flight test had been made from Wright field by a basic training plane, the fuselage of which had been moulded of glass-fibre, plastic resins and balsa wood.

At first, 'radomes', made for British aircraft, used materials imported from the USA. The Ministry of Supply then stepped in, and during 1946 **the first unsaturated low-pressure, home-produced polyester resins** became commercially available in the UK.

From experimental prototype-boats built in 1946, **the first marketable fgrp rowboats and dinghies** were exhibited at the 1948 US National Motor Boat Show.

On 3 November 1949, on the initiative of Ernest Scott Bader and Mr Brian Parkyn, **the first UK polyester technical forum** was held by the 30-year-old Scott-Bader Company at their Wollaston Hall HQ, Northamptonshire. Here, Dr Irving E. Muskat, inventor/president of Marco Resins Inc, New Jersey (USA) gave a lecture to representatives of British Industry on polyester resins. He stated that after severe trials in the Mediterranean and elsewhere, 28 ft (8·5 m) fgrp personnel carriers and 36 ft (11 m) landing craft were to go into mass production for the US Navy at the Bremerton (Seattle) Naval Yard. Muskat claimed that fgrp boats would be better than ones made of wood or steel on a strength/weight ratio – also more serviceable, lighter, leak-proof, fire-resistant, barnacle resistant and shrapnel proof.

In January 1950, an article appeared in the British magazine, *The Boatbuilder*, reporting in detail on Dr Muskat's talk, and entitled 'Enter Plastic Age for Boats'; it was to have a profound influence on the introduction of British fgrp craft.

The Marco vacuum process used to construct **the very first British fgrp boats** involved placing dry reinforcement into the cavity between two rigid moulds – often made of plaster-faced concrete – which were then sealed together. Resin was allowed access to the lowest point of the cavity and sucked upwards towards one or more vacuum take-off points at the top of the mould. In passing upwards the resin impregnated the reinforcement and the air was drawn off. The Marco was an expensive and difficult process to master and limited the size and shape of articles that could be produced.

Before long, the more economical wet lay-up process, known as **contact moulding**, using the newly introduced glass chopped strand matting (introduced in 1951) had taken over. This began with the construction of a high-polished 'male' timber mould, coated with a separating compound, followed by a coat of pure or pigmented resin, accelerated to give a fast setting time. Chopped strand glass-fibre matting was then laid up and impregnated with resin, by spraying or brushing. Bands of electric heating elements

were then embedded in this ¼ in (6 mm) thick shell, the 'female', which was then framed in either timber or metal to hold it rigid when used as a mould.

Manufacture of each boat again involved a coating of separator, followed by the painting-on and curing of a quick setting resin to act as the boat's outside surface; the chopped strand glass matting was then tailored into the mould and saturated with polyester resin. The curing then took place at 120° C without any pressure. The complete shell of the hull was then lifted out of the mould, ready for its fittings. Any desired colour could be incorporated into the polyester resin from which the boat was made. Minimum maintenance, comparative lightness and resistance to oil, salt, acids, alkalines and the teredo wood beetle (!), were claimed as the advantages of a resin glass-fibre boat. In terms of productivity, a boat could be cured, ready for removal from the mould, every four hours.

The first resin glass-fibre motor-cruiser was the *Dreadnought 23*, exhibited at the 1951 US National Boat Show, and described as 'a plastic sports cruiser', designed by M. Rosenblatt & Son, and built using the Marco vacuum process without any seams or joints by the Dreadnought Cruiser Company.

Dreadnought 23 had a raised deck, with a streamlined trunk cabin forward, while a short permanent after-top with full headroom was available at extra cost. Colour was fused into the plastic construction, but a varnished mahogany trim had been used in sufficient quantity to give a rich appearance.

To prove that resin-impregnated glass-fibre hulls developed three-quarters the tensile strength of steel, one of these Dreadnoughts was dropped from a considerable height into the water; it was reported that no damage was sustained.

The first British inboard-engined craft to be contact-moulded in fgrp was an experimental 20 ft (6·1 m) motor-dory for the Royal Navy, built by Messrs W. & J. Tod of Ferrybridge, Weymouth, Dorset. In 1951, Tod Brothers, under their dynamic Managing Director, Norman Wright, had produced a 12 ft (3·7 m) glass-fibre dinghy on the Marco vacuum process, suitable for rowing or outboard engine; by

1951: The first fgrp Tod was a 12 ft (3·7 m) outboard-engined dinghy

Perpetua, *the first large motor yacht in fgrp to have diesel engines (1954) (Halmatic Ltd)*

October 1952 they were producing one dinghy per day. In 1953, after discussions with the Naval Construction Department, the dory (LOA 20 ft 4½ in (6·2 m) × B 6 ft (1·8 m)) was constructed using six layers of glass-fibre, lapped at the keel to form a backbone of twelve layers; colour was given by a grey-impregnated resin. Weighing 16 cwt, a 5½ hp Enfield air-cooled diesel engine propelled the dory to a speed of over 7 knots. Hull, decks, seating, floors, engine-casing and fuel tank were all moulded.

Designated 'Landing Craft Personnel (Small)', this boat was extensively tested by the Royal Marine Commandos in landing on all types of coast with great success, and was exhibited on the RN Stand at the 1955 Boat Show. This was followed by a batch of larger boats, including two 27 ft (8·2 m) × 7½ ft (2·3 m) Whalers. In 1961, the Admiralty stated that all future procurements of small boats – up to 27 ft (8·2 m) – would be in reinforced plastics.

The first UK motor cabin cruiser in fgrp was again produced by Tod Brothers in 1954. Called the *Tuna*, it was 20 ft (6·1 m) long and powered by a single Watermota/Ford 10 to 30 hp engine.

The first UK speedboat in fgrp was designed by F. Hutchings & Son, and made by British Resin Products Ltd in 1954.

The first large glass-fibre motor-cruiser to be built on either side of the Atlantic was the 48 ft 8 in (14·8 m) *Perpetua*, designed by Peter Thornycroft in 1954 to prove to officials of the Procurement Branch of the Admiralty that a large resin-impregnated glass-fibre boat could withstand the vibration of twin diesel engines. The male mould was made by Messrs Attrill & Sons of Bembridge, Isle of Wight, while for the first time Crystic 189 polyester resin, developed by Scott-Bader Ltd to be especially resistant to deep water conditions, was used by Patrick de Lazlo's Halmatics firm in Portsmouth to saturate the chopped strand glass matting. Halmatics then used the trade name of 'Deborine' (a combination of de Lazlo's daughters' christian names) to describe their hulls.

Perpetua's specification was very similar to that of an Admiral's barge and her twin Gardiner LW6 107 hp engines gave her a speed of 13 knots at 1600 rpm.

Perpetua travelled widely throughout Europe under her own power and whilst on a voyage to Copenhagen withstood a formidable gale which damaged the Royal Yacht, *Britannia*. Returning home via rivers and canals from a trip to the South of France, *Perpetua* negotiated 227 locks *en route*, and suffered only slight scoring from a damaged lock. The scoring proved to be little more than a scratch barely $\frac{1}{16}$ in deep, which was easily filled (overall thickness of hull was $\frac{1}{4}$ in, thickening to $\frac{3}{8}$ in below the water line). *Perpetua* was surveyed in November 1965 and passed 'A1' by Lloyds. Unfortunately the mould for this boat was damaged beyond repair and *Perpetua* was the only hull of her class.

The first use of fgrp as shroud material for an outboard engine was for a 1956 engine produced by Scott-Attwater, at that time the Marine Products Division of the McCulloch Corporation (USA).

The first British luxury motor-yacht in fgrp (53 ft 8 in (16·4 m) LOA), was designed and tank-tested by Burness, Kendall & Partners Ltd, and built in 1956 with a 'Deborine' hull by Halmatic Ltd for Mr Jack Gerbere of London. She was to be powered by twin 220 hp Rolls-Royce diesel engines. During her early trials, the 20 knot *Bebe Grande* collided with a tug and was holed in her stem above the waterline. Repairs to the localised damage took two days and cost £5 – a marked reduction in time and expense when compared with a timber-hulled craft. One decade after construction, *Bebe Grande* was still being used in South Africa by her original owner.

Halmatic Ltd now went into mass production with their 'Deborine 31' and '56' motor-craft. In 1960, they produced the 67 ft (20·4 m) *Ocean-Commander*, **the then largest one-piece fgrp moulding yet made.**

Meanwhile other forms of construction were being investigated which would be suitable for larger craft. In 1954, Cdr T. F. Crang and Mr E. R. Cooper, a plastics engineer, had set up a research division at the J. Samuel White yard, Cowes to look into those possibilities. Two years later, a 16½ ft (5·1 m) Admiralty Fast Motor Boat, powered by a Coventry diesel KF4 engine developing 50 hp at 2000 rpm, became **the first craft to be built using foamed plastic cores (pvc) sandwiched between layers of polyester-glass**; this was an attractive innovation since it produced strong laminates with built-in buoyancy. But it was expensive and did not take full advantage of reinforced plastic construction. However, once innovated, fgrp sandwich construction was soon improved, until multi-decker sandwich construction – using sheets of pvc foam, alternate layers of chopped strand glass mat and woven glass rovings, each layer im-

pregnated with polyester resin, polyester gelcoat and polyurethene paint – was commonplace for motor-craft in excess of 90 ft (27·4 m). But this technique, together with the problems of surface pinholing, blistering, wrinkling, yellowing, etc, was to take another two decades to slowly overcome.

It was estimated that between World War II and 1960, some 500000 fgrp boats had been built in the USA alone. At the 1955 International Boat Show in London, four per cent of the craft on show were in fgrp; at the 1965 Show this figure had risen to 39 per cent; by 1968 it stood at 60 per cent; by 1971 it stood at 75 per cent, whilst the other 25 per cent included a fair number of inflatables.

The official seal of approval for the fgrp boat came with the publication, in 1961, of Lloyds Register of Shipping Provisional Rules for the Construction of Reinforced Plastic Yachts up to 120 ft (36·6 m) in length.

The largest boat to be built so far in fgrp is the 150 ft (47 m) minehunter, HMS *Wilton*, moulded by Vosper-Thornycroft and launched on 18 January 1972. HMS *Wilton* was the first all-fgrp vessel of her class. From her successful trials the Navy proceeded to order four mine-counter-measure vessels in the 725-ton Hunt class to be built at Yarrows and Vosper Thornycrofts. It was considered desirable to have a design which could be mass-produced in British shipyards in an emergency, whilst the use of fgrp would make the Hunt class largely immune to magnetic mines. HMS *Brecon* was launched on 29 June 1978. Two more of this type are under construction.

STEEL

By 1858, Henry Bessemer was making a mild steel for sale, which was actually **used for a merchant ship in 1858**, and in 1859 for a 375 ft (114·3 m) troop vessel for service on the Lower Indus. In 1862 the Siemens-Martin process introduced open-hearth steel; **the first steel-hulled vessel to cross the Atlantic Ocean** was the paddle-steamer *Banshee* of 325 tons, built at Liverpool in 1862 for use as a blockade runner in the American Civil War. Lloyd's Register permitted the use of steel in 1866. In 1871 John I. Thorny-

Galvanized steel motor tug, Sharpness, *built in 1908 by Abdela & Mitchell used for towing through tunnels and as an ice-breaker on the Worcester and Birmingham Canal (Hugh McKnight)*

croft built his 60 ft (18·3 m) *Miranda* using $\frac{1}{8}$–$\frac{1}{16}$ in thick plates, together with a steel boiler, and achieved speeds of 18 mph (29 km/h) which was very fast for that period. **The first three warships to be steel-plated were** built in France in 1874, whilst HMS *Iris* and HMS *Mercury* were **the first two British Naval vessels to be built of steel**. With the launching of the *Rotomahana*, **the earliest large ocean-going steel steamer** (1777 gross tons), built by W. Denny & Bros in 1878 for the Union Steamship Company of New Zealand, the iron age of the steamer began its decline. But it was only after 1880 that steel costs came down from twice that of iron to a reasonable figure. Riveting was then the only method, and the Cunard express steamer, the 790 ft (237·8 m) *Mauretania*, for example, used some 26 000 steel plates (the largest being about 48 ft (14·6 m) in length) and over 4 000 000 rivets.

S. F. Edge's *Napier I*, which won the very first British International (or Harmsworth) Trophy contest of 1903, was one of **the first steel-hulled motor-launches**, using 20-gauge cold rolled steel.

The costs of labour, the noise of riveting, and the excessive heaviness of the clumsy, leakable plates, called out for a new process of ship-building in steel. In the 1860s, an Englishman called Wilde succeeded in using an electric arc to weld together two small pieces of iron, and in 1865 he was granted **the world's first electric welding patent**. By the 1890s the Russians were using a clumsy form of arc welding in the Baltic shipyards, but with the problem of oxidisation (ie when the steel was melted by the heat of the electric arc) the steel was corroded by the gases in the surrounding air, and this weakened the join. In 1902, Oscar Kjellberg, a Swedish marine engineer solved this problem, establishing ESAB, his own welding company, in 1904, for the speedy repair of ships and their boilers.

The first all-welded vessel was a 125 ft (38·1 m) long barge, built at Richborough in 1917, on government orders, largely to test the speed and efficiency of this process. In 1918, Lloyd's Register published their **first regulations for the construction of welded ships**.

The world's first all-welded sea-going ship was the *Fullagar* (LOA 150 ft (45·7 m) × B 23 ft 9 in (7·2 m) × D 11 ft 6 in (3·5 m)), built by Cammell Laird of Birkenhead in 1919 for the Anchor Brocklebank Line of Liverpool, and launched in February 1920. It sunk in 1937 after a collision off Mexico.

The *SAF No. 4* was **the first French all-welded craft** (LOA 65 ft (20 m) × B 13 ft (4 m) × D 7½ ft (2·3 m)), her keel being laid after that of the

Fullagar, but having been built by wartime female labour and launched the year before.

The oldest all-welded ship ever built, and still in service in the Kockums Shipyard in Malmö, Sweden, is the 52 ft (16 m) tug *KMV 1* (formerly the *ESAB IV*) launched on 29 December 1920.

Apart from these famous prototypes, very little welding was done in the 1920s. In 1932 Lloyds Register revised its original welding regulations and the notation 'Experimental' was abolished. In the 1930s a few all-welded tankers were built, together with the partly-welded aircraft carrier, *Ark Royal*. Tests in the USA showed that if two ships, 425 ft (129·5 m) in length, 57 ft (17·4 m) beam and 28 ft (8·5 m) draught were built using the rival systems, the welded one would use 2450 tons of steel compared with 2944 tons for the riveted version. The welded vessel would have a deadweight – that is, a cargo-carrying capacity – of 11 039 tons, compared with 10 539 tons, and the total cost would be 3·7 per cent lower.

It was not until World War II, and the resulting demand for merchant shipping by the allied nations, that welding became established and used in the construction of large and small motor-craft.

NON-MAGNETIC

In 1933, Vickers-Petter Ltd was commissioned to construct a **non-magnetic engine** to propel the expedition motorboat, *Research*, for its investigation of the earth's magnetic field. *Research* was to have been built of teak and brass, whilst all metal parts of her construction and furnishings had to be of bronze alloy or non-magnetic steel. Many months of development went into the construction of the Atomic 160 hp engine in bronze alloy, with only the steel crankshaft and cylinder-liners being made in non-magnetic steel. Unfortunately the advent of World War II brought about the end of expedition preparations.

ALUMINIUM

The world's first aluminium boat – even to its smoke stack and rigging – was built in 1891 by Escher, Wyss & Co. of Zurich, Switzerland. It

Advertisement in the Leipzig Illustrated News *of 1900 (Mary Evans Picture Library)*

was powered by a 2 hp naphtha engine, had a speed of 6 mph (10 km/h), weighed 1000 lb and carried eight passengers. Escher, Wyss later built an all-aluminium naphtha yacht, *Mignon* (LOA 43 ft (13·1 m) × B 6 ft (1·8 m) × D 2 ft 2 in (0·6 m)). All machinery, including the 6 hp engine, was of aluminium except for the cranks and shafting; the shell, stretched over forged aluminium frames, was $\frac{3}{32}$ in (2·5 mm) thick; on a trial trip *Mignon* attained a speed of 8 mph (13 km/h).

The first 60 ft (18·3 m) aluminium torpedo boat was built by Yarrow for the French Government, and powered by a set of three-stage compound steam engines and a Yarrow water-tube boiler. It attained trial speeds of 20·5 knots – three knots faster than any other torpedo boat of her time. Several other torpedo boats – the *Sokol* (Russian), *Dahlgren* (GB) and *Craven* (GB) – were noted for their marginally extra speeds.

The first American aluminium boats were built in 1894 – for both the Walter Wellman and the Jackson Arctic Expeditions.

Between 1926 and 1934, 50 aluminium pontoon boats were built for the US Army, and were still in service 10 years later.

The problem with aluminium, despite its lightness, was its softness and liability to 'metal fatigue'. A harder and more resistant aluminium-magnesium-manganese alloy was first developed and patented in Britain for marine use in 1929 – called duralmin. By 1930, the Birmingham Aluminium Castings (1903) Co. Ltd of Birmid Works, Smethwick had built **their first two 'Birmabright' motorboats**: a 16 ft (4·9 m), 32 hp Johnson-outboard-engined hydroplane and a 22 ft (6·7 m) inboard motorboat. After continual tests on the Severn at Worcester and on the sea, Birmingham Aluminium Castings Co. formed a subsidiary, Birmal Boats of Southampton, to further develop an economical and durable marine aluminium, impervious to saltwater. From 1930 to 1938, a larger number of design studies were completed and over 200 small and medium size craft were built, including 31 rowing boats, 26 powered dinghies, 54 motor-launches, four racing hydroplanes, three cabin cruisers, one experimental 70 ft (21·3 m) motor-torpedo boat and 70 lifeboats. This was the hey-day of aluminium boating.

The most famous boat to be built by Birmals was the express cruiser, *Diana II* (LOA 55 ft (16·8 m) × B 12 ft (3·7 m) × D 3 ft (0·9 m) × Dp 6 ft 3 in (2 m)), with a net tonnage of 16·15 tons. She was built for RMYC member, Donald van den Bergh. Apart from bronze prop, stainless steel prop-shafts and certain bolts, all metal parts of the *Diana II* were in $3\frac{1}{2}$ per cent magnesium BB3 alloy; in wrought form, this alloy was used for all hull constructional members, tanks, masts, davits, companion ladders and dinghy;

in cast form, BB3 was used for prop-shaft logs and brackets, window fittings and door furniture and deck fittings; the hull was plated with ten and eight gauge material.

Lloyds Register granted the boat an experimental classification 'for service in enclosed waters'.

Originally engined with twin 235 hp Kermath petrol units, giving her a speed of 20 knots, *Diana II* first saw service around the Mediterranean, but was to change owners several times; her varied life included an engine-room explosion (which did very little damage to the structure). She also lay for twelve months in a mud berth on the Isle of Wight and for three years afloat in Ramsgate Harbour. In 1942 she was requisitioned by the Royal Navy; after the war she was completely stripped of paint, and it was found that the original mill finish on the sheets was undisturbed and the reflectivity unimpaired. In 1951 *Diana II* was bought by the British Aluminium Company Ltd and in 1955 motored up the Thames on the occasion of the Aluminium Centenary Exhibition. It was only in 1961 that it was found necessary to replace any of her original plating.

Birmabright also supplied the metal for **the first large vessel to be built with an aluminium hull on the American continent**; this was the 65 ft (19·8 m), twin-Gleniffer diesel-engined patrol boat, *Interceptor*, built at Mansau Shipyards Ltd, Sorel, Quebec and commissioned in 1934 by the Royal Canadian Mounted Police for service

Diana II, *a pre-War aluminium express motor cruiser*

on the St Lawrence River and on the coast of Nova Scotia. *Interceptor*, her hull in excellent condition, was still in service in 1945.

In 1933, Hubert Scott-Paine's high speed aero-engine hydroplane, *Miss Britain III*, clocked a new sea-mile saltwater record for single-engined boats of 100·132 mph (161·147 km/h) on the Solent. She was plated with 14 and 16 gauge lengths of a German aluminium alloy, called 'Alclad', fastened by duralmin nuts and bolts, with countersunk heads. That metal is still in good condition today, and is on show at the National Maritime Museum, Greenwich.

In 1934 a 30 ft (9·1 m) Fleming-type all-alloy ship's lifeboat, something of a prototype, was given one coat of aluminium-pigmented varnish outside the hull and one coat of grey zinc oxide primer on the inside, then deliberately neglected for $2\frac{1}{2}$ years, moored in water containing factory effluent on the River Itchen, where she rested on the mud at each ebb. She quickly acquired the name *Barnacle Bill* because of the thick crust of barnacles she collected on her hull. In 1937 she was loaned to the Dutch for investigation, preceding the adoption of aluminium lifeboats for the *Nieuw Amsterdam*. She was returned to England in 1939, fitted with a diesel engine and put into harness as a work boat. No painting or repairs to plating or metal work were done during that period of her life. In 1955, *Barnacle Bill* was another 20-year-old exhibit at the Aluminium Centenary Exhibition in London.

In 1938 the US magazine *Motor Boating* published an article by Walter Leveau, advocating the construction of an all-aluminium hydroplane for the US Gold Cup Powerboat Race.

In 1940, a 103 ft (31·4 m) all-alloy yacht, called the *Edi*, was built in Sweden.

In 1945, the US Bureau of Ships, realising that their small fighting ships were becoming obsolete, commissioned the construction of four experimental patrol boats in aluminium. Two of these were all-welded, one was riveted-welded and the fourth riveted-throughout. The easier process of welding had begun to be adopted.

Aluminium boats received **their worst publicity image in America** just after World War II because vast quantities of ex-Government aluminium sheeting was being turned into pleasure craft by manufacturers who, even if they had known that it was the wrong grade for marine use, would not have been disturbed. Pleasure boats were also being built in Britain using an alloy called Hiduminium.

During this time, experiments in aluminium welding were proceeding apace in the USA and Canada. In 1948, the Tacoma Boat Building Co. Inc. of Washington had a $500 000 plan to mass produce an all-welded alloy 23 ft (7 m) cruiser. The following year, Deluxe Welding Co. of Detroit produced a 34 ft (10·4 m) boat, powered by two 1750 hp Allison engines for racing on the Detroit River. This was sheathed, using countersunk screws with $\frac{1}{8}$ in (3 mm) alloy sheet, the fabrication of which involved 125 ft (38 m) of corner welding, 85 ft (26 m) of fillet welding and 92 ft (28 m) of butt welding, all by the Heliarc process. After all this the boat was a failure – it would not take the turns. A more successful racing craft was *Aluminium First*, owned by Oakland billionaire industrialist Henry J. Kaiser, but this was of riveted construction.

One of the first attempts to use inert-gas shielded, self-adjusting arc-welding techniques in the construction of aluminium alloy craft was the building, in 1951, of two patrol boats for the Venezuelan Government by Marine Industries Ltd of Sorel, Quebec.

To demonstrate to British shipbuilders the superiority of this process over riveted construction, a twin-screw auxiliary motor-yacht was designed by Laurent Giles in conjunction with Saunders-Roe (Anglesey) Ltd and the British Aluminium Company Ltd. During the early 1950s, *Morag Mhor* (LOA 72 ft 3 in (22 m) × B 16 ft (4·9 m) × D 7 ft (2 m)) of 45 tons displacement and powered by two Gleniffer 72 bhp DB6 engines, cruised to almost all the major ports of the UK and Northern Europe and became **the most well-known and influential example of the advantages of an all-welded, aluminium (LM10) motor-sailer**. She also crossed the Atlantic under her own power.

John Cobb's high-speed, turbo-jet-engined craft, the *Crusader* (1952), was built of birch plywood reinforced by DTB 610 B, a high tensile alloy, produced by the British Aluminium Company.

Possibly the greatest single-factor to recommend aluminium for marine purposes is its weight saving. In 1951, the *Ain-Al-Bahr*, a 60 ft (18·3 m)

Morag Mhor

aluminium survey vessel, had a displacement of 11 tons and a draft of 2 ft 9 in (0·8 m), whereas her sister vessel, built of teak, had a displacement of 70 tons and a draft of 4 ft 6 in (1·4 m). The *Ain-Al-Bahr* proved during weeks of trials that she could achieve 13 knots using half the power and fuel that was necessary for her teak sister vessel.

In 1955 there were an estimated 55 builders of aluminium craft in the USA, with a total production of 90 000 boats. Of all the outboard craft produced, 31 per cent were aluminium.

In 1960, the Burger Boat Co. of Manitowoc, Wisconsin, one of **America's biggest producers of 'aluminium' boats** (since 1954) launched the 72 ft (22 m) motor-yacht, *Jigmil IV*. An amount of 35 000 lb of alloy was used in her construction – 26 000 lb in her $\frac{1}{4}$ in (6 mm) and $\frac{1}{3}$ in (8 mm) hull and deck plating and $\frac{3}{16}$ in plating for cabin and interior decks. Extrusions totalled 8500 lb. Soon afterwards, Berger built **the then largest all-welded alloy motor-yacht in the USA**, the 83 ft (25·3 m) luxury twin-screw *Ceriel*.

The **first all-alloy powerboat to compete in the Daily Express International Offshore Powerboat race from Cowes to Torquay** was the 27 ft (8·2 m) Brigand-class *Impetus* (1963), engined by Rolls-Royce petrol units, developing a total 490 bhp.

In 1964, the largest all-aluminium motor-yacht was the *Aurora* (LOA 114 ft 8 in (35 m) × B 22 ft (6·7 m) × D 6 ft 1$\frac{1}{2}$ in (1·9 m)), built to the US designs of Sparkman and Stephens at the Cantiere Navale, Apuania, Italy, and powered by two Mercedes 820-DB turbo-charged 1350 hp engines, giving her a speed of 20 knots under full load.

Between 1969 and 1973 Don Shead designed, and Ernie Sims of Enfield Marine built **the most successful aluminium alloy powerboats to be raced in offshore conditions**. *Miss Enfield* was followed by *Miss Enfield 2*. The latter became *Yellowdrama* for Ken Cassir (1972–73), *Blitz* for John Davey (1974–75), *Blitz* for Alf Bontoft (1976) and re-engined with diesels, *British Buzzard* for Roger Allen (1977–78).

Enfield Avenger (1971) became perhaps **the most well-known and successful Shead hull ever from the yard**, not in her first year under Tommy Sopwith and Pascoe Watson, but subsequently as *Unowot* and then *UNO-Embassy* for Shead, Col Ronnie Hoare and Harry Hyams. A winner of Cowes–Torquay–Cowes (1973 and 1975), she entered her eighth year of top-class competition in 1978.

FERROCEMENT

The first concrete boats to be built by plastering a sand-cement mortar over a framework of iron bars and mesh, were the work of Joseph Louis Lambot, French horticulturalist in 1848 and 1849; they were used for rowing and still survive today.

Between 1917 and 1922, due to World War I steel shortages, over 150 000 tons of concrete shipping was built on both sides of the Atlantic, **the smallest vessels being small tugs and lighters**. In 1943, Nervi carried out **the first recorded experiments on ferro-cement** and sought to understand its properties – before building several vessels immediately after the war.

The firm that has built **the most number of British ferro-cement boats** since then is Windboats Ltd of Wroxham, Norfolk, using the Seacrete process. **The first motorboat to be thus built** was a 1961 Norfolk-Broads-type cruiser (LOA 34 ft (10·4 m) × B 11 ft (3·4 m) × D 3 ft (0·9 m)), powered by a BMC Commodore engine; now 19 years old, she is still cruising.

On 24 August 1964 *Mars*, a 24 ft (7·3 m) Seacrete-hulled motor-cruiser, exploded and caught fire on the Norfolk Broads. The explosion blew the boat's wooden cabin tip 50 ft (15·2 m) in the air. The mast landed in a garden 200 yards (182 m) away; the whole of the interior was gutted by fire. Other than a 1½ in (38 mm) wide crack tapering from 24 in (0·6 m) to nothing on the port side, and a ¾ in (19 mm) crack tapering from 24 in (0·6 m) to nothing on the starboard side, there was no other damage to the hull. This was **the best example possible** for the advantages of ferrocement hulls.

By just under two decades, 350 Seacrete hulls had been built and put into operation in eleven different countries, including police boats in Nigeria, 35 ft (10·7 m) pilot boats in the Middle East, 30 ft (9 m) fishing boats in Iran, Kenya and Somalia, 39 ft (11·9 m) tugboats in Guyana, 50 ft (15·2 m) trawlers for Somalia and South Yemen – and the *Caranx*, a 55 ft (16·8 m) fisheries research vessel. Seacrete hulls ranged in thickness from ⅝ in (15 mm) up to ⅞ in (22 m) up to 1⅛ in (27 mm) thickness, but were flexible with a higher density than either wood or fgrp.

Possibly the smallest concrete motorboat was built in 1974 by Ferro-Boat builders of Owings, Maryland (USA). She is a 10½ ft (3·2 m) outboard-engined dory with carrying capacity for three adults. The hull weighs only 250 lb, and she is still in service.

INFLATABLES

In 880 BC, King Ashurnasirpal II commanded his Assyrian soldiers to cross a river, using animal skins which they continually inflated to keep afloat. During the Sung Dynasty (AD 960–1274) and the Ming Dynasty (1368–1644) of Ancient China, inflated goatskins were used as floats for primitive raft-ferries, which might have been described as **the very first inflatable boats**. This was also the custom in Tibet.

At that time, 'Hsieh-fa' or the spear-raft was possibly **the largest application of floating bags** whereby a raft was made from some 5000 spears and supported by two sponsons, made up of some 20 inflated skins each side. But by the 1930s in China, ox-skin and goatskin rafts (pa-fa or pi-fa-tzu) could use sometimes as many as 800 inflated skins!

Again in India, the 'samai' rafts on the Ganges river were also supported by inflated skins, as was so in Persia and Mesopotamia.

The first inflatable pontoons constructed out of strong canvas, rendered air-proof by india-rubber, to support military floating bridges, were first tested in 1839 by the Duke of Wellington. Forty foot-guards were placed on the raft and towed down river some distance. To test stability, the Duke of Wellington commanded that the guards first sit, and then lie down on the raft. Fully satisfied, the raft was then towed to shore and the men landed.

The first artificially constructed inflatable boat was invented and tested by Lieut. Peter Alexander Halkett RN in 1844. This was the 'Boat Cloak', a semi-circular piece of material, 9 ft (2·7 m) wide × 4 ft 4 in (1·3 m) deep. Inset in this was the inflatable body of the boat, oval in shape, about 7 ft 1 in (2·1 m) in length × 3 ft 6 in (1·1 m) beam. On land, the middle of the diameter of the semi-circle formed the collar of the cloak. There was a nozzle for inflating the boat.

Halkett's first trial run in the Boat-Cloak was from Kew to Westminster Bridge (12 miles (19 km)) during which voyage he was nearly run down by a Metropolitan paddle-steamer. Trial trips at Brighton, Portsmouth, Spithead, Plymouth, Firth of Tay, Cove of Cork, Bay of Dublin – finally took Lieut. Halkett to the Bay of Biscay, where he successfully paddled with a convertible umbrella-sail from HMS *Caledonia* to HMS *St Vincent* of the Experimental Squadron. During 1845, the Admiralty tested a larger version of the Boat Cloak at Portsmouth and Spithead. While deciding that it would be ideal for geographical expeditions, their Lordships rejected it for Naval Service.

Between 1846 and 1857, Halkett's inflatable cloth-boats were used in several Arctic expeditions, particularly by Dr John Rae who was so impressed by its performance that he named a

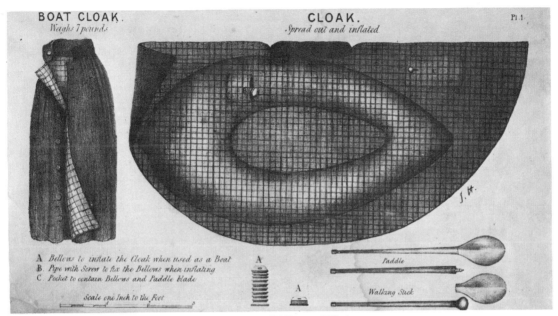

BOAT CLOAK.
Weighs 7 pounds

CLOAK.
Spread out and inflated

Pl.1

A *Bellows to inflate the Cloak when used as a Boat*
B. *Pipe with Screw to fix the Bellows when inflating*
C. *Pocket to contain Bellows and Paddle blade*

Scale one Inch to the Foot

Paddle

Walking Stick

Lieut. Halkett's inflatable 'Boat Cloak' of 1844 (Courtesy HM Patents Office)

point on the West Coast of Melville Peninsula, after Halkett. By fortunate circumstances, Rae's boat can still be seen at Stromness Museum. Despite many favourable comments, Halkett's boat never came into general use.

The first artificially constructed inflatable india-rubber boat, or 'Gutta Percha' boat, was also made by Halkett during the same period, and he also began to design a 30 ft (9·1 m) inflatable canvas lifeboat, to take 30 to 40 persons, but his services with the Royal Navy prevented its completion. He died at Torquay on 23 March 1885, aged 65.

The first motorised inflatable three-pointer was designed by the French inventor Clement Ader in 1901. Its sponson-type wings and tails were inflated by a pump driven by its inboard engine, whilst propulsion was by a submerged propeller. Though the boat worked fairly well, it was considered too complicated and unwieldy for practical use.

The first inflatable boat to be built by the English inventor, Reginald Foster Dagnall (RFD), was tested by the inventor on Wisley Lake, near

Byfleet, Surrey, England in 1919. On its success, the RFD Company was formed to produce flotation gear for aircraft made by Short Brothers. In 1926, R. F. Dagnall's 'Doughnut Ring', for marking the site of crashed aircraft, was being manufactured at the Guildford works, Surrey. In 1932, in conjunction with R. T. Youngman, R. F. Dagnall developed the first inflatable life-rafts for aircraft.

Reginald Foster Dagnell, testing his inflatable boat on Wisley Lake, near Brooklands Motor Course, in 1919 (RFD)

In a pre-1936 catalogue, the RFD Company advertised two sizes of portable inflatable boat: a standard 10 ft (3 m) × 4 ft (1·2 m) × 2 ft (0·6 m) craft, costing £16, which could be powered by a 4 hp obm; and a large 11 ft 6 in (3·5 m) × 4 ft 6 in (1·4 m) × 2 ft 6 in (0·7 m) craft (as had been used by the British African Trade Development Expedition) costing £21, which could be powered by a 10 hp outboard; but they could build any craft up to 20 ft (6·1 m) long. Although bellows could be used, it was recommended that an RFD portable could be inflated in three minutes by the exhaust gases from either a car or motorcycle engine; but buyers were asked to state the size of exhaust pipe of their car or motorcycle! Deflating, rolling up and packing into a valise would normally take no more than five minutes.

Soon afterwards, Dagnall had patented a device whereby his life-rafts, fitted with CO_2 cylinders, could be automatically inflated – an advance adopted by the RAF in 1937.

The first inflatable pontoon boats to be manufactured by the Austrian Semperit concern in 1932 were made with a rubberised sailcloth and had rubber inner tubes. The Semperit concern had grown out of a factory built up by Johann Nepomuk Reithoffer, who in 1824 had taken out a patent for the waterproofing of garments for industrial and agricultural workers.

The first inflatable boat to be built by the Société Zodiac was a two-seater kayak, designed by the French engineer Pièrre Debroutelle in 1934. Zodiac concern had grown out of the balloon workshop founded in 1896 by Maurice Mallet, and re-named the French Airships Society in 1908.

'Duprene' (later known as neoprene) was the first commercially successful synthetic rubber, developed by Dr Wallace Carothers at E. I. DuPont de Nemours in 1931. As such, Zodiac were soon experimenting with duprene for the construction of an inflatable catamaran incorporating parallel buoyancy chambers pointed at each end, together with a centre-board that could carry an outboard engine at its stern (1936). The boat's design was eventually modified to the shape of a 'U', with connecting lateral buoyancy chambers meeting at the bow. The stern was enclosed with a wooden transom. After some exhaustive trials, this was **the first**

inflatable boat to be built for the French Navy, to carry bombs and torpedos to seaplanes (1938).

The German armaments build-up after the Austrian Anschluss, put pressure on the Semperit concern to improve their inflatable boat, and by 1938 they were producing 15 ft (4·6 m) craft powered by 40 hp outboard engines.

The first pneumatically inflated canopied life-rafts were produced by RFD at their Godalming works in 1938 and the Royal Canadian Air Force was the first organisation to adopt them. During the Battle of Britain (1940), working closely with the Ministry of Aircraft Production, R. F. Dagnall developed **the one-man yellow inflatable dinghy**, and by 1 April 1941 all fighter pilots in the RAF were equipped with a single-seater dinghy pack fitted to the parachute pack. During World War II, it was estimated that 40000 sailors lost their lives at sea, after successfully abandoning ship, whereas 17000 allied airmen were saved after ditching. R. F. Dagnall died in 1942.

After the war, these dinghies came onto the market as Government surplus, selling for as little as 50p each.

In 1945, Zodiac manufactured their **first four-man inflatable life-raft** for the French Air Force, and in 1947 a one-man lifeboat was made to be used in sea operations.

The first mass-produced inflatable boats to be put on the pleasure market in France were produced from rubberised cotton, cut into shaped panels and welded together in an autoclave, by Werner Philip of La Nautique Sportiv.

Until the 1950s, inflatable craft had suffered from the effects of sunlight. But from 1952, they could be coated with chloro-sulphonated-poly-ethylene, given the tradename by DuPont de Nemours of 'Hypalon'. It was in 1952 that Prof. Alain Bombard crossed the Atlantic Ocean single-handed in a standard Zodiac Mark III inflatable – **the first man to use this type of craft**.

The first Avon inflatables were produced in 1959 by the Avon Rubber Company's Marine Division, then based at Melksham, Wiltshire. The initial reason for producing craft was to tender for Government contracts, but it was soon realised that great potential lay in the leisure market. The Company moved to Dafen Llanelli, South Wales in 1964 in order to expand. (In 1978, Avon Inflatables exhibited a 12-year-old Redstart dinghy at the London Boat Show. This had been used as a tender to Maj. Pat Steptoe's yacht, *Silhouette II*, since 1962.)

The world's largest inflatable boat was the *Amphitrite*, used to carry a mini-submarine during Capt. Jacques-Yves Cousteau's airborne undersea expeditions. *Amphitrite* (LOA 65 ft (19·8 m) × B 29 ft (8·8 m) × D 1 ft 2 in (0·35 m)) took Zodiac just eleven months in 1960 to construct. Her mainframe was of magnesium-aluminium alloy tubing, weighing 5700 lb and held together by only 57 bolts. Her 5 ft (1·5 m) high nylon cylinders were made up of nine separate air-filled inner tubes. Originally powered by quadruple 80 hp outboard engines, *Amphitrite* was soon given Hispano-Suiza diesels, powering Berkeley water-jet units, giving her a loaded speed of 30 knots. Compared to 55 tons for a conventionally built hull, she weighed only 6 tons.

The first batch of inflatables to be accepted into service by the RNLI were RFD 15 ft 6 in (4·7 m), 40 hp outboard engined craft, capable of 20 knots. They were distributed around the British Isles in 1963. **The first rescue** was reported from Aberyswyth, Wales in August when three people and a dog were saved. By 1968, 1500 people had been rescued by the Inshore Rescue Service.

The most successful inflatable racing driver has been Tony Williams. He had already won the Amsterdam Three Hours of 1967 and 1968, among many other international class placings, when he tackled inflatables. In 1970, Williams took 1st Overall in the Powerboat National Inflatable Race, defending that title for three subsequent years. On Lake Windermere, in 1972, he also created UIM Speed Records in his 12½ ft (3·8 m) Aeroazur inflatables: in the PE Class, using a 55 to 60 hp Penta outboard, he was clocked at 62·094 mph (99·930 km/h); in 1974 Angelo Vassena of Italy lifted that record to 64·51 mph (105·27 km/h) in a Carniti-engined Dorati inflatable; a record which has remained unbeaten for four years.

In its heyday, every major club organised inflatable races, including the BP-sponsored Somo Trophy held at the LMBRC, Iver – sometimes as many as 30 boats competed. But by 1975, inflatable racing had died away, possibly because an embryo British Inflatable Powerboat Club never took shape with a regular venue/ headquarters.

The first rigid inflatable for use in rough seas was the *Atalanta*, designed and built in 1963 by Rear Admiral D. J. Hoare (RN Rtd), Headmaster of Atlantic College. She was made by glueing the tubes of an inflatable to a flat piece of plywood with a small central fin. It proved seaworthy and won a prize in the 20 hp class of a local powerboat race on a rough day when conventional small speedboats were either breaking up or flooding.

Working with his students and later a full-time carpenter, Rear Admiral Hoare went on to design and produce the Bravo fleet of rigid-hulled inflatables, including the well-known *Psychedelic Surfer* which successfully competed in the Round Britain Powerboat Race (1969).

From the flat piece of plywood, Hoare progressed to a deep 'V' hull, made of ply and packed with polystyrene and decked over. The tubes were glued and nailed to both the deck or platform and the sides of the 'V' hull with strips of rubber. In the early designs for use with 20 hp motors, the hull was set back about 2 ft (0·6 m) from the bow tubes which gave a pocket of air up front, producing a much softer ride. Before long, the design took the bow of the rigid hull right up to the front of the tubes. The pocket of air was no longer required because better design and construction enabled 50 hp outboard motors to be used, which meant that once the throttle was opened up, the rigid inflatable went straight onto the plane.

Before long the RNLI were considering the possibility of adopting the rigid-inflatable and decided on the *Atlantic 21*, a 16-footer (4·8 m) powered by twin 40 hp outboard giving 27 knots with a crew of three on board, developed from the *Atlantic 17*, driven by a single 40 hp outboard giving 22 knots with a crew of two on board. While the original models used plywood, production boats for service around the coast came to be made in fgrp, moulded by Halmatic.

Inflatables come in different shapes and sizes (Avon)

The first rigid inflatable to be powered by an inboard diesel engine was the *Osborne Pacific 30*, the first of which was built in the summer of 1976 by William Osborne Ltd of Littlehampton. The *Pacific 30* (LOA 30 ft (9 m) × B 9 ft 9 in (3 m) × D 3 ft (0·9 m)) was powered by a 180 hp turbo-charged diesel engine to travel at 26 knots. The deep 'V' round bilge rigid hull could either be cold-moulded in marine ply, or in fgrp by Halmatic, whilst large inflatable tubes with nine separate air chambers were supplied by FPT. The *Pacific 30* was specifically designed as a rescue craft operating from supply vessels to the North Sea oil and gas rigs.

In France, where a company called Alsthom Atlantique had developed a dynamic oil-skimming unit called the Cyclonet (in 1974), it was decided to make use of Zodiac inflatables to carry it out to the site of an oil spillage. The cyclonet permitted recovery of up to 30 cu m (39 cu yards) per hour of oil spillage or other polluting liquids from areas of water other than high seas.

Current estimates as to the number of in-flatables commercially produced so far must go far above the total of estimates given by Avon (over 150 000 units since 1959); Zodiac (over 150 000 since 1934); RFD (500 000 life-rafts since 1932) – reaching the million mark. Given the average length of an inflatable as 13 ft (4 m), if every inflatable hitherto constructed were to be placed bow-to-stern, it would create a chain, some 2460 miles (3960 km) long.

Showing the versatility of a light racing Air Cushion Vehicle (Courtesy Neil MacDonald)

Shearwater, the very first Red Funnel hydrofoil (a Seaflight H57) to go into service between Southampton and Cowes on 5 May 1969 (Courtesy Red Funnel Group)

The summertime joys of inflatable motorboating (Courtesy Avon)

Typical Marine Compression Ignition engine of the 1930s. 140 parts were tabulated by Shell-Mex & BP for this diagram. The internal workings were numerically displayed by lifting cardboard cut-outs and flaps (Courtesy British Petroleum Limited)

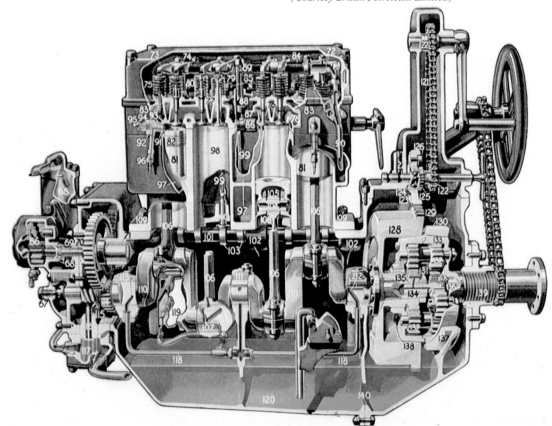

KEVLAR

In 1969, DuPont de Nemours developed a new family of petroleum-based high-strength, organic fibres, different from regular nylon fibres; one of these, designated PRD-49, was made available to selected US Government Departments. By 1970 it had begun to be developed for the rubber reinforcement of motorcar tyres of the radial type and very soon afterwards was being employed to reinforce the interior panels of both the Lockheed L-1001 and Concorde Supersonic airliners. In July 1973, DuPont first introduced this patented fibre commercially as 'Kevlar 49', offering excellent tensile strength and twice the stiffness of glass-fibre at approximately half its weight. 'Kevlar', like most DuPont trademarks, was selected by computer. The normal procedure was for basic requirements – two syllables, X number of letters, beginning and ending with a consonant – to be fed into the computer. This was how the best-known DuPont trademarks like 'Teflon', 'Dacron', 'Antron', 'Aldyl', 'Tyvek' – and 'Kevlar' – came about.

The generic term 'aramid' was adopted by the US Federal Trade Commission to describe the family of fibres (chemically known as aromatic polyamides) in which Kevlar 49 was included.

Available from European weavers such as Fothergill & Harvey (UK), SAATI (Italy), Brochier et Fils (France), etc – in yard, roving, mat and woven fabric forms – an increasing number of applications soon came to be found for this Kevlar 49 aramid: lightweight bulletproof clothing, heat-resistant garments, shockproof helmets, aircraft fuselage parts, exterior fairings and helicopter rotor blades.

The first motorboat to be built in Europe, using Kevlar 49, was constructed in 1974 by Fabio Buzzi.

In 1975 the McLaren M23 Ford racing-car used resin-impregnated Kevlar 49 as a reinforcement for non-structural panels, thus replacing the aluminium alloy panels previously used, with a weight saving of 35 to 40 per cent. The following year the McLaren 1976 Ford racing-car, driven by World Champion James Hunt, incorporated nose cone, radiator covers and airbox moulded from glass-fibre, Kevlar 49 and heat-resistant Nomex (DuPont tradename) paper honeycomb.

That same year, a number of rigorous field tests were run on wild rivers in California, Idaho and West Virginia with **the first inflatable boats to be constructed of woven Kevlar 29**, coated with urethane by the Maravia Corporation of San Leandro. River trials included running the inflatables down rapids and deliberately into and off sharp rocks and boulders; the bottom fabric was only slightly scraped. Because Kevlar/urethane inflatables were as much as one half lighter than their nylon counterparts, they were much easier to manoeuvre in rough water – less air pressure was needed to inflate them and when inflated they were ten times stiffer than nylon-based inflatables, with five times the 'tear' strength.

In September 1976, the 29 ft (9 m) *Scarab M-9* became the first Kevlar powerboat to create a speed record when it set a new mark of 72·57 mph (116·79 km/h) in the American Power Boat Association Modified IV (multiple-engine) production class. This official speed was clocked during the Sixth Annual Powerboat Magazine Offshore World Speed Trials at Marina del Rey, California.

Smith's Scarab Marine now offered Kevlar 49 as an optional hull reinforcement material in its 29-foot (8·8 m) production model, whilst building several Kevlar 49, 38 ft (11·6 m) racers to run in the Open Class Offshore circuit for 1977.

By spring 1977, five American boatbuilders were offering a Kevlar 49 hull option for their standard motorboats, whilst one of them, **Hydra-Sports, who were the first to use Kevlar**, had already sold more than 2000 boats reinforced with the DuPont aramid, and were expecting to double production during the subsequent year. The Maravia Corporation was also planning mass-production of Kevlar 29 urethane inflatables.

The first public showing of Kevlar 49 hulls in Europe took place at the 17th International Nautical Salon at Genoa, Italy from 14–24 October 1977. A section of a 16 ft (5 m) Zodiac inflatable, with 100 per cent Kevlar reinforcement, was displayed alongside a Kevlar speedboat hull on the DuPont stand, whilst Italcraft, Cigala Bertinetti, Abbate, and several other

Italian boatbuilders, displayed sports motor-cruisers reinforced with Kevlar.

In offshore powerboat racing, Bertram, Cobra, Scarab and Cigarette boatyards reinforced their hulls with Kevlar 49. Indeed it was in the face of rough seas at Key West, during the World Champion Offshore race in November 1977 that the Kevlar-hulled Scarab *Kaama*, piloted by Betty Cook, survived the course to win the race, followed by the Kevlar-hulled Cobra, *Beep Beep*, with the Kevlar-hulled Cigarette, *Powerboat Magazine Special*, driven by Bob Nordskog in 4th place. From these performances, it was becoming apparent that Kevlar was liable to make a complete take-over of fgrp motorboat hull construction by the 1980s.

The first British boatyard to experiment with Kevlar-hulled motorboats was Fletcher Marine. After finding the right saw and drills, the Burntwood yard together with SRL developed a new resin to speed up the curing process. From June 1978, a Mercury 175 hp Arrowshaft 25, built with Kevlar 49, ran trials against a Mercury 175 hp Arrowshaft, conventionally built of fgrp. The Kevlar Arrowshaft was a $\frac{1}{2}$ ton lighter due to its stringers having been lightened, and driven by McKinnol at 85 mph (135 km/h), it proved some 6 mph (10 km/h) faster, and won the third race for which it entered.

On 7/8 October 1978, Fabbio Buzzi of Italy, driving a VM 3·5-litre powered hydroplane, shattered world diesel records on Lake Sabaudia, near Rome. His boat, **built in Kevlar 49** by F. B. Marine, set up a speed of 102·83 mph (165·59 km/h) which beat the previous record of 87 mph (140 km/h) set up earlier in the year by Giulio Abbate with a Fiat-powered boat. In the one-hour Endurance Test, the previous record of 47·5 mph (75·6 km/h), held by a Perkins-engined craft, was almost doubled with a speed of 79·6 mph (128·2 km/h). New records were also established over 24 miles (38 km) – 79·964 mph (128·689 km/h), and in the two-hour Endurance Test 89·760 mph (144·456 km/h).

In the late 1970s, Dr Bob Magoon, 45-year-old Miami eye surgeon is to make an assault on the speed record for crossing the Atlantic Ocean under power. To succeed, Magoon and his four-man crew will have to endure nearly 80 hr and 3440 miles (5535 km) of non-stop pounding across the ocean at better than 41 mph (66 km/h). Their boat, *Citicorp Traveler*, a 45-ft (72 m) Cigarette design is **built in Kevlar 49**.

PAINT AND VARNISH

The first technical description of the paint and varnish industry was made in Jean Felix Watin's *Formulary* (first published in the 1770s). It described how, using copals and amber as the principle varnish resins, with turpentine as a thinner, a typical varnish recipe required 1 lb of resin to $\frac{1}{2}$ lb of oil. Pigments were ground with the aid of a large stone trough and ball muller. These methods remained unchanged up to and including the dawn of the motorboat. Indeed as late as 1910, so few chemists were occupied with paint technology that it was said that one of them could probably name all the others.

The first daylight fluorescent pigments, now known by the tradename of 'Day-Glo' colours, were produced in 1933 at a Los Angeles drug store by a young amateur magician called Joe Switzer. Inspired by an article about 'black light' (invisible ultra-violet light), Switzer discovered that several drugs in his father's store, glowed in the rays of an improvised lamp; by mixing the drugs with shellac, he painted some props and put on a magic show which amazed his high-school classmates. Together with his brother Bob, Joe Switzer proceeded to market his invention. Before long the Switzers were

Kevlar-built Citicorp Traveler *on trials in 1978 (Mercury Marine)*

Early 1951: Joe Switzer and Dick Ward, inventors of 'Dayglo' colours (SWADA)

joined by a chemist called Dick War and they ran a lithography company in Cleveland, Ohio, producing fluorescent inks. Day-Glo colours were three times as brilliant as their conventional counterparts and during World War II, the former were used to great advantage in air/sea rescue operations.

The first company to introduce fluorescent colours to the British market in the form of Day-Glo silk screen process inks in the early part of 1950 (these inks being manufactured with pigments imported from Joe Switzer's US company) was Dane & Co. Ltd. Because of considerable demand, in 1951, Donald Dane had soon combined the names *Switzer* with *Dane* to produce the name Swada (London) Ltd, to manufacture fluorescent pigments in England and export them into Europe.

In March 1953, on the recommendation of the Vision Committee of the Flying Personnel Research Committee, trials were arranged to determine more accurately the ideal colour and type of fluorescent dyed materials for use on survival equipment – inflatable boats and lifejackets. The trial was conducted at RNAS Culdrose, Cornwall in July 1953. Some 7 miles

(11 km) offshore, six inflatable dinghies, interlinked at 100 ft (30 m) intervals, were inverted to show: standard yellow, aluminium foil cloth, neon-red on cotton, neon-red rubberised, flame orange on cotton, flame orange rubberised.

An aircraft equipped with radar (200 yd (183 m) range) located and homed in on these targets at 120 knots air/sea search speed, at heights of 500 ft (152 m) and 1000 ft (304 m). The moment a target was seen, two observers called 'Contact!' and named the colour, whilst the radar operator collated the distance from aircraft to inflatable; this test was carried out a number of times in different conditions (cloudy, cross-sun, against sun, sunset, dusk). It was found that 'standard yellow' was the least conspicuous, whilst **rubberised flame-orange material was the most conspicuous**, with flame-orange dye on cotton next. RFD supplied the inflatables.

In 1958, Dane and Co. Ltd received the following telegram: 'Donald Campbell officially stated on breaking World Water Speed Record today that if it hadn't been for Day-glo covered marker buoy he would have missed Record.'

Fluorescent colouring first appeared on lifeboats in 1969 when the first Day-Glo orange moulded fgrp McLachlan inshore lifeboat appeared. The rest of the RNLI's fleet had their superstructures painted orange after that.

The specific claim made by fgrp boatbuilders that no paint maintenance would be necessary was, in the course of time, proved to be inaccurate, and by the late 1950s many such motorboats had become discoloured and lost their gloss. In 1960, the International Paint Co. Ltd (founded in 1881 by the Holzapfel family at Felling-on-Tyne, near Gateshead, England) were **the first to develop and market a two-component polyurethene finishing system for fgrp craft** – it was given the tradename 'International 708'. In 1978, this two-pot system was improved so that boats would have a gloss-permanence of four years, and would last over ten years without any reduction in weather resistance; this was called 'Perfection 709'.

11 ENGINEERING

Petrol-driven boat on Lake Victoria, Africa, in 1904 (Mary Evans Picture Library)

INBOARD ENGINES

Ailsa Craig

Founded as the Craig Dorwald company by Ellis A. D. Kisch, this company soon changed its name to the Putney Motor Company. The most powerful petrol motor built for motor-launches in 1904 was the 150 hp 12-cylinder Craig-Dorwald (4 ft 3 in (1·3 m) long × 2 ft (0·6 m) high × 2 ft 8 in (0·8 m) broad, and weighing 950 lb). Originally built by the Putney Motor Co. for an airship, it was installed in Fred May's 40 ft (12·1 m) racing boat, *Defender*;

fitted with two six-cylinder magnetos, the first made, to overcome salt water damp tracking of the HT distributor; the crankcase was of aluminium, and as with other Craig-Dorwald engines, the crankshaft was set in advance of the cylinder axis. Unsuccessful for racing, this pioneer V-12 engine was ultimately exported to China, where it was installed in a junk.

Soon after this the company again changed its name to the Ailsa Craig Motor Co. Ltd of Chiswick, London (Ailsa Craig is a small, domed island in the Firth of Clyde, Scotland). Until the mid 1930s, the company produced some 20 types of petrol/paraffin marine engines

The 150 hp 12-cylinder Craig-Dorwald engines of 1904 (Robert Kisch)

(developing up to 90 bhp), the most popular being the LA4, LB4, Z4 and a two-stroke horizontally-opposed twin, developing 4/6 hp, the R2 (known as the 'Pup' and selling for £54). Ailsa Craig engines proved so reliable for every type of craft, that before long, Mr Kisch, Managing Director, had been appointed Engine Manufacturer to His Majesty King George V.

Marine diesel engines were added to the range from 1934, starting with the 8/12 bhp DD1, with split sump and external plunger oil pump. The DD, CF and DF ranges of diesel which soon followed, incorporated Acro pistons (developed since the early 1920s by Bosch of Stuttgart, who was a friend of Kisch), with the choke in the piston crown; the DD's had a bore of $3\frac{7}{8}$ in, whilst the CF's and DF's had $4\frac{1}{2}$ in bore; the 32 cwt DR 12-cylinder engine, developing 96 to 144 hp, and capable of powering vessels up to 150 tons, cost £960 in 1936. A great many Ailsa Craig DD4 engines were used for the war effort. Post-war the company moved to Ashford, Kent where 'batch' production began on their RF series, fitted with Ricardo Whirlpool combustion chamber (first adopted in 1937), choke in the head and a flat top piston; the most popular engine in this series was the RF2. By 1961, RL, RK and RA engines went on the market, the RK gearbox allowing reverse engines at full power for an indefinite period. In 1979, Ailsa Craig demonstrated their new T 4·5, 4 hp engine. Ailsa Craig are now based at Redhill, Surrey.

Austin-Morris

In 1910 **Herbert Austin** designed and installed a 300 hp engine, of his own design, into the motor-launch *Irene I*, named after his daughter, and became the fastest man on Southampton Waters. The following year, the output was increased to 380 hp and the engine installed in an improved *Irene II*. In 1912 'Pa' Austin installed two new 400 hp engines, built at Longbridge, Birmingham, into the racing hydroplane *Maple Leaf IV*, which reached 50 mph (80 km/h). He also developed small, 2-cylinder 20 hp, and 6-cylinder 60 hp, engines before World War I.

During the 1920s and 30s, whilst Austins of Longbridge produced the four-cylinder 8 hp 'Thetis', and the four-cylinder, 12 hp 'Triton' marine petrol engines, Wortham Blake Ltd, of Whetstone, N. London, were supplying conversion kits for the marinisation of the Austin Seven motorcar engine (they also did the same for Morris Cowley and Model-T Ford engines). During World War II, very many hundreds of Austin 'Thetis' engines were converted for ships' lifeboats. Post-war, Austins abandoned their Thetis and brought out the six-cylinder 4-litre 'Skipper 100', the four-cylinder 2-litre 'Skipper 60', and the four-cylinder $1\frac{1}{2}$-litre 'Skipper 35' marine petrol engines; also the Austin 'Chief' range of petrol-paraffin equivalents, with a 'bi-fuel' automatic fuel changeover system developed by James G. Allday of Weybridge Motors Ltd.

When Austin merged with Morris in 1951 to form the British Motor Corporation (BMC), it was mutually agreed that the Austin 'Skipper/Chief' range should be faded out; spares for these engines ran out in the early 1960s.

In 1929 **William Morris** (later Lord Nuffield), became interested in the marine market because of its possibilities and began to build a marine engine up at Coventry, based on the 'Bullnose Morris' car engine, as developed by Hotchkiss of France. He produced a four-cylinder monobloc unit with a rating of 12 to 24 hp at 1000 to 2000 rpm. The prototype was thoroughly tested in the 30 ft (9·1 m) cruiser *Nymphaea* on a canal, on the Upper Thames, and in the Thames Estuary.

With immense foresight, Morris registered a series of trade-names for the marine engines he would be developing: 'Navigator', 'Vedette',

'Commodore', 'Sea-Lord', 'Commander', 'Captain', and 'Admiral'.

His first engine, the Navigator Mk I of 1930, was followed by the four-cylinder side-valve Vedette Mk I (1933), based on the original Morris Minor car and fitted with a Gleniffer marine gearbox (later abandoned for a Morris design). Followed the Commodore Mk I (1934), an OHV, OHC engine, with dry sump lubrication based on the early Morris Oxford car. 1936 saw the four-cylinder 6 to 12 hp Vedette Mk III, which was a thoroughly waterproof version of the Mk II. Very many hundreds of Vedette Mk III's were built for ships' lifeboats. 1936 also saw the Commodore Mk II, six-cylinder 20 to 40 hp, based on the engine used in Morris Commercial vans and trucks, and in every wartime ambulance; this engine went on selling until 1957!

Post-war, **Morris produced their first marine diesel engine**, the aluminium-based six-cylinder OHV 'Sea-Lord' of 1949.

On the Austin-Morris merger of 1951, the BMC Marine Division at Coventry brought out the Vedette Mk IV and its lifeboat version, the Mk V, together with the Navigator Mk II petrol engines.

In 1957, the 3·4 litre 38 to 52 hp BMC Commodore and 2·2 litre, 22 to 31 hp Commander diesel engines were brought out alongside the 950 cc BMC Vedette Mk IV (based on the later Morris Minor car), and also the BMC Navigator (as used in the MG Magnette, Austin Cambridge and Wolseley cars).

The Newage (Northern Electrical Welding and General Engineering) Co. Ltd had been founded by Sid Harris in the 1930s. In 1951 Harris obtained a concession to industrialise any of BMC's engines. In 1960, Newage (Manchester) Ltd bought out the Marine Engine Division of BMC Coventry. In 1961 BMC/ Newage brought out the 5·1-litre Sea-Lord petrol engine, followed by the Newage Commander and the Newage Captain in 1962. In 1964 the 1622 cc Newage Navigator and the 1098 cc Newage Vedette Mk VII appeared. In 1965, Newage (Manchester) Ltd became Newage Lyon Ltd, based in Stamford, Lincs. In 1966 appeared the Vedette Mk VIII 1100 cc 19 to 23 hp petrol engine. Soon after Newage further changed their name to Newage Engineers, and then Newage Marine, until in 1972 Charterhouse Industrial Developments, who owned

Newage, decided to 'hive off' the marine engine side, and the name 'Tempest Diesels Ltd' came into being, progressing to the 6·98 litre, 105 to 110 hp Tempest Sea Lord and the 1·8 litre Tempest Captain. In 1979, Tempest Diesels Ltd were exhibiting a range of engines from 31 to 180 bhp based on 'Leyland' and 'Ford' units.

The most ironic part of this complicated pedigree of marine engine manufacture is that, of the trade-names originally registered by Lord Nuffield in 1930, 'Admiral' has yet to be used!

Brooke Marine

Although Walter Brooke of Lowestoft had installed a reciprocating steam engine into the launch *Nellie*, built by Sam Richards, in 1887, it was only during J. W. Brooke & Co.'s expansion as an iron foundry that Mawdsley Brooke was inspired by a Mr Estcourt's 16 ft (4·8 m) Daimler-engined, 'The Old Tub', and built the first three-cylinder Brooke marine engine, installed in Estcourt's houseboat on Wroxham Broad. The central cylinder worked on steam from the heat generated by the water-jackets of the other two petrol-fired cylinders. Parallel with motorcar development, Mawdsley Brooke teamed up with Reynolds and Miller, local boatbuilders, to

Mawdsley Brooke

'The English chaplain here (Arcachon, France) is credited with having described Brooke I, *after hearing her deafening exhaust and seeing her big bow wave, as an infernal monster with angels' wings!' (1905)*

produce a series of racing boats called either 'Baby' or 'Brooke'. *Brooke I* was powered by a special, six-cylinder, 400 hp racing-engine, whilst *Brooke II* was powered by a 100 hp engine. Meanwhile, the more standard Brooke units were a single-cylinder, 4 hp/two-cylinder, 8 hp/three-cylinder, 12hp/four-cylinder, 18 hp. Foreign exports included the *Marquita*, shipped to Buenos Aires in 1906, and a 27 ft (8·2 m) auxiliary yacht, built for Argentina the following year.

By 1911, Brooke gave up sub-contracting to separate boatbuilders and established their own boatyard of Brooke Motor Craft Co. beside Lake Lothing, the outlet from Oulton Broad to Lowestoft Harbour. Brooke's most affluent customer was Howard ('Bourne &') Hollingsworth, who commissioned *Crusader* and the *Cordon Rouge* series of racing boats; *Cordon Rouge IV* was, at one stage, experimentally powered by two 300 hp V8 Brooke-designed engines. At the same time, passenger and cargo motor-launches were being sold as far afield as Bombay, Greece and the River Plate. During

World War I, 230 service craft of various types were built for Government Departments, including Brookes' first steel ships – minesweepers for the Navy. The HMD class were laid down for naval use, but after the war were sold into private ownership to become steam drifters at Lowestoft. The 1920s saw Mawdsley Brooke' sons, Jack and Waveney ('Pick'), using the basic design of the Universal engine to develop the 5½ hp, two-cylinder Brooke Dominion and the 10 hp, four-cylinder Brooke Empire marine engines, installed in both motor-yachts and fishing craft, exported to Russia, Central and South America and the Sudan.

In 1929, Brookes received an order from the Brazilian Government for 30, 30 ft (9·1 m) fast sea-going launches with 100 hp motors and a speed of 20 knots, together with three 44 ft (13·4 m) express cruisers with two 100 hp Brooke motors and a speed of 17 knots. Standardised craft eventually came into being and Brookes' contribution was the 100 hp *Seacar* and the 18 ft (5·5 m) Standard runabout, many of which were built.

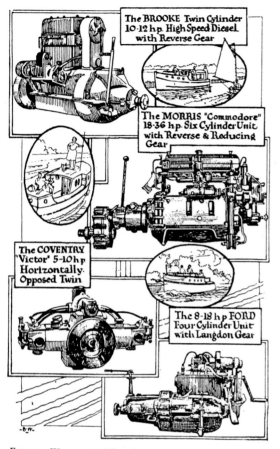

Four pre-War marine inboard engines

Jack Brooke also developed the first British 1½ litre marine engine, installing it in the hydroplane, *Mr Poo*, then after modification in the highly successful hydroplane *Bulldog*. In 1925 he set a world record of 38·17 knots for the 1½ litre Class. Mawdsley Brooke retired in 1935 and Jack Brooke left the family business to join the Rootes group in 1936. In 1939, Brookes were taken over by the Harry Dowsett Group. The yard was expanded to cope with Royal Naval contracts for motor-launches, motor-torpedo boats, motor fishing vessels, seaplane tenders and supply launches for the Fleet Air Arm. A slack period followed the war, the company's apprentices even having time to build a yard boat. The old boatyard was closed down in 1955 and Pick Brooke severed his connection with Brooke Marine in 1956. Both Mawdsley and Jack Brooke died in 1958, within a few weeks of

each other; the racing Brookes had won over 370 trophies since 1904.

By this time the Dowsett Group were completing an order for £6½ million for 20 distant water Soviet trawlers. They went on to build trawlers for British and South African owners, tugs for New Zealand and Pakistan, steel lifeboats for the RNLI and oil rig supply vessels for the North Sea. In addition the yard built vessels for the Royal Navy and the Navies of the USA, Pakistan, Libya, the Sheikdom of Oman, Nigeria, New Zealand and Kenya. The *Constance*, a refrigerated meat and fruit ship, is the largest vessel built at the Brooke Marine Yard.

Chrysler

From its formation in 1925, by Walter P. Chrysler, the Chrysler Corporation began to marinise automobile engines; Chrysler himself used to commute to work in a motorboat. By 1926, the company had received so many orders for conversions that they opened a Marine and Industrial Division. Beginning with the Imperial engine, developing over 100 hp, incorporating an extra large seven-bearing counter-balanced crankshaft with webbed crankcase, a great many Chrysler marine engines were used in Chris-Craft runabouts.

Fiat (Fabbrica Italiana Automobili Torino)

Established in 1899 as a motorcar factory in Turin, this company entered motorboat racing

The 960 hp Fiat marine engine, M.905, developed for racing in the 1930s

at the earliest possibility, taking first and second prizes at the 1903 Stresa Regatta on Lake Maggiore. Their first successful petrol engine was the 53A, a four-cylinder unit with magneto ignition, developing 24 to 35 hp at 1200 rpm. Installed in racing hulls, such as the FIAT X, constructed at Fiat's Muggiano boatyard at Spezia, this motor scored up several race victories. By 1911, Fiat was offering five types of four-cylinder petrol motor, developing from 12 to 50 hp, and in 1913 a hydroplane called *Le Quatre* was powered by a 300 hp engine.

Alongside this development, the Fiat San Giorgio Company, under their · Development Chief, Giovanni Chiesa, had been developing progressively larger two-stroke marine diesel engines for ships, and post-war, the Italian MAS craft were powered by such engines. By the 1930s, a four-stroke high-speed diesel (the V 1616), developing 720 hp, had been evolved for high-speed gunboats.

Simultaneously, standard Fiat car engines were marinised for use in motorboats, namely the M914 (four-cylinder, $1\frac{1}{2}$ litre, developing 18 hp at 2300 rpm); the M921 (six-cylinder, $2\frac{1}{2}$ litre, developing 32 hp at 2200 rpm); and the M925 (six-cylinder, $3\frac{3}{4}$ litres, developing 45 hp at 2000 rpm). While for racing, the M905 was specially developed; in May 1931, its 960 hp propelled Count Theo Rossi's *Torino* to a circuit-racing speed of 60·377 mph (97·167 km/h).

Gardner

Founded in 1868 by Lawrence Gardner in a Manchester cellar, his six sons soon became involved with the oil engine in 1894, moving to Barton Hall Engine Works, Paticroft in 1898. The early 1900s saw Gardner two-stroke 'hot-bulb' semi-diesels sold for marine use. Their first four-stroke, high-speed marine diesel, carefully developed since 1925 by Joseph Gardner and his son Hugh, made its first appearance at the 1929 Engineering and Marine Exhibition at Olympia as the '4L2', and was at once successful. During the 1930s this was followed by the lightweight 'LW', the bigger 'L3', the '4LK'; post-war saw the introduction of horizontal high-speed engines such as the 'HLW' and the 'LX'. From 1954, Gardner Engines Ltd began supplying units to the RNLI.

Gleniffer

Named after Gleniffer Braes, a ridge of low grassy slopes, south-west of Glasgow, this company was founded in 1908 at Paisley, moving to Anniesland, Glasgow in 1913. That year the Scottish Motor Boat Racing Championships saw sweeping victories for craft engined with either the 8 to 10 hp or 20 to 28 hp 'Gleniffer' engines. The first Gleniffer marine high-speed diesel engine, developing 80 hp at 900 rpm, with its marine-type bedplate and clerestory head, having horizontally opposed valves, was also first exhibited at the 1929 Olympia Motor Show. Gleniffer Engines Ltd produced the first British V-12 marine diesel engine and also the first V-16. The Vee-type engines were abandoned post-war and the DH and DB series introduced. The DB4 and DB6 cylinder engines developed 48 and 72 bhp respectively, whilst the DH three-, four-, six-, and eight-cylinder engines developed 60, 80, 120 and 160 bhp respectively. Twin DH8's were often installed in ferries, fishing boats and fireboats, whilst DB engines tended to power motor-yachts and motor-cruisers. Gleniffer Engines were taken over by the Bergius Kelvin Co. in September 1963, and the Anniesland factory was sold in 1967.

Kelvin

In March 1906, Walter and Willie Bergius of Glasgow installed one of their four-cylinder, 12 hp Kelvin motorcar engines in a 23 ft (7 m) rowing gig, the *Kelvin* which was so successful in winning practically every race in its own class on the Clyde that the Bergius Car & Engine Company had soon changed over to marine engine production. A 7 hp unit was developed to drive an overside folding propeller. A 7 hp Kelvin engine was first fitted to a Scottish fishing boat, *The Brothers* of Campbeltown, in 1907. From then on the rehabilitation of the smaller, redundant vessels of the British inshore fishing fleet began.

In 1910, after superb publicity from nine firsts by their racing launch *Kelvin II*, and with a total of 700 marine engines, the Bergius Launch & Engine Company moved to a larger factory at 254 Dobbies Loan. By 1913 seven models, from 3 to 60 hp were on the market and by World War

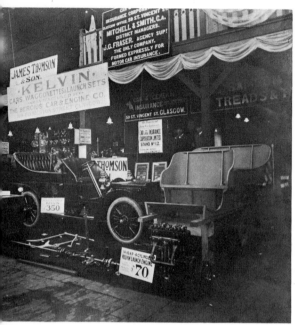

The Kelvin stand at the 1905 Motor Show; note the Kelvin launch engine at the bottom right

I, 1000 fishing boats and 250 sailing yachts had been fitted with auxiliary Kelvin engines.

Between 1908 and 1912, Bergius designed a series of standard motor-launches, ranging from 20 to 50 ft (6·1 to 15·2 m) plus, which he proposed to carry in stock. Hull construction was placed with various boatbuilders at home and abroad and the bare hulls sent to the company's boat shed in Glasgow, where engines, drives, and fittings were added. Specifications accompanying the designs were very complete, so as to ensure standardisation – even down to the size of the nails used. By 1939, the company had completed 1178 standard launches.

In about 1920, the company acquired the right to use the Burt McCullum single-sleeve valve originally embodied in the Argyll motorcar engine. Several thousand Kelvin-Sleeve engines were turned out before 1935, when manufacture was finally given up, mainly due to public prejudice against the sleeve valve. A series of poppet-valve engines, designed by Sir Harry Ricardo, was introduced as the Kelvin-Ricardo in 1927, which formed the bulk of the company's output until the first diesels were produced in 1932.

In spring 1930, the Newfoundland schooner, *Neptune II*, fitted with a 60 hp Model G4 'Kelvin-Ricardo' auxiliary, crossed the Atlantic in 20 days – the engine running at full power for 18 days, 4 hr. In summer 1934, *Neptune II* made a round trip from Newfoundland–Oporto (Portugal)–Newfoundland – a trip of 4850 miles (7805 km) – without even a grumble from the engine.

The Kelvin J and K diesel engines, which first appeared in 1933, soon replaced the petrol-paraffin engine. During World War II, Kelvin engines were used exclusively in the small craft which carried out Commando raids on the Lofoten Islands.

By 1954, about 80 of the 350 labour force had been employed by Kelvins for more than 25 years and 19 for more than 40 years.

Walter Bergius died in 1949, and in 1954 the J and K engines were replaced by the smaller Kelvin Model P monobloc diesel (developing 10 and 20 hp) designed by W. M. Miller (formerly Chief Development Engineer at Petters). These units, still produced, are possibly **the smallest water-cooled diesels in the world to be built entirely for marine use**. The 'T' and 'R' range are the current diesel engines being produced and marketed by Kelvin Diesels Ltd (currently a subsidiary of GEC Diesels); they range from 10 to 720 bhp.

Perkins

Frank Perkins MA (1889–1968) was Works Manager for Petters (see p. 183) in Ipswich in the 1920s, when he first met Charles Chapman, Chief Engineer for that company. In 1931, both Perkins and Chapman were working for Aveling & Porter of Rochester when Perkins decided to return to his native town of Peterborough to form a company to build diesel engines. From its foundation in 1932, Frank Perkins Ltd, with Chapman as both Director and Chief Engineer, began producing engines by the tradenames of Vixen (1932), Wolf (1933), Panther (1934), Python (1935), and Leopard (1936). **The first Perkins marine engine** was produced in 1936, basically a marinised version of the Leopard vehicle engine and marketed as the Birmal-Perkins. A demonstration of the engine installed in a motor-launch built by J. S. Whites of Cowes, was successfully carried out for Admiralty

Left to right: *Lumsden Collis (Chief Engineer, New Scotland Yard) and Frank A. Perkins inspecting a P6 marine diesel engine which had just completed 31000 hours of service while installed in a Police Patrol Launch (October 1953).* Inset: *The Perkins logo*

officials at about this time. From the P6M, developing 80 bhp at 2500 rpm, followed the S6M giving 100 to 130 bhp at 2000 to 2250 rpm. The power/weight ratio was 9·23 lb/bhp.

It was at about this time that the polychromatic blue livery which – apart from the brief use of silver – was to become the hallmark of a Perkins marine engine received the company logo, which is identical to the motifs of the huge bronze Mandorla door of the Renaissance-built Florence Cathedral in Italy!

During World War II, a total of over 7000 of these two engines were produced for launches of the three armed services. These were principally used for air/sea rescue launches, seaplane tenders, general service launches and torpedo recovery purposes.

During this period Perkins also developed the V12, 850 bhp, T12 diesel engine for high-speed launches for the RAF and Navy and two were installed in a 'B' Class Fairmile, but the war ended before it was put into production.

Peacetime activities saw many Perkins engines in private pleasure craft and in 1948 Perkins engine motor-yachts secured the first five places in the Pavillon d'Or event. Through to 1953

they remained prominent in this event and in 1949 out of 67 yachts entered, 33 were fitted with Perkins engines.

In 1951 Perkins-engined boats were present in strength at the ceremonial opening of the Thames Passenger Service and the year saw the first engines (P6M's) fitted in the launches of the Thames Division of the Metropolitan Police where they were later to be standardised. Engines were again supplied to the Admiralty for fast motorboats. By 1953 the first engine sold to the Metropolitan River Police boats had achieved a total of 31303 hours of service. Similar engines were supplied to the Admiralty for the motorboats carried on board HMS *Britannia*, the Royal Yacht. The Perkins 6·354 engine was first introduced in 1960, and in 1963 a large contingent of Perkins-powered boats were entered for the Cowes–Torquay Offshore Powerboat race – Perkins boats were among the award winners. In 1964, eight Perkins-engined boats started and all finished. In 1966, seven awards were won by Perkins-engined craft. In 1972, a Perkins T6 354–engined boat, *Four Winds*, set a new world diesel speed record of 78·350 mph (126·092 km/h).

Over the years, Perkins engines have been installed in a wide variety of craft which has included not only light high-speed private launches, but fast patrol launches and slow-speed commercial fishing boats. Hundreds of boats of the revitalised fishing fleet of Sri Lanka and hundreds of the small fishing boats around the shores of Norway have been fitted with Perkins 3·152 and 4·99/4·108 marine engines in recent years. A production of some 7000 marine units per year, places Perkins engines in the worldwide lead in its power class.

In 1979 Perkins offered their 'Range 4' series of six-cylinder marine diesels, including the '6·3544' (the turbo-charged version of the T6·3544) developing 124 bhp at 2800 rpm.

Petter

Established in Yeovil, Somerset (1872) as iron founders, by 1892 James B. Petter, founder of Petter & Sons, was already manufacturing a self-propelled oil engine. In the early 1900s, the Petter single-cylinder 120 lb cast-iron motorcar engine was first converted for marine use. By 1919, Vickers-Petter Ltd were marketing long-stroke marine engines (up to 540 hp) at their Ipswich factory, together with their smaller 'VS' engines. 1930 saw the arrival of their 'Atomic' range of marine engines developing up to 400 bhp. During 1940, the Petter PU8 engines were used to power tank pontoons for crossing the Rhine.

Power-Meadows

In 1929 Hubert Scott-Paine, Head of the British Power Boat Company (see p. 129), determined to develop British machinery for high-speed craft. He bought up the old motorcar concern of Henry Meadows and appointed Wilson Hamel (formerly Rolls-Royce, Scotland) as Managing Director. A new, streamlined factory was built and after developing a horizontally-opposed diesel engine for tanks, Hamel went on to develop a gearbox for the 100 hp Power Meadows, of which there were two versions: the 8/28 and 12/48. Production of this engine was limited to the 1930s decade.

Sabre

Sabre was founded in 1968 by John Freeman, whose success in racing his Fairey Huntsman *Seaspray* had encouraged him to believe that turbo-charged diesel engines could offer standards of performance previously associated only with petrol engines, and with much lower fuel costs. In 1969, a Sabre turbo-charged and charge-cooled engine was developed for racing to produce 210 bhp and the company achieved the team prize in the 1969 Round Britain Powerboat Race. As this racing engine was progressively boosted to 250, 300 and today 365 bhp, it saw such racing successes as an outright win in the London to Monte Carlo Marathon of 1972 – a gruelling race of over 2600 miles (4200 km). Today this young company offers a range of eight engines with power outputs from a four-cylinder, 80 hp unit up to a V-10, 400 hp unit.

In 1979 Sabre offered a new 500 hp turbo-charged intercooled V-10 engine.

Stuart

Founded by S. M. Stuart Turner in the early 1900s at Henley-on-Thames, Oxfordshire, manu-facturing castings for model engineers and small house-lighting, electric generating plants for both private customers and also as stand-by units for the Post Office.

In 1929, Mr Nagle, a Danish showman from the Royal Boat Building Corporation Ltd of Weybridge, Surrey, enquired of several companies for a small marine engine to be installed in hire boats for an ornamental lake. Stuart Turner won this contract by swiftly marinising 50 of their engines, with shaft extension on end opposite the flywheel, together with circulating pump and couplings (£18 8s each). These P5MC engines (named after Stuart Turner's design engineer, Alex F. Plint) were successful and led to further orders. Indeed, a single-cylinder, 3 hp marine engine was then designed and built from scratch (P5M), followed by a twin-cylinder engine (P55M). Altogether some 20 000 marine engines of P5 designations were sold.

Although S. M. Stuart Turner left the company in 1935, the company and Alex Plint produced a 1½ hp engine for small dinghies (the R3M and R3MC). Between 1941 and 1944, a number of these smaller engines were put in small boats taking intelligence agents, instructors, wireless equipment and stores from the Shetland Isles to the Underground Movement in Norway – known as the 'Shetland Bus'. Post-war, between a dozen and up to twenty of these Stuart-engined dinghies competed in an annual race for the Stuart Challenge Trophy; teams coming from Sandwick and Scalloway.

In September 1950 the 38 ft (11·6 m), 16-ton yacht *Boleh*, commanded by Robin Kilroy RN, arrived at Salcombe, S. Devon after a 12 000-mile (19 000 km) voyage from Singapore. *Boleh*'s Stuart P55ME 8 hp engine, supplied in Singapore in May 1949, had run for 700 hr without any attention except occasional changing of plugs and one adjustment to the water pump. With only 50 gallons (227 litres) of petrol a time, Cdr Kilroy estimated that the *Boleh* had travelled 500 miles (800 km) under power, besides which they also used the engine regularly as a generating plant for charging the batteries. The Stuart gave *Boleh* a regular speed of between 3½ and 4½ knots.

In the mid 1950s, Stuart Turner did introduce a small, two-stroke, 9 hp diesel engine (HZM), designed by the late Alex Plint's son, Michael; although reliable, when compared to the 8 hp

A 20 hp petrol motor, with gearbox, shaft and propeller, constructed by Thornycroft in 1904

petrol engine, it had a less than advantageous power/weight ratio and only 340 units were sold.

In 1975, Stuart Turner phased out their own engines, and started importing a 6 hp and 9 hp Spanish diesel engine, marketed as the Stuart Sole diesel engine. While still servicing post-1938 Stuart engines, the Henley works has had to say that, due to costs, the very early P-engines are obsolete.

Thornycroft

Established in the early 1870s by (Sir) John Isaac Thornycroft (KBE) and John Donaldson at Chiswick, London, between 1874 and 1891, 222 steam-propelled torpedo boats were built at this yard for British, Colonial and Foreign Navies. Thornycroft's son, (Sir) John Edward took over management of what in 1901, became known as John I. Thornycroft & Co. Ltd, moving their yard to Woolston on the River Itchen, Southampton in 1904; it was here that Sir J. E. Thornycroft carried out the thorough development work on petrol, paraffin, producer-gas and diesel engines. In January 1903, a Thornycroft four-cylinder, 20 hp motorcar engine was marinised and installed in a light, open, 30 ft (9·1 m) racing launch, called *Scolopendra*, which was raced with such success by John Thornycroft and his younger brother, Tom, that the company now began serious production of both their car and lorry engines, embodying as many standard parts as possible. Until 1909, a special test house was maintained at Chiswick, where all Thornycroft marine motors were brake-tested before delivery. The department then moved to Basingstoke, and to Reading in 1926.

The Chiswick yard had usually contracted out wooden boatbuilding to such firms as Burgoyne, Maynard, Simpson-Strickland or Luke Bros – until Thornycroft purchased the old Immisch Electric Launch Works on Platt's Eyot, near Hampton-on-Thames and converted it for boat-building. For the next 50 years, Mr C. E. Miles was Manager of this yard, where over 1100 boats were constructed.

All Thornycroft marine engines were distinguished by a letter and a numeral (this represented the type and number of cylinders). Between 1903 and 1908 the most popular models were the A/2 and A/4 of 10 and 20 hp. The slightly more powerful B/1, B/2 and B/4 engines were followed by the C/2, C/4 and C/6, developing up to about 65 bhp. In 1908 the famous M-type engines appeared: M/1 represented 7 bhp on paraffin; M/6 about 45 bhp on paraffin. Until production ceased in 1926, M-types were widely used for motor-cruising.

During World War I Thornycrofts, using the design of *Miranda IV*, built some 123 Coastal Motor Boats (CMB) for the Royal Navy at Platts Eyot. These torpedo-carrying craft were powered by Thornycroft V/12, 250 hp engines or the larger Y/12, and ranged in length from 40 to 55 ft (12·2 to 16·7 m) with speeds approaching 35 to 40 knots.

Post-war, Thornycrofts produced a stepped 30-footer (9·1 m), powered by an RB/6 engine developing 120 bhp (Prefix 'R' meant manufactured at the Reading Works). This was the prototype for the standard 'Sea Hawk' class of cabin hydroplanes.

During the inter-war years, Hampton produced a very large number of boats, varying in size from dinghies, up to the 92-ton yacht *Varis* (afterwards re-named *Altona II*). A large number of motor-cruisers were built to standard designs prepared by Thornycrofts' London-based 'Marine Motor Department'. The 30 and 40 ft (9·1 and 12·2 m) cabin cruisers were especially popular, and considerable numbers were built at Hampton, engined with the DB/2 or 'Handybilly' two-cylinder engine with heavy external flywheel and an integral reduction gear of about 1.5:1. 'Handybilly', first marketed in 1923, developed 9 bhp on petrol and 7½ bhp on paraffin; it could 'tick over' reliably at low rpm's; it was in production for about 35 years.

The first Hampton craft to be fitted with Reading-built diesels were two yachts, *Varis* and *Sinbad II* – 210 and 150 total bhp respectively – giving speeds of 11·7 and 11 knots respectively. During subsequent years, the RJ/4 and RJ/2 diesels went into many small craft. After World War II, Thornycrofts were producing six types of marine diesel engine for private yachts, up to 125 bhp (the RZ/6). Whereas between 1914 and 1945, boatbuilding at Hampton had produced about 28 craft per annum, in post-war years this average fell to about 14.

Yanmar

Magokichi Yamaoka of Japan introduced his first 3 hp vertical-type agricultural kerosene engine in 1920, following this with a horizontal-type where fuel delivery was automatically controlled by the load of the engine – naming it *Yanmar* ('King of the Dragonflies'). From 1921, Yanmar kerosene engines were widely used for industrial applications.

In December 1933, the first Yanmar high-speed diesel (Model HB) was developed by Yamaoka, as **the world's smallest horizontal-cylinder, water-cooled, four-stroke engine**, developing 5 to 6 hp. Post-war production began with production of the S3 Yanmar diesel, which was extensively used in the changeover of Japanese coastal fishing vessels from sail to power. Today Yanmar diesels are the largest producers of diesel engines in the world, and current production is reported to be over 1000 engines per day. This includes a range of marine engines from 8 to 30 hp, including their new 'M' series of 8 to 12 hp, single-cylinder engines.

Mr Yamaoka, founder of Yanmar with his first engine (1920)
(E. P. Barrus Ltd)

At the turn of the century a 35 hp petrol marine engine with reversing gear, weighed 1586 lb and occupied 34·5 cu ft. By the 1970s, an engine with the same output and with reversing gear weighs 530 lb (about one third of the 1902 figure) and occupies 75 cu ft (less than a quarter of the space).

In 1914, a four-cylinder, 40 hp marine diesel engine with reversing gear weighed 6600 lb and occupied 142 cu ft. Today's diesel engine of the same output weighs 520 lb (about a twelfth of the earlier engine) and occupies 12·5 cu ft (again about a twelfth of the 1914 figure).

Other marine inboard engines (petrol/paraffin/diesel) manufactured during the past 80 years include, in alphabetical order: AEC, Albin, Alfa Romeo, Allen, Allison, Atlantic, Atlas, BMC, BMW, Bolinder, Brit, David Brown, Buda, Buffalo, Caterpillar, Chevrolet, Coventry Victor, Crossley, Cummins, Deutz, Dorman, Ducati, Ellwe, Feffles, Ferry, Ford, General Motors, Gray, Kermath, Kromhaut, Lister-Blackstone, McLaren, Meadows, Mercédès-Benz, Morris, 'Nat' National, Russell Newbury, Nohaub-Polar, Packard, Palmer, Parsons, Davey Paxman, Pelapone, Peugeot, Plenty, British Polar, Rapp, Renault, Rolls-Royce, Ruston-Hornsby, Ruston-Lister, Sabb, Hall Scott, Scripps, Seal, Sterling, Sulzer, Superior, Universal, Van Blerck, Widdop, Wickstrom.

OUTBOARD ENGINES

British Anzani

After the crack Italian motor-bicycle rider, Signor Anzani had founded this company on Hampton Hill, Middlesex in the early 1900s, British Anzani became a household name at Brooklands motor racing track in the inter-war years. With its special 10 hp overhead camshaft, V-twin air-cooled engines installed in either Morgan three-wheeler cars or OEC-Anzani motorcycles, speeds approaching 100 mph (160 km/h) were achieved round the Outer Circuit.

Ownership of this company changed in 1938 and development work began on a stationary industrial engine, driving through a flexible underwater unit, to propel landing craft; this

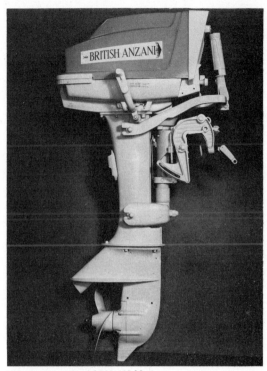

British Anzani Model 180 (18 bhp)

went into full-scale production. At the same time, British Anzani produced a single-cylinder, 158 cc, 4 hp outboard, tradenamed the 'Super Single' for Admiralty requirements. This was eventually modified for the pleasure market and became a long-term seller.

During the early 1960s, British Anzani outboards ranged from 2½ hp up to the 40 hp Super Twin, the then largest outboard offered by a British manufacturer. In 1965 Anzani took over the Perkins outboard interest (see p. 183). In 1967 the Super Twin 'B-Class', 'Jet' and '180' models had been discontinued. British Anzani engineering division was then taken over in 1973 by Boxley Engineering of Maidstone, Kent who limited their production to a 3 hp 'Pilot 30' and 5 hp 'Super Single 50'.

British Seagull

In 1931, John Marston Ltd of Wolverhampton (makers of the Sunbeam 'top quality' motorcycle and a subsidiary of ICI Ltd) presented their 'up-market' 78 cc, 2 hp single-cylinder Marston Seagull Super Lightweight outboard, tury', 'Silver Century Plus', and '110'. The sealed coil and condenser unit, cast iron cylinder block and non-corrosive phospher bronze bearings are unique to Seagull. Sales since 1931 have totalled half a million units.

Evinrude

In 1908, 31-year-old, Norwegian-born, pattern-maker and engineer, Ole Evinrude, was persuaded by his wife Bess that it would be a shrewd move to market the single-cylinder iron and brass detachable rowboat motor, which he had taken a couple of years to quietly develop and now successfully test on the local Kinnikinnic River (near Milwaukee, Wisconsin State, USA). Having cleaned up its ugly 'coffee-grinder' appearance, Evinrude now bought and made parts for 25 engines. After a friend's demonstration of the motor on Pewaukee Lake, Evinrude received orders for ten motors, which he hand-

British Seagull's logo for a detachable outboard motor

designed by J. E. Greenwood; a basically simple, saltwater-resistant design. This engine had been built of stainless steel monel metal and other non-corrosive metals. It had an underwater exhaust, Lucas flywheel magneto and Amal carburettor. In 1933, they followed this up with a special 10 hp, twin-cylinder unit. These units were completely re-designed in 1935–36 as 102 cc units.

Up to this time the 'Sunbeamland' engine was being sold by the Bristol Motor Boat Co. But before long Marston sold out his outboard interests to Bill Pinniger and John Wayhope, who set up business as The British Seagull Co. Ltd, in Poole, Dorset.

During World War II, the company contracted to supply 10000 engines at short notice for barges and small assault craft; with materials in short supply, some of these engines were built up from scrap metal.

Post-war saw the '102' (1946 onwards), then the Forty series (1950 onwards), followed by the Century (1956 onwards), Silver (1966). Most recent models are the 'Forty Plus', 'Silver Cen-

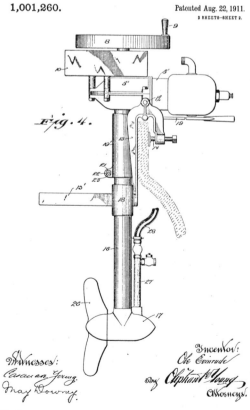

1,001,260.

Patented Aug. 22, 1911.
2 SHEETS—SHEET 2.

Fig. 4.

Witnesses:

Inventor:
Ole Evinrude
By Clephan & Young
Attorneys.

Ole Evinrude's patent for a detachable outboard motor

built himself and sold for £12 ($62) each. These were single-cylinder, water-cooled units, developing 1·5 hp at 1000 rpm, and weighing 60 lb. Following many orders promoted by Bess Evinrude's publicity campaigning and business acumen, in 1911 Chris Meyer, President of Meyer Tug Boat Lines, put up $5000 and became a 50 per cent partner in the Evinrude Motor Company. By 1913 the family firm of Evinrude was employing 300 people and working furiously in a specially built factory to satisfy export orders at home and abroad; Ole's friend, Olaf Mikkelsen, was exporting Evinrudes to Scandinavia by the thousand. The Evinrude Motor Co. established itself in south-east London, England as British importers of these engines. They offered two single-cylinder, two-stroke units, ranging from 2 to 5 hp, and a single-cylinder, four-stroke motor (4 to 6 hp). In 1914, the overworked, exhausted Evinrudes sold out to co-director Meyer for $140 000 and went on an extended vacation, on the understanding that Ole would not re-enter the outboard market for five years. Seven years later, the Evinrude family team was back in business with **the first outboard motor to make extensive use of aircraft aluminium alloy.** Called by Bess the 'Evinrude Light Twin Outboard' or ELTO, it weighed only 47 lb. This was a horizontally-opposed unit developing 2½ hp, with its underwater exhaust through the propeller hub as another innovation. The Elto was first exhibited in England by Bramco Ltd at a Motor Boat Show held at the White City, London in 1921. With its lightness, particularly advantageous for racing, the Elto set a trend in light alloy outboards, and after some six years of success it was superseded by the Elto Quad, as **the first four-cylinder, two-cycle outboard to be built in the United States**; the Elto Quad was even more successful in outboard racing leagues (see p. 36).

During the 1920s, the Evinrude (as opposed to Elto) Company's fortunes dwindled from bad to worse until Stephen F. Briggs, President of Briggs and Stratton industrial motors complex, bought up the Milwaukee company in 1928. Briggs then followed through by merging Evinrude with Lockwood and also with Elto, and whilst retaining their individual brand names, formed the Outboard Motors Corporation (OMC) with Ole Evinrude as President, in March 1929. A 38 lb folding motor by Elto was now prepared for production, together with the incorporation of experimental electric starting generators as developed by the Owen-Dyneto Corporation of Syracuse, New York, for Packard cars. Seven months later came the Wall Street stock market 'crash'. Lockwood was discontinued in 1930, whilst OMC survived by selling left-over engines and making motors such as the Evinrude-Elto 'All Electric' in 1932 from a surplus inventory of electric starter units.

But by 1933 a new range of nine models was launched, including the 5·5 hp Evinrude Lightwin Imperial and the 9·2 hp Lightfour Imperial. The largest Elto four-cylinder, 973 cc motor, developed some 60 hp. A special feature of these engines was that **the whole of the power head was shielded for the first time** by a streamlined alloy hood, keeping the motor clean, dry and protected from damage.

In 1934 'honest' Ole Evinrude died, aged 57 – only fourteen months after the death of his wife, Bess; his son Ralph took over the Presidency of OMC almost immediately (see p. 190).

In 1935, the 25 lb, 1·5 hp Evinrude Sportsman was offered for $55; this streamlined motor was **the first to use the reed valve intake.** By the mid-1940s, OMC were offering four Elto models, including the 5 hp Elto Cub and ten Evinrude models, including the 16 hp four-cylinder Evinrude Sportfour. In 1953 Evinrude reverse-gear models were introduced, while in 1956, Evinrude Duck Twin, Fleetwin, Fastwin, Big Twin and Lark models were marketed. In 1958–60, the first Evinrude V4 50 and 75 hp engines were developed. In 1962 the Evinrude Selectric (electro-magnetic) push button gear shift was offered on 40 hp and 75 hp models – and in 1965 the Evinrude 100 hp outboard came on the market as the Starflite.

By this time, only two Elto outboard models were being manufactured in Ontario, Canada and these were faded out with the brand-name in the late 1950s.

In 1977, Evinrude were offering some 39 different models, ranging from 2 hp to the 200 hp Starflite; every model above 4 hp incorporated breakerless CD-ignition. In 1978, the range had been reduced to 33 models, the brand-names (Sportwin, Speedtwin, Starflite, Swinger, etc) had been dropped, but **the power output had been increased to 235 hp, the most powerful production outboard yet built.**

Honda Motor Co.

Established in Hamamatsu in 1948, they produced their first, twin-cylinder overhead camshaft water-cooled four-stroke B75 outboard in 1973, following this with the B75 K1 in 1973, and then the B 10 hp 100 (long-shaft and short-shaft).

Johnson

In 1908, Lou Johnson (of Danish origin) with the help of his younger brothers, Harry, Clarence and Julius, whittled the first model of his marine engine from a pine block; the Johnson brothers then built a 3 hp, single-cylinder brass inboard, developing some 400 rpm and installed it in their 16 ft (4·9 m) boat, which they used along the Wabash River from Terre Haute (Indiana State). In 1909, the brothers built a lightweight two-cycle, V-type aircraft engine, which they eventually installed in an aluminium-framed wooden monoplane. In August 1911, the Johnson aircraft became **the first American monoplane to make a successful flight**. With the money from their newly-formed Johnson School of Aviation at Terre Haute, the Brothers had soon installed two 180 hp, V-type inboard motors of their own design in a racing hydroplane, the *Black Demon III*, capable of over 50 mph (80 km/h). Despite their plant being wrecked by a tornado, by 1917 the Johnson Motor Wheel Company was offering a twin-cylinder, 1½ hp, air-cooled detachable bicycle engine, built largely of aluminium alloy.

Lou Johnson with a Sea-Horse 24 in the 1930s

In March 1918, Warren Ripple, dynamic President of the Quick Action Magneto Company, had taken over the business side from the Johnsons and moved their factory to South Bend, on the banks of the St Joe River. When their motor-bicycle venture failed, the Johnsons – particularly brother Clarence – changed over to the development of a 2 hp lightweight aluminium alloy outboard, working in close conjunction with a Norwegian engineer called Finn T. Irgens. After experimenting with hand-built models, the Johnson Motor Company put their Light Twin into production in 1922. Otherwise known as the 'Waterbug', not only was this the first lightweight outboard (only 100 lb), but the first to be fitted with reverse lock.

In 1926, the company was offering a 7 hp Standard Twin, an 11 hp Big Twin and a 17¾ hp Giant Twin (which could be boosted up to 25 hp for racing). The Big Twin was the first outboard to incorporate die castings.

In 1927, Johnson Motors moved to a new, custom-designed factory at Waukegan (Illinois State). In 1929, Indiana Advertising Agency copy-writer Carl Prell coined the words 'Sea Horse' to describe the Johnson Sea Horse 16 and Johnson Sea Horse 32 racing engines, which were to be marketed alongside six other utility models that year. The Sea Horse engines incorporated underwater exhaust, offset cylinders, twist-grip throttle control and a rotary valve that boosted power by 50 per cent by permitting a larger charge to be taken into the crankcase.

At the time of the Wall Street stock market 'crash', despite a highly expensive advertising campaign, Johnson's President, Ripple, was unable to sell his vast stock pile of engines and boats – including the first inboard/outboard device, and between 1931 and 1935 Johnson Motors gradually ground to an almost bankrupt halt.

But in November 1935 Steve Briggs, Outboard Motors Corporation (OMC) Chairman, and Ralph Evinrude, OMC President, purchased two-thirds of Johnson outstanding shares – and in 1936 Johnson Motors and OMC were reformed as the Outboard Marine & Manufacturing Corporation (OMMC). Despite top-level control, it was decided that Evinrude-Elto and Johnson outboards would remain arch rivals for sales at both dealer and consumer level.

During World War II, many thousands of 5 and 10 hp Johnson Sea Horse outboards were used to power inflatable landing rafts, together with a 22 hp Johnson Twin (POLR-15) to power 'floating-bridge' pontoons in both European and Pacific theatres of war. (Other outboards used during the war were 50 hp Evinrudes.)

On 6 November 1952, **the millionth Sea Horse outboard rolled off the Waukegan assembly line**; this was the 10 hp QD-14; some 60 000 of these motors had been produced over a four-year period; it featured a forward-neutral-reverse gear shift innovation and connections for a Ship Master remote control unit. Only seven years later, in 1959, the two millionth motor, a V-75, was produced – one year after Johnson had developed their first V four-cylinder motor. Nine years later, in 1968, the three millionth motor was produced; this was loop-charged Sea Horse 55; by this time, Johnson had developed the power output of their V-type motors to 100 hp.

In 1972, Johnson were offering 12 models, ranging from 2 hp to 125 hp, whilst they used a scorpion logo and the 'Stinger' name for their racing engines. In 1974 power output had been increased to a maximum of 135 to 140 hp. They then developed a V-six-cylinder motor to raise that output to a further 235 hp in 1976–77, which was further increased to 240 hp by 1978. By this time, the name Stinger had been adopted for the more standard 75 hp engine.

Mercury

In 1939, E. Carl Kiekhaefer, engineer in the field of magnetic separators, magnetic clutches and magnetic brakes, purchased the assets of the Cedarburg Manufacturing Corporation in Wisconsin, including 300 Thor outboard motors that had been rejected by a major mail order firm because they would not perform satisfactorily. Sorely in need of capital, Kiekhaefer decided to rebuild and improve these Thor engines to the satisfaction of the mail order firm, who not only accepted them, but ordered more. From this, Kiekhaefer progressed to design both a single-cylinder outboard and an alternate-firing twin, incorporating abrasion-resistant, rubber rotor water pumps and stream-lined housings and cowlings, which he launched at the 1940 New York National Boat Show. Kiekhaefer named his new engines after the Roman god of commerce, the winged messenger – Mercury.

In March 1941, the US Government restricted the use of aluminium to military projects – and by the end of the war, the Kiekhaefer Corporation was the largest chain-saw engine builder in the world and a recognised authority on radio-controlled target aircraft. Experience gained in manufacturing two-cycle engines for this purpose, saw, in 1947, the 10 hp alternate-firing Mercury outboard, incorporating anti-friction

The Mercury Marine conference room, showing early engines in the foreground, later models to the left and latest models at the back

The endurance run to inaugurate Lake X in 1957 (Courtesy of Mercury Marine)

ball, roller and needle bearings in its connecting rods, crankshaft, driveshaft and prop-shaft. With the establishment of a new factory at Fond du Lac in 1949, the Kiekhaefer Corporation developed the first four-cylinder-in-line, two-cycle, 40 hp Mercury outboard – with one-piece die-cast aluminium block and integral single coil magneto system.

When the Korean War (1950–53) again saw restrictions in the use of aluminium, Kiekhaefer developed and produced an 85 hp, V4 target drone engine with fuel injection, weighing only 103 lb, which could fit into a 14-in fuselage. By 1957, the Corporation was offering **the world's first 60 hp, six-cylinder outboard, the Mark 75**; this came either as the standard Mark 75 Marathon, or as the March 75H racing version, incorporating a world's first with single lever remote controls. Mercury now offered 12 models ranging from the 10 hp Mark 10 Twin-Trol, up to the Mark 75; the colour of the cowlings of these engines varied from bright red to scarlet, to green, to blue – although at this stage, black was not used.

Two Mark 75's played a thrilling role in 1957 at the inauguration of Lake X, Mercury's, and the outboard industry's, first 100 per cent private 'proving waters' near St Cloud, Florida. Each engine propelled a family-sized runabout 50 000 miles (80 000 km) in 68¾ days of continuous night-and-day running, at an average speed of 30·3 mph (48·7 km/h).

The Kiekhaefer Corporation was now spread between Cedarburg, Fond du Lac, Oshkosh, Sarasota and Lake X.

In August 1961, the Kiekhaefer Corporation merged with Brunswick Corporation of Chicago.

All Mercury models were given a white livery in 1961, followed in 1962 by one black model, then in 1963 three black models, and by 1964, with the introduction of their first 100 hp outboard dubbed the 'Black Widow', all Mercury outboards were given the jet-black livery which has remained with them for the past 15 years. Before long, the brand-names Tempest and Hurricane had been replaced by the Twister for Mercury racing engines.

Outboard motor horsepower advanced to 110

in the 1966 Mercury line and to 125 in 1968. During this period, **Thunderbolt ignition, the industry's first capacitor discharge ignition system**, was introduced by this ever-expanding Wisconsin manufacturer, that now began branches in both Toronto and Dandenong. By 1971, a new three-cylinder Merc 650 and the 140 hp Merc 1400, both with direct charge, were introduced. Mr K. B. Abernathy, President of the Mercury Division of Brunswick, now became President of the Brunswick Corporation – succeeded at Mercury Marine by Mr J. F. Reichart.

In 1974, Mariner outboards were introduced (see p. 197). 1975 saw production of the Black Max, a loop-charged, 175 hp, V-6 outboard – together with the Gnat, a 4 hp, two-cylinder, loop-charged outboard, manufactured at the company's plant in Belgium.

1976 saw the introduction of the quiet Thruster electric outboard, which by using a planetary gearbox and 10½-in diameter polycarbonate propeller, gave a thrust of some 20 lb whilst drawing 20 A at only 12 volts – both remote and manual steering models were offered to fishermen. In 1978, Mercury Marine offered 15 models, ranging from 4 hp to the 200 hp V-6 racing engine, dubbed the Black Max. Six of these were mounted onto the transom of Dr Robert C. Magoon's trans-Atlantic sprint boat, *Citicorp Traveler*, to give its 45 ft (13·7 m) Kevlar hull the necessary thrust to get across the Atlantic. This is **the greatest number of outboards and total power ever fixed to the transom of a boat** (ie 1200 bhp) (see p. 174).

By 1979 Mercury were offering 40 models.

Selva

Prior to the formation of this company in 1945, Lorenzo Selva spent 18 years in the Italian Navy as a marine engineer. During the late 1940s, assisted by his eldest son Ezio, an expert engine tuner, Lorenzo built up a business specialising in the design/production of parts for the two-stroke motorcycles, such as the Innocenti, Lambretta, Vespa, and Piraggio machines. In 1954 Luigi Selva, Ezio's younger brother, joined the company. With the success that followed from the Selva marinisation of Ferrari and Maserati engines in the late 1950s, Selva brothers now introduced a two-stroke outboard and gave it good promotional publicity by clean-

ing up both the Italian and European Championships for 1961–62, at the end of which Selva withdrew from racing. By 1971 the company was offering 50, 65 and 80 hp models, manufactured at their new Tirano factory, north of Lake Como, Italy.

Suzuki Motor Co.

This firm was formed in 1909 at Hamamatsu by Mickio Suzuki to manufacture weaving looms. Suzuki began building motorcycles in 1952 and outboard motors in 1968 (a 4½ hp and 7 hp unit). The first Suzuki outboard motors were marketed in the UK in 1973. By 1978, Suzuki presented a range of 12 outboards in their DT series, ranging from 2 hp to 65 hp; they entered NE 'stock' powerboat racing during that season, whilst two 25 hp units were sent out to the *Chagos Archipelago* to power Avon inflatables during the Joint Services Expedition in unexplored islands in the mid Indian Ocean. In 1979 they increased their range to include an 85 hp unit.

The Japanese 'Kinuta' outboard motor of 1940, was the Daddy of present-day Japanese outboards such as the Honda, Suzuki and Yamaha

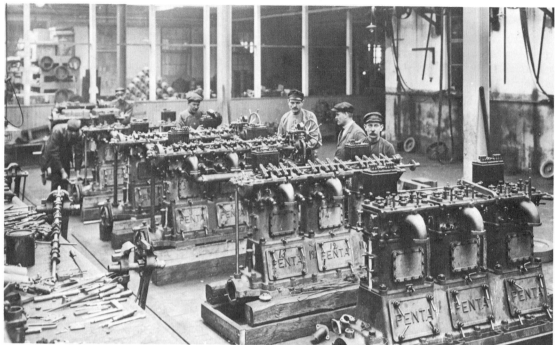

D6 Penta marine engines being assembled in Skövde

Volvo Penta

In 1907, John Gronwall's 40-year-old Skofde Mekaniska Verkstad (Foundry and Engineering Company), directed by consultant engineer Friz Egnell, built the B1 'Penta' Swedish marine internal combustion engine, designed by combustion-engine specialist, Edvard Hubendick. This single-cylinder overhead camshaft engine was either called by the Greek word 'penta' ('five') because it was Egnell's fifth great idea, or because there were five people round the table when the challenge of an all-Swedish engine was conceived. With its success, the two-cylinder B2 engine was built, and by 1910 a four-cylinder, 28 hp overhead camshaft engine followed; by 1911 Egnell had ordered 275 two-cylinder engines, marketing them as 'Penta Minor'. In 1919, as new Board Chairman, Egnell, renamed his company 'Pentaverken'.

Simultaneous to this progress, in 1912 the Swedish engineering brothers, Carl Alrik and Oskar Walfrid Hult, built and internationally patented the world's first two-cylinder production detachable motor, employing the so-called

'balance system', with one cylinder on each side of the crankshaft; it was also **the first outboard motor in the world that could be tilted up**. This first 2·5 hp 'Archimedes BS' engine was soon followed by a 5 hp unit, primarily intended to propel barges and workboats. At the 1914 Baltic Exhibition, 148 000 people went on trips round the exhibition in small boats, reliably equipped with the Archimedes engine. AB Archimedes now became the largest manufacturer of outboard motors in Europe. In 1916 they produced **the first outboard motor in the world with a leg that could be swung all the way round for reversing**; this ABEA engine was fitted with two tillers. In 1918 Archimedes introduced a reverse control on the tiller and in 1919 a co-pilot device to keep the boat running on a straight course when the tiller was released. The 1922 Archimedes BR10 was **the first known attempt to balance a piston engine with the aid of separate rotating counterweights**.

In 1922 Pentaverken presented its first twin-cylinder outboard (the U2, designed by Carl-Axel Skarlund). This was **the first production outboard in the world with two cylinders arranged**

above each other. This cylinder arrangement was so advanced that the U-2 and U-21 remained in production until 1953. It is reported that through the immense popularity of this engine, the word 'penta' came to mean 'outboard engine' in many native dialects.

In 1926 the Pentaverken-built engine of the first Volvo motorcar was working so successfully that in 1927, Volvo founders, Assar Gabrielsson and Gustaf Larson, made an order for 700 four-cylinder, two-litre, 28 hp engines to be built. In 1930, 2500 car engines were built and 1742 Penta marine engines. By 1935, Pentaverken had become a wholly owned subsidiary of Volvo, and AB Penta was established in Gothenburg to design and sell marine engines.

Meanwhile, AB Archimedes developed a rotary throttle on the tiller of their 1928 outboard, following up with the robust 8 to 9 hp B2 and 10 to 12 hp B22 outboards, fitted with reverse gear with slipping-disc clutch units. During the 1930s, Archimedes dominated all outboard racing events in Sweden and abroad with its largest B2 model. In 1940 the Swedish Army bought Archimedes engines, fitted with double reduction gear housing to drive their pontoon ferries.

The Electrolux group took over Archimedes in 1941 and Penta's outboard production in 1944. Archimedes then took over the right to manufacture Penta outboards, whilst Penta concentrated on inboard engines, such as the Penta 80 to 90 hp BB70, launched onto the US market in 1957.

From 1953, Jim Wynne, Mercury test driver, came to the belief that the huge, clumsy 'high rise' units he was testing on Lake X might be better replaced by locating a four-stroke, 70 hp Volvo Penta inboard engine inside the transom, whilst retaining the manoeuvrability advantages of the outboard in the leg and gear housing. When Karl Kiekhaefer, Wynne's boss at Mercury, rejected this inboard/outboard concept, Wynn resigned from Mercury and did the necessary welding job in his own garage, installing it in a hull borrowed from the Thunderbird Boatyard in Florida; **the first successful trial of this inboard/outboard took place in March 1958**.

The idea was not new. **The first inboard/outboard drive to be put into production was the aluminium-built Lautonautile** 'portable', introduced in 1899 by the Société du Propulseur

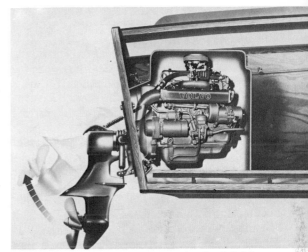

The first Aquamatic assembly to be introduced included the Volvo B-16 engine

Universel Amovable of Neuilly, France; the vertical shaft housing and prop tilted up and rotated to provide steering and reverse action. The $1\frac{3}{4}$ hp version burned either alcohol or petrol and weighed 144 lb. Inboard/outboard models were unsuccessfully launched by Gierholt (1921), S. E. Saunders (1922), Comet (1923), whilst in 1928, Joseph van Blerck put an outdrive system on the market and over the next five years sold about 2000 of them. In 1930 Johnson Motors brought out a tilting inboard/outboard which died quickly in the Depression. In 1932 the Motonautica Lario di Milano constructed a 'stern-oar' system weighing only 33 lb, for use with 20 to 30 hp inboards, while in 1936, Guido Cattaneo, engineer in Milan, had fitted an outboard leg, with two three-bladed props on the same shaft, to a 90 hp Alfa Romeo; but neither Italians had followed this up commercially.

By December 1959, with the interested backing of Volvo Penta at Gothenburg, Sweden, Jim Wynne saw the first patented 'Aquamatic' inboard/outboard successfully tank-tested, prior to its shipment and unveiling at the 1959 New York Boat Show. During the show itself, 100 Aquamatic units were sold, and later during the year Jim Wynne gave the Aquamatic superb promotional publicity by winning most of the offshore races, held in the USA, in his 'Aqua-Hunter' powerboat, *Moppie*. Over 1000 Aquamatic units were sold in the USA alone during that first year; it was the start of a new era of motorboats, many of which were being moulded in fgrp (see p. 158).

The first company to get round the Aquamatic patents was Mercury, who in 1962 developed the more expensive Mercruiser. Outboard Marine Corporation followed suit with the 'Z-Drive' or 'Sterndrive', where gear-changing was carried out electrically.

During the next decade Volvo Penta sold some 300 000 Aquamatic units. In 1963 spur gears were replaced by bevel units and a 'Silent Shift' clutch was introduced. Series 100 was followed by '200', then by '250', then the '270' (suitable for US V8 engines), and then the '280' (with underwater housing). Finally there was type '750' for large, six-cylinder diesel engines developing up to 280 hp.

Parallel with this, in 1953, the Swedish bicycle and motorcycle manufacturer, Nymans Verkstader at Uppsala, had presented its first 4 hp Crescent outboard. Ten years later Nymans combined forces with Monark motorcycles and both Crescent and Monark outboard engines were now mass-produced. With their three-cylinder, loop-charged two-stroke engines, Crescent and AB Archimedes became pioneers in the modern fuel-saving, two-stroke technique. In 1965 the 25 hp Crescent outboard was the first to have throttle control and reverse gear control in the same handle. That same year, AB Archimedes transferred outboard manufacture to the Crescent factory in Uppsala, and all Swedish outboard production was concentrated at the Uppsala plant. The 10 hp E12 outboard, produced in 1967, was **the first multi-cylinder outboard in the world with both loop-charging and a die-cast cylinder block made of aluminium.** In 1970 Archimedes and Penta model ranges were finally combined under the name Archimedes-Penta, and three years later Volvo Penta took over outboard manufacture at Uppsala.

From 1975, Volvo Penta outboard engines, Volvo Penta MD inboards, Volvo Penta Aquamatic inboard engines/outboard drives, Volvo Penta six-cylinder 342 hp turbo-supercharged marine diesels have been on the market, on a production rate of about 50 000 units per year.

In 1979 the Volvo Penta engines ranged from 3·5 to 580 hp, and they offered a new inboard, the MB2/505 four-stroke engine developing 7·5 hp.

Waterman

Cameron B. Waterman was a Yale law student, keen on motorcycling, when he hit on the idea of converting his Curtiss air-cooled motorcycle engine into a chain-drive boat motor. Back in his Detroit home city, after graduation in 1904 and after tests on the Detroit River and tank tests at home in his 'converted' piano box, Waterman and his friend George Thrall (owner of a local boiler factory) soon found that the answer lay in a two-stroke, single-cylinder motor, the drive being transmitted from the crankshaft to the driveshaft through a vertical sprocket; the driveshaft remained absolutely unprotected. No silencer was fitted and the fuel tank was fitted to the tiller arm. This was placed high above the cylinder head of the vertical motor. Waterman now hired a production engineer, Oliver E. Barthel, to convert the experimental model to a production model; in 1906 Barthel designed a water-cooled unit, with its flywheel enclosed in the crankcase. However, an air-cooled version of the 'Waterman Outboard Porto' was first exhibited at the National Boat Show in the old Madison Square Garden that year: 25 motors were sold and the Waterman Marine Motor Company came into being. **It was Cameron Waterman who first coined the word 'outboard'** to the detachable type marine motor.

In 1907 the design was revised, substituting a water-cooled cylinder – and some 3000 units were manufactured and sold. In 1908 a horizontal model with top flywheel was designed and put into production: another 3000 units were sold. **The Waterman Porto was the first mass-produced outboard in the world.** By 1909, production had risen to 6000. In 1914, the 3 hp C-14 engine was equipped with a magneto, and the following year they were equipped with a fly-wheel magneto. In 1917 the Waterman Co. was taken over by Arrow Motor & Marine Company of New York and production continued under the Arrow tradename until 1924. Cameron Waterman died in 1956, aged 79 years, a successful lawyer and devoted sportsman.

Watermota

Founded in 1911 by Walter D. Fair at the Pembroke Engineering Works, Hampton Wick to import and market the US Waterman (see p.

Colin Fair raced the Watermota-engined British Maid *boats with great success in the late 1920s (Motor Boat & Yachting)*

196) detachable engines. During World War I, working in close collaboration with British Admiralty engineers, Fair developed a two-stroke, 3½ hp unit known as the Mark I, later marketed as the 'Watermota' Outboard Detachable Marine Motor; it had a comparatively large rudder, an aluminium piston and a copper water jacket, amongst other things. Together with a smaller 2 to 3 hp unit, these were **the first British-built outboards**.

The 347 cc, single-cylinder Watermota Speed Model, 4 to 11 hp, was the only, and first, British outboard which was successful at race meetings during the 1927 and 1928 seasons; raced by Walter Fair's son, Colin, the 10 ft (3·1 m) Watermota-engined *British Maid* made the fastest lap of the first major outboard race in England on the Welsh Harp and would have made an easy victory at 28 mph+ (45 km/h+) had not a deluge of water shorted the sparking plug, causing Fair to re-start the engine again, with no difficulty at all. On the strength of continued successes with other *British Maid* boats during 1928 and 1929, with increased speeds of 36 mph (58 km/h), the Fairs were able to ride fairly high on the outboard engine boom with the Silent Speed Eleven and the 'Utility Eight', producing 8 bhp at 2150 rpm.

In April 1931, Miss Gladys Clements and Richard Cole used a silent speed eleven-engined 13 ft (3·9 m) dinghy to make a 700-mile (1100 km) day trip from Westminster Pier to Dover,

Calais, Ostend, Bruges, Ghent, Gaveres, Antwerp, Calais and back to Dover.

In 1931, after the outboard engine slump, the Watermota 10 hp SK2 inboard engine was marketed, to give 30 ft (9·1 m) cruisers up to 10 tons, a speed of around 7 knots. In 1934, the company decided to adapt a standard production engine – the Ford Model C which, with the Watermota marinisation, developed 10 to 32 hp. This was the first time that the company had departed from the two-stroke to the four-stroke principle. The unit would drive a 15 ft (4·6 m) runabout-type dinghy at 25 knots, or an auxiliary cruiser at 6 knots. By this time the company had moved to a one-time cider works outside Newton Abbot in Devon, and Walter D. Fair had sold out his interests.

In the 1970s, Watermota were manufacturing only inboard engines: Sea Cub, Sea Panther, Sea Scout, Sea Wolf and Sea Lion, with a power range of from 7 hp up to 250 hp.

Yamaha Motor Cycle Co. Ltd

In 1955 Yamaha separated from Nippon Gaki Co. Ltd and entered into the production of motorcycles. In 1960 they began the manufacture of outboard engines with a 7 hp single-cylinder piston valve unit (P-7k); the following year Yamaha marketed the world's first 3 hp air-cooled, rotary-valve outboard. During the next decade, nine 'P'-type Yamaha outboards were presented.

In 1971 Mercury Marine (see p. 193) decided it needed a new line of outboards to increase its market share; in 1972 Mercury purchased an equal shareholding with Yamaha, and during the next two years, with joint research at Fond du Lac and Sanshin, the first 5 hp **Mariner** outboard was developed.

To test and promote this new outboard in Australia, South America and the USA 17 engines were used in five expeditions to power 13 different boats over 40 000 miles (65 000 km) of tough-water conditions. In May 1975, a single-engined and a twin-engined boat broke, by nine hours, the ocean speed record for the 546 mile Sydney–Brisbane run. Between December 1975 and March 1976, Chilean engineer, Enrique Gundermann, took a Mariner-engined, barrow 50 ft (15·2 m) 'bongo' (hollowed-out tree) some 8000 miles (13 000 km) along the Orinoco,

Amazon and Parana Rivers to prove that a navigable inland marine route lay across South America from Venezuela to Buenos Aires; Gundermann was 100 days on the water during one section.

The 1976 'Spirit of Adventure' run saw four Mariner-engined cruisers successfully retrace the 1926-mile (3100 km) route of Capt. James Cook (1770) despite storms with 50-knot winds. In September 1976, six men – two each from Australia, Venezuela and the USA – ran three Mariner-engined boats some 1500 miles (2400 km) up the Mississippi and Illinois Rivers against the current from Orleans to Chicago, in just two weeks.

The Mariner first appeared at the US Trade Show in Chicago in 1976, then in London in 1977. The range had been developed from a 2 hp, 43 cc unit up to a six-cylinder, 115 hp, 1636 cc unit. This was extended to a six-cylinder, 140 hp in-line outboard in 1978, as the fifteenth of the range. Crossflow fuel/air charging and loop-charging had been combined and 'power-ported' pistons innovated. During this period a Mariner outboard sank in Foley Bay, Alabama (USA) to be salvaged some 60 days later, en-crusted with barnacles and filled with mud; it is reported that it worked reliably after only several hours' overhaul and that no new spare parts were found necessary. The 175 hp Mariner V6 came onto the market in 1979.

The longest standing British concessionaires for outboard engines are E. P. Barrus Ltd, founded in Upper Thames Street, London by the European representative for Starrut Tools (USA), Ernest Philip Barrus, in 1917. During the 1920s and early 1930s they dealt mainly with auto-motive equipment, but from 1937 they began to import Johnson outboard engines, following this with Lycoming-engined Ventnor three-point hydroplanes in 1938. During 1973, Barrus imported and sold some 4000 Johnson outboards. More recently they have been concessionaires for Zodiac inflatables, Yanmar diesels and Mariner outboards. After 40 years in London, they are now based in Bicester, Oxfordshire.

The longest-serving British marine rep 'on the road' was Bert Savidge who started work in the Barrus workshops in 1938; he then became mechanic to H. C. Notley (Sales Manager of the Barrus marine section) when Notley raced Johnson outboards and his Lycoming-engined Ventnor three-pointer, the *Blue Ace*. Savidge went 'on the road' for Barrus in 1956, and when he retired in 1977 he had become known as 'Mister Johnson'!

Other outboard names manufactured during the past 80 years include, in alphabetical order:

Aerothrust, Albin, Ali, Amagi, Amarc, Amphion, Apex, Aquajet, Arrow, Ascoy, Aspin, Atco, Bantam, Beckett, Bendix, Bermuda, Britannia, Brockhouse, Brooke, Buccaneer, Bucol, Bundy, Caille, Carniti, Champion, Chrysler, Clemenson, Clinton, Comet, Commando, Corsair, Coventry Victor, Crescent, Cross, Danette, Diesella, Dragonfly, Dunelt, Eclipse, Effzett, Elgin, Eska, Esturian, Fageol, Farrow, Ferrier, Firestone, Fisherman, Flam-beau, Fortis, Gale, Garelli, Gierholt, Giorgi, Gregg, Harbormaster, Homelite, Husqvarna, Ilo, Indian, Jewell, JLO, Kelston, Kinuta, Koban, König, Laros, Lauson, LeJay, Lock-wood, Lutetia, McCulloch, Mallard, Man-U-Troll, Medina, Miller, Minn-Kota, Mobo, Moscone, Moskva, Motogodille, Motor Guide, Muncie, My-Te, Nautilo, Neptune, Oliver, Perkins, Peter Pan, Peugeto, Pioneer, Puffin, Revley, Riley, Roness, Rootes, Royal, Sachs, Safix, Saunders, Scott, Scott-Atwater, Sharland, Silvertrol, Simplex, Soriano, Spartan, Spinaway, Swallow, Taifun, Tasman, Thor, Tidemaster, Tomos, Trim, TSD, Turner-Bray, Viking, West Bend, Wizard, Woodson, Yamato.

MARINE GAS TURBINES

The success of the steam turbine soon led to attempts to apply its principles to a gas turbine in the early 1900s. R. Armengaud and C. Lemale built **the first – albeit inefficient – gas turbine unit in 1903**.

In 1947, the British Admiralty was sufficiently impressed by the possible advantages of gas turbine propulsion that **the Royal Navy's first gas turbine ship** was built and tested; she was a 122 ft (37·2 m) 115-ton Camper & Nicholson boat, called *MGB 2009* (later re-classified *MTB 5559*). Powered by a 2500 hp Metropolitan-Vickers G2 gas turbine, *MGB 2009* had a speed

12 October 1950: First marine application of the Rover T8 gas turbine: two of these units each developing 200 bhp were installed in M.Y. Torquil

of 31 knots, and was distinguished by her exhaust funnels.

In 1950, the Rover Car Company of Birmingham, who had been engaged in the development of gas-turbine engines, not only exhibited a gas turbine motorcar, but also a gas-turbine powered 60 ft (18·3 m) ex-RAF pinnace, called the *Torquil*. As **the first application of the small gas turbine to marine propulsion**, *Torquil*'s Rover T8 turbines had a maximum output of 200 bhp each, with a compressor designed for a maximum speed of 40 000 rpm; this gave her a speed of about 13 knots. Before long the Admiralty had placed an order with the Rover Company for a number of these units.

From the 'Bold' class built in 1951 and following closely on construction of the 'Brave' class triple turbine-propelled fast patrol boats, Vospers Ltd of Portsmouth built, in 1961, the 88 ft (26·8 m) *Ferocity*, with a maximum speed of 50 to 54 knots; the powerplants were twin Bristol Siddeley Marine Proteus gas turbines (each rated at 4250 hp maximum) and alternately twin Mathway-Daimler diesel engines, developing 150 hp each. This system was known as Combined Diesel Or Gas (CODOG). Once the gas-turbine had been shown capable of sustaining high speeds, the racing world soon became involved.

The fastest private motor-yacht in the world in the early 1960s was millionaire Stavros Niarchos's

Mercury, built by Vosper Ltd, and also powered by three Bristol Siddeley Marine Proteus engines.

In 1963, the Rover 2S/150 twin-shaft 150 bhp gas-turbine engine was installed in a high-speed launch, ironically and fittingly called *Turbinia*. The following year, Rover developed the first application of a 107 bhp engine driving a variable pitch propeller, using their high-speed cabin launch *Rover Argo*.

In 1966, two Molinari powerboats, fitted with the Rover 2S/150M Marton shaft marine gas-turbines, coupled with Mercruiser stern-drives developed by Karl Kiekhaefer and driving a single propeller, were entered in the Paris Six Hour Race. This was the first time a gas-turbine-

Millionaire Stavros Niarchos's 102 ft (31 m) Mercury *was powered by 3 Bristol Proteus 1250 gas turbines (British Leyland)*

engined boat had competed internationally. The engines of these Mercrover Turbocruiser boats were installed centrally with a specially designed air-intake to prevent ingress of water, and an exhaust extractor which assisted compartment cooling. Driven by Roy Ridgell and Don Pruett, these boats achieved fantastic speeds, but were unable to achieve swift enough deceleration for rounding the buoys; before long, one boat had broken down and the other one was holed. So far, no gas-turbine circuit boats have been built since.

With offshore racing, the **first British power-boat to be propelled by the gas-turbine system** was *Miss Embassy*, with a Rolls-Royce Gnome, piloted during the 1973 Season by Tommy Sopwith. This boat was soon followed by Tim Powell's *Marlborough*, Gordon Proctor's *Passing Cloud* and several other craft; indeed, an experimental gas-turbine class was established to fit in these potentially very fast boats.

MARINE PROPELLERS

The Daimler Launch Motor Catalogue of July 1899 advised that their 17 ft (5·2 m) 1½ hp motor-launch be fitted with a two-bladed bronze propeller of 15¾ in diameter, whilst their 40 to 50 ft (12·2 to 15·2 m) 10 hp launch be fitted with a two-bladed prop of 25½ in diameter. For small motor-boats, it was soon recognised that a reversible propeller was the simplest, cheapest and most convenient method of control. In 1905, the best-known types were the Gaines (British) and the Meissner (German).

In the days before the motor-sailer, **the first Overside Propelling Outfit** was fitted by its inventor, Lord Ardee (later Earl of Meath), to his 40 ft (12·2 m), 22-ton TM cutter, *Patience*, in 1906. A 30 hp, four-cylinder Fafnir petrol engine was mounted fore and aft, which drove by belt a pulley on a shaft which was mounted on a spar over the side of the vessel; this could be lifted inboard and carried on deck when not required. The propeller was fitted to the aft end of the shaft, which ran in plummer blocks. The engine was installed on anti-vibration mats of cork and felt.

In 1909, a 70-ton ketch, *Rubicon*, owned by H. W. Longbottom, was fitted with the Overside

Propeller: a 30 hp, four-cylinder Ailsa Craig engine was mounted athwartships, the drive to the 2:1 bevel reducing gearbox being through universal joints. The shaft was enclosed in a tube and the speed attained was 6 to 7 knots. Risk of noise and vibration from so light a mounting as the deck, immediately above the saloon, was overcome by sandwiching a mat of cork and felt between it and the galvanised steel bedplate. This was **the first use of anti-vibration mounting of this type**. A second 30 hp Ailsa Craig Overside Propeller was fitted to a Mevagissey fishing vessel. Several other installations followed, many of small size, and the largest some 35 hp. Once auxiliary engines were accepted by yacht owners, the overside propeller disappeared from the scene.

F. Bamford & Co. Ltd

At the turn of the century, Fred Bamford, a qualified engineer and skilled craftsman of Stockport, Cheshire, installed his version of the marinised internal combustion engine in his launch, *Ajax*, running it on the Manchester Ship Canal at High Lane. In 1904 Bamford founded a company in Waterloo Road, Stockport to manufacture marine engines complete with shafts and propellers. From 1906, Bamfords also made the propellers and stern-gear for the Mirrlees portable diesel engines. Before long, they were marketing the Ropner 'Patent' Safety Speed Controlling and Reversing Propeller from their Ajax Works: the Roper prop gave Full Ahead, Slow Ahead, Neutral, Slow Astern and Full Astern; at the neutral point, when the two sets of blades were working in direct opposition, the motorboat could be kept stationary. Separate Bamford propellers ranged from a two-bladed unit (12 in diam × 14 in pitch) for £1 2s up to a three-bladed unit (18 in diam × 24 in pitch) for £2 18s. Special finish for racing would cost 30 per cent extra.

By the start of World War I, F. Bamford & Co. Motor Engineers' sale of propellers had exceeded those of engines, Fred had become an acknowledged expert in hydrodynamics, and the company was re-named 'Marine Propeller Manufacturers'.

Post-war racing saw the 1½-litre Sunbeam and Aston-Martin-engined hydroplanes competing for the Duke of York's Trophy, and much in

The first Bamford marine engine, fitted with the first controllable pitch propeller. Inset: *Fred Bamford*

need of high-revving propellers; Bamfords offered two types – for saltwater racing and for freshwater racing.

But possibly **Bamford's greatest challenge** was to produce a successful propeller for Sir Henry Segrave's Rolls-Royce aero-engined hydroplane, *Miss England II*, whose engine revs were experimentally stepped up by 1:4 to spin the propeller at 12550 to 13000 rpm (200 revs per sec); the prop diameter would have to be small enough to avoid 'torque'.

At first Rolls-Royce designed a two-blader using aircraft propeller principles and employing a totally new constructional technique. A solid billet of Stan Royal – high-speed nickel-chrome steel, instead of being forged – was literally carved down to nine-tenths of its size. This left 100 in (254 cm) for final machining after heat treatment which involved heating to 840° C, quenching in oil, tempering by heating to 570° C and quenching once more. This gave a tensile strength of 120 tons per sq in. The billet weighed 170 lb and the finished prop 17 lb, being polished

so finely that it could cut the finger of the highly-skilled operator who carved it. When one of the blades of this propeller snapped at high speed, adding to the growing pile of broken props (some of them produced by Bamfords), Segrave began to despair. However, on her fatal 120 mph (193 km/h) flat-out run on 13 June 1930, *Miss England II* was driving a manganese bronze prop designed and forged by F. Bamford & Co. Ltd.

During World War II, props were manufactured for high-speed naval craft. Post-war, Fred Bamford Jr sold his business to Assistant Manager Frank Smith and Works Manager George Robinson. By 1948, **the first modern type of 'Ajax' controllable pitch propeller**, incorporating two pins working in cycloidal slots, were supplied for the Navy's torpedo recovery vessels.

When the British Motor Corporation began manufacturing marine engines in 1951, Bamfords won a world franchise for the manufacture of their propellers and sterngear. Soon after, Bamfords merged with the Warwick Motor Engine Co. to form Ajax Marine Engines Ltd. It was also in the early 1950s that the company developed **the world's first pure cold cast, flexible nylon propellers** for use in shallow waters.

Prop-shaft manufacture received a boost in 1952 when substantial work was carried out in survey ships and seaward defence vessels for Italy, Yugoslavia, Canada and the UK.

Today Bamfords are based at the Whitehill Industrial Estate, supplying manganese bronze and nickel aluminium bronze props for every conceivable type of motorboat. **The biggest fixed pitch propeller yet made by the company** has a diameter of 12 ft 4 in (3·7 m), weighing about 4½ tons, for the *Lady Howard*, an offshore supply ship; **the largest controllable pitch propeller** was manufactured in 1970 for the *Sandwader*, and measured 12 ft (3·7 m). **The largest nylon propeller** is a 5 ft (1·5 m) unit for a container ship on the Panama Canal. Bamfords are still the only company making pure nylon propellers.

Bruntons Propellers Ltd

This company was established in 1868 by Mainprice Barton as the Stour Valley Iron Works, in Sudbury, Suffolk. In 1908 Philip Ransom, an apprentice with a lively interest in motorboats, made some wooden patterns for two- and three-bladed model propellers; the foundry was quick to cast them in iron. Both designs were soon being sold through advertisements in a model makers' magazine. Before long, Barton & Stern Ltd were supplying larger propellers, some made in brass. In 1911, Harold Brunton had bought up Mainprice Barton's Company and formed Bruntons (Sudbury) Ltd. By World War I, several thousand marine propellers had been made, including hand-operated designs for lifeboats, reversible pitch propellers, together with stern gear, stuffing boxes and bearings. In 1949, J. Stone & Co. Ltd

Three-bladed 12 in diameter propeller, supplied by Bruntons in 1920 for a Boulton & Paul launch (Bruntons Propellers Ltd)

A one-metre diameter propeller finished to ISO Class S Tolerances. It transmits 3500 hp at 1500 rpm in fast patrol boats (Bruntons Propellers Ltd)

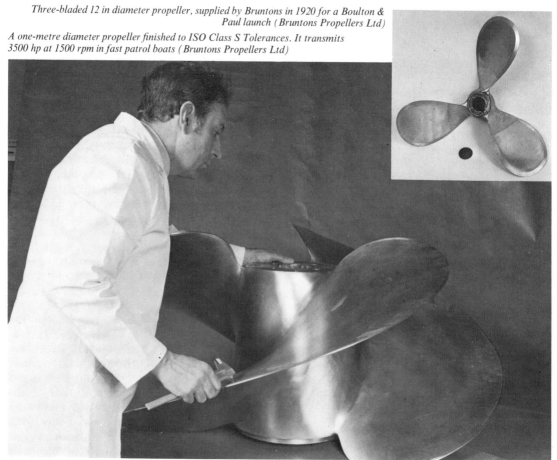

took a financial interest in Bruntons, and by 1958 Bruntons were wholly owned by Stone-Pratt Industries Ltd, and a subsidiary of Stone Manganese Marine Ltd, **the world's largest manufacturer of ship's propellers.**

During World War II, Stone Manganese had moved away from the traditional high tensile brass (manganese bronze) and begun to develop a new family of alloys which could be favourably employed in marine propeller manufacture. The first of these 'complex aluminium bronzes' was Nikalium (composed of 80·2 per cent copper/9·3 per cent aluminium/4·3 per cent nickel/5 per cent iron/1·2 per cent manganese), used since 1945. This was followed by Novoston (composed of 75 per cent copper/12 per cent manganese/8 per cent aluminium/3 per cent iron and 2 per cent nickel) with the first Novoston propeller spinning into operation in 1951. More recently Sonoston has been introduced.

In 1963 Bruntons produced their **first 'Caledonian' propeller**, specifically designed for motor

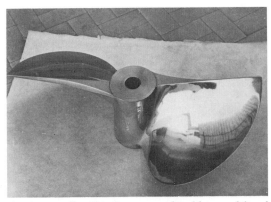

A racing propeller, 13 in diameter, machined from a solid steel forging for the US unlimited hydroplanes, with over 3000 hp to turn at over 12000 rpm. Price: US $1350

fishing vessels in service off the north-east coast of Scotland – in predominantly rough water conditions. 'Caledonian Mark II' was produced a few years later as the experience-improved version of this propeller.

Kort nozzle rudder, fitted to the motor tug Fiery Cross *in 1957*

The first motorboat to use a prototype Kort nozzle method of propulsion was the DB9, built in response to the concern stated by the German minister in charge of canals that the wash of powerful motor-tugs was eroding the canal banks. The aerodynamicist, Herr Ludwig Kort, proposed that a streamlined shroud should be fitted around the propeller. After model tests, the DB9, with two oblique intakes forward, joining into a single discharge tunnel ending at the stern, was built. The propeller worked at the narrowest portion of the tunnel just behind the junction of the two side intakes. On 7 June 1932, a 'tug-of-war' was publicly staged on the Mittelland Canal between the 120 bhp DB9 and a normal 180 hp tug. DB9 towed the conventional tug backwards. Soon after, Kort reduced his 'tunnel-hull' system to a simple nozzle ring, fitted round the propeller and separate from the hull itself. From now on the Kort nozzle could be easily fitted to existing vessels without any alteration to the hull at all. **The first American tug to be fitted with the fixed Kort nozzle with flanking rudders** was the Dravo Corporation's *Pioneer* in 1937. **The first UK tug to be fitted with the Kort nozzle rudder** was the *Fiery Cross* in 1957. A conservative estimate of the number of nozzles supplied to date is 6000 worldwide.

The first motor-vessel to be fitted with the combined marine propeller and rudder as invented in 1926 by M. E. Schneider of Vienna was constructed in 1929 by Messrs J. M. Voith of Heidenheim, and called the *Torqueo*. The bronze blades of aerofoil section projected vertically downward into the water, under the vessel. As the ring, in which the blades were pivoted, rotated about the central axis, the blades themselves were made to 'feather' on their own trunnions. This 'feathering' action could be set to propel the vessel ahead or astern, or to steer it in any desired direction.

Voith-Schneider propellers were fitted in 1938 to the 200 ft (61 m) motor-ship *Vecta*, built by Messrs John I. Thornycroft & Co. Ltd; each of the two props carried six bronze blades of aerofoil section 3·94 ft (1·20 m) long, which were rotated at 135 rpm around the central axis in an orbit 5·9 ft (1·8 m) diameter. The two diesel engines were supplied by English Electric Co. Ltd producing 550 hp at 325 rpm. *Vecta*'s speed on trial was 15·6 knots.

The first Schottel-Rudderpropeller to be sold was an SRP 75 unit in 1950 for the propulsion of

Schottel-Rudderpropeller, built in 1957

a 60-ton gravel barge, owned by the West German waterway control board. Joseph Becker founded his works in 1921, aged only 24. 'Die Schottel' is a section of the Rhine River between Boppard and Spay. Joseph Becker gave his enterprise the name of this part of the river. As well as building some 11 000 one-design jolly-boats, Becker started building motorboats in 1928. The Schottel Rudderpropeller was designed so that the underwater part of the unit with the propeller could be turned through 360° in both directions. Thus a ship could be steered by the full power of its propulsion machinery. By July 1978, with branches all over the world, Schottel-Werft had manufactured 16 750 Rudderpropeller units. The company is at present headed by Joseph Becker's son-in-law, Franz Krautkremer.

COMPARATIVE PROPELLER SPEEDS

	Revolutions per minute	Prop Diam. (in)
Super-Tanker	80	150+
Motor-Tug (2500 hp)	180	120
70 ft (21·3 m) Motor Fishing Vessel (400 hp)	300	80
30 ft (9·1 m) Motor Fishing Vessel (140 hp)	500	30
Fast Patrol Boat	750–1000	25
Outboard-engined racing powerboat (200 hp)	8250	16
Unlimited aero-engined Thunderboat (3000 hp)	12 000	13

(These figures are only averages – the designs of each propeller will vary in the extreme. Metals range from cast iron to solid steel forgings. Boat speeds also vary.)

WATER-JET PROPULSION

The first patent on record for jet propulsion by water was taken out by Thomas Toogood and James Hayes in February 1661. In 1783 Daniel Bernouilli published his 'Hydrodynamics' talking about water-jet propulsion. In 1729, John Allen wrote of his experiments with an 11-in water-jet propelled model.

A 2 hp Evinrude 'detachable outboard motor' of 1922–24, fitted with reverse gear (Courtesy Stuart Delf)

A 2 hp Johnson Light Twin aluminium outboard motor of 1925, nicknamed the 'Waterbug' (Courtesy Stuart Delf)

A typical 10 cc multi-hull model powerboat in action at the 1977 European Championships (Courtesy John Cundell, Model Boats*)*

The first boat to be powered by a water-jet apparatus was designed by the American pioneer, James Rumsey, and built near Bath, Virginia in the summer of 1785, whence it was transported down the River Potomac to Sheperdstown to be fitted with an experimental steam engine, built in Frederickstown and Baltimore by three separate companies.

Water was taken in through brass valve cocks and then pumped out from the stern of the boat by the action of steam pressure on the iron cylinder. On trial in December 1787, Rumsey's 18 ft (5·5 m) boat moved against the current of the Potomac with 2 tons on board, exclusive of machinery, at the rate of 4 mph (6 km/h). One year later the Rumseian Society was formed in Philadelphia and the inventor arrived in London to secure British patents.

The first steam-engined water-jet-propelled craft to be built in England to Rumsey's patents was the *Columbian Maid* (101 tons) constructed at Dover and fitted with a water-trunk 6 in square, and a pump 24 in diameter. Rumsey

reported that on 15 December 1972, the *Columbian Maid* worked well at Greenwich. Before she could be given further trials, Rumsey suffered a stroke and died in London. The boat was later tried on the Thames in February 1783, reaching 4 knots.

The first military vessel to be propelled by the water-jet system was HMS *Waterwitch*, a 162 ft (49·4 m) armour-plated gunboat designed by the Admiralty and launched at Millwall in 1866. She was propelled by a hydraulic reaction arrangement introduced by Mr J. Ruthven. HMS *Waterwitch* could also go into reverse by switching over the valves that controlled delivery, and not by reversing the 150 nominal hp engines.

(For the first steam-engined water-jet propelled lifeboats, see p. 75.)

The first water-jet propelled motor firefloat was constructed in 1905 to protect the biscuit factory of Messrs Huntley & Palmers Ltd on the River Kennet. Built by Messrs Merryweather & Sons of Greenwich, this 32 ft (9·8 m) firefloat was only

C. W. F. Hamilton testing out his waterjet-powered craft in New Zealand in the late 1950s (Popperfoto)

4½ ft (1·4 m) high so as to enable it to move under the bridges of the Kennet. Two 30 hp, four-cylinder petrol motors drove three-cylinder sets of Hatfield pumps, each delivering 300 gallons (1365 litres) of river water per minute – either to propel the firefloat forward or astern, or to enter six hose outlets. Speed of the firefloat was some 4 mph (6 km/h).

There was a water-jet propelled launch stationed at the Royal Albert Docks, London from 1925 to World War II.

The first successful motorboat where the water-jet was directed straight out through the transom above the waterline was developed by New Zealander O. W. F. Hamilton in the 1950s. He wished to gain easy access to the beautiful high country regions near his South Canterbury holding. The obvious route into this wild country was up the fast-flowing, rocky rivers. In the little workshop 'half-way up Mt Cook' many experiments took place with propellers, submerged and aerial, with no success. So Bill Hamilton experimented with centrifugal marine jet units such as the Hanley Hydrojet (on the market since the late 1940s) with maximum speeds of 11 mph (17 km/h) from the steerable nozzle. When Hamilton moved the nozzle from below to above waterline level, speeds increased to 17 mph (27 km/h). Before long, close attention to small details made for even greater efficiency with the Quinnat unit, which was Hamilton's first unit.

In 1954 the first batch of 'Rainbow' jet units were marketed. A direct-drive centrifugal type, the Rainbow gave good performance in a suitable craft; some 40 units were manufactured and marketed in New Zealand.

1956 saw the birth of the two-stage axial-flow turbine, christened the Chinook unit, closely followed by the three-stage unit.

The most challenging test for the development of the Hamilton Jet came in 1960 when three jet boats successfully completed the hazardous two-way run through the Colorado River. The first run of the expedition was down from Lee's Ferry to Lake Mead – over 300 miles (480 km) of water, sandbars, shoals and Grand Canyon rapids, the return run was all the more hazardous. Four reinforced 18-footers (5·5 m), American Buehler Turbocraft with American-built three-stage Hamilton jets, were powered by Dearborn V8 Interceptor engines on the down-run and Graymarine 188 engines on the return journey, during which time each boat was holed, then beached and patched up again. Only three boats arrived triumphantly at Lee's Ferry.

The first commercially produced water-jet propelled boats in England were the Dowty Turbocraft, fgrp hulls using Hamilton single-stage jets, powered by six-cylinder Ford Zephyr engines. A number of these were assembled at Sir George Dowty's Cheltenham factory. Donald Campbell took time off from creating world water speed records to become a Director of Dowty Marine and test-drive – among other craft – a 40 ft (12·2 m) cabin cruiser called *Desi*, powered by three Dowty jets, which was uncontrollably powerful.

Soon after, Campbell set to work with Peter Milne, the designer and magazine editor, and with Norris Brothers, his Bluebird engineers, to produce a less costly water-jet boat. In 1966, after some initial failures, the *Jetstar*, a 13 ft (4 m) plywood craft using the Hamilton Colorado Junior single-stage jet unit and powered by an 80 hp Evinrude, had been put through its paces at 40 mph (64 km/h) in front of an enthusiastic Mr Kilgour of the Malta Dry Docks Company, with the idea of establishing a jet boat plant in Malta, which would eventually turn out 5000 jet boats per year. Sadly, Campbell's tragic death on Coniston Water in 1967 precluded this ambitious project.

Since that period water-jet units have been manufactured by Castoldi, Jacuzzi, Berkeley, Panther, and PP. It was in 1960 that Ing. Franco Castoldi, the head of a large agricultural/marine machinery concern at Abbiategrasso, Milan, began design work to improve the intake, impeller and nozzle design of the jet package. By 1970 a Castoldi jet, complete with clutch and a pair of gears matched to the power output of the engine used, be it petrol or diesel, was launched into the market. In 1974, the Shead-designed, Enfield-built 37 ft (11·3 m) *Frediavolo*, powered by a modified Castoldi 06 unit with contra-rotating impellers, became **the first water-jet powered Class I powerboat to win an offshore race**.

The water-jet system has also been recently applied to commercial passenger-carrying hydrofoils (see p. 123).

National Lifeboatmen wore multi-segment cork lifebelts during the late Victorian era (RNLI)

LIFEJACKETS

In 1852, Capt. John Ross Ward RN of the National Lifeboat Institution (RNLI) carefully examined and experimented with every type of available lifebelt. He condemned the use of light-weight woods such as baobob from Senegal and balsa from Peru, because they were difficult to obtain in large quantities. He condemned rushes and horse hair because they absorbed too much moisture, and objected to the air-belt as prone to fatal puncturing. Capt. Ward concluded that the cork belt, made of multi-segments strung and sewn together to a stout linen or canvas belt, despite its cost, was the best.

In 1856 some 800 of these were supplied to lifeboat crews who wore them as standard issue until 1904.

The first kapok lifebelts were issued to the RNLI Stations for trial in 1904, and by 1906 there had been a complete changeover from cork to kapok at all RNLI stations, soon to be followed by its adoption by the Board of Trade for the Mercantile Marine. Kapok is a vegetable fibre, found chiefly around Java, Indonesia; although resembling cotton its follicles have a natural oil which makes them entirely resistant to water; per weight of lifejacket, the supporting role of kapok is $3\frac{1}{2}$ times that of cork.

The first RAF Mark I inflatable lifejackets, made by the inclusion of thin rolls of kapok inside a luminescent orange stole and fully inflated by the manipulation of a small lever which released CO_2 gas from two metal capsules, first saw service during the Battle of Britain. It was popularly nicknamed the 'Mae West' after the Hollywood sex symbol and film star of the late 1930s.

From 1943, the RAF Physiology Laboratory at RAE Farnborough carried out work to improve the Mae West design, under the supervision of Dr E. A. Pask, who realised that an effective lifejacket could only be designed around data from an induced state of unconsciousness in the water. Surface and underwater photographs were therefore taken of the anaesthetised and fully clothed Dr Pask at the freshwater pool of the London hospital, the saltwater pool at Farnborough and finally at Ealing Studios' saltwater pool where 3 ft (1 m) waves were simulated by a machine. From these films and allied research, after several years of experimentation, **Pattern 5580 was first produced in 1952**.

Its 'bubble' chest chamber was inflatable through a spring-loaded, non-return nylon valve. It was 'traffic yellow' in colour, resistant to jumps of over 30 ft (9 m), impervious to oil, and provided adequate support at the sides and back of the head so as to prevent immersion of the nose and mouth. It was equipped with a lifting becket, a whistle, a water-activated battery and light, and a toggle line as standard accessories.

During the late 1950s/early 1960s, Dr Pask continued to work with the Board of Trade to improve the buoyancy, minimum freeboard, etc of their lifejackets. They found that kapok was particularly susceptible to oil, but overcame this

problem by heat-sealing each section of kapok inside a polythene envelope. The standards set by the Department of Trade differed from those of the British Standards Institute and the Ship & Boatbuilders National Federation who specified some 18 to 20 lb of permanent buoyancy as opposed to 35 lb specified by the Board of Trade. This enabled less bulky items to be designed for the active enjoyment of watersport; **simplified 'buoyancy aids' began to appear on the market**. One of the first commercial buoyancy aids was the Marksway.

Before long, competition had grown up with companies such as Beaufort, Avon, etc, and instead of the 'trapped air' method, the sponge sandwich came in, followed by **closed-cell foam rubber buoyancy aids**.

In 1960, the Inter-Governmental Maritime Consultative Organisation (IMCO) – a branch of the United Nations – held their Solus Convention on International Safety. It was specified that lifejackets 'Shall be of a highly visible colour'. Although the phrase 'International Orange' was used, it was soon found that there was no strict definition of this – although the public were already referring to the colour popularly as **'Dayglo Orange'** (see p. 174). During the early 1960s most lifejacket and buoyancy aid manufacturers changed over to 'International Orange' – Beaufort, for example, in 1964.

Although it was proved by an American that the 'best colour for seeing' is a yellow lime-green, such a colour has only really been found effective on land, whilst in sea-green water conditions it does not contrast so favourably.

The problem of nocturnal maritime search and rescue operation had yet to be solved. Pre-war, the 3 M's Corporation in the USA (originally known as the Minnesota Mining & Manufacturing Company) had pioneered – alongside 'masking tape', 'wet-and-dry', and 'underseal' – **a retro-reflective, nocturnally visible tape called 'Scotchlite'**, which could be used for road signs, automobile numberplates, etc. Millions of microscopic glass beads embedded in the material acted as lenses to reflect light shining on them directly back to source, with undiminished intensity. Scotchlite first appeared in the UK in 1952.

It was in 1959 that Trinity House started using Scotchlite sheeting on its steel buoys so that they

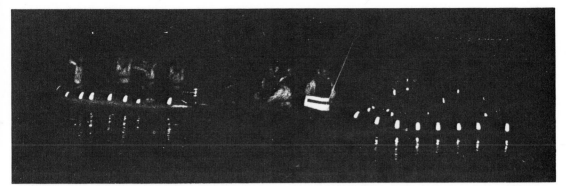

Scotchlite reflective patches can be seen in a searchlight beam, as demonstrated by the visibility of the life-rafts to the left and right of the unmarked one in the centre (3 M's)

might be seen in the searchlights of a marine vessel. In 1964, both the Royal Navy and RAF began to use Scotchlite on their larger inflatable life-rafts, but found that the tape tended to crack when these inflatables were folded up. 3 M's set about developing a flexible sheeting.

Stemming from the report of the International North Atlantic Air and Surface Search and Rescue Seminar of 1970, the US Coast Guard instructed all its operating units to apply retro-reflective tape on all non-inflatable lifejackets and life-rings by the end of June 1971.

In May 1973, the National Coastal Rescue Training Centre gave a demonstration of re-flectorisation as an aid to night-time sea rescue at Aberavon in South Wales. Reflectorised boats and swimmers could be spotted by a search-light from a distance of some 700 yards (600 m), whilst those not reflectorised could not be seen until they were within 75 yards (69 m) of the shore.

On 25 June the 90 ft (27·4 m) ketch *Sea Star* left London for a round-the-world voyage of at least two years to raise funds for the United World Colleges. All life-saving equipment was reflectorised using Scotchlite sheeting and tape – on the recommendation of IMCO.

In November 1973, another demonstration of reflectorisation was given to the Marine Superintendents of the major shipping companies to the RNLI, HM Coastguard, the Board of Trade and representatives of the Press. Boats and lifejackets and buoys, floating down on the Thames from Tower Bridge to Greenwich Reach, could be seen from some 700 to 800 yards (600–700 m) distance when picked up by six Coastguard searchlights turned on and off, one after the other.

One year later, the Department of Trade officially recommended that retro-reflective Scotchlite tape and sheeting be fitted to life-saving appliances on board every British Merchant Ship, of which there were an estimated 4000 registered at over 100 tons, and more than half a million pleasure craft.

IMCO, to whom some 20 countries are con-tracted, is already considering making their recommendation for reflectorisation into a regulation, although it is already in force in half a dozen countries. Wiser motor yachtsmen have also made use of this inexpensive accessory.

FIRE EXTINGUISHERS

Hand appliances were the first form of fire extinguisher, and water-filled syringes were be-ing used in ancient Greece and Rome.

In 1761, grenades were being made with gun-powder, alum, sal-ammoniac and other chemi-cals, which when thrown into a fire exploded and instantly quenched the fire.

In 1816, Capt. Manby of London invented **the first high-pressure chemical fire extinguisher**. This was a 2 ft (0·6 m) long copper cylinder, charged with 3 gallons (13·6 litres) of water, in which carbonate of potash had been dissolved. The remaining space in the cylinder was filled with compressed air through a lock by means of a pump and on the jet being replaced it was ready for action. Single cylinders could be con-veyed on men's backs by straps. Despite suc-cessful experiments, Manby's extinguisher was rejected by the insurance companies.

Possibly the most famous fire extinguisher company during the 20th century was 'Pyrene'. Their standard 14 in polished brass model projected a special liquid, having a carbon tetrachloride base, which on meeting the fire formed a blanket of vapour which excluded the oxygen necessary to combustion. The double-acting pump by which the Pyrene extinguisher was operated gave a powerful jet no matter which side up or at what angle the extinguisher was held, to a distance of 25 to 30 ft (7·5 to 9 m). During 50 years, some 17 000 000 Pyrene fire extinguishers were supplied – thousands of which were installed onboard motorboats, cabin cruisers and yachts. Pyrene is now owned by the Chubb Group, who still produce fire extinguishers alongside other companies such as Antifyre, Kil-fire, Minimax, Nu-Swift, Stand-by, etc.

THE COMPASS

The mariner's compass was already in fairly regular use around the 13th century, though **it is uncertain whether the Chinese, Arabs, Turks, Persians, Italians or Greeks were the first to use it**. This was a magnetic iron-ore 'lodestone' resting in a float in a bowl of water – or alternatively a magnetised iron needle thrust through a floating reed (hence 'sailing needle'). Sailing needles were essentially used to indicate 'North' in foggy or cloudy weather when the stars, particularly the Pole star, were hidden from sight – and astro-navigation impeded.

Before long the sailing needle was developed into a needle pivoted on a pin rising from the bottom of the compass box or bowl, around which primitive compass points were marked; then a graduated card came to be attached to the needle itself. It was the Flemish navigators who subdivided their compass cards into 32 points.

The problem of retaining magnetism in the compass needle was lessened by Dr Gowin Knight in 1766, who used better steel for the needle with a jewel cap (sapphire) for the pivot in the centre. Dr Knight's method of supporting the compass bowl and his design of the gimbal system were so successful that the Knight compass was soon adopted by the Royal Navy.

(Gimbals are a ring/pivot suspension system for supporting nautical instruments in a horizontal position.)

The extremely adverse navigational effects on the magnetic compass, brought about by the introduction of shipbuilding in iron and steel and the vibrational errors caused by steam-driven propelling machinery, were first investigated by Capt. Matthew Flinders RN during his voyage to Australia in HMS *Investigator* in 1801–4. As a means of compass correction, Flinders designed a vertical bar or soft iron – known today as the Flinders bar. The numerous marine catastrophes attributable to unreliable compasses and unknown deviations brought the Admiralty Compass Committee of 1837 to design a new compass, Admiralty Pattern 1, also laying down rules for the correct placing of the compass in HM ships.

The first liquid-filled compass was produced by Francis Crow of Faversham in 1813 – incorporating many of the features in present-day compasses. But leakage of liquid, expansion, discolouration and difficulty in repairing a damaged pivot still have to be overcome. Considerable advances were made by E. S. Ritchie's float-system of 1862 and W. R. Hammersley's expansion chamber, respectively preventing undue pivot stress and liquid leakage. Although the liquid compass was adopted by the US Navy, the Royal Navy continued to use the 'dry card' compass Pattern L, except in bad weather and during gunfire when liquid compasses were used.

The dry-card compass was given a new lease of reliable life by Sir William Thomson (later Lord Kelvin) who in 1876 produced an easily maintained, 'replaceable-parts' compass, which was encased on a gimbal-supporting binnacle, embodying all the correctors necessary and allowing for their easy adjustment. Not only did the Thomson compass replace Admiralty Pattern 1, but it also became a traditional compass for the Merchant Service. It sold in vast numbers, and spare parts were available at all the world's principal ports; from then on, it became commonplace to adjust compasses properly and to keep them accurately adjusted.

The liquid compass was officially introduced into the Royal Navy in 1906 by Capt. L. W. P. Chetwynd. This was filled with a rather weak mixture of alcohol and water, often suffering from 'bubbles' through poor gaskets and diaphragms, whilst the weight of the floats which carried the card, was still relatively heavy. It was only during World War II that the liquid compass was hesitantly adopted by the Merchant Navy.

The expensive, gyroscopic compass was developed almost simultaneously by Brown, Sperry and Anschutz in England, America and Germany respectively, during the first decade of this century. The gyro-compass, with remote indication by several repeaters and unaffected by magnetic materials and electrical appliances – made it immediately more popular than the magnetic compass, especially for larger naval and merchant ships.

During World War II, the Admiralty introduced their **first magnetic compass capable of remote indication by several repeaters**, for use in small high-speed coastal craft, made possible by recent electronic advances. This less expensive compass challenged the supremacy of the gyrocompass.

With the advent of the long-distance World War I aircraft, with its noisy engine vibrations, sharp turns and bumpy touchdowns, a new compass had to be developed where the gimballing was replaced by anti-vibration spring mountings, and where the only movement of the card was internal within the compass, allowing a healing movement of the card itself. Following this, during the inter-war years, a grid form of steering was introduced to overcome the parallax error developed in a pilot/co-pilot situation where the compass was positioned between the two of them.

After World War II, grid compasses were adapted for offshore powerboat racing drivers, several of whom were former RAF pilots. The gimballing system was abandoned for offshore racing in favour of the heavily oil-damped liquid compass using very lightweight spider-type systems to give an improved fluid reaction. The old-fashioned sapphire or steel pivot system was replaced by one of the new forms of hardened metal – such as iridium – capable of polishing down to an ultra-accurate radius, whilst new higher-powered magnetic materials such as Alnico and Alcomax were also incorporated, resulting in a much smaller and lighter magnet. For the less aggressive forms of water transport, external gimballing was maintained.

Ideally the highest performance from a compass is obtained by the largest possible compass bowl and the smallest possible card compatible with visibility. **Perspex domes were first incorporated into compass designs** in the early 1940s.

Compass cards were originally made nocturnally visible by the use of a radium-based luminous compound, which was later replaced by a prometheum-based pigment. Present-day luminosity is obtained from tritium cells, being glass capsules coated inside with phospher and then filled with tritium gas under pressure; the tritium gas excites the phospher and makes it glow – with a 12-year lifespan.

Henry Browne in 1908

Inter-war, Sestrel Grid-steering compass for motorboats. Notice the single-line grid, replaced after World War II (Henry Browne Ltd)

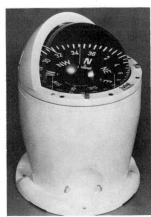

Sestrel 'Major' compass of 1978 (Henry Browne Ltd)

The oldest existing British manufacturer of compasses is Henry Browne & Son Ltd, formed by Henry Browne (1861–1929) in 1884 at Brightlingsea, the premier yachting port in England at the time. The company's main activities then were the painting of liquid compass cards, repair work of compasses and the manufacture of compasses for lifeboats.

During the inter-war years, the company became famous for its compasses and binnacles, named the 'Falmouth', 'Fastnet', 'Viking', 'Solent', 'Thames', etc after river or sea areas.

In the early 1930s the company moved to East London, and very soon afterwards to Barking, Essex. By 1939 the relatively small number of 14 employees had grown to 150. During the war years of 1939–45, the number of personnel trebled to provide compasses for the armed Forces.

Ernie Barlex, the company's present Technical Director, joined in 1936, and by 1944 had worked his way up from 'boy', to shop-foreman, to chief inspector, to designer. In 1945–46, Barlex designed the first custom-built compass for the pleasure-boating market – the Sestrel 'Major'. The word SESTREL was built up from **S**ensitive, **St**eady, **Rel**iable. Since then the Sestrel 'Major', 'Minor', 'Moore', 'Shoresight', 'Popular', 'Repeater' have sold in their thousands throughout the world.

In 1970, Henry Browne & Son Ltd were taken over by the public Winn Group, and by 1974 had moved into a new factory devised by Ernie Barlex to incorporate a 'flow-line' production where 200 personnel were turning out some 60 Sestrel compasses per week.

THE LOG

The earliest known attempt to estimate distance or speed at sea was made by Vitruvius and the Romans, who used a type of water wheel fixed to the hull of the galley which carried a drum on board filled with pebbles. Every time the wheel revolved, one pebble fell out into a tally box. By counting the number of pebbles in the box an estimate of distance travelled could be obtained.

From the late 16th/early 17th century, two methods of measuring distance run came into use:

The Dutchman's Log consisted of two marks on the ship's bulwark, the distance between which had been accurately measured. A float or similar object was thrown as far ahead of the ship as possible and timed, by counting the human pulse or saying a rhyme as it passed between the two marks. From the timing and the distance apart of the two marks, the speed of the ship could be calculated. The success of results depended on the accuracy of observation and timing.

The Common or English Log, first reported in 1574, usually consisted of a wooden board called the log-chip, weighed at its base to keep it upright on the water, with three holes, to which the log-line was attached by a crow's foot of three legs, to one of which a peg was attached. When heaving the log, the log-chip was hove overboard, well clear and to windward, the line being paid out from the reel on which it was wound. The first 10 or 20 fathoms of the log-line, marked by a piece of bunting, were called stray-line, which left the log clear of the disturbed wake of the vessel before timing was begun.

At first the line was run out for one min, timed by a log-class, but by the 17th century, for 30 sec. Initially the length of line run out was measured in fathoms in the traditional way against the stretch of arms. By multiplying the result by 60 (min) and dividing the amount by 2500 (fathoms in a league of 3 miles (5 km)) the speed of the ship in leagues per hour could be obtained.

Early in the 17th century, the line was marked by knotted cords (knots) inserted in the line at 42 ft (12·8 m – 7 fathoms) intervals, the number of knots in each cord increasing progressively so that the amount of log-line run out could be measured more accurately and quickly. The number of knots run out in 30 sec corresponded with the number of English nautical miles travelled in one hour, each mile traditionally considered to consist of 5000 ft (1500 m). This error was not corrected to 6080 ft (1850 m) until the mid 18th century.

The commercial introduction of the pendulum to control time-keeping clocks in 1657 made it possible to make accurate sand-glasses and from the 1680s the 'half minute' glass, filled to run for only 28 sec, was introduced to correct the log, it being easier to alter the amount of sand in the glass and use it with the customary 7 fathoms knots than to mark off the log-line in fractions of fathoms.

In 1747 Pierre Bouguer, a Frenchman, developed an improvement to the Common Log which counteracted the effect of wind and sea upon the surface of the log-chip, and overcame the friction of the log-reel which tended to cause the log-chip to be dragged along with the ship. It consisted of a cone of varnished wood to which was attached a metal sinker of a weight sufficient to allow only the top of the cone to appear on the sea surface. Two parts were connected to each other by a line of about 50 ft (15·2 m) in length. The ordinary log-line was attached to the cone, and the whole was hove and used in the customary way.

When the sand ran out of the hour-glass, the log-line was quickly nipped and the knots counted. The nipping of the line was simplified by the use of an instrument called 'Burts Nipper' which was a device consisting of a handle and rollers through which the line was allowed to run. When the sand-glass ran out the line could be jammed on the rollers. When the log-line was nipped the bone peg in the log-ship was pulled away allowing the log-ship to be heaved in.

The Common Log remained in widespread use until the 1920s and was still being used by some Belgian fishermen in the 1960s.

Mechanical Logs – the first commercially successful recording 'perpetual' log was patented by Edward Massey in 1802. This consisted of a shallow rectangular box, with a float plate on its upper side, which contained the registering wheelwork. The dials on the register were exposed and showed 10th's miles and 100 miles. The rotator consisted of a thin metal tube, coned at the fore end, carrying flat metal vanes set at an angle. The rotator was connected to a universal joint on the first spindle of the register by four 17-in lengths of cane jointed together; later these were replaced by a 6 ft (1·8 m) length of line. The whole mechanism was towed astern of the ship. It had to be hauled in, read and reset at each alteration of course or change of watch. Massey's log is known to have been fitted as early as 1805 in HMS *Donegal*; trials were carried out in the Bay of Naples to everyone's satisfaction.

Thomas Walker, Edward Massey's nephew, introduced his 'Harpoon Log' in 1861; it was an improvement on the Massey Log in that the

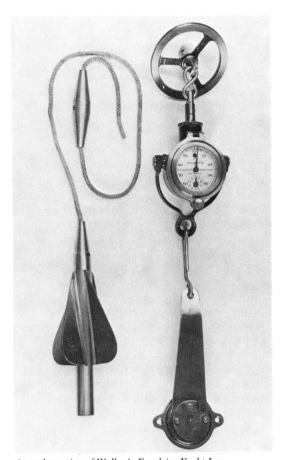

An early version of Walker's Excelsior Yacht Log

rotator and registering mechanism were in one unit, but the log still had to be hauled in when readings were required. The Harpoon log was still being used a century later in Arctic waters, where, unlike later types, it did not suffer from icy conditions.

In 1878 Thomas Ferdinand Walker Jr patented his 'Cherub' taffrail log which had a towed rotator, connected by a log-line, to a register mounted on the taffrail. This was convenient, involving only a walk to the stern of the ship to read the dial when required. It embodied all the principles on which the modern towed log is based. It was named 'Cherub' after a cartoon which appeared in Punch magazine, depicting Joseph Chamberlain, then President of the Board of Trade, hovering in the shape of a cherub, over one of the over-insured 'murder' ships which were then under severe criticism.

In 1890, Walker patented a method in which the rotator was suspended from a spar projecting from the side of the ship, and was made fast to a line secured to an eye on the primary spindle, which through a bevel gear and universal joint, rotated a line which transmitted the movement of the rotator to the indicator on the bridge. This arrangement was still in use in the 1950s.

Over the past century, Thomas Walker and Son of 58 Oxford Street, Birmingham have manufactured and marketed the most number of ship's logs; they have lost count of this number, but estimate it to be in the hundreds of thousands. With the advent of the motor-launch, Walkers brought in their Excelsior ('Higher') towing-type logs, which existed in various models from the turn of the century; 'Walker's Excelsior Yacht Log Register for Yachts, Motor Launches and Fishing Craft', came with Walker's Ship Log Oil either in ½ pint or 1 pint tins. In 1912, the Excelsior log was manufactured with a distance repeater in the wheelhouse, operated from electrical contacts within the log register itself; this accessory was known as the 'Trident Electric Log Register', which was either part of the instrument panel or on the ship's bulkhead, complete with resistance box when the electrical supply was over 24 knots. The Excelsior Yacht Log Mark IV was designed in 1936 and still sells in considerable quantities. The standard form has an 'outrigger' by which it is attached to the deck or taffrail with a form of bayonet fitting. Secondly, is the 'sling' pattern where it can be lashed to the rail.

In 1917, Capt. B. Chernikeef of the Russian Naval Hydrographic Department developed a log which consisted of a casing containing a small rotator attached to the ship's bottom. The rotator drives an electrical transmitter which is connected to indicating and recording apparatus carried inboard. **The Chernikeef Log** was demonstrated to the British Admiralty in 1921 – and it is still widely used today, particularly on submarines.

The Electro-Magnetic Log was developed in the late 1960s, based on the principle of Faraday's law of magnetic induction. Two sensors are mounted below the ship's hull. A voltage directly proportional to the speed of the ship through the water is induced across the sensors when the magnetic field is cut by a conductor, which in this case is the seawater passing the sensors. This type of log is capable of measuring speeds up to 40 knots.

RADAR

Radio waves were first discovered by Heinrich Hertz, who conclusively demonstrated in 1886 that they were reflected from conducting objects such as metal sheets. In 1904 a German engineer was granted a patent in several countries on a proposed way of using this property in an obstable detector and navigational aid for ships. In June 1922, Marconi strongly urged the use of short waves for radio detection in a paper read before the American Institute of Electrical Engineers and Institute of Radio Engineers. In Autumn 1922 a Dr Hoyt Taylor and his assistant Leo C. Young, working for the US Navy, observed a distortion or 'phase shift' in the received signals due to the reflection from a small wooden steamer on the River Potomac. Taylor suggested to the Navy Department that 'destroyers located on a line a number of miles apart could be immediately aware of the passage of an enemy vessel between any two destroyers of the line, irrespective of fog, darkness or smoke screen'.

The principle of 'pulse ranging' which characterises modern radar was first used in 1925 by Dr Gregory Breit and Dr Merle A. Tuve of the Carnegie Institution of Washington for measuring the distance to the ionosphere, which is the radio reflecting layer near the top of the earth's atmosphere.

In June 1932, Sir Robert Watson-Watt, the Scottish scientist, showed that aircraft interfered with radio signals and re-radiated them, deducing that an aircraft would act as a reflector of short-wave radio pulses.

In 1932, Marconi demonstrated a form of radar while experimenting with microwaves. It was found that a man walking in front of the aerials could also be detected. It was in the field of microwaves that Marconi gave one of his most spectacular demonstrations: that of guid-

Marconi's famous yacht Elettra, *which he acquired in 1919 and used as a sea-going laboratory (Marconi)*

ing a ship through a narrow entrance to a harbour in conditions of zero visibility (1934).

Two broad beam reflectors at right angles to each other, were mounted as the navigational beacon on the promontory at Sestri Levante, Italy (300 ft (90 m) above sea level). On board the ship *Elettra*, a four-valve receiver was mounted. Two buoys were then anchored 300 ft (90 m) apart at a distance of 2600 ft (800 m) from the shore to simulate a harbour entrance. On 30 July *Elettra* steamed out to sea for her anchorage, with representatives of all the big shipping lines and from Trinity House on board. With all the blinds of the chartroom drawn, so that it was impossible for the navigator to see, the yacht was successfully steered through the two buoys safely by means of the indication given by the beacon. The manoeuvre took little skill and many of Marconi's guests tried it out for themselves and became very excited about its potential.

Marconi had next arranged for two similar buoys to be anchored at the entrance to the harbour at Santa Margherita. By turning the receiver to face the stern, and by reversing the connections to the indicator, he then proceeded to carry out the same manoeuvre – this time at a distance of 10 miles (16 km) from the beacon!

RADAR, a reversible word, was first coined by the US Navy in 1940 as an abbreviation for 'radio detection and ranging' – the term was soon adopted by common consent in the USA and UK. Radar was born when it occurred to different persons independently, in America, England, France, Germany and Japan that the pulse technique could be used to detect objects such as aircraft and ships. Scientists in these countries worked secretly on problems of increased power output, shorter pulses, directional antenna systems, plan position indicators (PPI), etc.

In America, during the late 1930s much Government-sponsored work went on at the Naval Research Laboratory (Radio Division) towards the problems of getting the transmitter and receiver in the same ship, generating pulses of the proper length and shape, building a receiver which would not be blocked by transmitter pulses and therefore pick up those extremely short pulses (a millionth of a second long, every few thousandths of a second) after they were reflected; and a common radio-telephony radar antenna or 'duplexer'.

The first set of US radar equipment to be installed and work aboard ship was built at the Naval Research Laboratory. In April 1937, it was successfully demonstrated over saltwater at the mouth of the Chesapeake on the old four-stack destroyer *Leary*. The next two years were spent in designing a practical shipboard model. In December 1938, an NRL-designed radar, operating on a wavelength of a metre and a half, was installed on the USS *New York*. So successful were its trials at sea on battle manoeuvres over the ensuing months that, in October 1939, the first Government contract was awarded to a commercial company for the manufacture of six sets of aircraft detection equipment.

In Great Britain radar was developed at a somewhat faster pace under the immediate threat of Britain's security. During the winter of 1934–35, the Air Ministry set up a Committee for the Scientific Survey of Air Defence, with Sir Henry Tizard as Chairman. Among the suggestions it received was a carefully worked-out plan for the detection of aircraft by the re-radiation of incident energy – the pulse method; this came from Watson-Watt, Superintendent of the Radio Department of the National Physical Laboratory.

The first experimental system was set up with extreme efficiency in the late spring of 1935, on the barren isthmus of Ordfordness, off the east coast of England. By 13 May a team under Watt had been assembled, special equipment had been constructed, and 70 ft (21 m) masts erected. On 31 May all was ready for the first tests. On 15 June, under poor conditions for radio reception, the Tizard Committee saw an aircraft followed by radar to a distance of 17 miles (27 km). By July, a range of 40 miles (64 km) was achieved.

By March 1938, five stations, about 25 miles (40 km) apart, to protect the Thames estuary, were complete and operating under RAF personnel. In September 1938, ASV radar (for detecting surface vessels) was successfully demonstrated during fleet manoeuvres.

The first usable sea-going radar was installed on HMS *Rodney* in 1938. Her captain complained bitterly at having to install such ugly aerials. The cruiser HMS *Sheffield* soon followed suit.

The next stage in the sophistication of radar was realised to be the further shortening of wavelengths from 5 ft (1·5 m) down so as to obtain sharper, narrower radar beams. This necessitated the development of a capable short wave-generating valve. After much Admiralty-sponsored research at the Birmingham University Physics Laboratory under Prof Marcus Oliphant, Dr John Randall and several others, **the first effective valve for centimetre radar** – the cavity magnetron – was tested on 21 February 1940. After the visit of a British Technical Mission under Sir Henry Tizard in September 1940, where there was a free mutual exchange of discoveries, the US version of the cavity magnetron was soon being manufactured. In January 1941 the US Radiation Laboratory obtained echoes from **its first microwave radar set**, and by late spring of that year an experimental microwave sea-search radar was equipped with cathode-ray tube. Plan Position Indicator was installed on the venerable destroyer *Semmes* and in operation by 14 May. By 1943 the new microwave radar was in production on a large scale and beginning to have a significant role in maintaining the Allied margin of radar superiority. Many motor-torpedo boats and motor gunboats were adapted to take a radar set. By 1 July 1945 some $500 000 000 of radar equipment had been delivered to the US Navy.

Between 1945 and 1950, merchant ships tended to be fitted with heavy ex-Naval radar sets, until three or four companies, headed by Cossor, produced their own commercial version of radar. The first slotted aerial was developed by 1953 at Kelvin-Hughes for use on Lancaster bombers then flying for the RAF; a 40 kW marine version, range 48 miles (77 km), followed in 1956 – using the newly introduced fgrp in its construction. The first company to make a big commercial success of radar was Decca with their 'Type 159'.

Although small American radars had been manufactured by Raytheon, Apelco and Sperry, **the first truly small boat radar** that appeared in the UK (in 1959) and was subsequently exported, was the Marconi Consort of 240 watt consumption. This was push-button activated, cost £890 in 1959 and gave a good picture on a cathode ray tube.

But these radars, with their powerplants, their generator, their cathode ray tube, their transceiver with wave-guide going up to the aerial guide unit, were still bulky and heavy, not easily installed in pleasure motor-yachts below 150 ft (45·7 m); they also took up an enormous amount of power from the battery of the ship's supply.

With the advent of the germanium transistor, first successfully used with the US Army's radio transistorised receiver man-packs, it was realised that the power consumption and size of a

The Marconi Consort radar of 1959, fitted to Elettra II, *Marconi Marine's demonstration yacht (Marconi)*

The 'Seascan' 16-mile range radar, as produced by Electronic Laboratories Limited in 1970, was – along with the Decca 050 – the first transistorised radar

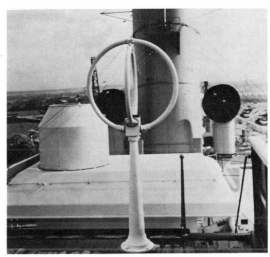

A Bellini-Tosi direction-finding aerial on board a merchant vessel in 1948 (Marconi)

transistorised solid state radar might be considerably reduced. During the early 1960s Marconi, Decca and Kelvin-Hughes (with their highly successful 'Type 17') introduced **the first 'tranny' radars**. It now became possible to install these on board smaller motorboats – be they cabin cruiser, patrol boats, lifeboats, etc. This period also saw the introduction of the first raydomes which could protect radar from severe weather effects.

In 1970, Decca produced **the first two unit radar** (the '050') with cable connections, thus eliminating the wave-guide, thus bringing down the power required, the range (to 12 miles (19 km)) and the size on to a practical pleasure boating basis. The following year, Electronic Laboratories at Poole produced their first 16-mile (26 km) range 'Seascan' radar – as **the smallest commercially produced radar**.

The main bugbear of radar was to develop a way of automatically clearing the radar screen of 'clutter' caused by the reflections of rough weather waves and rain drops. The first company to solve this was Decca, with their 'Clearscan' of 1977.

RDF

Prior to the advent of radar, motor yachtsmen and merchant shipping captains often used a bulky radio direction finder called the RD Loop,

consisting of the Bellini-Tosi sense aerial mounted on a cast bronze pillar bolted on the deck, which was connected to a sonometer, the tuning device of an MF radiotelephone in the wheelhouse below. By carefully tuning into such stations as London, Paris, Hilversum, Athlone, etc the captain was able to establish his bearings in relations to the 360° direction of the RD loop.

Post-war this device has also been miniaturised so that a ferrite aerial picking up the carrier wave of beacons, and coupled direct to a hand-held compass, was successfully developed by Maj. Richard Gatehouse in 1955 and dubbed the Heron. Apart from its immediate marine success, the Heron DF set was also used by Sir Vivian Fuchs on his South Polar Expedition of 1956.

Electronic Laboratories produced their first **Seafix** RDF hand-held set in 1965, geared to the mass market. By 1977 nearly 50 000 Seafix units had been sold and the company was maintaining an output of 1000 units per month.

ECHO-SOUNDERS

Depth-sounding afloat, by means of a lead line swung overboard, may be traced back to Ancient Egypt and is also mentioned in the 'Acts of the Apostles'. By the 18th century this method could go down as far as 20 fathoms (120 ft).

During the 1830s and 1840s, both log-designers Edward Massey and Thomas Walker developed sounding-apparati geared to measuring dials which lock when they hit the sea-bottom. The disadvantages of pulling up heavy, hemp line from great depths were tackled by substituting with either copper or iron wire, which also tended to snap in deep-sea sounding.

In 1872, Sir William Thomson (later Lord Kelvin) experimented with a sounding machine of his own design, on the drum of which was wound 3 miles (5 km) of piano wire. Using a 30 lb lead he successfully obtained a sounding of 2700 fathoms. When he came to heave in, however, he found there was far more strain on the wire than he had anticipated and this collapsed the drum of the machine. But Thomson persisted until he was able to patent a successful machine in 1876. It was soon universally adopted, its final modified form appearing in 1905. A thin chemical glass tube was attached to a 28 lb lead; the tube was sealed at one end, its inside coated with chromate of silver. As the tube sank to the bottom with the lead, the air in it was compressed allowing the saltwater to enter. The distance to which the saltwater penetrated was dependent upon the depth of the water and was marked by the chromate of silver becoming discoloured by the salt. When the lead had been recovered, all that was necessary was to measure the length of the tube which had not been discoloured against a special scale.

In 1911, Dr Alexander Behm of Kiel, showed that it might be possible to measure depth of water **by timing the echo of an underwater explosion**. The foundering of the *Titanic* on 14 April 1912 spurred Behm on to an experiment whereby the sound waves emitted in a small aquarium were photographed and shown to be well reflected.

The first practical Anti-Submarine Detection Indicator Chart (ASDIC) was developed in 1918 by Paul Langevin in France. In 1919 the Hayes Sonic depth finder had been developed at the US Naval Engineering Experimental Station. This consisted of an electro-magnetic device that sent sound waves to the ocean floor. By 1922 echo-sounders (otherwise known as Fathometers) were considered as a practicable reality. By 1924 the Behm system was being tried in the UK. In this system a cartridge was fired on one side of

the ship and the echo was recorded by a hydrophone on the other. An instrument measured the time between the two sounds and consequently the depth of water. In the same year the Royal Navy was experimenting with other equipment which had been developed on its behalf by Henry Hughes. **The first Royal Naval vessel to be fitted with an echo-sounder**, incorporating a gong, was the MV *Asturias* in 1925. **The earliest echo-sounding survey** of the Challenger Bank, WSW of Bermuda, was made by HMS *Ormonde* between 6 April and 1 May 1925. By 1926 HMS *Endeavour*, HMS *Kellet*, HMS *Beaufort* and HMS *Fitzroy* had been fitted with echo-sounding equipment. From the experience gained, the system of single soundings was replaced by a continuous automatic record which provided a traced curve showing the depth of water at all times.

In December 1930, the Marconi Sounding Device Company Ltd was formed, with capital provided by the Marconi Marine Company, to market the newly-developed '**Marconi Echometer**'. In April 1931, the first Marconi Echometer was installed on board a British merchant ship, giving a continuous and reliable indication of the depth of water under her keel from 2 to 360 fathoms. The apparatus was a separate unit, operated from a small battery.

Beginning of year	Total British vessels fitted with the Marconi Echometer
1932	110
1933	328
1934	514
1935	906
1936	1188
1937	1378
1938	1541
1939	1717
1940	1790
1946	1824
1950	2500

In 1947, a new series of Echometers had been designed, using a new type of magneto-striction projector. The recorder was named 'Seagraph' and the visual indicator 'Seavisa' – when combined they were called the 'Visagraph'. The advantages for trawlers using echometers and visagraphs during this period were notable.

Marconi Marine quartz steel shallow echo equipment installed in a motorboat, July 1938 (Marconi)

With the advent of the pleasure-boating boom, it was only a question of time before a smaller version of the echo-sounder was produced. **The first point-contact type transistor** had arrived in 1949, developed as an alternative to the radio valve. It was only on the introduction of the germanium-type transistor in 1956, that transistors became a viable and practical proposition.

In the winter of 1958, Maj. R. N. B. Gatehouse (formerly of the Royal Radar Establishment), a keen Lymington yachtsman and navigator, set about producing **the world's first transistorised echo-sounder**, the Hecta Mark I. Tests of this hermetically-sealed unit, with metre-dial calibration, were initially in Gatehouse's Lymington one-design sloop, *Wavecrest II*, fitted with an auxiliary Watermota engine. After only six intensive months, two working models of the Hecta were demonstrated at the 1959 Boat Show. The first one to be sold to the Royal Artillery Yacht Club's 20-ton sloop, *Santa Barbara*, and between April and August of that year some 35 more were sold. Hecta Mark I could not at first overcome the problems of noise and the air-bubble layer created by fast motorboats, until 1961 when a high powered mains operated model of Hecta, suitable for powerboats, was used by three offshore powerboats competing in the August Daily Express Cowes–Torquay race.

The first transistorised echo-sounder where the depth was displayed on a gas-filled neon tube was developed by R. R. Clark (1918–76) who had worked on radar in the RAF, with Wellington bombers and Mosquito fighter-bombers – and was also a keen yachtsman. The first 'Fairway' transistorised echo-sounder (costing only £39) was produced by Clark's company of Marine Electronics in 1959. It gave ranges of 0 to 100 ft and 0 to 100 fathoms in a tin box. In the first year some 600 'Fairway' echo-sounders were sold. In 1961–62 production at the Brent factory had reached 1300 units per year.

In 1963, a new company, Electronic Laboratories, began mass-production of the transistorised echo-sounder – with the Seafarer Mark K, costing only £25, based on the rapid drop in the costs of transistors and diodes and the introduction of Japanese motors. During their first year, Electronic Laboratories produced some 3500 units. Current production at the Poole factory is **3500 per week**.

When it was found that neon-tubes were almost invisible after 150 hr running and blacked out after 300 hr, the search began for a longer-lasting valve. The light-emitting diode was introduced into echo-sounding in 1971 – with a vision-durability over 1000 hr.

WIRELESS TELEGRAPHY

Morse was invented by Samuel F. B. Morse, in collaboration with Alfred Vail in 1837 for the purposes of sending messages by telegraph.

The first successful ship-shore wireless telegraphy (w/t) was demonstrated in June 1897 by Guglielmo Marconi to officers of the Italian Navy from the San Bartholemew Shipyard at Spezia with the Italian cruiser *San Martin* – at a range of 11 miles (18 km). Six months later Marconi gave **the first British ship-shore w/t demonstration** between the Needles Hotel, Isle of Wight and two small steamers the *Solent* and the *Mayflower*, while they cruised around Alum Bay, often in very bad weather, at ranges of up to 18 miles (29 km).

In July 1898, the *Daily Express* of Dublin became **the first newspaper in history to obtain news by w/t**. It asked the Marconi Company to report the Kingstown Regatta and reports were sent by Marconi himself from the steam tug, *Flying Huntress*, to a land station set up in the grounds of the Harbour Master.

Marconi giving a demonstration of wireless telegraphy to Italian officials at Spezia in 1897 (Marconi)

In August 1898, Marconi installed his wireless in the Royal Yacht *Osborne*, so that Queen Victoria at Osborne House might communicate with the Prince of Wales, who had hurt his knee, while he was cruising.

In 1899, on Admiralty invitation, three Naval vessels (HMS *Alexandra*, HMS *Europa* and HMS *Juno*) were fitted with w/t apparatus.

The first commercial ship in the world ever to be equipped with w/t for the purpose of sending and receiving paid messages was the German liner, *Kaiser Wilhelm der Grosse*, in March 1900. In November of that year, the Belgian mail packet *Princesse Clementine*, on the Ostend–Dover route, was fitted out with Marconi w/t.

The first British liner to carry w/t was the one-funnel, four-masted *Lake Champlain*, which sailed from Liverpool bound for Montreal on her historic voyage on 21 May 1901.

The first w/t interchange between two ships took place in summer 1901 between the *Lake Champlain* and the Cunard liner *Lucania*.

By June 1907, 139 ships of all flags had Marconi's system with a range of 150 to 300 miles (240 to 480 km).

Possibly **the smallest vessel to be fitted with Marconi w/t apparatus by 1912** was the Swedish motorboat, *Max*, powered by a 35 hp engine and owned by herring exporters. Her business was to follow the fishing fleet from 20 to 25 miles

(30 to 40 km) to sea and communicate to the shore news concerning catches. The installation consisted of a coil, condenser and NF jigger, electrical energy being supplied by a battery of eight accumulators. To provide an aerial, *Max*'s mast was increased about $16\frac{1}{2}$ ft (5 m) in height and strengthened considerably to hold an aerial of the umbrella type consisting of six wires.

The first British trawler to be fitted with Marconi w/t was the *Othello*, owned by Hellyers' Steam Fishing Company of Hull. A $\frac{1}{2}$ kW portable installation was installed in 1913 and *Othello* was able to communicate from 180 miles (290 km) to Cullercoats. By 1928 there were 191 trawlers and drifters carrying wireless telegraphy apparatus. By communicating with each other as to the location of a good catch, trawlers thus fitted could sometimes double their earnings.

WIRELESS OR RADIO TELEPHONY

The first experiments with wireless telephony were made in March 1914 by Marconi on board the Duke of Abruzzi's flagship *Regina Elena* in the Mediterranean off Augusta, Sicily. With ordinary apparatus, speech communications were kept up between several warships, including torpedo boats, three-fifths of a mile apart – but when Marconi's new apparatus was used, communications were possible between ships 18

The Johnson Super Stingers go through 'The Greatest Fire Jump in History' at Cypress Gardens, Florida, USA

Scene from Lucky Lady, *20th Century Fox's film about rum-running during the 1930s, starring Gene Hackman, Liza Minnelli and Burt Reynolds*

A French chocolate manufacturer's 1900 picture-card prophecy of 'Motorboating in the Year 2000' (Mary Evans Picture Library)

to 43 miles (30 to 70 km) out at sea. He also succeeded in communicating with a ship 12 miles (19 km) distant, despite intervening land. Valve transmitters and receivers were used of the round 'soft' type of tube. By this time, wireless **telegraphic** communication had been established between South Africa and Germany – a distance of 5300 miles (8500 km).

In 1920, delegates to an Imperial Press Conference sailed to Canada in the liner *Victorian*. Marconi wireless telephony kept her in touch for practically the whole voyage and concert programmes were exchanged with the shore while in mid-ocean. This was one of the first notable broadcasting successes.

In 1919, Marconi decided to leave his house in Rome and live where he could not so easily be disturbed; he would go and live at sea. So he bought a 220 ft (67 m) yacht called the *Rowenska*, built at Leith in 1904 for the Archduchess Maria Theresa of Austria. Marconi had the yacht converted to a floating home, a workshop and research laboratory; and changed her name to *Elettra* (Electra – the mythical daughter of Agamemnon, after whom the word electricity is named). During the 1920s, Marconi and his colleague, C. S. Franklin, experimented with short waves – with Franklin stationed at Poldhu, directing short-wave transmissions in one 'beam' to Marconi in the *Elettra*.

In May 1923 a wireless telephone transmitter was installed on board the SS *Olympic* of the White Star Line and good clear speech from the *Olympic* at sea was received on the *Celtic*, which was then in New York harbour.

In August 1923 the Marconi Company fitted a wireless telephone installation on the SS *Lorina* belonging to the South Railways Company. Good clear speech was maintained both ways between Marconi House and the *Lorina* while crossing the Channel. This was the first direct conversation between passengers on a ship at sea and an ordinary telephone subscriber on land in this country, as distinct from a telephone conversation between a wireless station on board a ship and a wireless station on land, or between two ships at sea.

By 1924, Marconi apparatus specially designed for the reception of broadcast programmes at sea had been fitted satisfactorily on a dozen ships. One of these Marconi Marine V4 sets was carried by the motor-yacht *Naz-Perwr*

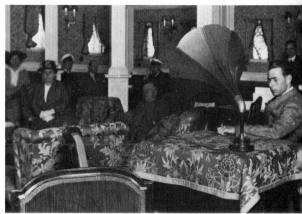

Marconi Wireless telephony entertained delegates to an Imperial Press Conference en route to Canada in 1920 (Marconi)

on a recent voyage to Norway. At Bergen the Aberdeen broadcasting station was received clearly during daylight and the Chelmsford station was received during practically the whole of the cruise, including times when the *Naz-Perwr* was landlocked in the fjords 200 miles (320 km) north of Bergen. A special single-wire aerial had been erected for use with the broadcast receiver so as to avoid any interference with the ship's ordinary wireless services.

In February 1925, the Marconi Company installed Duplex wireless telephone apparatus on the SS *Princess Ena*, belonging to the Southern Railway Company, and good speech was maintained between the *Princess Ena* when crossing the Channel and telephone subscribers in London, Glasgow, Leeds, Cardiff, Bristol, Portsmouth, Southampton and Bournemouth. This installation was subsequently dismantled as the owners found that the demand for the facilities did not justify the cost.

In January 1927 telephone communication was carried over the Arctic circle at distances of 600 and 1100 miles (950 and 1700 km) between the Hudson Bay Company's ships *Bayrupert*, *Baymaud* and *Baychimo* by means of Marconi Wireless telephone apparatus.

By July 1929, in England, over 30 Marconi wireless telephone stations were in constant use between the lightships, lighthouses and shore stations of Trinity House, the Mersey Docks and Harbour Board, the Dundee Harbour Trust and the Northern Lighthouse Board, while a number of similar wireless telephone stations had been

Wireless telephone installed in the Dover lifeboat in December 1929 (Marconi)

installed for other Port authorities in different parts of the world.

Also in 1929 a wireless telephone was installed in the Dover lifeboat. With two 375 hp engines this was the fastest lifeboat in the world and was specially designed to rescue aircraft from the sea. The totally enclosed installation, Type XMB1, was designed for use in the roughest conditions and was intended for communication with aircraft, aerodromes, ships and coastal wireless stations. Transmitter power was 100 watts, on a wavelength of 900 metres.

Early in 1930, the *Elettra* was in the Mediterranean when Marconi spoke from a telephone aboard the yacht to telephone subscribers in many cities all over the world including London, New York, Sydney, Buenos Aires, Bombay, Cape Town and Montreal. This was **the most comprehensive demonstration yet given to the world of the efficiency of the line possible between telephones ashore and afloat**.

VHF (VERY HIGH FREQUENCY)

In continued search for a new and economical means of reliable radio communication, free from electrical disturbances, eminently suitable for use between islands and also between other places separated by moderate distances, in 1931 Marconi resumed experiments with microwaves, and assisted by G. A. Mathieu and G. A. Isted developed valve transmitters and receivers

for 50 centimetres operation. By October, demonstrations of this equipment were given to the Italian Ministry of Communications between Santa Margherita and Sestri Levante, near Genoa, a distance of 11 miles (18 km) over sea. Two months later a demonstration over 25 miles (40 km) was given to representatives of the Italian Government. In April 1932 duplex telephony using two-wire telephone terminal apparatus was demonstrated between Santa Margherita and Sestri Levante to experts of the Italian Government and University representatives. A four-unit 57 centimetre transmitter, working with a five unit reflector and using Marconi's yacht *Elettra*, achieved a maximum range of 28 miles (45 km). In August, the *Elettra*, began a series of long distance trials up to 58 miles (93 km), with signals eventually perceived up to 168 miles (270 km). **VHF radio telephony had been proved a practicable reality**. **The first VHF-r/t sets were installed on RAF aircraft** in October 1939 after a lengthy development programme at the RAE, speeded up by the threat of war. An air-to-ground range of 140 miles (225 km) was obtained at a height of 10000 ft (3000 m). One aircraft could speak clearly to another at a range of 100 miles (160 km). This set was known as the TR 1133. By September 1940, some 16 squadrons had been equipped with VHF.

Until the late 1960s, the cost of a bulky VHF radio telephone was so prohibiting that there were perhaps only 1000 registrations. But the best frequency for short-wave communication with either the local Coast Guard or another motor-yacht or motor-cruiser nearby was VHF. By using the latest techniques of solid-state microcircuitry and mass production, Electronic Laboratories were able to radically bring down the price of VHF radio telephones with their **Seavoice** unit, the first of which was sold in 1973. By 1977 there were some 20000 VHF licensees using Seavoice sets – and this was 93 per cent of the VHF holders. Today one such r/t will be equipped with 55 channels covering all the International Maritime Band. Channel 16 was the emergency channel, for which there are the following emergency statements:

1 'Mayday! Mayday! Mayday!' (M'aider (French) 'to help me'). This should only be used where there is imminent danger.

2 'Panne! Panne!' This should be used when assistance is required or a doctor is needed.
3 'Securité! Securité! Securité!' This should be used when a marker buoy has come afloat or a hazard has appeared in the form of a floating wreck.

Channel 16 should be listened to by the motor-yachtsman as often as possible. It has only been with the advent of the Dual Watch Facility that motor-yachtsmen had been allowed to converse with each other, whilst their radio telephone flip-flops back and forwards between their own channel and Channel 16. Should any distress call be broadcast on Channel 16, the alternating system is abruptly halted as both radio telephones lock into 16.

SHIPPING FORECASTS

From February 1919, ships were being encouraged to exchange weather messages using Morse code. **The first 'weather bulletins for ships in coastal waters'** were given in Morse for Stornaway, Black Sod, Scilly, Holyhead and Dungeness, starting in June 1921.

The first BBC weather forecast for the London area was broadcast on 14 November 1922; provincial city weather forecasts followed as their stations were opened. **The first general UK forecast**, broadcast by the BBC, took place in 1924.

With the successful construction of a new higher-powered transmitter at Daventry, **the first BBC shipping forecast** was heard in July 1925. By 1928, 'The Daventry Shipping Forecast' was being broadcast at 10.30 a.m. and 9.15 p.m. This forecast briefly covered the various coastal areas giving probable weather and winds. When given at 10.30 a.m. it was read twice – once at normal reading speed and again at long-hand dictation speed so that ships' captains could have it taken down for reference. These forecasts were supplied by the Meteorological Office of the Air Ministry at Adastral House.

The first TV charts to illustrate the weather forecast were experimentally transmitted from Alexandra Palace during November 1936.

The most popular long-wave weather broadcasts ever attempted were transmitted between 1946 and 1950 by 'Air-Met'. Ten-minute weather bulletins were broadcast twice an hour right round the clock.

The worst possible forecast has been 'Severe – Storm Force 10', although this is not a frequent occurrence.

The Shipping Forecast is currently broadcast on 1500 metres Long Wave.

SOS

The question of an international distress call was discussed at a wireless conference in Berlin in 1903, but nothing was decided. From 1 February 1903 the Marconi Wireless Telegraph Co. decided officially that 'the call to be given by ships in distress, or in any way requiring assistance, shall be CQD (Come Quick Danger)'. CQD came to be regarded as an international call for help.

But in the international conference, again held in Berlin, in 1906 the Germans suggested that their general call SOE which was, in terms of Morse Code, quicker to send than CQD, should be adopted. Objection was raised that the letter E, in which Morse Code is a single dot, might be lost in the atmosphere with its many noises – apart from, of course, ship noises. Finally it was decided to use SOS (···---···). This was internationally ratified in 1908, although the British were slow to drop their CQD signal.

More recently International Radio Regulations prescribed for radio telegraphy:

1 The Alarm Signal – twelve dashes, lasting a prescribed time.
2 The Distress Signal – SOS.

BAROMETERS

The mercury column barometer was evolved from the experiments of Torricelli in the early 17th century; **one of the first instruments** was Hooke's Syphon Wheel Barometer of 1665, developed in 1670 by Sir Samuel Morland, 'master mechanic' to King Charles II. Basically the instrument consists of a small vessel containing mercury and a vertical glass tube exhausted of air, the upper end of which was closed and the lower end submerged beneath the surface of the mercury. The atmosphere, in pressing down on the surface of the mercury, forces some up inside the tube to a height depending on the pressure of the atmosphere at the time. As the pressure of the atmosphere varies according to the existing weather conditions, the height of the mercury column varies, and is read according to the scale graduated in inches – providing an indication of the likely changes in the weather and of the short-term outlook.

The first mechanic to try to determine the height of the mercury column accurately was Berham in 1698.

The first barometer maker to boil mercury in the tube, in order to drive out the last traces of air, was Charles Orme in 1738.

The first Aneroid (without liquid) Barometer was designed by Zaiker in 1758 for use at sea; the concept was further developed by Vidie of Paris. With no mercury, the pressure system involves a closed spring hollow metal box from which most of the air has been withdrawn and which is compressed to a varying extent by changes in the atmospheric pressure; by a system of levers the movement of the box is magnified and transferred to a pointer pivoted at the centre, so that with changes in atmospheric pressure the pointer moves on a scale graduated in inches in mercury, from which the barometric reading may be made directly.

The finest barometer makers have been Negretti and Zambra, Casartelli, Patorelli and Casella.

The oldest existing British company to have constructed barometers was founded in 1850 by two Italians, Henry Negretti and J. W. Zambra; proof of their quality came when they were appointed as meteorological instrument makers to Queen Victoria, soon after the Great Exhibition. In 1857, the company devised and constructed for Admiral Robert Fitzroy, the eminent hydrographer and meteorologist, a double bulb thermometer for taking sea temperatures at great depths (Negretti and Zambra eventually per-

fected this to withstand 7 tons pressure at 15 000 ft (4572 m) depth). Negretti and Zambra were also the first to enamel the backs of thermometers to make the mercury thread more visible. At Admiral Fitzroy's suggestion, the firm developed the shock-absorbent mercurial barometer for heavy duty work on board HM warships. Fitzroy was the first to introduce weather indications ('Stormy, Rain, Change, Very Dry') and later this system was introduced on Negretti and Zambra's improved Aneroid barometer.

All Expeditions – polar, jungle, mountain, etc – equipped themselves with Negretti and Zambra's instruments. In 1920, at the Air Ministry's request, the company produced and patented a Mercury in Steel Distance Thermometer for taking oil and air temperatures in aircraft; this marked their move towards industrial instrumentation and process control equipment as is manufactured at their Aylesbury factory today.

Of the barometers for marine use currently supplied by Negretti and Zambra, one is the Fisherman's (Lifeboat) Aneroid, the design of which has not changed for many decades; its dial is enamelled with black and red markings and it is protected in a black stove-enamelled case. For the smart motor-yacht wheelhouse, there is a 5 in diameter barometer with a solid, lacquered brass case, whilst the dial is of silvered metal.

SEARCHLIGHTS AND SIGNALLING LAMPS

The first electric arc lamps to be used for signalling from onboard ship were successfully tested by American gyro-compass inventor Elmer Sperry in the late 1860s. Following from work done by a British Naval Officer, Capt. Philip Colomb, **the first British naval vessel to have a searchlight was HMS *Minotaur*** in 1868. By 1875 good electric searchlights were being installed on board a number of British Naval ships. By 1880, a searchlight range of 250 yards (230 m) was thought to be an effective maximum range.

The first ship to have a complete marine electrical system for lighting and subsidiary power sources was the battleship HMS *Inflexible*,

In 1934, a Francis searchlight was installed on Mrs Clare Sydney Smith's speedboat, Biscuit, *by Aircraftman T. E. Shaw (Lawrence of Arabia)*

launched in 1881. Wiring and lighting elements used the Swan principle and the inventor himself supervised installation. The Birmingham firm of Joseph Lucas also played a major part in developing and improving marine electrical lighting and searchlights – rivalled by such companies as Siemens in Germany.

At the 1905 Olympia Motor Boat Show, Messrs Weldhen and Bleriot, who had long supplied lamps of all sorts to the French Navy, exhibited a powerful acetylene searchlight, designed to light up objects at a distance of 1000 yards (900 m); its six lenses were all caladioptrique, whilst a double burner was employed.

In 1901 Thomas Francis founded a company to supply lighting to theatres, buying in Westinghouse equipment and modifying it for this specialised field. During World War I, Francis & Co. expanded and produced lighting equipment for the Admiralty. In 1928, the Bentleys of Bolton, Lancashire bought the Francis company but retained its name. The eldest son, Norman Bentley, designed his **first Francis searchlight in 1933**. It had tungsten bulbs originally made for slide projection and reflectors manufactured by C. A. Parsons to inspect their turbines at electricity board installations. Before long, Francis tungsten bulb searchlights were being supplied to Scott-Paine's British Power Boat Company at Hythe (see p. 129) for use on board Imperial Airways seaplane tenders – and also to the motor police launches of Thames Division (Wapping). The Francis Company had their 12, 15 and 22 in searchlights on board HMS *Vernon*

at Gosport stringently tested by the Admiralty in 1937. The following year, Francis produced **the first portable searchlight with its own power source**. The late 1930s saw improvements in tungsten power sources so that searchlights could operate at lower voltages, and the mercury vapour principle was increasingly used on the larger lights.

The 1939 war brought many technical developments in searchlights and Francis produced **the first power-operated lights for remote signalling**. These had 22 in diameter reflectors and mercury vapour sources cooled by a rotary ventilation unit. They were invaluable for ships patrolling in poor visibility. The Admiralty were sufficiently impressed to give Francis a development contract for 5 in signalling lamps at the end of the war.

Post-war, Francis Searchlights continued the pattern of development – important technical breakthroughs included **hydraulically-operated remote control searchlights and radar units**; and special infra-red signalling devices for the Argentinian and Brazilian Navies. By the 1970s Francis Searchlights were being used by the Royal Navy, the British Merchant Marine, the RNLI, and motorboat builders for the leisure market.

Today Francis Searchlights, as part of the Lucas Marine Group, produce a wide range of searchlights, with their most recent development of the CSI (Compact Source Mercury Iodide) searchlights with exceptional range and illumination. Where a conventional 22 in (56 cm) searchlight, fitted with a 2000 watt tungsten filament lamp, provides a Peak Beam Candle Power of 2 588 000 and a range of 5220 ft (1590 m) – an identical searchlight fitted with a 1000 watt CSI lamp provides a Peak Beam Candle Power of 20 706 000 and **a range of 15 300 ft (4663 m)**!

Aside from this there is the M-range of conventional searchlights, M9 and M10, resistant to saltwater, with a fixed focus and toughened front cover glass, and a range up to 1350 ft (411 m), which are ideal for the motor-yachtsman. M11/M12 are manufactured from solid brass to give a special appearance. For lifeboats, the Mk 1 180 mm diameter searchlight, made with corrosion-resistant cast brass, using cable glands, a watertight frame, and toughened heat resistant front cover glass, is used by the RNLI.

Left to right: *The latest Francis Searchlight – the 28 in – 2000 watts and 240 volts, when equipped with a tungsten halogen lamp, has a range of 1½ miles (2260 m) (Lucas Marine). A Tannoy Portable Loudhailer in 1934. The super Hey-loh was introduced in 1976 (Tannoy). A ship's bell, as cast by the Whitechapel Bell Foundry*

Francis M12, M13 and M15, with ranges up to 3898 ft (1188 m), are used for police launches, patrol boats and fishing vessels. M17, M18, M20 and M21 are used for deep-sea trawlers. This makes Francis Searchlights the largest supplier of marine searchlights in the UK, if not in Europe.

PORTABLE LOUDHAILER – TANNOY

The Tulsmere Manufacturing Company was founded in 1926 by Guy R. Fountain, one of the early pioneers of radio, who designed, patented and produced a series of ingenious radio electrical services, including high tension and low tension charges and eliminators. One of these was an electrolytic rectifier using tantallum alloy. From these two words, the trade name Tannoy was derived.

In 1934, **the first transportable microphone equipment was marketed**; it consisted of a Tannoy Hand Power Microphone, a transformer unit, a co-axial loudspeaker and 12 volt accumulator, the whole being assembled on a transportable frame with folding legs, sufficiently light in weight to enable one man to carry it. Guy R. Fountain was possibly **the first motoryachtsman to use a 'tannoy'** on board his motoryacht *Naiad*. These early loudhailers came to be nicknamed 'collapsible calamities' but, nevertheless, did see early use in the field of motorboating. Indeed in 1936, Arthur Bray gave one of **the very first public motorboat racing commentaries** using a tannoy, at the *Daily Mirror* Outboard Trophy race on Oulton Broad, Suffolk. Indeed, this race was started by Commodore Gar Wood speaking on the phone from Detroit, USA, and his voice being amplified on

the tannoy could be heard by British spectators.

The experience gained in the 1930s placed Tannoy in a unique position to provide specialised communication and sound equipment to all branches of the armed services from 1939–45. In 1974 Tannoy merged with Harman International Industries.

The great grandchild of the 'collapsible calamity' – the Super Hey-Loh, was launched in 1976. It is a multiple-function, battery-operated loudhailer, enabling the user to speak, 'hoot', or listen.

SHIP'S BELLS

Ship's bells have been used for almost as long as bells have been in existence. The oldest existing bell-foundry in the UK, if not in the world, is the 400-year-old Whitechapel Bell Foundry in East London. Established by Robert Mot in 1572, this foundry of craftsmen can claim amongst other famous peelers, Britain's 'Big Ben' (1858) and America's 'Liberty Bell' (1752).

High quality bell metal is an alloy of approximately 77 per cent copper and 23 per cent tin. Today, the Whitechapel Bell Foundry continues to supply ship's and motorboat's bells, complete with cast lug and eye, flight clapper with lanyard. A typical bell, 16 in diameter at the mouth, turned and polished, sounding one of the 61 notes in the five octaves, was recently selling at £270, whilst a 6 in diameter bell was selling at £23.

The Lutine Bell in the rostrum of Lloyds is rung by the Caller before important announcements – two strokes if good news, one if bad. The bell was salvaged in 1859 from the wreck of HMS *Lutine*, which had foundered in October 1799.

13 MODEL POWERBOATS

Model boats and boaters: Victoria Park Lake in the Edwardian era (RTHPL)

Among the most notable early models of Egyptian sailing and rowing craft are those discovered at Thebes by Sir Flinders Petrie in tombs dating from the 11th Dynasty (approx 2500 BC).

During the early 1870s, the Rev. C. M. Ramus of Playden Rectory, Rye, Sussex spent a great deal of his time tying rockets to the sterns of model boats, pointing them at the other end of the local pond, then carefully observing them plane across the water at speeds of over 35 mph (56 km/h). His bisphenic (two-wedged) and polysphenic (multi-wedged) hulls were prototypes of the hydroplane.

The earliest record of a model jetboat is that of M. Salleron in 1880.

The oldest Model Power Boat Club still operating in the world is the Victoria Model Steamboat Club, which began using the Victoria Park Lake, near Bethnal Green and Hackney (East London) in 1904. One of the first secretaries was W. L. Blaney. Double acting model steam engines with water-tube boilers were in exclusive use in those days, constructed by Stuart Turner, Henry Greenly and others.

The first 'Steamer' competition to be run for speedboats, sponsored and organised by *The Model Engineer* magazine, took place in 1902. Nine model boats were entered, all steam-driven and of displacement toothpick-type hulls. With one exception all the boats were made by members of the Wirral Club and the speeds of the three fastest boats, *Express* (J. Tharme), *Darling* (H. Tharme) and *Fidget* (G. O. Klay) were 5 mph (8 km/h), 4·7 mph (7·6 km/h) and 4·56 mph (7·34 km/h) respectively. *The Model Engineer* Speedboat Competition was held annually thereafter until January 1939.

In 1902, a large petrol-driven model boat, constructed by the Foster brothers, could be seen on the Thames near Pangbourne; it carried a commercial engine, intended for a full-sized motor-launch. **The first company to custom-build petrol engines for model boats** was Arkell Brothers, whose 5 ft (1·5 m) *Moraima* reached 7·96 mph (12·81 km/h) in *The Model Engineer* Speedboat Competition of 1906, powered by a horizontally-mounted four-stroke engine ($1\frac{1}{2}$ in bore × $1\frac{3}{4}$ in stroke) with trembler coil ignition and gravity mixing valve type carburettor. In 1907 *Moraima* improved her speed to 9·71 mph (15·63 km/h). A popular pre-World War I model petrol engine was the Belvedere, manufactured by W. J. Smith.

The first model motorboat regatta to be held in the UK was *The Model Engineer* Regatta at Wembley (North London) in July 1908. The Arkell Brothers, *Moraima II*, reached a speed of 9·26 mph (14·90 km/h).

The first appearance of a flash steam, stepped hydroplane was made at this regatta by Herbert Teague and W. H. Delves-Broughton's *Folly*. The apparent advantages of the lightweight flash steam plant using coil boiler and torch blowlamp, installed in a successful planing hull, revolutionised model powerboating; for many years, petrol engines remained inferior to flash steam.

One of the next developments was the adoption of the circular course for racing craft, whereby a model powerboat was tethered to a

pole and ran round and round at increasing speeds. Most pre-war speed records were to be achieved using this system.

The first competitors to enter four boats in *The Model Engineer* Speedboat Competition were the Noble brothers, one of whose boats *Bullrush* achieved a record speed of 22·77 mph (36·64 km/h). Altogether G. D. Noble built a series of eight *Bullrush* model powerboats.

Mr H. H. Groves used lightweight aerodynamic principles to construct his series of *Irene* boats. In 1913 *Irene IV* achieved speeds of 21·19 mph (34·10 km/h) in the 'ME' Speedboat Competition.

In 1918 it was reported that a 29 in US flash steam hydroplane, *Elmara*, had become **the first model powerboat to achieve a speed slightly in excess of 30 mph** (48 km/h). In 1923, A. Norman Thompson, *Sunny Jim III*, succeeded in becoming **the first British model powerboat to reach 30 mph+ (48 km/h+)**. In 1924 Stan Clifford's (Victoria Model Steamboat Club) *Chatterbox III* reached 37 mph (60 km/h) round the pole, lifting that speed to 41·85 mph (67·35 km/h) in 1926 and 43 mph (69 km/h) in 1927. *Chatterbox II*'s record remained unbeaten for several years.

The Model Power Boat Association (MPBA) (today **the world's oldest model powerboat organisation**) was founded in 1924. John G. Philpot was the first Hon. Secretary. The first MPBA Grand Regatta was held in September 1925, including races and steering competitions for various classes – as well as a 100 yard (90 m) sprint race for internal combustion (i/c) model speedboats for the Hobbs Trophy. This regatta saw the appearance of a Frenchman, G. M. 'Jim' Suzor, with his 39 in *Canard* which won the Hobbs Trophy at 16 mph (26 km/h).

The first international ruling as regards engine capacities was drawn up between the MPBA and the Model Yacht Club de Paris, with a 30 cc restriction; one of the first successful boats in this class was 'Jim' Suzor's superbly constructed *Nickie II*, a wooden shallow-Vee step hydroplane (LOA 3 ft (0·9 m)). Many of the novel features in this hydroplane – two carburettors, spring-loaded syringe lubrication, articulated prop-shaft, etc – came to be universally copied.

Typical pre-war model racing hydroplane (Motor Boat & Yachting)

Nickie II won the international race for i/c boats in 1929, 1930 and 1931, also creating a world record of 31·95 mph (51·42 km/h) for i/c boats on Lake Damnesil, held for three years. Flash steam declined in popularity.

Racing Boats were now classified as:

Class A: below 30 cc i/c or under 16 lb steam-driven

Class B: below 15 cc i/c or under 8 lb steam-driven

Class C: below 10 cc i/c or under 5 lb steam-driven

In 1933, Messrs S. L. and J. B. Innocent's petrol-driven *Betty* returned a record speed of 36·03 mph (57·99 km/h). By 1945 S. H. Clifford's Class A model speedboat *Blue Streak* had attained a 500 yard (450 m) record of 55·6 mph (89·5 km/h), whilst K. Williams' Class A boat *Faro* had reached 48·7 mph (78·3 km/h) over 1800 yards (1650 m). By this time some 32 clubs were affiliated to the MPBA.

In 1898, an American electrician, Nikola Tesla, took out a patent for the land-based radio control of the propelling engines, the steering apparatus of a boat or floating vessel travelling at the highest possible speed, requiring 'no intermediate wires, cables or other form of electrical or mechanical connection with the object save the natural media of space. I accomplish nevertheless, similar results and in a much more practicable manner by producing waves, impulses or radiations which are received by suitable apparatus on the moving body . . .'

In 1904, Isaac Storey and Jack Kitchen used a paraffin-fired 27 ft (8·3 m) steam launch, the *Bat*, for some of the first experiments in radio control, using a Marconi spark transmitter and coherer-receiver. She was steered from a wireless mast on Queen Adelaide's Hill, whilst she steamed round the northern end of Lake Windermere with only a stoker on board.

In 1934 articles began to appear in American radio periodicals on radio control for models; but transmitting regulations excluded all but the licensed radio amateurs. In 1938 the RK62 thyratron valve, followed by the RK61 was developed specially for radio-control and put the device within the pockets of many more people.

Post-war several pioneers were working on radio-controlled motorboats using electric motors made up from Government surplus spare parts, using large twin-triode type valves. The first really commercial valve radio-sets were marketed by Triang from 1956. In 1957–58, Electronic Developments Ltd brought out a divisional voice-frequency multi-plex system whereby modifying a carrier wave to different tones, reed gear on board the model powerboat oscillated to work six independent navigational functions. Initially trade-named the 'Everest', this system, which was in use for at least ten years, was eventually re-named the 'Black Prince'.

The first and only model powerboat to make a successful radio-controlled crossing of the Eng-

September 1951: Miss E.D. *became the first and only model powerboat to make a successful radio-controlled crossing of the English Channel (G. Honnest-Redlich)*

lish Channel** was *Miss E.D.* (LOA 5 ft (1·5 m) ×
B 2 ft (0·6 m)), sponsored by Electronic Developments and controlled by George Honnest
Redlich. On 6 September 1951, this boat
travelled from Dover to Cap Gris Nez (near
Calais) accompanied by a 20 ft (6·1 m) cabin
cruiser, on a 32–35-mile (51–56-km) S-shaped
course from harbour to harbour. The journey
took 9 hr 9 min – at an average speed of just
under 4 mph (6 km/h).

In 1956 Col. Taplin, who ran a precision
engineering company in Kent, developed an in-
line diesel engine called the Taplin Twin. Up to
that time any i/c engine over $3\frac{1}{2}$ cc in a less than
20 in boat tended to cause vibration problems.
Taplin successfully combined two $3\frac{1}{2}$ cc engines
and easily overcame vibration problems. Until
the early 1960s the Taplin Twin ruled model-
powerboating.

During 1963, a great many surplus JAP motor
lawn-mower engines (30 cc) were bought up for
£5 each by model powerboat enthusiasts and for
a number of years the 30 cc class had a strong
following.

The most popular deep-Vee monohedron boat
for multi-hull racing over the years has been the
Jaguar (LOA 35 in (0·8 m) × B 12 in (0·3 m)),
whilst the major engine manufacturers have
been K. & B. (American) and Rossi (Italy).

**The first transistorised solid-state circuitry
radio-control sets** appeared in 1964–65, developed from proportional radio. By moving the
control stick a fraction of an inch, the servo-
mechanism in the model would move a fraction
of an inch and stay there. Within two years, the
old reed-gear system had become obsolete. This
method of pulse-code modulation has since
been developed to cater for eight independent
functions, including rudder, engine control
speed, engine control mixture, adjustable trim
tabs, etc.

The Germans began to use microprocessors in
1968–69, using integrated circuit 'chips'. Today
chip-technology has taken over in marine radio-
control for transmitters, receivers and servo-
mechanisms.

**The first fgrp-built model powerboats appeared
in 1958.**

The first radio-controlled multi-racing appeared in 1958 with pairs-racing, which grew to
six boats and today can go up to thirteen competitors racing simultaneously. This is **the most
popular type of radio-controlled model powerboating**. Eighty per cent of the 140 ·MPBA-
affiliated clubs participated, and there is an
average of three multi-race events every week-
end from April until October. The MPBA currently comprises 40 clubs in the North, 34 in the
Midlands and 66 in the South, with a total
membership of 2500 to 3000. The champions of
multi-racing have been John Stidwell (UK) and
John Melville (UK) and Giorgio Merlotti
(Italy). Merlotti won one race 140 laps ahead of
the runner-up, who himself had completed 200
laps.

*Giorgio Merlotti (Italy) International model multi-hull
racing champion (S.H.G. Marine Ltd)*

NAVIGA, the European Union for Ship-
Modelling and Ship-Model Sport, was founded
by Otto Kaiser in Basle, Switzerland in May
1959. Membership initially comprised Austria,
Switzerland, France and West Germany. The
European Model Powerboat Championships
have since been held 10 times every two years,
alternating between eastern and western Europe.
In 1977 NAVIGA became the World Union and
by 1978 with its seat'in Vienna, comprised every
other European country except Ireland, Denmark, Spain and Albania, as well as Canada and
New Zealand (21 countries).

NAVIGA will only respect one association
per country and therefore the USA with its rival
International Model Power Boating Association
(IMPBA) and National Association of Model
Powerboating (NAMB) has still not been
affiliated.

The USSR have claimed $1\frac{1}{2}$ million members enjoying model powerboating, whilst in Eastern Europe model powerboating is part of the school curriculum.

Since 1958, radio-controlled speed events have involved one person at a time, operating round a 100 ft (30 m) a-side, equilateral triangle, first anti-clockwise and then after a 180° turn, clockwise – proving the manoeuvrability of the model powerboat. This can take between 15 and 25 sec. Engine classes (national and international NAVIGA F1) range: 0–$2\frac{1}{2}$ cc; $2\frac{1}{2}$–5 cc (also $3\frac{1}{2}$ cc); 5–15 cc; 15–30 cc; and 35 cc.

Although the average multi-race lasts only 30 min, **an endurance record** was set by John Melville at Keighley at the World Multi-Powerboat Endurance Championships in 1974; his boat covered some 36 miles (58 km) in 2 hr.

On 6 August 1975, at Welwyn Garden City, the Czechoslovakian, Frantisek Dvoracek achieved a speed of 145·3 mph (233·8 km/h) with his tethered model powerboat (B-Class). At the NAVIGA 10th European Championships held at Kiev (USSR) in August 1977, R. Shaikov (USSR) set a new tethered record of 150·534 mph (242·261 km/h). This speed, set over a minimum number of five laps, is **the fastest speed that a tethered boat has ever travelled**.

The British Unrestricted Water Speed Record for internal-combustion radio-controlled boats, over 110 yards (100 m) was set on 17 June 1978 by Ray Varah (UK) with a speed of 38·46 mph (61·90 km/h) down the straightaway.

The fastest radio-controlled model powerboat is an American IMPBA Class E hydroplane, *Crapshooter*, owned and controlled by William E. LeFeber of Indianapolis, Indiana. On 9 October 1976, across a $\frac{1}{16}$th mile (0·1 km) straightaway course on Dandy 'T' Lake (Indianapolis), *Crapshooter* was timed by an electronic digital clock to a two-way average of 2·865 sec – otherwise 78·534 mph (126·388 km/h). With a fuel mixture of 65 per cent nitro, 20 per cent Klotz oil and 15 per cent alcohol, the fastest of LeFeber's two runs was 2·79 sec/80·645 mph (129·785 km/h). The previous Class E record was 74 mph (119 km/h), set by Don Pinckert in November 1972.

In January 1951, prior to the construction of John Cobb's full-scale turbo-jet-engined *Cru-*

sader, a $\frac{1}{16}$th scale, 5 ft (1·5 m), balsa-plywood model, powered by a cordite motor developed by the Rocket Propulsion Division of the RAE Farnborough and giving 30 lb of thrust for 20 sec, was tested on an artificial lake near Horsea Island. Controlled by an oscillating gyro, this model was clocked at $97\frac{1}{2}$ mph (157 km/h) over 700 yards (640 m); the equivalent full-scale speed was 240 mph (390 km/h).

In 1968, the magazine *Model Boats* ran a series of articles entitled 'Fast Electrics' by Philip Connolly, in which electrically powered model powerboats were explained and advocated. The development of the nickel-cadmium fast charge SAFT battery, superior to the traditional lead-acetate batteries, coupled with the public outcry against the noise and pollution made by i/c-engined model powerboats on public ponds and lakes – did much to escalate popularity in the 'Electrics'. NAVIGA had soon organised 1 kg and Unlimited Classes, although the British MPBA always preferred the $2\frac{1}{2}$ kg Class. The longest lasting multi-race for British electric boats lasted some 10 min. The champions of electric model boat racing are Rod Burman, Daniel Holder and David Harvey, using special silver-zinc batteries, developed at enormous costs in France. On 17 June 1978, Rod Burman set an Unrestricted Water Speed Record for electric radio-controlled boats over 110 yards

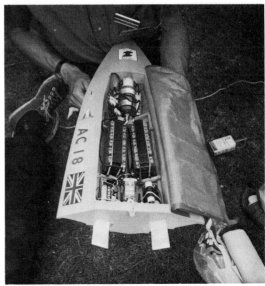

An electrically-driven model powerboat

Tony Faulkner and his historic model powerboat, Mary Dean

(100 m) at 32·85 mph (52·86 km/h), comparing favourably with the petrol-driven record of 38·46 mph (61·90 km/h).

Scale contests involve both the representation of a prototype (motor-torpedo boats, PTB's, tugs, trawlers, etc), its degree of accuracy and the quality of modelling (NAVIGA Class F2). **The biggest range of scale model plans** are published by Model & Allied Publications, comprising some 400 different types of vessel; **the most popular scale craft** are the Thames Sailing Barge, HMS *Victory*, Tugs, Trawlers and Fast Patrol Boats. **The finest quality plans** available to scale model makers are those of David McGregor and of Bassett-Lowk.

With radio-control scale models, precision manoeuvres in the water involve clover-leaf and christmas tree courses, steering through narrowly placed buoys, reversing, and completing a docking manoeuvre, which involves placing a boat within a U-shaped dock at the first attempt, without touching any part of the dock, without going through the dock, and keeping the nose of the vessel within a defined area, dependent on the length of the vessel for a period of 3 sec without controlling the transmitter. The most famous pre-war scale modeller was Norman Ough.

The oldest British model powerboat enthusiast is Bert Perman, an octogenarian who runs an unusual coal-fired steamboat called *Smoky*.

The oldest model powerboats still being actively run are Lieut. Greenhouse's 70-year-old *Leda III* and Tony Faulkner's steam yacht, *Mary Dean*. In the summer of 1974, there was a meeting at Victoria Park Lake where some half-a-dozen vintage model powerboats were operated; since then a vintage section has been formed.

14 MOTORBOAT PRESERVATION

In 1963, Mr and Mrs Alan Young of Clayton, NY felt that their antique wooden motorboat was such a joy, that a celebration should be set up to honour fine old wood-built motorboats. The first Annual Clayton Boat Show was staged in August 1964 with 15 boats on display; by 1977 the Clayton NY Boat Show saw some 100 boats of all classes on display.

The US Antique and Classic Boat Society Inc. was founded at Lake George in August 1974 by eight enthusiasts headed by Ray Nelson, and incorporated on 10 June 1975. By 1977 this Society had about 350 members from 25 States,

dedicated to the restoration and running of wooden motorboats. The first Lake George Antique and Classic Boat Rendezvous took place in 1974, sponsored by *Antique Boating* magazine and saw 36 entries, including six Chris-Crafts. The 1975 Rendezvous saw 59 boats, with 15 Chris-Crafts, the 1976 Rendez-vous saw 79 boats with 19 Chris-Crafts and 1977 some 130 old speedboats, seven of which were built between 1920 and 1934. The 1978 Rendez-vous, held last August, saw some 153 boats. These boats ranged from the 5 hp Elco-engined *McGuffy* of 1907, right up to *Sister Syn*, a 35-

T-108 hydroglider piloted by Colonel Prospero Freri, competed in the Pavia–Venezia race from 1933–38. Fully restored, it is now on permanent exhibition in Milan Museum

footer (10·7 m) powered by her original V-12 650 hp Curtiss Conqueror aero-engine and built in 1926 by Horace E. Dodge.

The largest and most famous vintage powerboats still in operation are *Miss America IX* (built 1930) and *Miss Canada IV* (built 1939), restored and maintained by Detroit businessmen, Harold and Chuck Mistele.

Miss America IX was kept in the old Gar Wood factory from 1933 until 1958 when she was donated to the Algonac Lions Club, Michigan. She sat in their barn until purchased by the Mistele family. After a year of restoration of her original wood hull, including the installation of twin 427 cu in, 525 bhp Chevrolet racing engines, transmission system and seats, *Miss America IX*, started giving demonstration runs up to 90 to 100 mph (150 to 160 km/h). In 1972, Gar Wood's brother George, accompanied by Orlin Johnson, had a ride in the old lady. She may be seen at the annual Gar Wood Memorial Trophy races in Detroit.

Miss Canada IV (later *Miss Supertest I*) was believed destroyed in a 1953 barn fire, until Mistele ultimately located her hull behind a barn in Tillbury, Ontario and persuaded her owner to sell the hulk. Much of her hull was replaced and she was fitted out with triple 454 cu in, 585 bhp Chevrolet racing engines. *Miss Canada IV*'s original pilot, Harold Wilson, found it a joy to ride in her after 30 years.

In summer 1976, 44 Richardson-built motorboats, dating from 1909 to 1962 celebrated the USA bicentennial by motoring from Lockport to Tonawanda, NY where the company was originally founded; a 1921 50-footer (15·3 m) led the fleet. Apart from the Richardson Boat Owners Association, there is also the Antique Outboard Motor Club, The Chris-Craft Antique Boat Club and the Elco Club.

The Napier-engined single-step hydro *Miss England I*, after a successful racing season in 1929, was presented to the nation by her sponsor, Lord Wakefield, and was on view in the Science Museum, South Kensington for several years until, because of her length, she was put into storage at the Museum warehouse in Knockholt until August 1971 when she was moved to Sydenham. After appearing at the Castrol Great Motoring Extravaganza at Olympia, she was transported, on permanent loan, to the Exeter Maritime Museum, where she is on display today.

Miss Britain III, on permanent exhibition in the Neptune Hall of the National Maritime Museum, Greenwich, was built and raced by Hubert Scott-Paine in 1933–34. During the war, she was stored in a barn at the Wiltshire village of Dowton, and then after a further move to Marchwood, from 1949–51 she was to be seen in the showrooms of Alick Bennett Ltd, Southampton. In 1951, Scott-Paine presented her to the Museum, where she has been ever since.

Bluebird K3, piloted by her owner, Sir Malcolm Campbell, to new world water speed records of 129·5 mph (208·4 km/h) (1937) and 130·86 mph (210·60 km/h) (1938) was sold to a Mr Simpson in the mid-1940s and in the late 1960s was purchased from a scrapyard by Lord Bolton. After appearing at the Castrol Great Motoring Extravaganza at Olympia in 1974, *Bluebird K3* was purchased by Leisure Sport Ltd, who are protecting her at their Thorpe Water Park, prior to complete restoration.

The Windermere Nautical Trust was established in 1971 to ensure that Mr G. H. Pattinson's collection of restored early steam launches could be preserved in perpetuity. The Steamboat Museum was built on the site of a former sand wharf in the first five months of 1977 with the help of the Maritime Trust and English Tourist Board. It was officially opened on the 18 May by HRH, Prince of Wales. The oldest British motorboat in operation is maintained by the Trust. This 16-footer (4·9 m) was purchased at the 1899 Paris Universal Exhibition and brought to Windermere soon after. The restoration of this boat began in 1963, eight years after George Pattison had found it on a compost heap.

The Steamboat Association of Great Britain (SBA) was formed in August 1971, during an informal steamboat regatta on the Beaulieu River in Hants. There are now about 300 members in Great Britain and 70 overseas in America, Canada, Australia, New Zealand, Scandinavia and on the Continent. The SBA's regattas have been held annually on the River Thames, Lake Windermere, Beaulieu River and other rivers, canals and coastal venues. Publications include the house journal *Funnel*, produced three or four times a year; the *Steamboat Index* (3rd Edition), which lists known vessels, and was published in

The twin-screw, steam yacht, Esperance, *is currently on view at the Windermere Steamboat Museum (Windermere Nautical Trust)*

1979. Membership Applications: Richard Bartrop, 24, Bankfield Drive, Bramcote Hill, Nottingham NG9 3EG.

The Historical Motor Boat Society was founded by Ian Wellcoat, Anthony Edwards, Kevin Desmond, Fiona Arran and Frank Bandy on 30 June 1977, at the W. Bates yard in Chertsey, with the aims of locating, restoring and running veteran and vintage motorboats in the UK and ultimately establishing a National Motor Boat Museum of static and working exhibits on the Thames. Beginning with *Lorita*, a restored 35 ft (10·7 m) Thornycroft motorcruiser of 1924, and *Dorothy*, a restored 25 ft (7·6 m) Borwicks-built, Morris-engined Windermere river-launch of 1926, the Society is at present continuing negotiations with the Surrey County Council for two acres of Chertsey Meads, where such a museum and vintage marina might be located. Membership Applica-

tions: Kevin Desmond, 122 Olive Road, London NW2 6UU.

The first British boatyard to take a serious interest in the restoration of wooden motorboats was Peter Freebody Ltd of Hurley in Berkshire. Since its change of policy in 1966, this yard has fully restored some 20 wooden boats, both steam- and petrol-engined; the oldest motor-launch restored has been the 45 ft (13·7 m) *Moe*, built pre-1920 by Burgoignes of Kingston-on-Thames. Freebodys are noted for their fine quality of craftmanship in woodwork.

To commemorate their 75th Anniversary, the magazine *Motor Boat and Yachting* has planned a Vintage Motor Boat Regatta, to take place at St Catherine's Dock on 9/10 June 1979, featuring 45 vintage motorboats. **This is the first vintage motorboat rally to take place in the UK.**

15 THE ARTS

The first book ever to be written by a famous author to include a section on powerboat history was *Life on the Mississippi* (published in 1883) by Mark Twain (the author's pseudonym for Samuel Langhorne Clemens; 1835–1910). From 1857 to 1861 Twain, who also wrote *Huckleberry Finn* and *Tom Sawyer*, was working with the Mississippi steam-boats as co-pilot to Capt. Horace Bixby. In 1875, he wrote a series of sketches for the *Atlantic Monthly* magazine under the title 'Old Times on the Mississippi'; these sketches eventually appeared in book form.

The first description of a powerboat chase in a work of fiction appears in 'The End of the Islander', Chapter 10 of Sir Arthur Conan Doyle's book, *The Sign of Four* (published in 1888), where Sherlock Holmes and Dr Watson, on board a swift Thames River Police steam-launch, give chase down the River Thames from Westminster to the steam launch *Aurora*, eventually catching up with her at Plumstead Marshes and shooting the villain dead.

The first manual ever to be published on motor-boating was W. J. Woodman's *Launch Motors Today*, published in Frome, Dorset in 1902. Price: one shilling.

The first fully-illustrated history of the motor-boat was. *Les Bateaux Automobiles* by Fernand Forest who was an engineer, a builder, and had a Naval Ministry degree. He was a member of the France Yacht Club. This book, with 692 illustrations, was published in 1906 by H. Dunod & E. Pinat of Paris.

The first mention of motorboats in an encyclo-paedia was a 185-word entry on page 366,

Mark Twain (alias Samuel Langhorne Clemens)

volume VII of the 10-volumed *The Harmsworth Encyclopaedia*, published in 1906. An entry on motorboats did not appear in the famous *Encyclopaedia Britannica* until the 1947 edition when pages 878–80 of Volume 15 were devoted to this subject.

In 1915, the poet John Masefield (1878–1966; Poet Laureate from 1930) collected enough money to purchase a 32 hp twin-screw ambu-lance motor-launch (the *Agnes*) and two smaller launches as well as a barge (to be named *John and Ada*, after the Galsworthys) which was to be fitted out as a Red Cross transport for the wounded. From 13 August for one month, Masefield journeyed with the *Agnes* from England to Lemnos via Gibraltar, struggling through stormy weather after Malta. He returned home in a transport by way of Alexandria. He never wrote any poetry about this voyage.

Possibly the most comprehensive guide ever published for the motor-yachtsman was the 640-page *Motor Cruising* (Volume XIX in the Lonsdale Library Series; published in 1935 by the Seeley Service Co. Ltd; 50 chapters, illustrated with 99 black-and-white photographs). This book was a compilation of articles by 17 well-known contributors. The most number of chapters to be written by any one contributor came from John Irving, Yachting Editor of *The Field* magazine.

The oldest surviving ex-editor of a motorboating magazine, is James G. Robinson of Fort Lauderdale, Florida. Originally a Canadian, Robinson was born pre 1890 and was active in the boat-building business from 1905 until 1914. After World War I, he moved to Detroit with the Hacker Boat Co. until 1920 when he went with the Hall-Scott Motor Car Co. and then to Penton Publishing Co. of Cleveland, Ohio as Associate Editor of *Power Boating*. He was editor of that magazine from 1921 until it was sold to *Motor Boat* in 1938. During this time Robinson was on the Harmsworth Trophy Selection Committee of the Yachtsman's Association of America, right up to the final race in 1961.

The oldest-living British motorboating journalist is the 83-year-old M. Ralph Horne (b 1895), who first wrote regularly for *The Motor Boat* magazine in spring 1915. He is still working actively as an industrial journalist.

The shortest-lived motorboating magazine was *The Outboard Motor & Light Motor Boat*, Number One of Volume One appearing in October 1928. No further issues were published!

The first authentic and romantic history of powerboat racing as centred around Detroit, Gar

Wood and the Harmsworth Trophy races was the 143-page *Speed Boat Kings – 25 Years of International Speedboating* by James Lee Barrett; published in Detroit 1939, by Arnold-Powers Inc. Its 18 chapters include 36 photographs. Barrett was not only Secretary of the Yachtsman's Association of America, but also US representative for the International Motor Yachting Union and the Olympic Games; he was also a very eloquent publicist for the city of Detroit.

In the Cumulative & Annual Fiction Indices, published between 1945 and 1976, by the Association of Assistant Librarians, under the heading *Sea Stories – Steamships and Motor Vessels*, no less than 326 titles have been recorded. **The author with the most number of those titles to his credit** has been Ernest Laurie Long with 18 novels (published between the 1930s and the early 1960s, for the greater part by Ward Lock & Co. Ltd, London). Other authors included are Joseph Conrad, C. S. Forester, Hammond Innes and Dennis Wheatley.

Thomas Fleming Day, was the founding Editor of *The Rudder*, **America's first boating magazine**, dealing also with motorboats.

The longest British editorship of a motorboating magazine was that of A. P. Chalkley who became Editor of *The Motor Boat* (Temple Press, London) in 1912 and – except for service in World War I – held that post until 1955: a period of some 40 years. He was also Editor of *The Motor Ship* and *The Oil Engine* (two separate magazines) for many years. He died in 1959. His post was taken by F. H. (Frank) Snoxell, who was Editor of *Motor Boat & Yachting* (published by IPC) from 1956–62.

One of the finest journalists to write about the motorboat was Clarence Earle Lovejoy (1894–1974) on the staff of the *New York Times* from 1915–20, and Boating Editor of that newspaper from 1934–62.

Other famous journalists to write about the motorboat were Charles F. Chapman (former Editor and Publisher of *Motor Boating & Sailing* magazine, who died in March 1976, aged 95); Harry Leduc (*Detroit News*); W. W. Edgar (*Detroit Free Press*); Harold Kahl and Bud Shaver (*Detroit Times*); Paul Gallico (*The Snow*

Goose and other novels); William Atkin – and so many others.

The first woman editor, and possibly the youngest ever editor, of a motorboating magazine was Rosalind Nott, a former fashion model, who took up editorship of *Powerboat & Waterskiing* (Ocean Publications Ltd) in November 1977 when she was 23 years old; at the time of this book going to Press, she has edited 15 issues of that British magazine. She is also powerboating correspondent for the *Daily Telegraph* newspaper.

The most celebrated electric canoe in history is the *Beazie* (LOA 28 ft (8·5 m) × B 7 ft (2·1 m)) owned for the past 33 years by 'the funniest woman in the world', the celebrated stage and film actress, Beatrice Lillie, Lady Peel. Kept in a thatched boathouse opposite Marsh Lock, Henley-on-Thames, with its own charging station, the 70-year-old *Beazie* (built by J. Bond *circa* Edwardian era), powered by 36 below-deck batteries, driving a three-bladed propeller, can carry a maximum of eleven people at half/full speed, ahead or astern. Since owned by Lady Peel, Sir Noel Coward, Ivor Novello, Lord Olivier, Sir John Gielgud, Sir Ralph Richardson, Ben Johnson – and many other celebrated actors, playwrights and critics, have enjoyed the pleasures of 'electric-canoeing' in *Beazie* along the Thames from Henley. Of necessity, *Beazie* is fitted with three bulb-horns.

In his poem, 'McAndrews' Hymn', published in 1893 when marine steam propulsion was at its height, Rudyard Kipling (1865–1936) warned:

'We're creeping on wi' each new rigless
   weight and larger power,
There'll be the loco-boiler next an' thirty
   miles an hour!
Thirty an' more. What I ha' seen since ocean
   steam began
Leaves me na doot for the machine: but
   what about the man?'

One of the earliest poems about a motorboat, entitled 'A Dirge' was published anonymously in the *Motor Boat* magazine for April 1905; it lamented the destruction by fire of a French racing motor-launch, *Trèfle-à-Quatre-Feuilles*.

One of the longest inter-war poems about a motorboat was 'El Lagarto's Answer', written by the powerboat racing driver, George C. Reis

This poster (124 × 89 cm) was designed by the Swiss artist Jules Alexandre Grün in 1905 (Lords Gallery)

The Beazie, *showing the plates to protect her propeller, whilst at the other end are three horns to herald her silent approach! (Motor Boat & Yachting).* Inset: *Lady Peel (Popperfoto)*

'Land Monster: "I hear you have a fine Launch on the stocks. What power is it?" Sea Monster: "A perfect leviathan – 14 whale-power!"' This cartoon appeared in The Motor *magazine of 14 June 1904.*

in the autumn of 1935, after he had won an unprecedented 30 successive victories in the US Gold Cup Powerboat contest in his Packard-engined hydroplane, *El Lagarto* ('The Lizard'). It ran to some 118 lines, including:

'The Instruments all say OK
and Dick calls out, "Well, whata you say?"
I jam the throttle to the floor,
and in response there comes a roar,
And now the motor starts to wind
As the far-flung spray streaks out behind...'

The first Poet Laureate to write verses against 'the hideous noise and exhaust of motorboats is Sir John Betjamin (b. 1906). His verses referred to the Camel Estuary in Cornwall and were broadcast in one part of a BBC TV series, entitled 'A Bird's Eye View of Britain'.

The first motion picture was publicly projected on a screen, as opposed to kinetoscope loops, in 1896 in St James's Hall, Piccadilly, London. **The first film of a powerboat at speed,** to be shown publicly, was entitled 'Turbinia – The Fastest Vessel in the World'. This was a 70 mm bioscope, taken in 1897 by means of a hand-cranked camera by Alfred J. West (1858–

1937). The film depicted *Turbinia*, steaming towards the camera, and also a shot from on board ship, 'showing the extraordinary effects of foam.'

Possibly the earliest film of a motorboat race was taken on a 'Biogen' of the 1904 cross-Channel race. This was viewed by the public at the stand of *The Motor Boat* magazine at the Motor Boat Exhibition at Olympia in February 1905. Two Biogens were working each day and it was thus possible for many visitors to view this contest simultaneously.

Whilst neither of these early films have survived, **the earliest surviving film in possession of the National Film Archive in London** (purchased from Mr E. G. Faulks in 1974) was made by Kineto (a subsidiary of Charles Urba Co.) in 1909 and entitled '*Ursula*, the fastest motorboat in the world'. This film was reviewed in *The Bioscope* magazine on 12 August 1909, and they commented:

'... Her immense speed is clearly seen by the enormous waves she throws up as she passes through the water, a long line of foam remaining in her wake. Her complete control is shown by the short curves she makes whilst going at top speed. Looking over her stern – at a speed of 35 knots – the sea has the appearance of a heavy storm and a very rough sea.'

This rare 35 mm film, on good quality nitrate stock, hand tinted in green, is 220 ft (67 m) long. It is almost unviewable because of the brittleness of its age, but it was re-copied in 1979 using modern processes and viewed previously in November 1978.

The earliest film of a motorboat to be preserved in the Motion Picture, Broadcasting & Recorded Sound Division of the Library of Congress, Washington DC, is entitled the 'White Fox Motor Boat' – 23 ft (7 m) of 16 mm taken by AM & B on 1 June 1906. The motorboat comes towards then goes away from the camera.

The earliest film at the National Maritime Museum, Greenwich, is a 1915 sequence showing Thornycroft motor-torpedo boats on trial.

The earliest film at the Imperial War Museum, London is a sequence entitled 'The Home of the Coastal Motor Boats'.

The earliest film in the Archives of Pathe News depicts motorboats racing for the Ford Liner Cup in Los Angeles (1922).

The first Walt Disney Mickey Mouse cartoon, 'Steamboat Willie' (1928), featured a riverboat. **The first Disney cartoon to feature a real boat with an outboard motor** appeared in 'Goofy & Wilbur' (1939) – although an earlier Mickey Mouse cartoon, 'Fishin' Around' (1931), featured a rowboat where to escape the sheriff, Pluto put his tail over the stern of the boat and spun it round so that it acted as an outboard propulsion unit!

'Gleeps! Pirates, Water Rats and Smugglers of the Seven Seas are fleeing from the Batboat! Holy Batboat!' (A Mercruiser-engined Glastron in disguise)

Steamboat Willie*: Mickey Mouse at her helm! (Walt Disney Productions)*

Jiminy Cricket perches on Goofy's finger in Goofy & Wilbur *(1939) (Walt Disney Productions)*

During the making of the 20th Century Fox feature film, 'Lucky Lady', about the Prohibition Days of Rum-Running (starring Gene Hackman, Liza Minnelli, and Burt Reynolds), some 80 vessels were used during the filming of the sea-battle; these included 25 50 ft (15 m) fishing boats, two tugs, 15 20 ft (6 m) sports fishing boats, and the 220 ft (67 m) *North Bay Star* – the funnels and superstructures of which were altered to conform to the 1930s period.

In 1933, the Russian emigré composer and concert pianist, **Sergei Vassilievitch Rachmaninov** (1873–1943), whilst living alongside Lake Lucerne, purchased a four-cylinder, redwood, motorboat at a local auction, and derived great enjoyment from it by racing the passenger steamers on that lake.

Sir Thomas Beecham (1879–1961), the English impresario and conductor, owned a motorboat, which he called the *MAHCEEB* (Sir Thomas's surname spelt backwards).

The most spectacular motorboat jump in the 1920s was possibly one made by Malcolm Pope during a race in Lake Wales, Fla. when he jumped over a dock sending the boat 10 ft (3 m) skyward and 50 ft (15 m) in distance – although this proved too much for the bottom of the boat which split.

In the 1960s, a five-motorboat stunt fleet, the Johnson 'Super Stingers', each powered by Sea-horse 20's, specialised in aquabatics. **Their most spectacular stunt** was to go over a ramp and through a wall of fire, made up of straw and lattice work and burning a mixture of gasoline and kerosene (petrol and paraffin).

In October 1972, 29-year-old Jerry Comeaux, driving a Glastron GT-150, powered by a 135 hp Evinrude Starflite on an isolated waterway in Louisiana, USA made a record jump of 110 ft (33 m). The take-off speed was 56 mph (90 km/h) and the jump was filmed for the eighth James Bond film 'Live and Let Die'.

In the Burt Reynolds' movie, 'Gator' (1978), a Johnson-powered Cobra made **a new world boat jump record of 138 ft (42·1 m)**.

One of the most spectacular marine stunts in cinema history was used in Warner Bros' 'Out-law Blues', starring Peter Fonda and Susan Saint James who were fleeing from the police in a Glastron – GT 150, powered by a Johnson 115 outboard. One scene involved the boat plunging over a dam near Austin, Texas to a fiery crash 150 ft (45 m) below. Two boats were used for the stunt, Boat no 1 being that boat that actually went over the dam and Boat no 2 which was the control boat. Steering linkage and throttle controls were designed with the use of model air-plane transmitters (radio signals either increased or decreased throttle and turned the boat left or

'A race between air, land and water.' M. de Havilland in an aeroplane, Mr J. W. Shillan, on the LNER express race along the River Ouse for 3 miles. The train – although travelling at 80 mph only – won, largely owing to navigational difficulties experienced by the aeroplane and speedboat.'

An outboard-engined seaplane at the Middletown Regatta of 1930 (Maurice Rosenfeld & Sons)

right). Of course, as the throttle setting was in-creased, torque was also increased which caused the boat to move left or right, which was com-pensated by the steering. These controls were anchored to the floor of Boat no 1. The radio operator and driver in Boat no 2 ran approxi-mately 100 ft (30 m) behind Boat no 1 in order to judge direction and speed. After approxi-mately a week of preliminary trial runs to be-come comfortable with the feel of the equip-ment and its reaction, Boat no 1 was sent over the dam at approximately 50 mph (80 km/h). A ramp, 16 ft (5 m) wide by 8 ft (2·5 m) long, was built so that Boat no 1 did not touch the dam itself, but slid across this ramp into the air over the dam.

The Dam sequence from Outlaw Blues *(Warner Brothers)*

16 AD 2000

The marine vapour-trail from 200 mph (320 km/h) (Crusader on Loch Ness 1952)

In 1894, *A Journey in Other Worlds, a Romance of the Future* was published by J. J. Astor, an American capitalist and inventor, who perished in 1912 in the *Titanic* disaster. *A Journey* describes an interplanetary journey in AD 2000, but also made reference to flying machines, magnetic railways, cars, television – and air-cushioned ships. The latter were dubbed 'marine spiders' and had 'large bell-shaped feet' through which 'a pressure of air' could be 'forced down upon the enclosed surface of the water'. Astor narrates a scene where delegates returning from a conference boarded one of these water-spiders at Key West. This craft was 600 ft (180 m) long by 300 ft (91 m) beam, and its deck was a 100 ft (30 m) above the sea. It bore its passengers 'over the water at a mile a minute'.

In 1900, a French chocolate manufacturer issued a series of cigarette-type cards, predicting life in the year AD 2000. His vision of a hydroplane bears a strong resemblance to a hovercraft superstructure and catamaran hull as may be seen today.

In 1902, M. Cvetkovic, a well-known Croatian engineer, drew out the details of a flat-bottomed ship which, when driven forward, would be raised to the water's surface and glide over it like a skate skims over the ice. This Aero-hydrostat, as Cvetkovic called his craft, would be powered by gas and propelled by peculiarly constructed screws. He calculated that with engines of 28 000 hp his Aero-hydrostat would travel at 600 mph (965 km/h) and circumnavigate the world in a matter of days.

Writing in Munsey's magazine in **August 1904**, Parker Newton wrote: '**The motor catamaran**, showing in the drawing, is put forward as a suggestion to auto-boat designers. Its advantages are cheapness and seaworthiness. Its twin hulls may be built in the same way as a fisherman's dory, with about two strakes in each side of a hull 40 ft (12·2 m) long. The deck beam is 22 in, depth of the hull 26 in amidships, shallowing toward bow and stern. In profile the bows will be similar to those of the cup defenders *Columbia* and *Reliance*, the stern coming down square and straight. Each hull has a keel 3 in wide, 8 in deep amidships and tapering to nothing at the bow and stern. Each hull also has a 12 hp motor, just forward of amidships. Over the motor is an open hatch with a high gunwale, to give easy access to the machinery. The hatch should be covered with canvas when there is a sea. The fuel tanks are well forward, and the extreme bow and stern have airtanks or collision bulkheads. The two hulls of the catamaran are fastened 8 ft (2·4 m) apart and decked over for a length of 12 ft (3·6 m). The whole craft will be light, and its draft will be extremely small. Its stability will make it perfectly safe in a sea that would swamp a single-hulled boat. Its roomy deck, whereon one can move without drawing a warning cry of "Trim Ship!", will add greatly to the comfort of its passengers.'

(The first motor-racing catamarans, built by Angelo Molinari and raced by his son, Renato, were built and tested in 1955 – some 50 years after Newton's imaginative suggestion.)

Lifting the Veil – 'Some Random Speculations on the Future of Motor Boating' by C. Oracle (F. H. Snoxell). Published in *Motor Boat & Yachting* in **July 1954**, these predictions were made for the year 2004.

'The United Kingdom will hold a First Class International Race Meeting; the British International Trophy will come home; the Transatlantic Race for motorboats, first mooted in 1905, will take place; General agreement will be reached amongst all the motorboat racing clubs and all their members, as to racing classes and rules; London will be the destination of the Pavilion d'Or; a silent outboard motor will go into production; the new British canal system, linking all important industrial centres with each other with the sea ports, carrying 250-ton barges, will be completed. With the perfection of the miniature atomic power plant, gas turbine propulsion for boats will be on its way out (per-

haps I am being too conservative about this date); the futility of trying to keep a flying jet boat in contact with the surface of the water having at last been realised, the water speed record will be abolished. The last straw will be the abortive discussion at the UIM Meeting when delegates will fail to agree as to the permitted distance for a record contestant to remain out of contact with the water.'

Design for a motor catamaran, published in Munsey's Magazine *in August 1904, long before James Beard and Cougar's successes (Mary Evans Picture Library)*

From the earliest dynastic times of Ancient Egypt (from 3100 BC) the mysterious fear of the one-way passage of the sun from East to West, was expressed by the religious symbol of the sun-god *Ra*, who travelled across the sky in his *Solar* boat. Hence in the tombs of the great kings, *Solar* boats have been re-discovered in perfect condition.

Recent predictions that within the next ten years the cost of solar cells will be reduced to 20 p/W with an increase in output to 10 W/ft² prompted a 65-year-old former consultant on railway electrification, Alan T. Freeman of Rugby, to make a practical study of the viability of future uses of this form of energy.

In 1976 an 8 ft (2·4 m) catamaran was constructed out of marine plywood and duralmin. Its powerplant was an electric motor converted directly from the energy of the sun's rays – and the craft was appropriately named *Solar Craft I*. Fifty circular silicon cells, divided up into 10 modules and mounted on a solar panel gave

Alan Freeman on his Solar Craft I, *powered by four 7-watt Ferranti Solar modules (1978) (A. T. Freeman)*

good results, but were later replaced by two 60-cell Ferranti solar (4×7 watt) panels, mounted on tripods fore and aft. The electric motor turned an aluminium alloy propeller. With the maximum speed of 4 mph (6 km/h) imposed on Inland Waters, on 10 May 1978, this revolutionary craft made a trip of 4·1 miles (6·6 km) in 2 hr on the British Waterways Canal at Rugby. It was an extremely sunny day, although Freeman found that his power efficiency was interfered with by the vapour trails left by jet aircraft.

On 31 October 1963 at 2.30 p.m., a saucer-shaped UFO was sighted, reportedly out of control, as it crashed into the Peropava River in Sao Paulo Province, Brazil. Witnesses said later that when the UFO came into contact with the surface, it was as if a hot iron had fallen into cold water. For the water at that spot began to bubble and surge up, then became exceedingly muddy and continued to boil. At that point the Peropava river is about 12 ft (3·6 m) deep with about 15 ft (4·5 m) of clay and mud at the bottom. The police questioned the witnesses and established that the disc, which resembled an aluminium basin was about 16 ft (5 m) in diameter and 3 ft (1 m) thick. It was extremely bright, almost luminous and it travelled at a fairly slow speed. Numerous salvage attempts failed to recover the object . . . As yet there is no vehicle which can fly low like a seaplane and then penetrate the air-water interface to move equally at ease in the ocean depths like a submarine.

During the 1960s, the Convair Division of General Dynamics, leaders in nuclear submarines and advanced military aircraft development, designed a seaplane hull with conventional wings and tail for airborne flight. Three engines would be installed, one on top of the hull to provide thrust for flight while the other two would be used for take-off. The engines would be sealed off for submerging with alternative means for underwater propulsion. The flight radius would be between 300 and 500 nautical miles at speeds between 150 and 225 knots, whilst 75 ft (23 m) underwater, it could travel at 5 knots. When not travelling it would float on the water surface like an ordinary boat.

So far, only two creatures in the Animal Kingdom have succeeded in this manoeuvre: The Tropical Flying Fish, of which there are 100 species, used their long pectoral fins to act, when distended, as parachutes, sustaining them in the air against the wind, sometimes for 500 to 600 ft (150 to 180 m) at 10 mph (16 km/h). Compound glides time as long as 43 s, may cover one-fourth mile. The Dipper (or Water-Ousel) is a thrush-sized bird, capable of flight, of swimming on the water and also of walking underwater on the river-bed, using its wings as a means of propulsion.

On 27 November 1975, under the auspices of the Small Craft Group, a symposium on 'The Future of Commercial Sail' was held at the Royal Institution of Naval Architects.

With the cost of diesel fuel escalating, the world's supply of oil in doubt, designers were returning to the idea of using natural forces, albeit with modern technology, to tackle these problems:

Dynaship. Corporations have been established in California and Copenhagen to put into practice the designs of a Mr Prolss, developed since the mid-1950s at the Hamburg Schiffbau Institute, from prolonged wind-tunnel and tank tests. The concept is one of a commercial bulk carrier (LOA 500 ft+ (152 m+) and of many thousands of tons), capable of 20 knots in a Force 9 wind. A Dynaship rig consists of six large sectional elliptical, hollow, cantilever masts (without stays), aerodynamically profiled, which turn about their axes to meet the apparent wind. Dacron sails are set horizontally (from being furled within the mast along the aerodynamically curved yard-arms). The entire manoeuvring of the masts and sail winches is hydraulically remote-controlled from the wheelhouse. The fully automated sailing rig and weather routing principles held to achieve remarkably competitive voyage times and costs per ton delivered. It is not expected to resort to auxiliary propulsion (diesel/gas turbine) for more than about 15 per cent of the passage time. A propeller nacelle can be withdrawn into the hull when idle to reduce unnecessary hydrodynamic drag. The Dynaship Corporations are still looking for a sponsor to pay for the construction of a prototype.

The Windmill Ship. Calculations have been carried out for a single-screw vessel with a fixed pitch propeller (15 ft (4·5 m) diam) driven by a variable pitch windmill (545 ft (166 m) diam), through a suitable gear train. It was found that a Windmill Ship could travel directly to windward, without tacking, since its water propeller thrust could exceed the windmill drag by a margin sufficiently great to achieve a useful speed through the water. With a Beaufort Force 8 wind, the windmill ship should achieve speeds of 13 knots, with the prop spinning at between 180–250 rpm.

The Flettner Rotorship derives its propulsive thrust from the lift and drag forces developed in large rotating cylinders mounted above the hull. Two small ships were converted to this form of propulsion in the early 1920s and one of these, the *Buckau* (680 tons), made a transatlantic voyage. She was reported to have achieved speeds of 5 to 6 knots in a 10-knot wind.

In 1897, an ex-sailor named Percy Pilcher, who had already experimented with his *Hawk* glider flying to distances of 250 yards (230 m), constructed a 17 ft (5·2 m) 'umbrella boat' with cyclone sail. The sail worked on the principal of the kite and exerted a lifting effect so that the

Thornycroft-built hull sailed on an even keel. With her 360 sq ft of umbrella sail, the Pilcher boat sailed quite swiftly and efficiently; Pilcher was killed two years later in a gliding accident.

The following experts have kindly contributed their view of motorboating in the year 2000.

'During the 1960s, I was developing a reverse three-pointer, which was driven by a second-hand Mercury outboard and with only 100 bhp reaching the propeller, this achieved over 80 mph (128 km/h). It consisted in a fore body fairly well Veed and leading to a step roughly under the driver who was seated amidships. The aft two sponsons were connected to the hull by aerofoils acting and placed in such a manner as to make use of the ram wing effect or what in aircraft is called the ground effect.

'However, despite the fact that we arranged a spray rail each side with the object of concentrating the spray in such a manner as to avoid splaying out on to the inside of the sponsons, there was considerable difficulty in turning at high speed. By fitting the engine and mounting with "power trim" the turning trouble was eliminated by altering the trim from the alteration in thrust line causing the nose (bow) to lower itself sufficiently to dig in and cause the boat to swivel round pretty quickly . . . too quickly if you were not careful! The control of the power trim was placed on the steering wheel to make things easier for the pilot. I saw my son-in-law, Nigel Tunnicliffe, drive her in to a wave which threw her into the air and which would undoubtedly have flipped a catamaran, which was encouraging. It was the sweep back of the sponsons which achieved this. I suspect that with sufficient patience in the trial stage and a bit of luck, success will eventually accrue to the Ram Wing reverse three-pointer . . . at any rate by AD 2000 in all classes including offshore.

'The development which would really help both hydrofoils and hovercraft, would be if some bright team could develop a really small nuclear plant, suitable for such waterborne vehicles as I have mentioned above, as this would get over the necessity for complicated arrangements for obtaining range through hullborne auxiliaries. I well know the present difficulty in accomplishing the light weight of shielding and in producing reactor units. I can hear loud cries from the experts that I am suggesting the impossible but to be fair I have been asked to put forward some targets.'

Cdr Peter du Cane
MINA, MI MechE, AFRAeS
County Cork, Eire
(1978)

'The future of powerboat racing lies with the aerodynamic boat, because aircraft wings work even more efficiently when flying just above a surface. Lift can be almost trebled and the drag more than halved when a wing operates in full "surface effect". The very efficient form of "aerofoil boat" developed by the later Dr Alexander Lippisch of sailplane and rock fighter fame, will become a major influence in high speed on water. This vehicle requires only 50 per cent of the power of similar water craft and has a commercial potential of 50 ton-miles per gallon in the 90 to 180 knot range. The first seven-seater production prototype has achieved speeds of over 100 knots and an endurance of 20 hr with only 200 hp. For propulsion, experiments have also been conducted with new types of high speed paddles which could match the surface propeller for efficiency without its disadvantages of torque and side thrust. Finally, with the rapid increase in development, it is quite possible that a new method might be devised which enables energy in the fuel to be transformed into a continuous change in water momentum, generating thrust, at efficiencies greater than that of the present engine and propeller. We can expect speeds over water of 150 knots, at much greater efficiency and comfort.'

W. H. Maloney
BSc C.Eng. MRINA MI MechE (1978)

'One suspects that circuit racers will eventually get up to speeds of around 160 mph (275 km/h) and will have lap times not far short of present day Formula 1 Grand Prix cars. Offshore boats will probably never go much over 120 mph (193 km/h) and the trend will be to get the same performance and sea-going ability with smaller engines. The craft will be multi-hulls of some

sort, as monohulls have obviously reached their limit, and will have a very large aerodynamic lift component. Electronic trim devices will possibly be used to help keep the craft stable although the driver will still need his skill to control it all. I suspect that propellers may be replaced by some sort of underwater jet device by then when a rule is introduced against it.

The more commercial forms of high-speed waterborne transport will probably be wing in ground effect machines flying 100 ft (30 m) or so above the sea. The hydrodynamic contribution will be to allow the craft to take off and land in rough conditions and "ride out" bad storms. It is in this area that powerboat racing may be of some use.

Of commercial craft, I feel that planing load transporters could be possible for coastal routes and could replace some road transport. If some of the principles for the designing of high-speed hulls which were investigated before World War I and developed between the wars were remembered now and developed further, much could be achieved in the field of fast commercial carrying. Also many of today's highly inefficient pleasure boats could be drastically improved by the judicious use of transverse steps in the hull and the sort of thinking which provides particular portions of the boat for it to ride on, instead of general vaguely outline area.'

Lorne F. Campbell
(1978)

'Hydrofoils have proved themselves both an economical and fast means of water-transportation, capable of successfully competing with any type of ship on the basis of their high-speed level, and also with short haul aircraft both because of their much more economical operational costs and also by their port-to-port, rather than airport-to-airport performance. Undoubtedly hydrofoils will keep this position and in the year 2000 we shall see them plying on comparatively shorter routes, probably with augmented speed and size.

We often read prophetic articles on ocean-crossing hydrofoil ships and we see, with admiration, artists' impressions of "what the new liners will look like" depicting gigantic hydrofoils flying over the ocean on towering struts safe and untouched by the stormy waves. It is predicted that a rapid and smooth ride will be combined with the amenities which we enjoy today on a luxurious passenger ship.

These dreams will never come true. A giant hydrofoil vessel could not compete with a long distance intercontinental jet aircraft because of her incomparably longer travelling time, her increased operational costs and her engineering problems. From studies it can be concluded that commercial hydrofoils up to 1000 tons – too small for ocean crossing – are technically feasible. However, it is believed that a 300-ton craft is already in the range of the largest size of commercial hydrofoils from which successful operation and adequate return on investment can be expected. Larger ships may be envisaged only if unforeseen inventions reducing foil-drag or increasing propulsion effectiveness, should turn up.

Baron Hanns von Schertel
Supramar AG, Switzerland
(1978)

'Examine World Unrestricted Water Speed Record holder, Ken Warby's vehicle, *Spirit of Australia* and what do we see perched purposefully on the aerodynamic fin at the aft end? An aerodynamic tailplane, a truly aerodynamic, force-generating lifting device, fitted no doubt for stability and damping purposes, without which the story could well have been one of disaster instead of success, and despite the fact that the current (1975) UIM rules clearly state that "any device which tends to lift the boat by means of an aerodynamic effect, including any extension of the size and shape of the hull intended for the purpose, is *prohibited*." However, the Australian World Water Speed Record of 317·186 mph (510·452 km/h) has been ratified and rightly so. After all, the basic hull of the vehicle itself is an aerodynamic lifting body, inefficient though it may be, and the efforts of our intrepid record-breakers must be recognised, even though the rules are bent.

To peep at things to come therefore, if we examine the various ways in which rules may be broken or bent, we may well reveal the future vehicles and from this, the future rules.

A simple analysis of the basic vehicle requirements of Support, Drive, Stability and Control for vehicles principally immersed in air indicates that there are 81 distinct vehicles, one of which is truly thoroughbred and two of which are nominal thoroughbreds, the remaining 78 being crossbreds. Of these vehicles 40 are landborne, 40 waterborne (or boats as we categorise them) and only one is truly airborne. Extensions of this analysis to include vehicles principally immersed in land and in water, indicate that there are 243 vehicles, three of which are true thoroughbreds and 240 are first generation crossbreds. It is variations of these crossbreds which have in the past violated the rules of the time, and it is crossbreds which will undoubtedly have the most impact on the rules of the future. Of the air-immersed vehicles, the three thoroughbreds, the nominally landborne, the nominally waterborne and the airborne vehicles (each with all of its basic vehicle requirements of Support, Drive, Stability and Control being supplied respectively from the land, the water and the air) will still be there, hammering away at class records; but the vehicle variants, the crossbreds, will be the pacesetters in the ultimate records and rules.

What will these vehicles look like?

The spectrum of potential speed record-breaking vehicles for the year 2000 is vast and exciting and the opportunities for our up-and-coming designers are legion. Will there be supersonic vehicles? Yes, on land and water, the same vehicle being used for both, running without wheels and using "ground effect" for support. Altitude and displacement from land or water surface will be indicated by mechanical and by electro-magnetic or electrical-type probes and manual-, or auto-control will be effected from this indication to maintain the required positioning from the Interface. Will these vehicles be streamlined? Yes, but with drag penalties perhaps resulting from careful attention to Stability and Control requirements.

Under today's rules, an aircraft cannot break a land or water speed record, but future aircraft-type vehicles will break ultra low-level speed records over both land and water. The rules governing such attempts will limit the daylight clearance of the major part of the vehicle's underside to 15 cm or thereabouts.

Under-water type vehicles travelling on the sea bed will also break speed records as well as more conventional types of submarines.

Drive will not be a major problem for these

future record-breakers; there will be plenty of power. Support may be difficult but Stability and Control will be paramount and the time and attention of our future designers will be directed accordingly.'

(From an unpublished dissertation by **K. W. Norris** BSc(Eng), ACGI, FRAeS, FIMechE and Co-Designer with L. H. Norris of *Bluebird K7* and *CN7*)

'The microprocessor will have a very great impact on the marine electronics industry in the next two decades. The microprocessor is an integrated circuit providing extensive computing power at remarkable low prices requiring very little space. This means that the average boat owner will have this large computing power at his finger tips at a price he can easily afford.

The larger powerboat owner will have the advantage of **integrated electronics**. This means that not only will all the navigational aids and other electronic equipment be physically integrated into a control and display panel similar to the dashboard of a car but all the sensors such as echo-sounders, transducers, log transducers, compass sensor, wind vane sensor, radar receiver, etc will be fed into a central processing system using microprocessors. Signals from this central processor will be fed to various displays and digital readouts providing the boat owner with a vast amount of information for safe navigation.

Marine Radar will begin to achieve its full potential, the improved digital processing due to microprocessors, daylight viewing solid state displays (replacing cathode ray tubes) and the use of higher microwave frequencies in Q band will enable relatively compact low cost docking and river radars to be developed. These high definition radars will provide such an accurate picture of the harbour, other boats, moored and moving that navigation should not be hindered by foggy conditions and low visibility.

VHF Radio Telephones will be fairly integrated into the domestic telephone system and each boat so equipped will be assigned a telephone number. The equipment will be synthesised, fully duplex and transmissions scrambled

to ensure privacy, it will be possible for the Coast Guard and other Government Agencies to place priority calls to any selected boat. All VHF installations will automatically carry out a watch-keeping function on distress channels. In the event of a boat owner wishing to place a distress call a series of standard coded signals identifying the boat and describing his predicament will be available at the push of a button and the equipment will automatically transmit the signal at regular intervals until help is available.

Compact low cost Echo-Sounders similar to SEAFARER will be developed using microprocessors with bright solid state displays with the storage of information on mini-cassettes. The use of the transducer as a hydrophone for identifying fish and other underwater objects is also feasible; the transducer could also be used as part of an acoustic data or telephone link to enable communications with underwater installations, submersibles and divers.

Scanning Sonars will be developed with solid state bright displays and electronic scanning transducers. With the use of microprocessors and digital signal processing radar like displays will provide a picture of the 'underwater world'. It should also be possible for suitable acoustic reflectors to be placed at harbour entrances and mouths of rivers to assist navigation in poor visibility (this will be equivalent to underwater 'cats eyes').

Low cost hand held RDF's such as SEAFIX we believe will still have a place in the market for the small boat owner but will be synthesised and almost fully automatic using microprocessors. With the installation of improved land based radio beacons it should then be possible to obtain an accurate fix of the boat's positions with the various error corrections already incorporated. The boat's present position, previous position and ETA should be available at the push of a button. It is possible that this instrument will also automatically record all the relevant weather information broadcast by the BBC and stored on a miniature cassette for playback when required.

F. P. Andrews
Technical Director, Electronic Laboratories
(July 1978)

INDEX

Jacket details:

FRONT

Top left : London Fire Brigade at work on River Thames.   Victorian Era (*London Fire Brigade*).   *Top right* :
Sea Panther, a 34 ft (10.4m) Halmatic 110 Shead-designed express motor yacht (*Halmatic*).   *Bottom left* : 1935
3½ hp Marston Seagull detachable outboard motor. Labelled 'John Marston Sunbeamland, Wolverhampton'
(*Stuart Delf*).   *Bottom right* : Fierce circuit competition around the Bristol Docks, June 1978 (*All-Sport*).

BACK

Top : Bill Munsey piloting the 12 cylinder 2500 hp Rolls-Royce Merlin-engined thunderbolt Atlas Van Lines
(*Atlas Van Lines*).   *Middle left* : The 40 ft (12.2m) Edwardian beaver-sterned, river launch *Lady Geneviè*. At Peter
Freebody and Co.'s, Hurley, Berkshire (*Peter Freebody*).   *Middle right* : Super wide-angle view of the 'innards' of
an offshore power boat entered for the 1978 Cowes–Torquay–Cowes race (*All-Sport*).   *Bottom left* : The 52 ft
(15.8m) Arun class lifeboat, *Spirit of Tayside*. Named by the Duke of Kent 17 July 1978 and on service at Dundee
(*RNLI*).   *Bottom right* : 1938 John Player cigarette card of the 45 knot HM Torpedo Boat 102 (*WD & HO Wills*).